INTERNATIONAL
AND
DEVELOPMENT
COMMUNICATION

INTERNATIONAL
AND
DEVELOPMENT COMMUNICATION

A 21st-Century Perspective

Bella Mody
Michigan State University
EDITOR

SAGE Publications
International Educational and Professional Publisher
Thousand Oaks ▪ London ▪ New Delhi

For information:

Sage Publications, Inc.
2455 Teller Road
Thousand Oaks, California 91320
E-mail: order@sagepub.com

Sage Publications Ltd.
6 Bonhill Street
London EC2A 4PU
United Kingdom

Sage Publications India Pvt. Ltd.
B-42, Panchsheel Enclave
Post Box 4109
New Delhi 110 017 India

Printed in the United States of America

Library of Congress Cataloging-in-Publication Data

  International and development communication : A 21st-century
perspective / editor, Bella Mody.
    p. cm.
  Includes bibliographical references and index.
  ISBN 0-7619-2901-0 (pbk.)
  1. Communication, International. 2. Communication—Developing
countries. 3. Intercultural communication. I. Mody, Bella.
  P96.I5I4847 2003
  302.2—dc21   2003005218

03 04 05 06 10 9 8 7 6 5 4 3 2 1

Acquiring Editor:	Todd R. Armstrong
Editorial Assistant:	Veronica K. Novak
Production Editor:	Sanford Robinson
Typesetter:	Christina Hill
Indexer:	Molly Hall
Cover Designer:	Michelle Lee

Contents

Foreword
Global and Local Influences on the Shape of Media Institutions

This book is intended to provide a historical perspective and a contemporary analysis of the field of international communication and its application to development communication. It revolves around media institutions and the conditions under which they have been used by the state and private capital. Part One on international communication presents the thinking of seven well-known authors spanning South Asia, East Asia, Europe, and North America. Part Two focuses in on development communication applications by seven active researchers and professors, drawn from Latin America, South Asia, and North America.

This foreword addresses the present-day context of globalization in comparison to its earlier eras. Communication media and telecommunication are considered central to globalization and to national development. Hence, before looking at applications of the media to international communication and development communication, I start out by looking at biases in the organization of media institutions. I then analyze causes of the change in media ownership and financing from public to private and illustrate implications of the change with two examples, one from international communication and another from development communication applications.

Taking over from modernization, globalization has become the primary intellectual theme in the social sciences and a buzzword in trade and industry in the past two decades. The term is used to describe a range of processes and outcomes. To illustrate:

- increases in international trade and foreign investment

- increases in information flows

- increased promotion of Western values such as markets and democracy

- increased attention to intellectual property regimes

- increases in the number of international nongovernmental organizations

- increases in the number of international governmental organizations

- increased number of international laws applicable to national policies, e.g., the UN Convention on Human Rights, the Millennium Round of the World Trade Organization, the Kyoto convention on greenhouse gas emissions

- increased migration

Globalization in History

The modern capitalist world system began in the 16th century when surplus accumulation in Western Europe, new shipping technology, and cannons enabled European traders to launch voyages for gold, spices, silks, and such. Globalization may be considered a new phase in capitalist development beginning in the 1980s, initiated by the needs of financial capital, energized by neoliberal policies such as deregulation and privatization, and facilitated by digitized information flows. Some structural power has now devolved from the state to global markets and firms. An argument rages on about whether the current process of global capitalist market expansion is stronger than in previous eras. Suffice it to say that this stage is *different* from the global intrusions/expansions of imperialism, colonialism, and even the high levels of international trade and investment in the 1890-1914's free trade capitalism. It may be distinguished by, first, the intensity of capital and information flows, and second, by the particular pattern of implicated locations. Some countries are more integrated into interactions with the rest of the world than others; the names change from year to year. *Foreign Policy* magazine's annual Globalization Index (created in 2001 with several indicators spanning information technology, finance, trade, personal communication, politics, and travel) showed Singapore and Ireland at the top of the ranks of political, economic, and technological integration from among 62 countries in 2001 and 2002. The United States, the world's dominant market power, ranked 11th in globalization in 2003.

The Role of Media

Castells (1989) places communication media at the center of changes that are driving globalization, as service delivery platforms for business transactions, and as carriers of information content and images central to the global push. While pace, scale, and pervasiveness of the Internet are unique, communication media have played central roles throughout history. Postal communication helped the Roman Empire to manage its far-flung properties. The telegraph helped Europe and Britain to manage their colonies. The telephone, the wireless, the television, coaxial cable, and the digital computer were all major influences in early periods of global expansion, as were popular print media and international news agencies. The geostationary satellite made electromagnetic transmissions global.

Considerable research on the influence of global forces focuses on the content and consequences of entertainment programming for cultural homogeneity and diversity (Kraidy, 1999, also Chapter 6 in Part I) and the impact of telecommunication services on global market integration. Media institutions and telecommunication institutions that provide entertainment programming and telecommunication services are considered major social forces that enable a range of changes—be they marketing and sales promotion, war, peace, or national development. In this chapter, I focus on media institutions and telecommunication organizations in the current era of global capitalist expansion. I analyze the causes of change in the ownership (private, foreign) and financing (private foreign and domestic investment, advertising). My purpose is to identify the bias inherent in the institutional organization (Innis, 1951) of media as infrastructure for further globalization, to be able to identify its influence on the content and form of information flows in international and development communication. I draw loosely from the literature on the social construction of technology (Williams & Edge, 1996) and on structuration (Giddens, 1979).

Print media organizations in most countries were organized as private initiatives in the 1800s and 1900s and remained so, except for those newspapers and magazines started after the 1940s by the governments of newly independent nations in Asia and Africa. Except for the United States and postcolonial Latin American countries in the U.S. hinterland, radio and TV stations were initiated by the state in European nations and in countries they colonized. Until the mid-1980s, the state owned and controlled the telecommunication system in most European and developing countries (except the Philippines). In the past two decades, a new global-local oligopoly has emerged. Whether it continues to exclude the majority is the primary question for policy.

Changes in the Structural Biases of Media and Telecommunication Institutions

An investigation into organizational design requires an analytical framework that links political and economic forces, including markets, firms, and regulatory organizations. I use an institutionalist perspective to understand the dynamics of entertainment programming and telecommunication services under conditions where there are substantial variations in market power.

My account of the privatization of public media organizations (primarily telecommunications and broadcasting) is a structuration argument. Following the agent-structure debate, the structure of organizations might be driven by the accumulation of initiatives taken by persons, individuals institutions, or civic organizations (methodological individualism), by deeply embedded social structures (e.g., capitalism as a production structure, patriarchy as a gender structure) with no individual influence, or by individual actor *and* structural forces that mutually influence the

other. Structural forces establish the range of options that are available to actors in a given historical context.

The growth of privately owned media organizations is neither random (by individual whims) nor predetermined (by structural formulas). Structural forces connected to capitalism at the national and global levels set the stage for the change. To illustrate from the case of telecommunication, these *global forces of capitalism* in the 1980s included

a. Large users like transnational corporations for whom telecommunication services are central to their business transactions. These include financial firms like J P Morgan, Chase Manhattan, and G.E. Capital; software developers like IBM, Hewlett-Packard, and Microsoft; manufacturing firms like GM and Ford; oil companies like Shell and Aramco (the Arab American Oil Company); and insurance, medical, and airline firms that send their back-office business processes (e.g., data entry, transcription, call centers) offshore to low-wage countries, to name a few

b. Telecommunication providers in near-saturated plain old telephone service markets in the United States, Western Europe, and Japan searching for new markets

c. The International Monetary Fund, The World Bank for Reconstruction and Development, and the World Trade Organization founded after the Great Depression of the 1930s to prevent such recurrences

National forces of capitalism that set the stage for the privatization of their public telecommunication entity included

a. Domestic firms that needed seamless voice and data communication to coordinate national business and to access global market opportunities for exports of goods and services (e.g., software development, data entry);

b. International and global firms that needed voice, video, and data to keep in touch with their command and control centers in headquarters

c. Middle-class residential users who wanted reliable local and long-distance telephone service like their counterparts in other countries

Crucial among individual initiatives were a number of technological innovations and deregulatory initiatives. Technological changes, that is, digitization, opened the door to flexible and multipurpose applications. Firms selected a *particular* organization of technology from the range of alternatives possible under digitization to maximize their own profit-making goals. Thus, the biases and imperfections of market conditions are embedded in the design of the organization. The type of deregulatory initiatives (namely, neoliberal) taken by the United States, the United Kingdom, and Japan enabled the change toward present-day global-local private oligopolies that have the power to select the content and form of their services.

Biases in International and Development Communication Messages

Chua (2003) points out that the United States is promoting "bare-knuckled capitalism" *without* social security provisions or antitrust laws around the globe. She shows how the unqualified simultaneous promotion of markets and this particular form of democracy have had disastrous consequences in countries where minority ethnic groups control markets: With no viable recourse through a workable ballot box, the majority ethnic group have seen no recourse to their marginalization but murderous direct action against the market-dominant Chinese minority in Indonesia and the Philippines.

Rodrik (2001) points out that governments in developing countries who receive information promoting global integration and act accordingly are diverting their scarce resources away from education, public health, industrial capacity, and social cohesion. Development strategy is thus selected by global prescription rather than by national public debate.

In the frenzy of strategic alliance formation between Internet service providers, traditional broadcasters, and the press jostling for profit from common digital platforms, the fundamental question of information asymmetry (e.g., between the global North and South, between media owners and users within a country) is often forgotten. An increase in the number of information technologies (e.g., wireless, satellites, cable) will need to be accompanied by customized content selection and access strategies in development communication to solve the basic problem of structured inequalities of wealth and status across the globe.

This volume is divided into two parts: I. International Communication, and II. Development Communication. Young scholars of development communication might wonder why this literature is housed in a book with international communication research. This is because applications of media technology for agriculture, health, education, democracy, social change, and poverty eradication were initially foreign aid initiatives. These were promoted, to a great extent, by practitioners, scholars (e.g., Schramm) and organizations (United Nations, foreign aid donors) interested in international communication. The use of communication to support development in the 21st century presently consists of national projects and researchers with strong domestic roots in many countries, industrially advanced and industrially less advanced. Each of the two parts begins with my introduction, followed by chapters authored by leading scholars. The book ends fittingly with Everett M. Rogers's analysis of how these fields are faring as areas of scholarship.

All of us would like to thank the invisible people who make books possible: In this instance, Sanford Robinson, Senior Production Editor at Sage, and Rachel Rivard, our careful proofreader. Without them, we could not communicate.

Bella Mody
Michigan State University

REFERENCES

Castells, M. (1989).*The information city: Information technology, economic restructuring and the urban-regional process.* Oxford: Blackwell.

Chua, A. (2002*). World on fire: How exporting free market democracy builds ethnic hatred and global instagbility.* New Yok: Doubleday.

Giddens, A. (1979). *Central problems in social theory: Action, structure and contradiction in social analysis.* Berkeley: University of California Press.

Innis, H. A. (1951). *The bias of communication.* Toronto: University of Toronto Press.

Kraidy, M. (1999). The global, the local and the hybrid: A native ethnography of globalization. *Critical Studies in Mass Communication, 16* (4), 454-476.

Measuring globalization: Who's up, who's down? *Foreign Policy* (Jan.-Feb. 2003). Retrieved Feb. 1, 2003 from http://www.foreignpolicy.com/wwwboard/g-index.php

Rodrik, D. (2001). Trading in Illusions. *Foreign Policy, 123*, Mar.-Apr. 2002, pp. 54-62.

PART I

International Communication

Introduction

Bella Mody

The seven chapters in this section on international communication are a historical and critical analysis of how communication between nation-states has been studied over the past 70 years. Researchers in this area have been blessed with a lot of international communication activity to analyze, many new forces and some old continuing factors, and fortunately, we have risen to the challenge by drawing on different disciplines to study these complex historical changes. When social research tools developed at the end of the 1920s, the state was the primary agent of communication between nations. International communication researchers studied how states used media to win on the world's battlefields. By the end of World War II, U.S. firms were expanding domestically and internationally. The Hollywood dream factory was making itself felt globally. The U.S. state became a supporter and facilitator of its private capital seeking new markets just like the European city-states in the 16th century supported their traders' voyages for spice and silver. This political economy of state support for private firms has grown stronger. A major contribution in the past half-century was the prophetic voice of Herbert I. Schiller stridently pointing to the implications of selling entertainment and news (culture) globally as a business commodity just like any other. His concern was that Hollywood and capitalist cultures would dominate the imaginations of two thirds of the world's population who live in very different situations from their on-screen heroes and heroines. The grip of high culture and propaganda provided by state-controlled media gave way in technologically less advanced nations to electronic fantasies of "any local girl can make good if she works hard enough" although on the ground in South Asia and Africa, economic mobility was quite different from that of the United States.

The global expansion of stand-alone and converged (i.e., the Internet) electronic delivery systems for data, voice, video, and text has enabled the growth of new local and regional firms, some in collaboration with international firms. Simultaneously, this expansion of technological infrastructure for private profit has enabled nongovernment, nonprofit organizations to reach out to each other across national boundaries in ways that were not possible under state and corporate monopolies that offered limited infrastructure. These public-interested alliances have networked globally to defeat the World Trade Organization and state-supported private empires on questions of labor rights, a multinational carte blanche on investment, peace issues, and biotechnology at the turn of the century. At the national level, women's groups are asking how their voices can be heard.

Some things change, many remain the same. This broad background is intended to highlight the question of power, who has had it over time, and how it has been manifested in words and images in different national, international, and now global transnational corporate epochs.

The first chapter in Part I, Chapter 1, by political scientist and communication professor Stephen McDowell, presents a history of the theoretical traditions in international communication. It is unparalleled in its breadth and analysis: Few would agree to do the large amount of reading that McDowell did. The benefits are there for all, particularly for younger researchers just entering the field.

In Chapter 2, on media corporations, political scientist and communication professor Edward Comor analyzes the current consolidation of private corporate power in the form of transnational media corporations and the different ways these firms have been studied.

Those of us who have moved to social constructionist paradigms of knowledge that affirm the partial, imperfect, and relative nature of ways of knowing will welcome the recommendation for the use of multiple frameworks.

In this corporate era, Oliver Boyd-Barrett in Chapter 3 analyzes the rise and fall of the dream of equal independent states in dialogue called the New World Information and Communication Order (NWICO). Boyd-Barrett is respected widely for his empirical definition of medium-specific imperialisms (Boyd-Barrett, 1998).

Drawing on philosophy and politics, Tom Jacobson and Won Yong Jang in Chapter 4 address the space for media to contribute to peace and public interest norms distinct from the interests of the state and private capital. They conclude that hopes for global peace through media must be contextualized in terms of the possibilities for global democracy. Lessons from the NWICO case have some implications for the possibility of a global public sphere.

Students will be grateful to Drs. Viswanath and Zeng, in Chapter 5, for identifying the ideological debates, reviewing the macro- and micro-level evidence, and presenting a research agenda on international advertising.

In Chapter 6, doctoral student Anselm Lee and I review the history of research traditions on international media influence (from propaganda to modernization to political economy to media effects to media-in-culture reception analysis).

With great verbal facility, Sandra Braman concludes this section, in Chapter 7, with her unique systems-theoretic perspective on where international communication should go from here.

There was a lot more each chapter author wanted to say. Some had to reduce their early drafts substantially to meet chapter size limitations. In addition, there were other topics that could have been included if there was space. There wasn't. These chapters are an introduction to the past and a taste of the future written by leaders in the field. I hope you find them a rich source of ideas for doctoral dissertations and future research.

REFERENCE

Boyd-Barrett, O. (1998). Media imperialism reformulated. In D. K. Thussu (Ed.), *Electronic empires: Global media and local resistance* (pp. 157-176). London: Edward Arnold.

1

Theory and Research in International Communication

An Historical and Institutional Account

STEPHEN D. McDOWELL
Florida State University

When undertaking research in international communication, several topics might come to mind. These include the more traditional subjects of international communication, such as studies of propaganda, the unbalanced flows of news and entertainment between countries, the dominance of Hollywood in world motion picture production and exhibition, and the factors underlying and the implications of the rise of the large digital delivery corporations (such as telecommunications, software, or online media companies). Thematically, one might also consider the role of the state in shaping national media, and the roles of intergovernmental organizations in shaping world media industries, flows, and uses—whether the United Nations Educational, Scientific and Cultural Organization (UNESCO), the International Telecommunication Union (ITU), the World Intellectual Property Organization (WIPO), or the World Trade

Organization (WTO). Effects of the dominance of media corporations on individuals, cultures, and politics across national boundaries have been debated at different times, whether called cultural imperialism or transnational media. More recently, new types of questions have also been considered, such as the importance of local and global processes; the rise of the transnational media firm; the shape of corporate information orders; the significance of transnational advertising; how transnational media and cultural studies can be situated in contexts of race, class, and gender relations or focus on national diasporas; and the use of new media by civil society movements in support of human rights, peace, or environmental protection objectives.

A field of inquiry, however, is not just a series of substantive topics. It should also be a set of core problems, concepts, theories, and

5

methods and an ongoing discussion among practitioners about theory and research (Kuhn, 1964). This chapter introduces some of the main bodies of theory and research in international communication over the past half-century. It outlines the analytic and conceptual characteristics of the different approaches to international communication, making reference to the institutional and political context of this work. Along with the broader historical context, this chapter makes reference to the institutions that supported and allowed for scholarly communication in this emerging field and served to build the careers of the practitioners of international communication theory and research.

The chapter closes by raising two questions for the field at the turn of the 21st century. How can a variety of questions and concerns be imported from other social sciences while retaining the distinctive contributions of a communication approach? What is the short-term and long-term significance of the contemporary lack of institutional support for theory and research in international communication?

PROPAGANDA STUDIES AND PSYCHOLOGICAL WARFARE

A most puzzling and troubling question for the study of international communication is that concerning the origins of the major questions, concepts, theories, and methods in the field. Numerous authors (Buxton, 1994; Simpson, 1994) claim the problems and purposes of international mass communication were developed in the context of two sets of social and political questions at the end of the 1930s and early 1940s. One set of questions concerned the role and importance of mass communication processes in general. As William Buxton (1994) argues, the work of the

Rockefeller Foundation was of primary significance here. It was in a series of seminars that aimed to bring focus and direction to, and published results from, studies by Paul Lazarsfeld that had already been funded that the formula associated with Harold Lasswell—"who says what in which channel to whom with what effect"—was developed.

This approach joined the concept of "public opinion" arising from the work of Walter Lippmann (1922) with a model that attempted to identify both the factors shaping public opinion and effective action by leaders in shaping and directing public opinion. The domestic set of problems that oriented communication studies was matched by international concerns. The propaganda efforts of the National Socialist party in Germany in the 1930s, and the beginning of war in Europe, eventually provided a threat to the United States. It was also an opportunity for the tools of analysis of public opinion and the processes of mass communication to be applied to war fighting. Christopher Simpson (1994) notes this involved research on how to mobilize the public and obtain consent for the war at home in the United States and developing methods of communication to sow doubt, suspicion, and misinformation with enemy populations. Psychological warfare was one more tool in the toolbox of the military strategist, and more specifically, strategists based in the United States.

Simpson (1994) argues that the journal *Public Opinion Quarterly* was throughout the 1950s essentially the academic organ of a network of government officials and agencies and university-affiliated research centers. These activities were in many cases funded by the federal government—or private philanthropic agencies working in cooperation with the government to circumvent prohibitions on certain types of funding—and advanced the respectability and objectivity of a field of research that had priorities and agendas set as part of the national security agenda. The list of authors of a special issue of this journal in 1952-1953, which provided an update on recent trends and research in the field of international communication, reads like those that are most often presented as the foundational figures for mass communication research in general (Lasswell, 1952-1953; Lazarsfeld, 1952-1953). The field that emerged as communication studies or international communication at the end of the 1950s was U.S.-based and U.S.-centric, and it was shaped by the choices made in the ideological and historical contexts of two decades earlier. Simpson argues that the "legacy of psychological warfare" was reflected in the "inheritance" that makes up mass communication studies, and it includes effects research, studies of national communications systems of the Soviet Union or other countries that might pose problems, refinement of scaling techniques for opinion surveys and analysis techniques, creation of opinion and audiences research techniques for areas outside the United States including hostile areas, early diffusion research, early development theory and research, Schramm's articulation of "zeitgeist" in the field of mass communication, refining the concepts of "reference group" and the "two-step flow" theory, and contributions to motivation research (Simpson, 1994, p. 111).

A fuller consideration of why these theoretic choices and research steps were taken would require an extensive and critical review of the historical evidence (Chaffee & Rogers, 1997; Delia, 1987; Dennis & Wartella, 1996; Mowlana & Wilson, 1990; Rogers, 1994; Schramm, 1997). The field emphasized elements of control and manipulation offered by new techniques, and it de-emphasized the investigation of the requisites of democracy that had initially given rise to Lippmann's concept of public opinion. Lasswell (1941) pres-

ents this move as merely a tactical choice. Whereas democracy is "the practice of justice by majority rule," he begins *Democracy Through Public Opinion* by stating, "Democracy depends on public opinion in support of the ends and means of democratic governance. The ends of democracy are permanent, but the means must fit the needs and opportunities of the hour" (Lasswell, 1941, p. 1).

The famous dictum of von Clausewitz (1984) that is mentioned in strategic studies is that "war is politics continued by other means." The early generation of international communication theorists and researchers, based in the United States, seemed to assume that communication was war continued by other means. The context in which they worked shifted quickly from an armed struggle by the United States against fascism to a Cold War against international communism. The task of communication scholarship was to explore public opinion in different countries and to develop the tools and technologies to ensure that Western values triumphed, even if some of the means, fitting "the needs and opportunities of the hour," were not those that might fit other times. Those same "means" became the concepts, theories, research methods, and defining characteristics of the field of international communication, and they did not fade away when the context changed.

COMMUNICATION AND DEVELOPMENT: MODERNIZATION

A second generation of international communication studies moved away from the explicit focus on control of public opinion in other countries in the service of war fighting, and more toward the mobilization of public opinion and the resources of a country in the service of national development. However, the modernization model of development should also be situated in the context of purposes and goals set in the Cold War framework, and state agencies with specific political interests that funded this work. U.S. president Harry Truman first articulated the goals of development assistance and set these up as ways to counter the spread of communism in countries of Europe and the South (Lerner, 1977). By offering a future or direction for countries that advanced economic growth and prosperity, the human misery that formed the basis upon which communist messages might find a receptive audience would be reduced. Economic development in the South would be good not only for the countries involved, it would, in the view of practitioners, serve the larger purpose of limiting the international spread of communism.

Communication could assist in advancing economic development in a number of ways. Because economic growth was most likely to be enhanced by changes in social attitudes and economic practices and relationships that would lead to greater productivity of workers; better use of technologies in sectors such as education, health care, and agriculture; enhanced efficiency of markets; and more effectiveness of state institutions, communication campaigns could assist in multiple modes. Mass communication campaigns could provide images of certain practices and behaviors that would provide opportunities for social learning. More directed local campaigns for certain sectors would involve the equivalent of agricultural extension workers, the on-the-ground change agents who would work with persons and groups on an interpersonal basis to reinforce specific types of innovations or adoption of new technologies and practices. Research on mass communication effectiveness had identified the importance of local opinion leaders, and the "two-step flow"

models provided a direction for development communication.

Many of the same figures that had dominated the first generation of propaganda or psychological war studies in international communication also emerged as the predominant figures in this new field (Lerner, 1958; Lerner & Schramm, 1967). Although a handful of university research centers funded by U.S. federal agencies dominated the agenda setting, problem formation, and project implementation in development communication, this model also was supported by international organizations, such as UNESCO or the World Food Organization. The professionalization of communication practitioners emerged and became more entrenched. Development communication projects could draw on persons trained in graduate programs to design and execute communication and development projects and undertake research that would advance and strengthen research in this area.

The involvement of international organizations moved the agenda solely from communication as a propaganda tool in interstate competition, to an institutionalized relationship in international politics. Along with the legitimacy provided by international organizations, the broader participation patterns and the more diffuse research programs of international organizations provided and exposed some contradictions. Numerous critiques of the modernization approach to communication and development were articulated, including some rethinking by practitioners (Lerner, 1977). Development communication was recast in the context of the North-South divide. The modernization agenda served to transmit specific cultural, economic, and political practices across borders, but in the guise of a universal model of development. This claim of universalism was questioned as explanations were sought for the failure of countries to develop as rapidly as expected.

NATIONAL STUDIES, UNDERDEVELOPMENT, DEPENDENCY

The consideration of comparative cases of media systems and media policy has become a major part of research and publication and has remained resilient over several decades. The initial propaganda research included a comparative dimension. Researchers were concerned about political communication in other countries, and how events in other countries might be influenced through the use of mass media (Schramm, 1948). The Cold War instrumentality that characterized the origins of comparative media research posed a problem for introducing a comparative dimension into the study of international communication. The major conceptual framework that was offered to provide guidance for the examination and categorization of different countries, Siebert, Peterson, and Schramm's (1956) *Four Theories of the Press,* was clearly situated in a Cold War context (see Berry, 1995). Comparative studies in communication were also prefigured by modernization studies (Lerner, 1958) that put much of the world in the "traditional" group. Mainstream comparative political research was influenced both by a systems analysis model (which viewed each country as a unique system) and by a drive to social scientific validity though the use of quantitative models. J. D. Downing (1996) argues that the *Four Theories of the Press* served primarily to celebrate the superiority of the Anglo-American models (libertarian and social responsibility) while placing non-Western and communist countries in the least favorable light (pp. xiii, 191). More recent theorizing (Curran & Park,

2000; Dissanayake, 1988; Martín Barbero, 1993; Mattelart, 1994; Wang & Dissanayake, 1984) is critical of this tradition, and it shifts the conceptual starting points of international and comparative work away from assumptions and questions that are set by the models of Western communication analysis.

The emergence of questions about international communication paralleled broader debates concerning power relations, in this case about the causes of and appropriate responses to a lack of economic growth and development. If national media systems were ineffective, this needed an explanation. Could this explanation be found in the characteristics of the national media systems themselves, or did part of this explanation lie in the linkage to international media structures? In the broad development debates, a new approach was signified by several terms and the research directions they entailed: underdevelopment, dependency, and core-periphery structures. Rather than speaking of the less developed countries, underdevelopment suggested that the faster and slower rates of economic growth and development in different parts of the world were related to each other.

The application of dependency models to the study of international communication patterns was reflected in similar types of research, both by academics and by bodies organized by international organizations. Among the most influential publications was Nordenstreng and Schiller's (1979) *National Sovereignty and International Communication.* This edited volume addressed theoretic issues, as well as noted the role of direct broadcast satellites as a challenge to national sovereignty and the role that international law might play in dealing with problems in international communication (such as the use of mass media, the right to communicate, and hostile propaganda). It also looked at the balance of flows of news and entertainment. In 1980, the International

Commission for the Study of Communication Problems, which was chaired by Sean MacBride and had been appointed following the UNESCO 1976 General Conference in Nairobi, published its report, *Many Voices, One World.* The report provided a comprehensive overview of research on the relationship between communication and society, as well as international imbalances and inequalities in the direction and content of information and communication flows. After providing an overview of the results on numerous studies on communication, the report addressed ways to deal with these imbalances, including strengthening communication policies, professional development for journalists, and rights, responsibilities, and ethics of journalists. It also proposed strengthening the national self-reliance of media systems.

NWICO AND INTERNATIONAL CRISIS

The reaction to the publication of *Many Voices, One World* reflected a watershed, both for defining approaches to international communication research and for the institutional support for international communication research. The debates over definition of appropriate international communication research and proposals centered around the MacBride Commission report and subsequent calls for a New World Information and Communication Order (NWICO). The focus on enhancing national sovereignty (meaning autonomy and self-determination) in the communication sphere was matched by an effort to enhance professionalism among media professionals, as well as to democratize media systems (Mowlana, 1985; Schiller, 1976). The basic underlying assumptions reflected a recognition of the need for strong national institutions to support and protect media profes-

sionals, to ensure democratic access to media, as well as to advance the idea of a right to communicate as a human right similar to those articulated in the International Declaration of Human Rights (McPhail, 1981). Arguably, interlocking networks of university researchers, government working groups and commissions, and peer evaluations of publicly funded projects still existed in international organizations in the 1960s and 1970s, but had different and broader sets of participants than nationally based international communication research.

In the study of international relations and world politics, the 1980s are seen as a period in which the crisis of Western hegemony was being played out, reflected by the New Cold War, the debt crisis, increased military spending, and decreases in official development aid. This crisis was to some extent resolved at the end of the 1980s in the collapse of the Soviet Union, the dispersion of the power of the Group of 77 developing nations, and the reemergence of GATT (General Agreement on Tariffs and Trade; replaced by the WTO after 1996) and the World Bank and International Monetary Fund as the preeminent international organizations. But during the 1980s, the modes of resolving the crisis had important implications for what types of communication research would be supported by governments and international organizations.

Along with journalism education, the dominant mode of international communication research that emerged in the 1980s could be called telecommunications for development (Hudson, 1984, 1997; ITU, 1984). The focus here was not on mass communication, but on the interactive telecommunications network, meaning the telephone, and how its use could enhance economic productivity and efficiency, social integration, and overall levels of social participation (Samarajiva & Shields, 1990). Again, research funded by international organizations, in this case the ITU and the international financial institutions, showed that there was a gap in the levels of access to telephone services between countries (Saunders, Warford, & Wellenius, 1994). Industrialized countries had the majority of households with telephone service, but in many developing countries there might be whole villages that did not have telephone services. Investment was needed in infrastructure and would be returned in fees provided for the services. At the same time, the uses of telecommunications services would result in savings in travel costs and travel time, more rapid filling of orders, and more rapid delivery of emergency services to rural areas.

Institutionally, research on telecommunications for development offered international organizations an alternative approach to dealing with international communication issues. Rather than addressing issues such as news and entertainment flows or divisive political issues such as the allocation of geosyncronous orbital spots for satellites, telecommunications for development framed a problem and a solution in such a way that could be supported by policymakers and researchers from different parts of the world. Developed countries saw ways in which they could provide official development assistance that would also benefit their own national groups, such as telecommunications firms. Less developed countries also saw new sources of development assistance and the possibility of the transfer of high technology and related expertise.

Critics argued that this approach to telecommunications as the infrastructure that would contribute to greater social integration and market growth was a revisitation of modernization approaches to development (Sussman & Lent, 1991). The central goal of international exchange was to bring the less developed countries to something resembling the conditions of the developed countries.

Among the beneficiaries of the attempt to address this gap would be telecommunications companies, and especially those from the North that had the technology, management expertise, and capital to offer in this type of project. The priority on telecommunications for development also fit with the effort of international financial institutions to promote investment in and privatization of telecommunications firms in different parts of the world. The point was less to promote national integration and social development, but to integrate at least parts of the economies of Third World countries into global political economy.

THE 1990s: FROM INTERNATIONAL TO TRANSNATIONAL TO GLOBAL

As the Cold War ended, some nation-states disintegrated, and many new nation-states emerged at the beginning of the 1990s, social scientists were once again enlisted in national development projects of regional and global scope. Nation-building was not just a public relations campaign. In this case, the project was to build the institutions of market economies and representative democracies in formerly communist states. Building these institutions, however, required once again educational or social change programs in the service of the creation of new individuals, the capitalist entrepreneur, the consumer, and the citizen. Once again social scientists were enlisted, in this case lawyers, regulators, economists, and business consultants, to jump-start social change and institution-building. Rather than attitude change among the common person, the focus had shifted to the managers and decision makers that would run businesses, courts, regulatory agencies, and governments. These programs were supported by the World Bank, regional banks, and private foundations.

However, much of international communication research was detached from this official agenda and examined a set of questions about international communication that states and international organizations were unable to address (Nordenstreng & Schiller, 1993). A much more diversified set of research concerns emerged. Although political economy perspectives were clearly evident in the dependency analysis as applied to international communication, these different traditions have flourished into a number of different types of research programs. Questions arising from political economy and communication and development are arguably the most significant contributions in the past decade, but they are joined by studies of the state and interstate competition, trade and investment in communication services, civil society, the transnational media firm, and national case comparisons in the context of shared liberalization of communication policies.

Some political economy perspectives retain the focus on the state and interstate competition. Anthony Smith (1980) and others took the issues that had been raised in the NWICO and UNESCO debates and situated these conflicts in a geopolitical framework of international power politics. The issues of international information and communication flow were not so much about the global problems of development and underdevelopment, but could be seen in the frame of the struggles among nation-states for power and prestige in world politics (Fortner, 1993; Headrick, 1991). Some of these studies have focused on the struggles over communication issues in international organizations (Lee, 1996; Zacher & Sutton, 1996); others have considered issues such as trade agreements (Aronson & Cowhey, 1988; Comor, 1998) and technical standards (Dupagne & Seel, 1998). It is notable that a number of theorists and

researchers coming from the field of international political economy and policy studies (rather than mass communication) began to publish widely in this area in the 1990s (Comor, 1994; Drake, 1995).

Legal and economic analysts have argued from a more deterministic or technological utopian perspective that state or national policies and international agreements become less relevant given the power of new communication technologies to allow communication and transactions to take place across borders (Pool, 1990). Kahin and Nesson (1997) and others argue that the institutions that are needed to govern international communication will emerge as key actors express a demand for such institutions. These may emerge in the form of industry self-governance rather than traditional communication law and policy. National regulatory efforts are seen as inflexible, and they will just cause more problems and a slower realization of what is inevitable about new technology and global change.

As communication technologies have become more important as an economic sector and facilitator of international trade, international economists have emphasized the benefits arising from open trade and investment in communication technologies and services, and the need for international agreements to preserve the openness of these exchanges (Jussawalla & Lamberton, 1982; Lamberton, 1996). In this approach, the emphasis is on communication as either an enabling technology and infrastructure for other services (Robinson, Sauvant, & Govitrikar, 1989), such as telecommunications for development or on communication technologies and services as growth sectors or new economy sectors. International communication studies and debates in the 1990s followed primarily from this economic analysis. If the benefits of new communication technologies stand ready for the taking, the role of trade policies, national information infrastructure initiatives, or global information infrastructure initiatives is to devise the best regulatory approach, economic incentives, or international trade and investment agreements to promote either national benefits or joint benefits in the international community (Drake, 1995).

Other theorists of international communication examined the complexity of relations between states, civil society groups, and private sector organizations. Karl Deutsch (1953), four decades ago, examined social communication and how it conditioned world politics. Pluralist perspectives in the 1980s and 1990s have emphasized the role of the uses of new information and communication technology in changing the actors and interactions that typify international politics and global culture (Braman & Mohammadi, 1996; Rosenau & Czempiel, 1992). In short, international communication is no longer about communication among states, or some states propagating ideas on the populations of other states, but is about citizen groups from different countries working together on issues such as the promotion of human rights, self-determination, environmental protection, or worker health and safety or opposition to nuclear weapons, land mines, or trade agreements, possibly making use of new communication technologies. This work has connected well with participatory and democratic approaches to communication and development (Jacobson & Servaes, 1999; Wasko & Mosco, 1992; Wilkins, 2000).

THE POLITICAL ECONOMY OF CONTEMPORARY COMMUNICATION

Political economy research has attempted to address in an integrated fashion the processes of formal political/legal power, economic relations (production, property, exchange), and

social patterns (Mosco, 1996). This research has refined questions and propositions arising from dependency models in a number of ways, with emphasis on the components that make up the global political economy of communication. First, a shift has been made to the examination of the firm and media industries, and the strategies and activities of these firms have been detached from a necessary link to a specific national interest, at least as an a priori assumption. Industry studies have traced the ways in which specific media sectors or media firms are organized on a global basis. This work includes studies of the international music industry (Burnett, 1996; Negus, 1999), the television industry (Gershon, 1997; Sinclair, Jacka, & Cunningham, 1996), the film industry (Hoskins, McFayden, & Finn, 1997; Wasko, 1994), and telecommunications (Mansell, 1993). Whereas states might have supported multinationals in manufacturing, resources, and communication in the past because they were tied to the national interest and were nationally based, media capital was now much more footloose. It is the firms that now set the agenda. "Home" states must compete like host states to retain desirable activities, offering tax incentives and other inducements to keep the jobs and investment of the transnational media firm located in their countries. At the same time, as some critics have noted, the interests of global media firms line up most often with governments and states with neoliberal politics.

A second shift in political economy has been toward the examination of national cases, including industry and policy change, and the specific examination of the processes of privatization, deregulation, and liberalization on a national basis rather than as a unified global process (Hudson, 1997; Mody, Bauer, & Straubhaar, 1995; Siune & Truetzschler, 1992). Article-length treatments of country case studies have also been joined by comprehensive review volumes that provide a number of pieces on different countries. These include the national handbooks on telecommunications policies by Eli Noam (1992, 1999). Shelton Gunaratne's (2000) *Handbook of the Media in Asia* provides 25 country case studies, focusing on mass media industries and policies.

A further contribution of political economy has been a renewed interest in cultural systems, and consumption and use of cultural and communication products and services. UNESCO studies also moved from national studies and news and entertainment flows to consideration of communication and culture industries (Guback & Varis, 1982) and global television industries (Varis, 1985). Others have examined shifts in industry structures, noting that media firms and industries are increasingly characterized by mergers, acquisitions, and partnerships. Barnet and Cavanah (1994) made the link between production, marketing, and culture on a global basis by examining specific firms and their strategies. Benjamin Barber (1995) presented a simple but fundamental and stark contrast between global cultural products and services, and local practices. This global-local dialectic has been explored by many, and in the strong version it seems to reproduce a modern-traditional contrast in a new form and does not take into account the mixing of a variety of influences and forms in media expressions and cultural practices.

Most strikingly, the shift to the use of *global* rather than *international* or *transnational* is evident in the titles of works in international communication. Recent books, in addition to those already mentioned, place *global* as the prominent question for theory and research (Demers, 1999; Herman & McChesney, 1997; Mowlana, 1986, 1997; Schiller, 1999; Sreberny-Mohammadi, Winseck, McKenna, & Boyd-Barrett, 1997; Sussman & Lent, 1998; Thussu, 1998). However, communication research has not been at the forefront of a care-

ful and critical assessment of the uses of the terms *global* and *globalization,* whereas this debate has been important in the field of international political economy (Hirst & Thompson, 1999). The global agenda of certain business and state actors has been presented as inevitable, and although communication scholars question this inevitability, the basic term has been adopted. Given this track record, more suspicion about the origins and usefulness of the "global" problematic will be a crucial challenge for international communication research (Thussu, 2000).

DISCUSSION AND CONCLUSIONS

The chapter has pointed to the recent use of policy studies, economic, and political economy perspectives in international communication research. In what ways—while a variety of questions and concerns are imported from other social sciences—can a distinctive contribution of a communication approach be retained? Work in international communication on long-term and global processes, whether technical, economic, or cultural, and their relation to local and specific experience has borrowed from a number of sources that appear throughout social science. Benedict Anderson's (1983) *Imagined Communities* addressed issues of the formation of intersubjective shared meanings and identities that were the core of nationalism and the sense of belonging to a national community. This approach contributed to the recognition of the importance of communication in contributing to nation-building. As well, the basic unit of analysis in comparative and international communication studies, the nation-state, was examined rather than assumed. David Harvey (1989) dealt with the question of postmodernity by making reference to political economy, culture, and technology in reflecting and shaping the changing experience of time and space. His work is most influential in geography, but it has had significant implications for examinations of communication technologies and the experience of geographic space, as well as in guiding attempts to situate media and cultural studies in a new global-local context. Both Anthony Giddens's (2000) and Manuel Castells's (1997) works on globalization were widely debated in the late 1990s. Castells's three-volume set on the network society relates very specific local, community, and identity formations to the social, economic, and technical networks that shape the new global political economy. Similarly, the structuring effect of decisions about technical communication infrastructure and standards is also reflected in Lawrence Lessig's (1999) *Code*. Many of these studies have been used by those with an interest in communication questions, but they do not share in the key assumptions and problems that led to the formation of international communication as a field of study. Academic disciplines are defined by concepts, theories, and methods rather than subject matter. However, with the rise of economic, political, and technical studies, any hold that international communication studies had on this subject has been loosened.

Throughout its history, the study of international communication has been related in some way both to the political context and the work of international organizations. What is the significance of the contemporary lack of institutional support for theory and research in international communication? What relationship might emerge between the configuration of economic, political, or social forces and the key questions pursued by the field in coming years? Although the field of international communication has embraced policy studies, institutional analysis, and industry studies, the affection has not been mutual. The international organizations involved in post-communist reconstruction look to lawyers,

economists, and business consultants rather than communication scholars. The international programs that support training and education for communication policymakers and regulators are directed most often to schools of business. The participation of some communication scholars in international policy research and analysis is notable, but with few exceptions communication scholars are outside looking in. This position may be appropriate and desirable, given the track record of close involvement in the 1950s. However, even a critical perspective requires an institutional base, whether universities, research institutes, international nongovernmental organizations, or advocacy groups. With decreasing public support for universities and international development programs not tied to trade and investment enhancement, the core academic and nongovernmental base for certain types of international communication scholarship is eroding, despite the flourishing of publications in the 1990s. At the same time, the growth of communication studies in centers outside the nexus of North America and Western Europe will bear watching in the decade ahead.

REFERENCES

Anderson, B. R. (1983). *Imagined communities: Reflections on the origin and spread of nationalism*. London: Verso.

Aronson, J. D., & Cowhey, P. F. (1988). *When countries talk: International trade in telecommunications services*. Cambridge, MA: Ballinger.

Barber, B. R. (1995). *Jihad vs. McWorld*. New York: Times Books.

Barnet, R., & Cavanah, J. (1994). *Global dreams*. New York: Simon & Schuster.

Berry, W. (1995). *Last rights: Revisiting four theories of the press* (J. C. Nerone, Ed.). Urbana: University of Illinois Press.

Braman, S., & Mohammadi, A. (Eds.). (1996). *Globalization, communication, and transitional civil society.* Cresskill, NJ: Hampton.

Burnett, R. (1996). *The global jukebox: The international music industry.* London and New York: Routledge.

Buxton, W. (1994). From radio research to communications intelligence: Rockefeller philanthropy, communications specialists, and the American policy community. In S. Brooks & A.-G. Gagnon (Eds.), *The political influence of ideas: Policy communities and the social scientists* (pp. 187-209). Westport, CN: Praeger.

Castells, M. (1997). *The information age: Economy, society and culture: Vol. 2. The power of identity.* Cambridge, UK: Basil Blackwell.

Chaffee, H. S., & Rogers, E. M. (Eds.). (1997). The establishment of communication study in America. In W. Schramm, *The beginnings of communication study in America: A personal memoir* (pp. 125-153). Thousand Oaks, CA: Sage.

Comor, E. (Ed.). (1994). *The global political economy of communication.* New York: St. Martin's.

Comor, E. (1998). *Communication, commerce, and power: The political economy of America and the direct broadcast satellite, 1960-2000.* New York: St. Martin's.

Curran, J., & Park, M.-J. (Eds.). (2000). *De-Westernizing media studies.* New York: Routledge.

Delia, J. G. (1987). Communication research: A history. In C. R. Berger & S. H. Chaffee (Eds.), *Handbook of communication science* (pp. 20-98), Newbury Park, CA: Sage.

Demers, D. P. (1999). *Global media: Menace or messiah?* Cresskill, NJ: Hampton.

Dennis, E., & Wartella, E. (Eds.). (1996). *American communication research: The remembered history.* Hillsdale, NJ: Lawrence Erlbaum.

Deutsch, K. W. (1953). *National and social communication: An inquiry into the foundations of nationality.* New York: Technology Press of the Massachusetts Institute of Technology.

Dissanayake, W. (Ed.). (1988). *Communication theory: The Asian perspective.* Singapore: Asian Mass Communication Research and Information Centre.

Downing, J. D. (1996). *Internationalizing media theory: Transition, power, culture.* London: Sage.

Drake, W. J. (Ed.). (1995). *The new information infrastructure: Strategies for U.S. policy.* New York: Twentieth Century Fund.

Dupagne, M., & Seel, P. B. (1998). *High-definition television: A global perspective.* Ames: Iowa State University Press.

Fortner, R. S. (1993). *International communication: History, conflict, and control of the global metropolis.* Belmont, CA: Wadsworth.

Gershon, R. A. (1997). *The transnational media corporation: Global messages and free market competition.* Mahwah, NJ: Lawrence Erlbaum.

Giddens, A. (2000). *Runaway world: How globalization is reshaping our lives.* New York: Routledge.

Guback, H. T., & Varis, T. (1982). *Transnational communication and culture industries.* Paris: United Nations Educational, Scientific and Cultural Organization.

Gunaratne, S. A. (Ed.). (2000). *Handbook of the media in Asia.* New Delhi: Sage.

Harvey, D. (1989). *The condition of postmodernity: An enquiry into the origins of cultural change.* Oxford, UK: Basil Blackwell.

Headrick, D. R. (1991). *The invisible weapon: Telecommunications and international politics, 1851-1945.* New York: Oxford University Press.

Herman, E. S., & McChesney, R. W. (1997). *The global media: The new missionaries of corporate capitalism.* London: Cassell.

Hirst, P., & Thompson, G. (1999). *Globalization in question* (2nd ed.). Cambridge, UK: Polity.

Hoskins, C., McFayden, S., & Finn, A. (1997). *Global television and film: An introduction to the economics of the business.* New York: Oxford University Press.

Hudson, H. E. (1984). *When telephones reach the village: The role of telecommunications in rural development.* Norwood, NJ: Ablex.

Hudson, H. E. (1997). *Global connections: International telecommunications infrastructure and policy.* New York: Van Nostrand Reinhold.

International Commission for the Study of Communication Problems. (1980). *Many voices, one world: Towards a new, more just and more effi-cient world information and communication or-der.* Paris: UNESCO.

International Telecommunication Union. (1984). *The missing link: Report of the Independent Commission for World Wide Telecommunications Development.* Geneva: Author.

Jacobson, T. L., & Servaes, J. (Eds.). (1999). *Theoretical approaches to participatory communication.* Cresskill, NJ: Hampton.

Jussawalla, M., & Lamberton, D. M. (Ed.). (1982). *Communication economics and development.* Honolulu, HI: East-West Center and Pergamon.

Kahin, B., & Nesson, C. (Eds.). (1997). *Borders in cyberspace: Information policy and the global information infrastructure.* Cambridge: MIT Press.

Kuhn, T. S. (1964). *The structure of scientific revolutions.* Chicago: University of Chicago Press.

Lamberton, D. M. (Ed.). (1996). *The economics of communication and information.* Cheltenham, UK: Edward Elgar.

Lasswell, H. D. (1941). *Democracy through public opinion.* Menasha, WI: George Banta.

Lasswell, H. D. (1952-1953). Psychological policy research and total strategy. *Public Opinion Quarterly, 16,* 491-500.

Lazarsfeld, P. F. (1952-1953). The prognosis for international communications research. *Public Opinion Quarterly, 16,* 481-490.

Lee, K. (1996). *Global telecommunications regulation: A political economy perspective.* London: Pinter.

Lerner, D. (1958). *The passing of traditional society: Modernizing the Middle East.* Glencoe, IL: Free Press.

Lerner, D. (1977). Communication and development. In D. Lerner & M. L. Nelson (Eds.), *Communication research: A half-century appraisal* (pp. 148-166). Honolulu, HI: East-West Center.

Lerner, D., & Schramm, W. (Eds.). (1967). *Communication and change in the developing countries.* Honolulu, HI: East-West Center.

Lessig, L. (1999). *Code and other laws of cyberspace.* New York: Basic Books.

Lippmann, W. (1922). *Public opinion.* New York: Free Press.

Mansell, R. (1993). *The new telecommunications: A political economy of network evolution.* Newbury Park, CA: Sage.

Martín Barbero, J. (1993). *Communication, culture and hegemony: From the media to mediations.* London: Sage.

Mattelart, A. (1994). *Mapping world communication: War, progress, and culture* (S. Emanuel & J. A. Cohen, Trans.). Minneapolis: University of Minnesota Press.

McPhail, L. T. (1981). *Electronic colonialism: The future of international broadcasting and communication.* Beverly Hills, CA: Sage.

Mody, B., Bauer, J. M., & Straubhaar, J. D. (Eds.). (1995). *Telecommunications politics: Ownership and control of the information highway in developing countries.* Mahwah, NJ: Lawrence Erlbaum.

Mosco, V. (1996). *The political economy of communication.* London: Sage.

Mowlana, H. (1985). *International flow of information: A global report and analysis.* Paris: UNESCO.

Mowlana, H. (1986). *Global and world communication.* New York: Longman.

Mowlana, H. (1997). *Global information and world communication: New frontiers in international relations.* London: Sage.

Mowlana, H., & Wilson, L. J. (1990). *The passing of modernity: Communication and the transformation of society.* White Plains, NY: Longman.

Negus, K. (1999). *Music genres and corporate cultures.* London: Routledge.

Noam, E. (1992). *Telecommunications in Europe.* New York: Oxford University Press.

Noam, E. (1999). *Telecommunications in Africa.* New York: Oxford University Press.

Nordenstreng, K., & Schiller, H. I. (Eds.). (1979). *National sovereignty and international communication.* Norwood, NJ: Ablex.

Nordenstreng, K., & Schiller, H. I. (Eds.). (1993). *Beyond national sovereignty: International communication in the 1990s.* Norwood, NJ: Ablex.

Pool, I. de S. (1990). *Technologies without boundaries: On telecommunications in a global age.* Cambridge, MA: Harvard University Press.

Robinson, P., Sauvant, K. P., & Govitrikar, V. P. (1989). *Electronic highways for world trade: Issues in telecommunication and data services.* Boulder, CO: Westview.

Rogers, E. M. (1994). *A history of communication study: A biographical approach.* New York: Free Press.

Rosenau, J. N., & Czempiel. E.-O. (1992). *Governance without government: Order and change in world politics.* Cambridge, UK: Cambridge University Press.

Samarajiva, R., & Shields, P. (1990). Integration, telecommunication, and development: Power in the paradigms. *Journal of Communication, 40,* 84-105.

Saunders, R. J., Warford, J. J., & Wellenius, B. (1994). *Telecommunications and economic development* (2nd ed.). Baltimore: Johns Hopkins University Press. (Published for the World Bank)

Schiller, D. (1999). *Digital capitalism: Networking the global market system.* Cambridge: MIT Press.

Schiller, H. I. (1976). *Communication and cultural domination.* White Plains, NY: International Arts and Sciences Press.

Schramm, W. (Ed.). (1948). *Communications in modern society: Fifteen studies of the mass media.* Urbana: University of Illinois Press.

Schramm, W. L. (1997). *The beginnings of communication study in America: A personal memoir* (S. H. Chaffee & E. M. Rogers, Eds.). Thousand Oaks, CA: Sage.

Siebert, F. S., Peterson, T., & Schramm, W. (1956). *Four theories of the press: The authoritarian, libertarian, social responsibility, and Soviet communist concepts of what the press should be and do.* Urbana: University of Illinois Press.

Simpson, C. (1994). *Science of coercion: Communication research and psychological warfare 1945-1960.* New York: Oxford University Press.

Sinclair, J., Jacka, E., & Cunningham, S. (Eds.). (1996). *New patterns in global television: Peripheral vision.* Oxford, UK, and New York: Oxford University Press.

Siune, K., & Truetzschler, W. (1992). *Dynamics of media politics: Broadcast and electronic media in Western Europe.* London: Sage.

Smith, A. (1980). *The geopolitics of information: How Western culture dominates the world.* New York: Oxford University Press.

Sreberny-Mohammadi, A., Winseck, D., McKenna, J., & Boyd-Barrett, O. (Eds.). (1997). *Media in global context: A reader.* New York: St. Martin's.

Sussman, G., & Lent, J. A. (Eds.). (1991). *Transnational communications: Wiring the Third World.* Newbury Park, CA: Sage.

Sussman, G., & Lent, J. A. (1998). *Global productions: Labor in the marketing of the "information society."* Cresskill, NJ: Hampton.

Thussu, D. K. (Ed.). (1998). *Electronic empires: Global media and local resistance.* London: Edward Arnold.

Thussu, D. K. (2000). *International communication: Continuity and change.* New York: Oxford University Press.

Varis, T. (1985). *International flow of television programmes.* Paris: UNESCO.

Wilkins, K. (Ed.). (2000). *Redeveloping communication for social change: Theory, practice, and power.* Lanham, MD: Rowman & Littlefield.

von Clausewitz, K. (1984). *On war* (Rev. ed., M. Howard & P. Paret, Trans. & Eds.). Princeton, NJ: Princeton University Press.

Wang, G., & Dissanayake, W. (Eds.). (1984). *Continuity and change in communication systems: An Asian perspective.* Norwood, NJ: Ablex: East-West Communication Institute.

Wasko, J. (1994). *Hollywood in the information age.* Cambridge, UK: Polity.

Wasko, J., & Mosco, V. (Eds.). (1992). *Democratic communications in the information age.* Toronto: Garamond Press; Norwood, NJ: Ablex.

Zacher, M., & Sutton, B. (1996). *Governing global networks: International regimes for transportation and communications.* Cambridge, UK: Cambridge University Press.

2

Media Corporations in the Age of Globalization

EDWARD COMOR
American University

As recently as the 1980s, the worldwide ambitions of large-scale media corporations were, almost exclusively, a subject of interest among so-called critical communication analysts. Herbert Schiller's (1969, 1976, 1989) writings on cultural imperialism, for example, are probably the best known of these. But following a series of remarkable developments—the end of the Cold War, the ascendancy of neoliberal economic policies, the rapid growth and dissemination of digital-based information and communication technologies—the political, economic, and technological conditions in which media interests operate have changed dramatically. The term *globalization* has become a commonplace way of characterizing these and related developments. Transnational media mergers and business ventures of unprecedented scale now are the stuff of almost everyday reading in the press, and their effects are being felt by more and more people around the world. As such, no longer is it just the critical analyst who is writing about worldwide media developments—relatively mainstream thinkers also are taking notice.

Governments around the world are enabling giant media corporations to make full use of new technologies through changes in policy and regulation. As Ben Bagdikian (1997) demonstrates in his book *The Media Monopoly,* as a result, fewer and fewer conglomerates are controlling more and more of the information and entertainment that is produced, distributed, and consumed through the media marketplace. Companies such as America Online (AOL)-Time Warner, Microsoft, Disney, News Corporation International, Sony, General Electric, and others all combine hardware and software, information and entertainment, production and distribution capabilities across formerly

19

segmented national and technological boundaries. The $179 billion purchase of Time Warner by AOL in 2000, for example, combines the world's largest Internet service provider with the audiovisual, broadcasting, cable, publishing, music, and other interests (including nearly 200 affiliated Web sites) held by the former. In the words of Robert W. McChesney (1999), increasingly, "the global media market more closely resembles a cartel than it does the competitive marketplace found in economics textbooks" (p. 91).

This chapter identifies and evaluates two general approaches that have been used by analysts in assessing media corporations in the age of globalization. Its first section provides a brief overview of the circumstances shaping the contemporary growth and integration of media and related corporations. The next section explains and provides some background for understanding the aforementioned approaches—what I refer to as the "liberal marketplace" and the "critical structuralist" perspectives. The third section evaluates these and shows that although some approaches are more helpful than others in the task of understanding media developments in the early 21st century, no one approach, by itself, is usually sufficient in this period of extraordinary change. The final section—the conclusion—briefly relates contemporary global media developments with these perspectives. Among other things, it concludes that we should be aware of the limitations of our favored approach and, when necessary, make use of the other to deepen our analyses.

UNDERLYING ECONOMIC FORCES

Not long ago, analyzing media developments mostly involved a detailed understanding of domestic political, economic, and cultural conditions in a particular country and how foreign interests and markets affected these.

But today, as McChesney (1999) points out, "one must first grasp the nature and logic of the global commercial system and then determine how local and national media deviate from the overall system" (p. 78). The economic logic directly shaping this shift predates those factors affecting globalization mentioned above. What economists call horizontal integration has long been a systemic tendency in the media marketplace. This refers to the interest of a firm to control as much of what is made available to consumers as possible. Not only does this provide the corporation with the opportunity to charge consumers higher prices for its information and entertainment products and services, it also gives it more power to dictate prices to suppliers. More generally, by forging such powerful positions, dominant interests make it difficult for others to enter the media marketplace unless the newcomer is extraordinarily wealthy and able to survive years of losses while it constructs its own distribution network and establishes a relationship with suppliers and consumers. Not surprisingly, then, until recently the general history of this particular marketplace has been one in which fewer entities gradually came to dominate particular media subsectors such as the press, cable, film, and the music industry (Demers, 1999, pp. 41-50).

Dating from the 1980s, another form of media integration has been on the rise—vertical integration. Unlike the tendencies described above, this form of integration is characterized by the dominant firms of different media subsectors merging, buying into, or taking over one another. As such, media conglomerates have emerged that include a range of strategic components often referred to as "synergies" (Turow, 1997, pp. 264-290). These usually involve the complementary integration of audiovisual or software interests, hardware production capabilities, and distribution entities. For example, although more than two thirds of Sony's revenues (totaling $63 billion in 2000) are derived from its manufacturing of electronics, its software interests—its music, television, film, and games divisions—are being developed with an eye on cross-media synergies. Headquartered in Japan, its acquisition of U.S.-based CBS Records and Columbia Pictures in 1989 directly reflects this strategy. More recently, digital technologies have enabled Sony to integrate and cross-market its highly successful PlayStation and related game interests (a media subsector whose overall revenues have surpassed those of the world's film industry) with its other holdings.

More fundamentally, the advent of digitalization, the Internet, and related technologies are making the transnational distribution of information and entertainment, when measured on a per unit basis, an undertaking almost free of monetary costs. Instead of packaging, transporting, and retailing information and entertainment to distant markets, online communications are directly connecting producers to consumers. This capability, in effect, is serving to intensify an economic dynamic that has long existed in the information and entertainment software business. As a result of the low costs involved in the reproduction of any particular software product (e.g., duplicating a film onto videotape or downloading a musical recording from the Internet), in relation to the costs involved in producing its prototype (e.g., the $50 million spent on a typical Hollywood film) and in relation to the per unit costs of reproducing "material" commodities (such as a car or a toaster), little economic risk is involved in contemporary efforts to saturate world markets with software commodities. Indeed, it has always made economic sense for media corporations to establish ever larger distribution networks. After all, if, for instance, the Walt Disney Corporation produces 10,000 more copies of the videotape version of *Fantasia* than it can sell, the costs of

doing so are minimal when compared with 10,000 surplus automobiles or even toasters. Now that Internet infrastructures are opening up seemingly costless distribution networks, the economic and technological barriers facing media corporations in their efforts to saturate global markets and grow ever more profitable have fallen more decisively in recent years than at any other time in history.

At the beginning of the 21st century, we are witnessing an unprecedented period of vertical integration in which corporations holding significant information, entertainment, and telecommunications interests are coming together. It is a process stimulated by economic opportunities, facilitated by emerging technological capabilities, and accommodated by government policies—including those that have relegated publicly owned forms of media into their now increasingly secondary status (Kellner, 1990; McChesney, 1999, pp. 63-76). It is also a process that some analysts believe will be economically, politically, and culturally beneficial.

Others, predictably, are more wary. Critics of these dynamic forces tend to view the Internet to be, among other things, a vehicle for the promotion of hyper-consumerist values and lifestyles (Comor, 2001) and the deepening economic exploitation of relatively less developed regions (Sussman & Lent, 1991). Rather than some kind of great equalizer (enabling almost anyone to gather information, mobilize a political constituency, take part in new economic opportunities, etc.), Internet technologies more likely will be used to extend the powers of giant media and other corporations through their growing influence over what people around the world see, hear, and read.

Proponents of new technologies and related reforms, however, counter that associated opportunities far outweigh potential problems stemming from the growth of media corporations. Two reasons are commonly cited. For one thing, new technologies are reducing the costs involved in entering the media marketplace. Almost anyone with advanced computer and Internet capabilities can, they argue, become a producer and distributor of an extraordinary range of information and entertainment commodities (Gates, 1995; Negroponte, 1995). The other reason for their lack of concern involves the view that regulations restricting concentrations of media ownership and local service commitments are outdated as a result of lower costs of entry and by the absolute growth in the number of Internet-mediated information and entertainment outlets becoming available. If a local (or any other) market is underserved, little will stop an entrepreneur from using the Internet to fill the gap. If the media marketplace is becoming a truly global marketplace, regulatory regimes surely must be refashioned and regulatory standards revised in accordance with this new reality.

Critics respond to this laissez-faire position by pointing out that, among other things, the vast majority of online information and entertainment providers are losing money even though the costs of entering the Internet marketplace, relative to the startup costs associated with other media, are negligible. Simply not enough revenue is being generated in relation to online information and entertainment investments. These investments include the costs of promoting the existence (not to mention the ongoing use) of a particular Web site in its competition with the hundreds and perhaps even thousands of choices available to the "surfer." The unprecedented multi-million-dollar advertising campaigns waged by a multitude of Internet startup companies and innumerable efforts to develop customer loyalty (such as the lottery giveaways conducted by iWon.com and others) all point to these high costs. In anticipation of the centrality of online communications, and in light of fulfilling the revenue opportunities that have emerged as a result of the digital integration of

newly acquired corporate assets, the Internet is becoming the global medium for the world's already dominant media conglomerates. As such, critics argue, new media most likely will be dominated by the biggest of the old media (McChesney, 1999).

COMPETING APPROACHES TO THE STUDY OF MEDIA CORPORATIONS

Social scientists and other analysts usually assess media corporations in ways that reflect ingrained views on the characteristics of the social-economic order and the nature of power relations in it. Here two such approaches are delineated—the liberal marketplace and the critical structuralist approach. Although these are assessed with one eye on their chronological development, with the other, the relationship of each to more general societal (particularly political and economic) developments is provided.

Proponents of the liberal marketplace approach have always emphasized the authority of consumers who, by spending their time and money, ultimately dictate what is and is not made available by the media. For these analysts, the media marketplace is inherently democratic. Through it, consumers enjoy the freedom to pick and choose the information and entertainment they desire as long as corporate interests are, in response, free to produce and distribute the information and entertainment people want. If consumer demands are not being met, existing or new commercial interests will fill the void. Alternatively, if corporations are supplying consumers with information and entertainment that is of little use or interest, the marketplace, again, will correct the apparent imbalance (Fowler & Brenner, 1982).

In sum, the proponents of the liberal marketplace approach have always had great faith in the market system and its capacity to send accurate signals to profit-seeking corporations about what people want and do not want in all cultural contexts. As such, whether one is looking at mass media activities in the United States, Iran, or Borneo, governments should only seek to facilitate these marketplace activities, acting as a kind of referee, ensuring that everyone plays by the same rules. The liberal marketplace approach thus places great emphasis on the notion of "consumer sovereignty." From a psychological and sociological perspective, people are assumed to be "rational" decision makers, knowing what information and entertainment are available and desirable. This approach sees the marketplace as a neutral structure, effectively matching up producer capacities with consumer demands. Because the consumers and corporations that buy and sell information and entertainment are assumed to be rational, self-serving, and knowledgeable, these actors and their decision-making capabilities generally are taken for granted. Proponents of the liberal marketplace perspective tend, therefore, to focus their attention on the immediate structural conditions in which these actors act—on the structural conditions of the marketplace itself.

Historically, for many proponents of the liberal marketplace perspective, media corporations were seen to be progressive forces in efforts to make more information available and modify the attitudes of people in Third World countries. In the 1960s, Daniel Lerner of MIT played a leadership role in promoting this "modernization" perspective—a perspective that informed U.S. foreign development policy for many years. For Lerner (1963), "The isolated and illiterate peasants and tribesmen [and women] who compose the bulk of the world's population" should be exposed to "clues as to what the better things of life might be" (pp. 341-342). Also articulating the assumption that the cultural "back-

wardness" of others constituted a significant barrier to development was Ithiel de Sola Pool. According to Pool (1966), "Newspapers and radio enable people to conceive what it is to be a ruler, or a foreigner, or a millionaire, or a movie star" (p. 110).

In sum, Lerner, Pool, and others assumed, first, that modern capitalism and liberal democratic institutions were universally desirable developments. Second, they assumed that Western media would help Third World cultures in their development of capitalism and democracy by stimulating previously unimagined questions and perspectives in the minds of various peoples. And third, it was assumed that once old ways of thinking were challenged and replaced through "modern" institutions, the people of Third World countries would be as "rational" and "free" to express themselves in the information marketplace as are the consumers of the United States and other "developed" societies.

As one of the most influential proponents of this approach, both the specificities of Pool's arguments and his political affiliations are of interest. Pool recognized that historically constructed institutions such as the nation-state, bureaucracy, cities, and class relations all mediate and shape the character of the social and economic structures in which people live and think. However, in the context of the Cold War and efforts to keep Third World countries in line with anticommunist interests, Pool applied his research in efforts to reconstruct non-Western cultures involving the imposition of a range of communication-related reforms. By changing the economic, political, and cultural structures of others—all in the name of "modernization"—it was thought that the capitalist-democratic model could be (and should be) grafted onto the histories of "transitional" societies with strategic benefits for the United States and its allies. In this context, Pool encouraged development policies that involved the opening up of foreign markets to Western media and tele-communications companies as these were seen to be the agents of cultural change and facilitators of capitalist investment.

The fact that know-how and capital can flow out of a country, as well as in, and that the cultural and economic implications of mass media and other Western influences can do more harm than good often escaped the analyses of Lerner, Pool, and their liberal marketplace contemporaries. Stimulating these lacunae, among other things, was the fact that many liberal marketplace theorists received significant research support from various branches of the U.S. government. Pool, for example, was a member of the Council on Foreign Relations and acted as an adviser to the U.S. government during the Cold War through his association with the RAND Corporation. Pool also worked for the CIA-supported propaganda radio stations Radio Free Europe and Radio Liberty (Pool, 1998, p. 3).

Quite unlike the critical structuralist approach, which, from the late 1960s, tended to sympathize or work in support of Third World interests and their calls for some kind of radical reorganization of world communications, proponents of the liberal marketplace perspective believed that corporate interests—including mass media firms—should be subjected to as little regulation as possible. Through their economic success, leading to their technological achievements, and their subsequent dissemination of Western and "modern" perspectives, Western media corporations would facilitate individual liberties and genuine choice in the Third World. As Pool's best-known book, *Technologies of Freedom* (1983), argues, capitalism and its corporate agents ultimately constitute the purveyors of the institutions, technologies, and liberties that most Westerners take for granted.

As critics of this perspective and the liberal marketplace approach pointed out, this position tends to underplay or ignore those complex (and often abstract) forces that might influence media production, audience reception, and a range of potentially undesirable consequences. Rather than the qualities of a given culture, the seductions of advertisers, the state of education in a society, and other such factors, the efficient functioning of the marketplace and, ultimately, the assumed universal superiority of Western models of "development" and rational thinking dominate the analysis. Moreover, this focus on the marketplace as the medium par excellence through which the needs of both producers and consumers are served involves two other questionable assumptions. First, as stated, it assumes that the marketplace is a relatively efficient and neutral arbiter of supply and demand. And second, it assumes that for this to work, it is essential to protect the marketplace from the potentially "harmful" effects of overly zealous government regulators or the "market-distorting" practices of monopolistic corporations.

In effect, the liberal marketplace approach to analyzing media corporations rarely questions status quo social-economic relations and the role of the media in these. Furthermore, the proponents of this perspective—given their inclination to solve problems associated with marketplace inefficiencies and other functional difficulties—are mostly mainstream policymakers, economists, and others interested in narrowly focused, relatively short-term issues (such as, in a contemporary context, the best remedy for Microsoft's anticompetitive practices, the implications of Viacom's holdings in a particular media marketplace, and so forth). As such, the liberal marketplace perspective is inherently uninterested in more complex historical issues, including questions concerning political-economic disparities, social stability and cri-sis, and the media's role in shaping the general cultural environment.

At the time of the predominance of the lib-eral marketplace position as represented by Lerner and Pool, representatives of the critical structuralist perspective were working in what can be described as the intellectual periphery. Many of these critics were either European Marxists or Third World anticolonial intel-lectuals. In the late 1960s and throughout the 1970s, Armand Mattelart, for example, argued that the messages conveyed by media corporations—including consumerism, mo-dernity, mass society, public opinion, and the like—function to mask the structural dispari-ties and injustices of the market system itself. According to Mattelart (1979), through the growing presence of commercial mass media, "public opinion and the concept of modernity become the imaginary actor sustaining the monolithic interests of class and allowing a particular vision to pass as that of the public" (p. 117). More generally, Hamid Mowlana (1975) argued that

> we can hypothesize that the power elite serves as gatekeeper in controlling the rate and kind of diffusion of technology into a system. It may prevent the diffusion of certain technological facts while favoring others that do not threaten to change its power and system structure. Once the diffusion process takes place, it is not always the new technology . . . that is the main source of rising discontent, but the social structure of the country and its bureaucratic and interelite rela-tionships that determine the nature and distribu-tion of that technology. (p. 89)

One of the best-known respondents to the liberal marketplace perspective and its politi-cal implications was Herbert I. Schiller. As Pool and others were supporting Western media activities in Third World countries,

Schiller's work was essential in bringing the writings of critical intellectuals out of the margins and into the center of both academic and popular debates. Importantly, historical developments dating from the 1960s—a ris-ing tide of resistance to Western, and particu-larly American, cultural influences—coin-cided with the publication of Schiller's (1969) *Mass Communications and American Empire*. More than just a defense of traditional cul-tures, Schiller's work stimulated a slew of fresh analyses on the more general power implications of media corporations and re-lated communications activities. These resis-tance efforts and critical writings culminated in the famous Mass Media Declaration of 1978, issued by the United Nations Educa-tional, Scientific and Cultural Organization (UNESCO), calling for a "wider and better balanced dissemination of [international] in-formation" (Preston, Harmen, & Schiller, 1989, p. xvi). Immediately following this was the publication of Sean MacBride's report, *Many Voices, One World* (International Com-mission for the Study of Communication Problems, 1980), on behalf of UNESCO and its articulation of Third World (and others') grievances against the influence of corporate media.

Unlike proponents of the liberal market-place approach, critical structuralists such as Schiller recognized that complex, historically generated structural conditions—conditions largely out of the immediate control of a cor-poration (or even a government) at any given place and time—are the most important fac-tors to take into account when assessing the thoughts and choices of various actors. Like the liberal marketplace tradition, critical structuralists see the marketplace itself to con-stitute a human-made institution. But unlike Pool and others, they take this point one step further and understand the marketplace itself to be an inherently power-laden (rather than

neutral) arbiter of producer-consumer relations. Moreover, critical structuralists tend to
focus on "capitalism" rather than just "the
marketplace" because the former constitutes a
far broader and more complex entity through
which to assess the thoughts and actions of
media executives, consumers, government
officials, technology experts, and others
(Garnham, 1990; Gitlin, 1980; Mosco,
1996). Schiller, for example, incorporates a
complex of structural factors and actors in his
assessment of corporate media power at the
end of the 20th century. An international
order, writes Schiller (1993), is being

> organized by transnational economic interests
> that are largely unaccountable to the nation-
> states in which they operate. This transnational
> corporate system is the product of a rationalized
> and commercialized communications infra-
> structure, which transmits massive flows of in-
> formation and has extended its marketing reach
> to every corner of every hemisphere. While the
> U.S. role in the creation and reproduction of this
> world-wide consumer society has lessened, the
> supporting institutions and the content of the in-
> formation still bear a heavy American imprint.
> (p. 47)

Reflecting the gulf between the liberal
marketplace and the critical structuralist
approaches—a gulf that remains with us in
the 21st century—is the text of a debate between Pool and Schiller recorded in 1980. For
Pool, the investments and activities of media
corporations around the world will provide
people with new technologies, more information, and ultimately, more freedom and
choice. Schiller responds by calling the commercial news, entertainment, and advertising being disseminated by corporate interests mostly "garbage information." Schiller
goes on to say that "Ithiel [de Sola Pool] says
we have to develop new electronic means of

retrieval—for what? To retrieve one pearl in
ten truckloads of garbage? I say get rid of the
garbage before you start worrying about the
pearls" (Pool & Schiller, 1982, pp. 178-179).
Pool's response involves several liberal marketplace assumptions, questioning Schiller
for raising abstract structural issues and sub-
jectively judging the quality of the information being generated by corporations. At the
end of the debate, Schiller sums up his position in relation to Pool's as follows:

> He [Pool] wants people to have a voice. He
> wants people to have opportunities to live more
> decent lives. Well, with electronic technology, as
> it is presently being structured and operating,
> what people will be receiving will be marketing
> messages. . . . [I]n countries which have essential
> needs, which have absolutely urgent priorities
> for food and medical care and similar basic
> wants, to promote a consumer society of the
> kind we [in the West] have—and even the words
> "consumer society" don't actually describe what
> goes on in our types of societies—with elec-
> tronic instrumentation acting as a vehicle to in-
> troduce and to inculcate it in the people of these
> countries, in my estimation, would be a very
> sorrowful development. (Pool & Schiller, 1982,
> pp. 180-181)

Subsequent discussions among liberal marketplace and critical structuralist theorists on
the subject of global media corporations have
taken various forms and directions. Among
the former, much work has been done on the
role of the practices, routines, and resulting
products of the people working for media
corporations. Analyses of concentrated ownership and monopolization tendencies and
their "distorting" effects on marketplace activities also are commonplace (Demers, 1999;
Gans, 1979; Gershon, 1997; Tuchman, 1978;
Tunstall, 1977; Turow, 1984). As for the latter, critical structuralist analyses have contin-

ued to focus on ideological effects, power implications, and the more general relationship of corporate media to global capitalism (McChesney, Wood, & Foster, 1998; Murdock, 1982; Sreberny-Mohammadi, Winseck, McKenna, & Boyd-Barrett, 1997).

One of several significant variations in the critical structuralist literature was initiated by Dallas W. Smythe (1981) and pursued by Sut Jhally (1987) and others. Generally referred to as "the audience as the commodity" perspective, rather than assessing the messages (or "use values") generated by media corporations, this perspective instead focuses on how, in many cases, advertisers are the media's "primary consumers" because they, in fact, most directly "pay the bills." As such, from this point of view, it is more important to assess the "exchange values" (i.e., the capitalist economics) of media messages in relation to their use values (again, their messages) because the structural conditions of this particular component of capitalism most fundamentally shapes why people get the media messages that they get. In stark contrast to liberal marketplace assumptions, for Smythe, Jhally, and others, "consumer sovereignty" does not refer to the individual watching commercial television, reading a newspaper, or listening to a radio broadcast. Instead, the entity that most directly pays for all or most of these services — the corporate advertiser—is ultimately sovereign in determining, through both structural practice and direct intervention, what information and entertainment will be made available and to whom. This, of course, goes some way in explaining Schiller's observation that much of what is being made available to audiences through the mass media (and other commercial sources) is "garbage." It is the structural conditions of the marketplace that underlies this condition rather than some kind of straightforward expression of what people really want to see, read, and hear. Rather than

a neutral arbiter of supply and demand, the media marketplace according to this variant of the critical structuralist perspective turns out to be not so neutral after all.

ASSESSING THE APPROACHES IN A 21st-CENTURY CONTEXT

To summarize, the critical structuralist position emphasizes the interdependence of structural forces in the context of capitalist social relations and its dynamics. Historically based economic inequalities and the status of the wealthy of the world as relatively desirable consumers have perpetuated ingrained disparities in the quality of information and entertainment made available to the world's rich in relation to its poor. Such complex structural conditions predicate that media-related disparities will not disappear overnight through the ascendancy of the Internet and related technologies. If anything, the rapid and widespread proliferation of what has been called "garbage information" or "infotainment" will take place in more of the world's markets. The consequences, generally, will not be good for those harboring aspirations for more thoughtful and democratic forms of global politics.

Essentially, the two approaches discussed in this chapter involve different views on the degrees to which structures influence decision-making capabilities and different perceptions regarding which structures (if any) are most relevant. Also underlying or shaping these positions are explicitly or implicitly expressed political orientations. For example, in assuming that the marketplace is a neutral and efficient arbiter of society's information and entertainment, proponents of the liberal marketplace approach ignore the inherent biases (recognized by critical structuralists) of a marketplace organized under the rubric of capitalism. For the critical structuralist, most fundamentally, if money constitutes the essential means of accessing information or entertainment, those consumers with more money will have more choice and possibly "better" (i.e., more useful or enlightening) information and entertainment available to them in relation to those possessing limited resources. The proponent of the liberal marketplace position tends to either ignore this fundamental disparity or dismiss it as an unchangeable fact of life and thus of little concern to the research agenda at hand.

For the critical structuralist, the social-economic system in which people live both contextualizes and directly shapes what most people do or don't do, imagine and can't imagine. To assume, for instance, that the executive of a transnational media corporation is more or less free to do whatever he or she pleases ignores the fact that human beings do not and, indeed, cannot act autonomously. Education, life experience, the parameters of government regulations, the state of technology, and other such conditions all shape how the individual thinks and acts. More generally, the fundamental conditions of capitalism itself will shape what any corporate official, including managers, technicians, and inventors, can realistically think about and do. The need, ultimately, to realize a profit, for example, imposes clear constraints. The cable television company executive, the computer engineer, the newspaper editor—all must be at least implicitly aware of this necessity. Otherwise, they will be out of a job, or worse still, their firm will be out of business.

There are, of course, cases in which extraordinarily hard-working, brilliant (and fortunate) entrepreneurs or executives have almost independently pushed an idea forward to a point at which that person has stimulated a more general change—has, in fact, altered the structural conditions in which people think and act. One example of this is the founder of Apple Computer, Steve Jobs, who, as its president in the early 1980s, developed and popularized the now ubiquitous graphical user interface (GUI—commonly pronounced "gooey"), which, despite economic losses and his subsequent dismissal by Apple's board of directors, made computing accessible to non-experts. Other such examples include the entrepreneurial zeal of media moguls Ted Turner (through CNN) and Rupert Murdoch (through News Corp.). Yet these, and others, do not belie the fact that structural conditions shape the thoughts and actions of *everyone*.

In sum, metaphorically speaking, no man or woman in the media (or any other) marketplace is an island. Structures—both explicitly recognized and implicitly socialized—affect what people think and do. Liberal marketplace media analysts therefore, inevitably, face difficulties in their efforts to fully evaluate why certain macrohistorical decisions are made, why other decisions are not made, and what ways of thinking and doing likely will emerge in the future. In the absence of a complex theory of structure, such perspectives can become overly descriptive, sometimes even resorting to psychological profiles. Media and related developments also tend to be assessed in terms of trends rather than on the dynamic forces and processes shaping the very conditions in which a whole range of agents and entities acts.

Again, this is not to say that the liberal marketplace approach is silent on questions concerning structure. It does, after all, place great weight on the structural conditions of the marketplace. From this perspective, the contemporary state of technology—involving seemingly fewer barriers to one's participation and apparently greater access to information—is thought to constitute the basis of ideal marketplace conditions. As Bill Gates (1995) puts it,

Capitalism, demonstrably the greatest of the constructed economic systems, has in the past decade clearly proved its advantages over the alternative systems. The information highway [i.e., the Internet] will magnify those advantages. It will allow those who produce goods to see, a lot more efficiently than ever before, what buyers want, and will allow potential consumers to buy those goods more efficiently. Adam Smith would be pleased. More important, consumers everywhere will enjoy the benefits. (p. 183)

Although it is ironic that the U.S. judicial system has found Gates's company, Microsoft, guilty of anti-competitive practices, certainly there are kernels of truth in this technology-induced "perfect market" scenario. The efficiencies lauded by Gates and innumerable others are indeed real (at least for those with adequate incomes, skills, and living in regions of the world maintaining the infrastructures required to take part in online activities). But still, the liberal marketplace approach can be questioned on at least two general counts. First, its assumptions regarding the marketplace as a neutral mediator of supply and demand are, as elaborated above, demonstrably false. And second, the limitations of any perspective that is focused on just one social-economic structure—the marketplace—are many.

Beyond these often overlooked problems, the assumption that consumers are rational decision makers and that they go into the media marketplace with particular demands also is false. Simply put, most human preferences and wants are learned and, more generally, are only comprehensible in the context of complex socialization processes (Comor, 2000). The demand for information and entertainment commodities in the media marketplace does not exist in anything approaching a state of equilibrium with supply precisely because the notion of equilibrium, in this context, is nonsensical. For the most part, people demand information and entertainment products and services only after they have been exposed to them (Babe, 1995). Who, for example, would look forward to the next Tom Cruise film if they have no idea who Tom Cruise is? The fact that supply usually precedes demand in this marketplace also explains the ongoing growth of a multi-billion-dollar worldwide advertising and marketing industry and, of course, the virtually free distribution of software and other such products to consumers during this formative stage of the Internet.

In light of these rather elementary points, not only is the liberal marketplace approach inherently limited, its deliberations regarding just one social-economic structure—the marketplace—itself both reveals a pro-status quo bias and, through its acritical application, ultimately serves to entrench its own analytical limitations.

Let us take this one step further. Imagine, if possible, that everyone in the world not only lives in a state of absolute equality in terms of income and access to media but also that the human mind is altogether capable of making rational decisions (in the mode of the television science fiction character Mr. Spock). Under such conditions, would people then not possess the means to express their needs and interests and, in fact, become the ultimate arbiters of what television programs survive, what magazines are popular, and which Web sites are being visited? The answer to this question is no because there is a range of other structural forces at work shaping the choices available to the consumer. One of the most influential of these, especially in the realm of "free" media, is the subsector primarily responsible for generating demand—the advertising industry (Jhally, 1987).

Returning to "the audience as the commodity" perspective discussed earlier, if the producers of goods and services, through advertising firms, pay for most of what is made available in the media marketplace, advertising clearly constitutes a significant structural component shaping the parameters of choice. Let us ask the following to illustrate this point: Would most advertisers sponsor media that consistently promote anticonsumerist messages, higher tax burdens on corporations, and other such positions? No doubt, niche programming of this type or specialized publications or Web sites can exist through the support of corporate sponsors. But to imagine that such perspectives could become the everyday norms of a world media system dominated by commercial interests is almost unimaginable given the systemic biases that infuse such capitalist structures. The most fundamental ideological component of these, of course, is the use of media to promote the general belief system known as consumerism (Lee, 1995).

The notion of consumer sovereignty, despite its status as a kind of "common sense" among both popular writers and proponents of the liberal marketplace approach, is itself nonsense precisely because one's very understanding of "rational" thought and action is not a simple result of having "all the facts" (or what economists commonly refer to as "perfect information"). The ways in which human beings assess their own and others' standards of what is "rational" is the result of socialization processes that involve a lifetime of media messages generated with an eye on promoting particular (and commercially compelling) ways of thinking, looking, and acting as "normal" or "desirable." Because standards of rationality are socially constructed "realities" (Berger & Luckmann, 1967), consumer preferences can be fully understood only when the structural biases of any particular marketplace and social-economic system are taken into account (Comor, 2001).

Given such fundamental problems, the critical structuralist perspective may appear to be the antidote to these analytical limitations. Its proponents, after all, place great emphasis on a range of interrelated historical structures, including the market system. However, the strength of the critical structuralist approach—its macrohistorical orientation and its concern with multiple and integrated levels of both structure and agency—also can constitute the bases of its own shortcomings. In examining media developments in the context of various and all-encompassing structures, the tendency of its proponents to play down the role of individual thought and action, and its general dismissal of the marketplace as a potentially efficient mediator of supply and demand, can lead to unnecessary analytical constraints. This usually takes place when the critical structuralist approach is applied to the exclusion of others on issues or problems that involve relatively limited time frames and the decisions of actors faced with the opportunity to make significant and potentially creative decisions.

For example, a critical structuralist perspective, although certainly of great value when used to frame the context and dynamics shaping thought and action, is limited in its capacity to fully comprehend the particulars of decisive actors and events in media history. If Steve Jobs had not been born, would the history of computing (and, thus, contemporary media developments) be significantly different? Proponents of the critical structuralist approach most likely would say no—history (i.e., structural conditions) forges human thought and action much more than agency shapes structure. At the very least, this response should be questioned in cases in which the importance of particular decisions and their subsequent implications constitute obvious turning points. In addition to the "heroics" of Steve Jobs and others, one can go still farther back in history to find illustrative examples such as the decisive changes to commercial broadcasting introduced by CBS president William Paley in the 1930s (Halberstam, 1979, pp. 21-33) and the role of William Randolph Hearst in establishing the so-called yellow press and its implications on the history of "the news."

Before proceeding to the conclusion of this chapter, it is important to point out that few academics work *entirely* within the parameters of just one of the approaches discussed. Arguably, the economic and technological opportunities facing media corporations, their strategic decisions, and the implications of these are more difficult to assess today than at any other time. More than ever before, in the words of the well-known sociologist C. Wright Mills (1970), our analyses must continually "range from the most impersonal and remote transformations to the most intimate features of the human self" (p. 13) as we aspire to understand global media developments in all their complexity.

CONCLUSION: UNDERSTANDING MEDIA IN THE AGE OF GLOBALIZATION

Global media corporations are important to a range of analysts for two fundamental reasons. First, media corporations are pivotal agents in the production and distribution of information and images throughout the world. Second, they constitute some of the most influential entities in the emerging history of the Internet and related digital technologies in terms of how these will be structured, who will have access to them, and how they will be used. In promoting and distributing information and entertainment commodities through various but increasingly interrelated means, and through concerted efforts to control the timing and pricing of this process, media conglomerates not only are becoming larger, they have become ever-growing components of everyday life for more and more people. Those who recognize the significance of media corporations at the beginning of a new century and the inherent complexities of the research before us may well want to consider the strengths and weaknesses of their own perspectives in relation to the two general approaches outlined in this chapter.

The relatively commonplace application of the liberal marketplace approach is understandable in terms of its emphasis on the problem-solving needs of the status quo. I am not implying that this way of assessing media corporations should be ignored. Indeed, in this period of rapid change involving arguably revolutionary developments in communication technologies, the role of both entrepreneurs and marketplace structures has been heightened rather than diminished. In an environment characterized by rapid transition and unpredictability, the communication scholar armed with an acute awareness of the potentially complementary aspects of different perspectives may find himself or herself in an appropriately flexible position to assess ongoing developments.

This is not to say, however, that both approaches are equally helpful. As I have implied throughout much of this chapter, the critical structuralist position constitutes the richer perspective. It is, after all, inherently more receptive in assessing periods of rapid change precisely because it is oriented toward the integrated and historical analyses of a complex of structures. But to repeat, this strength also can be its weakness. In its focus on structure, it can overlook the occasionally decisive role of agency in terms of both the relatively autonomous actions of individuals and, collectively, the demands of consumers.

In this age of globalization, international and transnational technological, political, economic, and cultural developments are inextricably interrelated. Analysts of media corporations can no more ignore this contextual reality than they can ignore the virtual annihilation of boundaries among media subsectors through the application of digital technologies. Beyond estimating the number of "alternative" information and entertainment providers that will survive to become established participants in the emerging media universe are questions involving the implications of the ongoing predominance of a corporate-run commercial marketplace on the world's political, economic, and cultural landscapes.

In a media marketplace characterized by an explosion of outlets, the competition to gain the attention and loyalty of an audience usually involves the promotion of ever more sensational images and ideas. In the struggle to attract eyeballs and credit cards, the progressive opportunities heralded by the arrival of the Internet may be drowned out as digital technologies are applied by corporate interests driven forward by the systemic compulsion to grow. For analysts of these and related developments, the approaches outlined in this chapter will no doubt continue to, in Pool's words, facilitate "a closer approximation to the truth." More ambitiously, as Schiller puts it, such analytical tools can help guide us in strategic efforts to "change the world" in the new century now upon us (Pool & Schiller, 1982, p. 174).

REFERENCES

Babe, R. E. (1995). *Communication and the transformation of economics.* Boulder, CO: Westview.

Bagdikian, B. H. (1997). *The media monopoly.* Boston: Beacon.

Berger, P. L., & Luckmann, T. (1967). *The social construction of reality.* Garden City, NY: Anchor.

Comor, E. (2000). Household consumption on the Internet. *Journal of Economic Issues, 34*(1), 105-116.

Comor, E. (2001). New technologies and consumption: Contradictions in the emerging world order. In J. N. Rosenau & J. P. Singh (Eds.), *Information technologies and global politics.* Albany: State University of New York Press.

Demers, D. (1999). *Global media, menace or messiah?* Cresskill, NJ: Hampton.

Fowler, M. S., & Brenner, D. L. (1982). A marketplace approach to broadcasting regulation. *Texas Law Review, 60*(2), 207-257.

Gans, H. (1979). *Deciding what's news.* New York: Vintage.

Garnham, N. (1990). *Capitalism and communication.* London: Sage.

Gates, B. (1995). *The road ahead.* New York: Viking.

Gershon, R. A. (1997). *The transnational media corporation: Global messages and free market competition.* Mahwah, NJ: Lawrence Erlbaum.

Gitlin, T. (1980). *The whole world is watching.* Berkeley: University of California Press.

Halberstam, D. (1979). *The powers that be.* New York: Knopf.

International Commission for the Study of Communication Problems. (1980). *Many voices, one world: Towards a new, more just and more efficient world information and communication order.* Paris: UNESCO.

Jhally, S. (1987). *The codes of advertising.* New York: St. Martin's.

Kellner, D. (1990). *Television and the crisis of democracy.* Boulder, CO: Westview.

Lee, M. J. (1995). *Consumer culture reborn.* London: Routledge.

Lerner, D. (1963). Toward a communication theory of modernization. In L. Pye (Ed.), *Communications and political development* (pp. 327-350). Princeton, NJ: Princeton University Press.

Mattelart, A. (1979). Communication ideology and class practice. In A. Mattelart & S. Siegelaub (Eds.), *Communication and class struggle* (pp. 115-123). New York: International General.

McChesney, R. W. (1999). *Rich media, poor democracy*. Urbana: University of Illinois Press.

McChesney, R. W., Wood, E. M., & Foster, J. B. (Eds.). (1998). *Capitalism and the information age*. New York: Monthly Review Press.

Mills, C. W. (1970). *The sociological imagination*. Harmondsworth, UK: Penguin.

Mosco, V. (1996). *The political economy of communication*. London: Sage.

Mowlana, H. (1975). The multinational corporation and the diffusion of technology. In A. A. Said & L. R. Simmons (Eds.), *The new sovereigns: MNCs as world powers* (pp. 77-90). Englewood Cliffs, NJ: Prentice Hall.

Murdock, G. (1982). Large corporations and the control of the communications industries. In M. Gurevitch, T. Bennett, J. Curran, & J. Woollacott (Eds.), *Culture, society and the media*. London: Routledge.

Negroponte, N. (1995). *Going digital*. New York: Knopf.

Pool, I. de S. (1966). Communication and development. In M. Weiner (Ed.), *Modernization: The dynamics of growth* (pp. 105-116). Washington, DC: Voice of America Forum Lecture Series.

Pool. I. de S. (1983). *Technologies of freedom*. Cambridge, MA: Belknap.

Pool, I. de S. (1998). *Politics in wired nations* (L. S. Etheredge, Ed.). New Brunswick, NJ: Transaction Books.

Pool, I. de S., & Schiller, H. I. (1982). Perspectives on communications research: An exchange. In International Association for Mass Communication Research (Ed.), *New structures of international communication? The role of research* (pp. 172-181). Leicester, UK: Adams Bros. & Shardlow.

Preston, W., Harmen, C., & Schiller, H. I. (1989). *Hope and folly: The United States and UNESCO*. Minneapolis: University of Minnesota Press.

Schiller, H. I. (1969). *Mass communications and American empire*. New York: A. M. Kelley.

Schiller, H. I. (1976). *Communication and cultural domination*. White Plains, NY: International Arts and Sciences Press.

Schiller, H. I. (1989). *Culture, Inc.: The corporate takeover of public expression*. New York: Oxford University Press.

Schiller, H. I. (1993, Summer). Transnational media. *Journal of International Affairs*, pp. 47-59.

Smythe, D. W. (1981). *Dependency Road: Communications, capitalism, consciousness, and Canada*. Norwood, NJ: Ablex.

Sreberny-Mohammadi, A., Winseck, D., McKenna, J., & Boyd-Barrett, O. (Eds.). (1997). *Media in global context: A reader*. London: Edward Arnold.

Sussman, G., & Lent, J. A. (1991). Introduction. In G. Sussman & J. A. Lent (Eds.), *Transnational communications: Wiring the Third World*. Newbury Park, CA: Sage.

Tuchman, G. (1978). *Making news: A study in the construction of reality*. New York: Free Press.

Tunstall, J. (1977). *The media are American*. New York: Columbia University Press.

Turow, J. (1984). *Media industries: The production of news and entertainment*. New York: Longman.

Turow, J. (1997). *Media systems in society*. New York: Longman.

3

Global Communication Orders

OLIVER BOYD-BARRETT
California State Polytechnic University, Pomona

DEFINING THE CONCEPT

The concept of the New World Information and Communication Order (NWICO) is 25 years old at the time of writing. As a political tool, it had little influence on the world's communication media. What then did it signify, and why am I writing about it now?

In this chapter, I review the definition and origins of NWICO and its political and intellectual contexts. I look at the various phases of its history, at differences of viewpoint about its significance, and at evaluations of communication experts. I examine the paradox of its political demise and continuing relevance.

NWICO was a position statement, molded principally by the countries of the developing world in alliance with the communist nations of the Soviet Union and Eastern Europe. Their voices were represented through the United Nations, and through the movement of the Non-Aligned Nations, whose purpose was to resist incorporation within the sphere of influence of either of the then two superpowers. NWICO was a protest, whose proponents argued that the structure and operation of global communication had grossly inequitable consequences. They said that this structure advantaged established media proprietors and their sponsors in the developed world, allowing them to dominate global communication with the perspectives of the developed world. Developing countries, on the other hand, lacked equivalent means to originate expression, were overly dependent on information transmitted from the developed world, and were largely dependent on Western-based media to articulate and disseminate information even about the developing world itself. NWICO signified a strategy to end such inequalities.

The NWICO debate is of historical interest for anyone wanting to monitor relations between developed and developing, rich and poor nations. It is significant for its contribution to the articulation of human rights within the United Nations. Many structural inequalities addressed by NWICO still remain in evidence; some have intensified. NWICO constituted a timely recognition that communications—then largely regarded as a national policy matters, except for esoteric regulatory issues concerning allocation of access to the electromagnetic spectrum—had acquired a significant global dimension. The operation of international communication had implications for national sovereignty, and therefore they had to be regulated for reasons of national security.

NWICO signifies a transition between world orders. Governance of the earlier order was articulated by nation states, whose dialogue was given form by national media. The new order is governed by a neoliberal economic presumption of an open and global marketplace regulated by rules of competition. This order is adjudicated and adjusted by "global" institutions such as the World Trade Organization, the World Bank, and the International Monetary Fund, in which the wealthy nations exercise most influence. The new order is associated with the ascendancy of transnational corporations in the global economy. It is identified with communication media that are increasingly owned by international capital. Communications facilitate the operations of the transnational corporations, of which there were approximately 60,000 in 2000, with 600,000 affiliates. In number and importance, most are based in the United States, Britain, and Japan, countries that constitute the most important transnational corporation markets and in which most of their direct employees are based.

NWICO emerged when the United States as a global superpower was threatened by its failure in Vietnam, a war that had been fought to contain the spread of communism, at the cost of many hundreds of thousands of lives. Coincidentally, it was a war whose U.S. objective was attained two decades later by the tentative

entry of Vietnam into the world economy. A further defeat, indirectly linked to Vietnam, was the exposure of U.S. government duplicity at the highest levels during Watergate. Such public exposure, leading to the successful ouster of President Richard Nixon, provoked a crisis of confidence both between press and government and between government and society. Vietnam and Watergate fueled a new radicalism in American society among those disillusioned by the economic, social, and foreign policies of their country's power elite. Adding to the general malaise of war defeat was the newfound strength of the Organization of Petroleum Exporting Countries (OPEC), which exerted its collective control over the volume of oil production and raised prices. Non-oil countries feared the economic impact of higher gasoline prices, and the possibility that the OPEC example might be adopted by other alliances of primary goods exporters in the developing world.

The economic miracle of Japan and its developing supremacy in the manufacture and global sale of audiovisual equipment and cars underlined U.S. vulnerability to labor at home, lower wages abroad, and global competition. The persistence of Soviet and Chinese communism and the nuclear arms race between the United States and the Soviet Union, and their global rivalry for political influence, constituted an all-absorbing investment of attention and resources. This atmosphere of fear and rivalry provided the pretext, in the name of "freedom," for U.S. support of outrageously brutal and corrupt dictatorships. In Chile, for example, the United States helped to overthrow a democratically elected socialist government and to install and sustain the murderous regime of a military dictator, Augusto Pinochet.

Computer innovation—benefiting from considerable military and defense investment—was beginning to demonstrate its technical revolutionary potential, aided in part by the relaxation of antitrust legislation to permit collaboration between otherwise competing corporations in research and development.

There is important work to be done in tracing linkages between the threatened supremacy of the United States in the 1970s and the new world order initiated by Republican Ronald Reagan in the United States and Conservative Margaret Thatcher in the United Kingdom from the early 1980s. This new world order rejected strategies of compromise with the developing world in the forums of the United Nations and its agency, UNESCO (United Nations Educational, Scientific and Cultural Organization). The number of members of the United Nations had grown significantly with the success of independent movements and the subsequent creation of new nations. The United States and its allies no longer enjoyed uncontested control over the United Nations. Debates about the new world economic order and its sister concept, NWICO, were nurtured precisely through such forums. In place of the old world order of sovereign national states operating autonomously in international trade, communications, and other flows, the United States and its allies, working through the General Agreement on Tariffs and Trade (GATT), the International Monetary Fund, and the World Bank, proposed an order of increasingly open markets. The prospect of opening up their domestic markets to greater external competition was a small price to pay for the immeasurably greater advantage, to already powerful economies, of gaining unfettered access to overseas markets. Whether this transition of world orders is an overall positive or negative thing is a matter of considerable contention. Advocates of the new world order may say that it has brought relief to the peoples of the erstwhile stagnant economies of the communist world and that free flows of capital distribute job opportunities and wealth globally. The large, continuous U.S. trade deficit demonstrates just how much the U.S. domestic market is open to foreign producers, and the fluid movement of capital undermines older oligarchies and supports democracy, where practicable, as providing a relatively stable business environment. Critics of the new world order are particularly concerned that the increasing volume and penetration of international capital weaken state control and undermine the health of the "public sphere." They fear that state-sanctioned, unfettered pursuit of corporate profit is dangerous to the environment, creates economic disparities within and between nations, and destroys cultural identity.

Communication industries are important to the neoliberal new world order. They are sizable industries in their own right, generate international trade, and grow more important as digitization enhances communication capacity and speed. Older regulatory structures were based on presumptions of the scarcity of communication space (airwaves), and on egalitarian ideologies of universal service, but have collapsed before the prospect of a seeming infinity of bandwidth. The conquest of space and time has been of great benefit to transnational corporations. These advances accelerate the distribution of global capital and financial markets. They consolidate alliances between financial elites around the world. They promote the emergence of a global class of the super-rich and yet they also promote alliances of movements of resistance. Applied to communication industries, neoliberalism intensifies the global process of communication commercialization—even of the "public service media." It subverts the authority and wealth of state-sponsored communication monopolies in broadcasting and telecommunications. Many of these have been privatized, or forced to compete with new, commercial competitors, domestic and foreign. The new order favors media products that maximize profit by attracting either large or wealthy audiences and delivering these audiences to advertisers. It favors a media environment that respects the needs of capital, at the expense of the state and civil society. But the decline of state involvement in media, where this has occurred, is not everywhere mourned. The "public service" models of Western Europe, best exemplified by the British Broadcasting Corporation, did not translate easily to other parts of the world. They had and still have much to commend them. But they have also been accused of cultural elitism, of being insufficiently vigorous in their resistance to contentious political controls and interference. The potential contribution of communication media to the wider civil society remains an inspiration for those who engage critically with current global trends and is reason in itself for pondering the fate of NWICO.

ORIGINS AND CONTEXTS

History of NWICO

Nordenstreng (1995) summarized the cornerstones of NWICO as the "four Ds": decolonization, development, democratization, and demonopolization. He traced its roots to the League of Nations. Many "international instruments"—resolutions or commitments agreed on between nations—have touched directly on communications and, less directly, on human rights as these might pertain to communications. The Universal Declaration of Human Rights was passed in 1948. U.N. consideration of freedom of information and an international code of ethics for journalists date back to the 1940s. A 1952 U.N. General Assembly resolution called for resources for independent, domestic, information enterprises, as contributors to the development of public opinion. The U.N. Economic and Social Council (ECOSOC) addressed the issue of global imbalance of information structures as early as 1961. The U.N. General Assembly in 1962 noted that 70% of the world's population lacked adequate information facilities and were denied the effective enjoyment of the right to information. The U.N. General Assembly, in 1966 and 1972, addressed issues of satellite broadcasting and resolved in favor of national sovereignty, upholding "the principle of prior consent" by the receiving country.

In 1974, the United Nations presented the Declaration on the New International Economic Order (NIEO). This advocated an equitable economic relationship between nations of the First and Third Worlds. It proposed improved terms of trade for the Third World, greater Third World control over productive assets, more interaction between Third World countries, more Third World presence in First World markets, and more Third World influence in global economic institutions. NWICO, sister to NWEO, was created to foster more equitable communications between First and Third Worlds. It proposed news-exchange agreements, greater Third World countries' control over their own communications assets, improvements in the quantity and quality of news about Third World countries in Third World media, a stronger Third World media presence in the First World, and enhancement of Third World influence in UNESCO/ International Telecommunication Union or other forums.

Specifically, Nordenstreng (1995) traces NWICO back to Tunis at the end of March 1976. Its emergence postdated the Helsinki agreements between 33 European nations, the United States, and Canada. These enhanced international cooperation in practically all fields—from commerce and industry to culture and communication. The Helsinki accords, says Schiller (1976), represented a U.S. relaxation of its doctrine of "free flow," a doctrine that employed the concept of freedom as an excuse for imperialistic domination. Another significant contribution to the birth of NWICO was the Intergovernmental Meeting of Experts at UNESCO in Paris, December 1975. Its purpose was to prepare the Declaration on Fundamental Principles Governing the Use of the Mass Media in Strengthening Peace and International Understanding and in Combating War Propaganda, Racism and Apartheid. This was a Soviet and East European initiative, backed by militant developing countries. It had been discussed at the UNESCO General Assembly in 1974. Progress was complicated by Arab countries' calls for the inclusion of references to Zionism as a form of racism and racial discrimination.

The 1976 Tunis Non-Aligned Symposium on Information was organized by the Non-Aligned Movement (NAM), based on a mandate by the previous NAM summit and bringing together nearly 200 representatives from 38 NAM member states, some international organizations (including the United Nations and UNESCO), and some countries as invited guests. In opening the symposium, Tunisia's prime minister made reference to NAM's "global majority" and its entitlement to readjustment of international relations leading to the establishment of a new economic order based on a more equitable distribution of resources. During the meeting, a Peruvian delegate, German Carnero Roque, noting that the fight for national emancipation was often distorted by international communication media, made reference to the "new international information order."

NAM had already helped to establish an alternative news agency, the Non-Aligned News Agencies Pool (NANAP). From the Conference of the Press Agencies Pool of the Non-Aligned Pool in New Delhi, in July 1976, there emerged the New Delhi Declaration. This referred to the inadequacy and imbalance of global information flows and noted that the right to freedom of information could be secured only by material means and that a new international order for information was as necessary as the new international economic order.

A resolution adopted at the fourth meeting of the Inter-Governmental Coordinating Council for Information of Non-Aligned Countries in Baghdad, in June 1980, was an outspoken articulation of NWICO principles within the context of international law. Its preamble invoked relevant decisions of NAM summits in Algiers (1973), Colombo (1976), and Havana (1979); the U.N. decisions concerning NIEO, disarmament, and information; and the Mass Media Declaration of UNESCO. The 1980 Baghdad document talks of

- the right of every nation to develop its own independent information system and to protect its national sovereignty and cultural identity, in particular by regulating the activities of the transnational corporations;

- the right of people and individuals to acquire an objective picture of reality by means of accurate and comprehensive information as well as to express themselves freely through various media of culture and communication;

- the right of every nation to use its means of information to make known worldwide its interests, its aspirations, and its political, moral, and cultural values;

- the right of every nation to participate, on the governmental and nongovernmental level, in the international exchange of information under conditions of equality, justice, and mutual advantage; and

- the responsibility of the producers of information for its truthfulness and objectivity as well as for the particular social objectives to which the information activities are dedicated.

Following publication of the MacBride report, *Many Voices, One World* (International Commission for the Study of Communication Problems, 1980), the UNESCO General Conference in Belgrade that same year passed a milder version of the NAM document. This noted that NWICO could be based on

- elimination of imbalances and inequalities;

- elimination of the negative effects of certain monopolies and excessive concentrations;

- removal of internal and external obstacles to a fee flow and wider and better balanced dissemination of information and ideas;

- plurality of sources and channels of information;

- freedom of the press and information;

- freedom and responsibility of journalists and all professionals in the communication media;

- respect for each people's cultural identity and the right of each nation to inform the world public about its interests, its aspirations, and its social and cultural values;

- respect for the right of all peoples to participate in international exchanges of information on the basis of equality, justice, and mutual benefit; and

- respect for the right of the public, of ethnic and social groups, and of individuals to have access to information sources and to participate actively in the communication process.

Postcolonialism

A full explanation of developing countries' interest in NWICO must extend beyond the internal dynamics of international organizations. Hamelink (1997) locates NWICO within the context of postcolonialism. He cites the challenges that recently liberated states faced when trying to achieve national

integration in territories whose boundaries were artificial constructs, many of whose peoples were multiethnic and multilingual and whose economies had been developed to suit Western business interests. Western technologies were transferred to cultural contexts for which they were not always suitable, at a high price in precious foreign exchange, often within programs of tied aid, and they created a dependent relationship on provider companies for spare parts and repairs. NAM forums offered an opportunity for dialogue both between the ex-colonial powers and countries of the South and among the countries of the South. Growing disillusion with postcolonialism contributed to suspicion of multinational corporations and cynicism about the Western political interests.

Intellectual Radicalism: New Waves

The arguments of developing countries drew in part on a new generation of communications thinking. Up to the mid-1960s, the United Nations and UNESCO promoted a two-dimensional approach: free flow of information and development communication. Development communication was conservatively defined as the transfer of technology, skills, and culture from prosperous Western countries to developing countries. Some experts tolerated government control of media: They believed media had a responsibility to facilitate modernization, defined in a way that prioritized state efforts to achieve national integration and industrialization. But they gave insufficient attention to which interests defined modernization and which interests were served by the media, or to media working practices that shaped their content.

NWICO debates corresponded with important shifts in scholarly thinking. A new radicalism was reflected in Third World voices such as those of Fritz Fanon (1967) and Paulo

Freire (1970); in protests against American intervention in Vietnam; in European student movements that rocked campuses in hostile reaction to Vietnam, cultural conservatism, and the "massification" of higher education. Social scientists such as Baran and Sweezy (1968), Noam Chomsky (1990), Herbert Marcuse (1964), C. Wright Mills (1956), and Herbert Schiller (1969) rediscovered and reinterpreted Marx. They subverted fundamental mainstream ideas about economics, history, language, psychology, social structure, and communications, mainly by tracing the links between micro and macro levels of analysis, and analyzed phenomena in their full historical, political, cultural, and economic contexts. With their help, communication research wrenched itself free of quantitative scientism and psychology that had numbed scholarly ability to ask socially relevant questions, think critically, and identify methodologies appropriate to the questions that were asked. Communication scholarship notably in the works of Curran and Seaton (1980), Murdock and Golding (1977), Halloran, Elliot, and Murdock (1970), Mattelart (1979), Nordenstreng (1984), Schiller (1969), Tunstall (1977), and Varis (1973) showed how media worldwide were subject to forces that filtered their representations of the world in the interests of hegemonic power. They fingered corporate and political interests of the United States, and of a small handful of other countries, among them Britain, France, and Japan. Some of the best work from this tradition became available only after NWICO had lost steam under counterattack.

These influences conceptualized significant issues, among them (a) the *imbalance* of communication flows between First and Third Worlds, (b) the *content* of that flow (which in news, for example, prioritized the First World and further undermined the Third World), and (c) *control* of that flow (principally by Western countries, in their own interests).

The NWICO movement's response to these issues, as reflected in the 1980 MacBride report, was to urge the development of national communication policies in developing countries, elaborate guiding principles for mass media in the international sphere, restructure the international information system to achieve greater national autonomy and equity between nations, and stimulate indigenous cultural expression and local communication industry.

PHASES

Nordenstreng (1995) identifies three different phases of the debate. The first was the "decolonization offensive," in which the Third World articulated a collective protest to the First World. Then the West counterattacked, with the help, among others, of the International Press Institute and the Inter-American Press Association. The U.S. Senate Committee on Foreign Relations prepared reports and hearings. Western governments prepared deals, offering material help to build mass media infrastructures. This led to the compromise Mass Media Declaration of 1978, and later to the International Programme for the Development of Communication (IPDC), whose purpose, said critics, was to deflect attention from ideology toward technical aid issues. Radical statements were still to be heard, as at the Intergovernmental Conference on Communication Policies in Asia and Oceania, in Kuala Lumpur in 1979, and at the Intergovernmental Conference on Communication Policies in Africa, in Yaoundé in July 1980. The latter noted that communication problems cannot be reduced to issues of technology transfer or resource distribution. These are essential, certainly, but there are more important issues of ideology and journalistic practice. These were expressed at a conference of 300,000 organized journalists in Mexico City in 1980, which proposed 10 principles for an international code of journalistic ethics.

But the United States was disengaging from the debate. Maintaining a semblance of accommodation, the United States walked away well satisfied from the 1979 World Administrative Radio Conference of the International Telecommunication Union in Geneva, which had met to allocate the international airwaves. Conservatives grew more vocal in opposition to NWICO, which *Time* (October 6, 1980) deemed to directly undermine press freedom. The managing director of Reuters opposed a policy that he claimed would support government control of expression. The United States and Western Europe supported the setting up of IPDC, a policy one U.S. diplomat described as the outcome of "our practical, nonideological approach" in place of "Soviet-inspired ideological approaches." Within six months of the UNESCO General Conference in Belgrade that had endorsed the MacBride report and established IPDC, came the Talloires meeting of 63 delegates from 21 countries to take a united stand against NWICO. Its main resolution urged UNESCO to abandon attempts to regulate global information and strive instead for practical solutions to Third World media advancement. The "Talloires approach" urged developing country media to cooperate with the private sector in the West in setting up, training, and maintaining media infrastructure and personnel.

NWICO references continued until the late 1980s. A compromise formulation by UNESCO's 1983 General Conference referred to "a new world information and communication order, seen as an evolving and continuous process, conducive to a free flow and better balanced dissemination of information." This was one year before U.S. withdrawal from UNESCO, followed by Britain and Singapore, actions that crippled UNESCO economically. Reference to NWICO appeared in a resolution from the 1985 General Conference. With the ascent of Federico Mayor as director general in 1987, UNESCO ceased to promote NWICO altogether, resorting instead to free flow. NWICO discussion continued in NAM, but NAM influence collapsed with the disintegration of Yugoslavia and the end of European communism. Annual meetings continue of the MacBride Round Table on Communication, a coalition of nongovernmental organizations and professional and academic supporters of NWICO.

KEY POSITIONS

NWICO was a dialogue between three distinct power blocs (Wells, 1987). The Soviets wanted resolutions to secure the conditions necessary for peace, including the responsible use of communications and information. They argued that information must serve the interests of the state as representative of the people. Journalists had to educate their reading publics in socialist principles and serve the cause of international peace. Their work was subject to state control, to prevent dissemination of undesirable material. The Soviets distrusted the Western presumption of "freedom of information" as an ultimate good. Individuals could not exercise their right to freedom unless they had access to the means of communication, and such access was denied when the means of communication were controlled mainly by the wealthy. "Freedom of communication" if applied internationally, contravened national sovereignty. Governments also had to guarantee that citizens had access to "correct" information.

The Soviet position was alien to the West. Of course, Soviet principles clashed with actual Soviet practice. Their media were no less concentrated in state hands than Western media were concentrated in the hands of commercial interests. But Soviet philosophy of the 1970s is still a challenge to the West, particularly with respect to the protection of national sovereignty. Global neoliberal hegemony rarely exhibits a defense of national ideology that does not prioritize openness to the global market. This perspective has attained the state of "naturalness" that in the West is a hallmark of the most successful, all-pervasive, and all-invasive of ideologies. Yet the self-definition of many states is emphatically ideological, unsympathetic to invasion of communication space from programming content that violates cherished social, political, and cultural beliefs and values. Why should communications not be directed by the state? The West argues that state control is dangerous to international peace and to human rights. Human rights, at least in theory, were respected both by Soviet insistence on the "responsibility" of journalists and the rights of citizens to "correct" information. The state had considerable power even in many countries of the West, for example, over national broadcasting institutions. The essential difference between the two positions was the higher value the Soviets placed on collective interest (even if in practice it was the party and state that were served) and to the higher value the West placed on the individual (even if in practice it was business that was served). For the West it was incredulous that anyone should seriously trust the state to police "correct" information; Westerners imputed the mere suggestion to nefarious motives.

The Western bloc held fast to the "free flow of information" and the principle of freedom from state interference with its presumption that actual state influences in the West are mostly benign. Not accepting the Soviet notion that the state ensures media responsibility, the West saw a relationship between international conflict and state manipulation of information flows. The West suspected that many of the collective "rights" referred to by NWICO were a cloak for reinforcement of state control. Advertising, far from being a pernicious barrier to the supply of public-serving information, was seen as the guarantor of freedom from the state and of media credibility. This argument underestimated public capacity to pay for media content without the intermediary filter of advertising. The West was concerned (sensibly) about loosely drafted legal and extra-legal propositions, and about measures that might justify the distribution of subsidies only to media that did the bidding of governments. Issues of responsibility and ethics, in the Western bloc, were considered best achieved voluntarily, through codes of ethics and journalist training. The West treated things that alarmed the non-Western countries as of only marginal concern: for example, the might of private capital through media ownership, advertising, and secret or informal alliances with political parties, and the power of even Western states to corrupt the validity, relevance, and accessibility of public information and to curtail the scope for public participation in social communication.

The developing world, represented principally by NAM, was closer to the Soviet than to the Western position, but distinct. It was hostile to Western laissez-faire principles of free flow, freedom that was of benefit mainly to countries and institutions that were already strong, freedom for Western media whose wealth derived from affluent domestic markets. Having covered their costs on domestic markets, they had an unbeatable advantage in foreign markets. They enjoyed links with big industry (through advertising) and with the state (through informal alliance and shared ideology). The main beneficiaries were media proprietors and their allies in government, defense, and other industries with which the media were associated through ownership and partnership. They had the freedom to push information, advertising, ideology, and propaganda anywhere in the world. Developing countries lacked the wealth to arrest this one-way flow, and they lacked the credibility and sophistication to penetrate Western markets. Their protests were more than an expression of hurt national pride. It was a question of investment. In "coups and earthquakes," Western coverage of the developing world (Rosenblum, 1979), Western media were "free" to construct whatever negative images they wanted, without fear of reprisal or serious challenge and with little concern for the damage that such coverage inflicted on investment flows.

Developing countries in the 1970s seemed unable to protect infant media industries. The "dumping" of Western television products at cheap rates made it difficult to nurture local production and talent at a competitive price. Simultaneously, they were targeted by developed country corporations, tying them into expensive media technologies that were not necessarily cost-effective in developing country conditions. Television in itself required an infrastructure of electricity supply that was not widely available. Content came mainly from developed countries, and much of it clashed with traditional values. Developing countries were strong defenders of cultural pluralism in international media flow (in strong contrast to their domestic policies). They were concerned about structured information imbalance and distortions in content, for example, Western news focus on elite countries, elite people, the exceptional, the trivial, failures rather than successes, entertainment rather than information, events rather than processes. These features did not serve long-term political and cultural interests. The developing world supported UNESCO attempts to secure rights to inform, to be heard, to full sovereignty over information, to a free and *balanced* flow, and the right to preserve a way of life. In this perspective, unfortunately, too little was heard of domestic tyrannies, of the absence of political and

media representation of many ethnic and other groups, of the use of cultural industries to establish ethnic and political hegemony, of political corruption, and of local alliances with multinational corporations.

ISSUES

The debate revolved around five critical contradictions:

Contradiction between ideas of freedom and of sovereignty, for example, between the freedom of publishers to disseminate their media products around the world and the sovereign rights of states to control information flows into and out of national territories.

Contradiction between ideas about media responsibility for the nation and about their responsibility to the people. The media, some say, have a responsibility for the achievement of national development, international peace, and other publicly desirable objectives, whether by actively promoting such objectives or passively declining to cover issues or ideas that might impede them. But the media may also have a responsibility to protect the people against the state as concrete representative of the "nation." The role of the press as a watchdog or a fourth estate pits it as ever vigilant against abuse of communications by the state, which typically appeals to national development, security, or integration as excuses for abuse or covers for factional interest. This contradiction can be thought of as a three-way tension between ideas of information as social development, information as political control, and information as social criticism.

Contradiction between freedom of the press (referring mainly to the rights of owners) and freedom of information (referring to the rights of individuals and groups to express ideas through media, exercise control over media, and to access media).

Contradiction between a communications ideology of professional service that positions audiences as clients or consumers, as against a communications ideology of social participation that engages audiences as equal partners with the media in debate about public issues for the public good.

Contradiction between principles of communications equity, requiring some form of state or other form of intervention to achieve equality of access to expression, representation, and reception, and principles of communications choice, which guarantee freedom for audiences to make market choices between technologies, content, and consumption behaviors.

EVALUATION AND CONTEMPORARY RELEVANCE

Outcomes of NWICO have been modest. NWICO was a victim of the very imbalances it critiqued, and it was the target of counterreaction from threatened interests. Antagonists included Freedom House, Heritage, the InterAmerican Press Council, the International Press Institute, and the World Press Freedom Committee. Their views were influential in the Western press. Among common misrepresentations was the charge that UNESCO (as opposed to particular UNESCO delegates) favored government control of information, and wanted governments to license journalists.

One significant outcome, IPDC, represented a victory for the United States. It restricted UNESCO to facilitation of communications infrastructure by technical assistance. It evaded issues of media ownership and content, and it preserved the principle of free flow. IPDC funds could be made available to capitalist interests in developing countries.

News-exchange agreements and alternative news agencies are often regarded as a positive outcome of NWICO. Some initiatives, such as NANAP and the Pan-African News Agency (PANA), date from early in the debate, or even preceded it. Subsequent evaluations (see Boyd-Barrett & Rantanen, 1998; Boyd-Barrett & Thussu, 1992) are not encouraging. The popularity of NANAP, never great, was undermined by the collapse of Yugoslavia, whose national agency, TANJUG, was the pool's main coordinator. PANA, once owned by the Organization of African Unity, became a semi-commercial agency in 1998, owned by national news agencies of African countries and African private or commercial interests. This change highlights a record of feckless government or intergovernmental intervention in efforts to transform information flow. Some news agencies that had been established in line with NWICO principles, such as Shihata of Tanzania, have disappeared. Others, such as the News Agency of Nigeria (cf. Musa, 1997), developed in ways that are not identifiably different in news philosophy from conventional agencies; others still are in political and/or economic difficulty. News-exchange arrangements in themselves are incapable of challenging dominant Western news agencies. Mainstream Western agencies have achieved vertical integration in their home markets, have gained privileged access to news clients and news sources in wealthy domestic markets, have the benefits of established worldwide first-copy costs, and have the safeguards of diversification (Somarajiwa, 1984). Effective operation of news-exchange mechanisms is undermined by the lack of credibility that results from dependence on governments for patronage and/or revenue, inability of many members to pay, excessive "protocol" news, lack of facilities and training, inappropriate editing for international markets, invisibility in developing world media, and little play in developed world media.

By 1980, NWICO had secured a place on the global political agenda. There were international mechanisms for the development of communications in the developing world, and basic principles had been articulated for mass media conduct in international relations. There were no legally binding obligations on nations to act on any of these principles. Little finance was committed. Some kind of U.N. intervention was necessary in support of NWICO, but the United Nations is made up of governments, and people who attend U.N. conferences are diplomats and bureaucrats. For NWICO supporters, these considerations presented no problem because of their belief that states must take responsibility for their respective media. But Western media philosophy is hostile to government intervention in media practice, even though this position sometimes may seem hypocritical.

Perhaps NWICO proponents focused too narrowly on news. Hamelink (1994) argued that there should have been more attention to media technology and communication policy, more demand for fundamental political changes within developing countries, more vigorous control by Western governments over transnational corporations, and more significant concessions to the role of market forces in socialist countries.

Nordenstreng (1995) argues that what emerged after NWICO was almost the opposite of what was intended, namely, a media world that was every day more concentrated in fewer hands. Yet NWICO did not disappear; many of its issues remain. The main lessons that Nordenstreng draws are that power rather than reason sets the rules of the debate and that in the final analysis it is the political that determines the global (political) agenda. The withdrawal of the United States and the United Kingdom from UNESCO was not due to any single issue but reflected increasing opposition to multilateralism. The anti-NWICO campaign, he argues, was a "big lie" that presented NWICO as an enemy to media freedom—quite the reverse of what it actually represented—and it claimed, wrongly as it happens, that Third World dictators would use NWICO as a pretext for information suppression. Nordenstreng recognizes that the concept lacked sufficient precision to survive politically. Self-critically, he notes that the NWICO concept remained relatively shallow and its relation to the big narratives of modernization, dependency, imperialism, and so on was left without sufficient articulation. He concludes that NWICO's significance lies in the debate and its lessons rather than in the actual operations of communication industries.

Is NWICO relevant to the contemporary world? Mainly, yes. The significance of geographical boundary has changed. The international media influence of a few countries (most notably the United States) in areas such as cinema, computing, and telecommunications is immense. The fundamental issue is control over communications space, which in almost every domain appears to be monopolized by the twin forces of either private capital or the state, or both, at the expense of the public sphere (cf. Boyd-Barrett, 1999). This battlefield is less about struggle between national interests than it is between corporate giants for global markets. Issues of equity, participation, corporate control, and responsibility are no less pressing now than they were in the 1970s. The role of the nation in communications analysis has been underrated in globalization discourse (Curran & Park, 2000). A worldwide process continues that redirects regulatory systems away from principles of public good toward principles of competition, and whose purpose is to articulate the rules of engagement for surviving oligopolies.

Writing in 1997, Hamelink looks at the MacBride report's five key areas: communication policies, technology, culture, human rights, and international cooperation. The proposal for national, comprehensive communication policies, he concludes, had little impact because communication issues reach the public agenda relatively rarely. The notion of integrated policy making usually runs against the preferences of powerful local lobbies for existing institutional and regulatory arrangements. The proposal did not chime with the mood for deregulation in the 1980s. In technology, the commission had proposed responsible technology decision making with extended public involvement and regulatory measures that favored developing countries. Again, this had little impact. The pace of technology change and anxiety not to be "left behind" militated against prudent, comparative assessment of different technologies from a public good perspective. In the meantime, business has become increasingly influential in regulatory forums. The commission recommended policies that fostered cultural identity and cultural dialogue. But national culture policies have not emerged. The commission simplified the notion of culture, underestimated the extent of cultural heterogeneity, and exaggerated the mutual interest that people have in each other's culture. In human rights, the commission recommended that the media expose human rights violations and support human rights. But in practice, media coverage of human rights is distorted and uneven, and the media themselves are part of the problem that NWICO addressed. The proposed right to communicate has not been codified. Finally, MacBride recommended the establishment of a New World Information and Communication Order and the improvement of multilateral assistance for communication development. In practice, both NIIO and NWICO have disappeared as formative concepts. IPDC never became a genuine multilateral fund, and it continues to be short of finance. Governments have given low priority to communication development, leaving this to "market forces." As a set of policies, the formulation of NWICO lacked precision and strategy: "Fundamental principles were taken for granted; wrong choices about major addressees were made; existing communication policies were ignored; and the commission's

work itself revealed an inadequate understanding of social reality" (Hamelink, 1997, p. 91).

Hancock and Hamelink (1999) reviewed the conclusions of the MacBride report's recommendations. MacBride's commitment to communication as a basic human right linked it to the concept of a free and balanced flow of information, and to the view that communication policies were necessary to realize communication rights. But the recommendations did not, nor could not, fuse together to form a coherent philosophy. The report had two somewhat incompatible audiences: the UNESCO and U.N. system, on the one hand, and the general audience, on the other.

The call for cohesive national communication policies, including language and literacy policies, had little response. IPDC has had some successes, but the emphasis on the national now seems insensitive to intra- and cross-national interests and has been subverted by the continuing internationalization of media and culture. Attempts to politicize communication and elevate investment in public communications infrastructure and capacity have been undermined by deregulation and commercialization. Some tariff reductions have been achieved, but spectrum division is still unequal. Communications is a more central component of both communication and development policies within international organizations such as UNESCO, the Food and Agriculture Organization of the United Nations (FAO), and UNICEF (United Nations Children's Fund), but public participation in communications has grown weaker, whereas media monopolization and commercialization is greater and more complex.

Recommendations to preserve national and cultural identity confused communication and culture and overemphasized national culture to the detriment of local culture(s). Development of informatics has been facilitated, mainly by the Internet. MacBride wanted to improve journalism through such means as educational training; strengthening values of truthfulness, accuracy, and respect for human rights, with mechanisms to hold journalists accountable (mainly voluntary measures); and codes of professional ethics. UNESCO has continued to be active in these areas, and the status of journalists has been enhanced in some countries (though there is a lamentable continuation of aggression against journalists worldwide).

The report wanted to widen the sources of information available to citizens in their everyday life, abolish censorship or arbitrary control of information, reduce concentration of media ownership and commercial influence, establish effective legal measures to circumscribe the actions of transnationals, and reduce the editorial influence of advertising. Progress toward these ends has been helped in part by the collapse of authoritarian regimes, yet political controls still range from severe to overwhelming in many parts of the world, and issues of concentration and monopoly are strong almost everywhere. Independence and autonomy are normally championed in relation to freedom from government, but much less is said in mainstream public discourse about the relationship between economic factors and editorial independence.

Positive endorsement of diversity and choice was to be achieved by strengthening infrastructure, increasing resources, securing a plurality of information sources, and safeguarding the needs of women and minorities. Hancock and Hamelink (1999) note that principles of individual and community participation are largely incompatible with the modus operandi of the mass media. There is now more abundant information and more sources, and more favorable attention is directed toward the interests of women and minorities, although there is considerable scope for improvement. Media management is hardly more democratic.

How has communication scholarship in general handled the NWICO debate? Broadly, it has been sympathetic to the original developing world perspective. Closer to the time of the debate, sympathetic analyses incorporated NWICO within a broader critique of cultural and media imperialism or dominance-dependency relationships, drawing on specific case studies of flows of television and news products (cf. Harris, 1977). This critique has been transformed subsequently into a broader critique of globalization, the neoliberal global order, relations between local and global, and the multimedia mega-corporations (cf. Golding & Harris, 1997). A related but distinct literature, also sympathetic to the original developing world perspective, has focused its attention on practical solutions, for example, the role of radio in health and agricultural campaigns. There has also been an important counter-critique to NWICO, which has used empirical study to challenge some of its presumptions (cf. Weaver, Wilhoit, Stevenson, Shaw, & Cole, 1980).

CHALLENGES FOR SCHOLARSHIP

Analysis of communications in national and international context has continued to improve since NWICO. Scannell and Cardiff (1990) and Martín Barbero (1993), among others, illuminated the relationship between the development of mass communication and the formation of national and cultural identities. Habermas (1988) contributed the concept of "public sphere" as an ideal type by which to judge the extent to which media nurture public dialogue. His main criteria were equality of access, relevance of content to the public good, freedom from the intervention of state or capital, and the role of rationality as the final arbiter of value. Curran (1996), Galtung (1999), and Winseck (1995) offered helpful models for depicting relationships between state, capital, civil society, and media. Notable North American scholars Edward Herman and Noam Chomsky (1988), Robert McChesney (1999; Herman & McChesney, 1997), Herbert Schiller (1976), and Dan Schiller (1999) charted continuing processes of concentration and convergence, and the capture of media by industrial, political, and military interests. Sreberny (2000) explored the complexity of relationships between the global and the local, and the many different influences that act upon culture. Hamelink (1994) identified the principal forces of change in international communication as digitization, deregulation, convergence, concentration, commercialization, and globalization. To these, Boyd-Barrett (2000, 2001) added *competitivization* and democratization. Competitivization happens when new markets are created or old markets are considerably expanded as the result of technological innovation or deregulation, in a way that temporarily reduces the costs of market entry. The result is a dramatic increase of new players, and a scramble for market influence among old and new. What starts as enhanced competition then leads to industrial consolidation through aggression and fear. Democratization also initially stimulates media abundance and diversity. In the 1980s and 1990s, democratization typically involved an opening up of national markets to the global market. This encourages the formation of alliances between national and international enterprises, and a gradual delocalization and consolidation of media interests. It reflects the ascendancy of neoliberal ideology, implemented through international financial institutions, which, as Braman (1990) observed, foster principles of economic exchange that do not distinguish cultural commodities from

any others. This ideology therefore is hostile to forms of state subsidy for cultural industries, or to state intervention to protect national media markets from foreign competition. It would seek to penalize states that persist in such subsidies and interventions.

The rate at which states subscribe to this regulatory order is uneven. At the end of the Uruguay Round of GATS (General Agreement on Trade and Services), only 13 countries made commitments (rising to 19 by 1998 as a result of accessions) in the audiovisual services sector. A substantially larger number sought exemptions. Only 2 countries, the Central African Republic and the United States, made commitments in all six subsectors. Most commitments are subject to limitations. The most common include limits on foreign shareholdings and on the share of screening time allotted to foreign productions, and exclusion from national treatment in respect to domestic subsidies. Several audiovisual industry representatives of member countries during the Uruguay Round suggested that the cinema and broadcasting sectors should be excluded from the agreement in order to protect national industries and cultures from being overwhelmed by foreign products. An alternative approach was to suggest exemptions from certain disciplines in recognition of the cultural specificity of these industries. No agreement was reached. Even where exemptions are sought, however, they are hard to police. The European Union's "Television Without Frontiers" directive to preserve a proportion of television time for local consumption has not been well enforced, and such standards are easy to evade (e.g., through coproductions) and are sometimes ignored with impunity (as in the case of many cable and satellite channels). Countries continue to be under pressure to reduce state protections, as a condition of full entry to global nontariff markets, and as a form of leverage for the securing of international financial loans. In summary, neoliberal ideology commits states to the principle of free flow and in relation to all commodities, cultural and other.

Assessing the actual balance between local, national, regional, and global factors in the functioning and role of communication media is a contentious exercise. Warning against errors of determination (e.g., attribution of deterministic power to concepts such as globalization rather than to actions of responsible human agents), I have called for a sharper focus on issues of access, fairness, and representation (Boyd-Barrett, 1999).

There are important lessons here for communication research. Research should be embedded within a thorough understanding of the social, cultural, political, and economic context of the subject that it addresses. It should consciously articulate and balance a range of theoretical perspectives available for making sense of its subjects. It should take equal account of each phase of the communication process, namely, production, content, and reception, and should build on and contribute to a solid framework of empirical data systematically collected, quantitative and qualitative. In international communication research, a strong ethnographic and empirical base of information concerning peripheral countries is as important as in the case of core countries. Special care should be taken when the subject under investigation is also high on political agendas. Advocacy is best left to politicians. Yes, scholars ought sometimes to identify themes and issues of public concern that have a sociological reality but have not penetrated political discourse. Otherwise, scholarship should examine the underlying premises and ideologies that inform political discourses, what is said and not said, holding them up against alternative perspectives and evidence. In the 1970s, NWICO was a sufficiently daunting challenge with respect to postcolonial theories of cultural imperialism and dominance-dependency. The challenge to scholars at the turn of the 21st century with respect to communications and globalization is even greater, even more interdisciplinary, macro, elusive, and enjoys much higher political visibility because it is more plainly relevant, in both positive and negative implications, to peoples of both developed and developing worlds. It is not different from NWICO: NWICO was an early manifestation of concern about processes that were later to be identified as component forces of globalization. Communication processes, as we have seen, are central to globalization. We have not been examining a concept that was alive and whose significance has now lapsed, but a concept that helps give us a purchase, albeit imperfectly, on the state of the world as it is today.

REFERENCES

Baran, P., & Sweezy, P. (1968). *Monopoly capital*. Harmondsworth, UK: Pelican.

Boyd-Barrett, O. (1999). Media imperialism reformulated. In D. K. Thussu (Ed.), *Electronic empires: Global media and local resistance* (pp. 157-176). London: Edward Arnold.

Boyd-Barrett, O. (2000). Cyberspace and the public sphere. In *DIAC-2000 symposium*. Proceedings of the Shaping the Network Society: The Future of the Public Space in Cyberspace. Seattle, WA: Computer Professionals for Social Responsibility.

Boyd-Barrett, O. (in press). Globalization and cyberspace. In D. Schules & P. Day (Eds.), *Shaping the network press*. Cambridge: MIT Press.

Boyd-Barrett, O., & Rantanen, T. (1998). *The globalization of news*. London: Sage.

Boyd-Barrett, O., & Thussu, D. (1992). *Contraflow in global news*. London: John Libbey.

Braman, S. (1990). Trade and information policy. *Media, Culture & Society, 12,* 361-385.

Chomsky, N. (1990). *Deterring democracy.* London: Verso.

Curran, J. (1996). Mass media and democracy revisited. In J. Curran & M. Gurevitch (Eds.), *Mass media and society* (2nd ed., pp. 81-119). London: Edward Arnold.

Curran, J., & Park, M.-J. (2000). *De-Westernizing media studies.* London: Routledge.

Curran, J., & Seaton, J. (1980). *Power without responsibility.* London: Fontana.

Fanon, F. (1967). *The wretched of the earth.* Middlesex, UK: Penguin.

Freire, P. (1970). *Pedagogy of the oppressed.* New York: Continuum.

Galtung, J. (1999). State, capital and the civil society: A problem of communication. In R. Vincent, K. Nordenstreng, & M. Traber (Eds.), *Towards equity in global communication: MacBride update.* Cresskill, NJ: Hampton.

Golding, P., & Harris, P. (Eds.). (1997). *Beyond cultural imperialism: Globalization, communication and the new international order.* London: Sage.

Habermas, J. (1988). *The structural transformation of the public sphere* (T. Burger, Trans.). Cambridge: MIT Press.

Halloran, J., Elliot, P., & Murdock, G. (1970). *Communications and demonstrations.* Harmondsworth, UK: Penguin.

Hamelink, C. J. (1994). *The politics of world communication.* London: Sage.

Hamelink, C. J. (1997). MacBride with hindsight. In P. Golding & P. Harris (Eds.), *Beyond cultural imperialism: Globalization, communication and the new international order* (pp. 69-93). London: Sage.

Hancock, A., & Hamelink, C. (1999). Many more voices, another world: Looking back at the MacBride recommendations. In R. Vincent, K. Nordenstreng, & M. Traber (Eds.), *Towards equity in global communication: MacBride update.* Cresskill, NJ: Hampton.

Harris, P. (1977). *News dependence: The case for a new world information order.* Final report to UNESCO of a study of the international news media. Paris: UNESCO.

Herman, E., & Chomsky, N. (1988). *Manufacturing public consent.* New York: Pantheon.

Herman, E., & McChesney, R. (1997). *The global media.* London: Cassell.

International Commission for the Study of Communication Problems. (1980). *Many voices, one world: Towards a new, more just and more efficient world information and communication order.* Paris: UNESCO.

Marcuse, H. (1964). *One-dimensional man.* Boston: Beacon.

Martín Barbero, J. (1993). *Communication, culture and hegemony: From media to mediations.* London: Sage.

Mattelart, A. (1979). *Multinational corporations and the control of culture: The ideological apparatuses of imperialism.* Brighton, UK: Harvester.

McChesney, R. (1999). *Rich media, poor democracy: Communication politics in dubious times.* Urbana and Chicago: University of Illinois Press.

Mills, C. W. (1956). *The power elite.* New York: Oxford University Press.

Murdock, G., & Golding, P. (1977). Capitalism, communication and class relations. In J. Curran, M. Gurevitch, & J. Woollacott (Eds.), *Mass communication and society* (pp. 12-43). London: Edward Arnold.

Musa, M. (1997). From optimism to reality: An overview of Third World news agencies. In P. Golding & P. Harris (Eds.), *Beyond cultural imperialism: Globalization, communication and the new international order.* London: Sage.

Nordenstreng, K. (1984). *The mass media declaration of UNESCO.* Norwood, NJ: Ablex.

Nordenstreng, K. (1995). *The NWICO debate.* Unit 20 of the M.A. in mass communications. Leicester, UK: University of Leicester, Centre for Mass Communications Research.

Rosenblum, M. (1979). *Coups and earthquakes: Reporting the Third World for America.* New York: Harper and Row.

Somarajiwa, R. (1984). Third World entry to the world market in news: Problems and possible solutions. *Media, Culture & Society, 6,* 119-136.

Scannell, P., & Cardiff, D. (1990). *A social history of British broadcasting*. Oxford, UK: Basil Blackwell.

Schiller, D. (1999). *Digital capitalism: Networking the global market system*. Cambridge: MIT Press.

Schiller, H. I. (1969). *Mass communications and American empire*. New York: A. M. Kelley.

Schiller, H. I. (1976). *Communication and cultural domination*. White Plains, NY: International Arts and Sciences Press.

Sreberny, A. (2000). Television, gender, and democratization in the Middle East. In J. Curran & M.-J. Park (Eds.), *De-Westernizing media studies* (pp. 63-78). London: Routledge.

Tunstall, J. (1977). *The media are American*. London: Constable.

Varis, T. (1973). *International inventory of television programme structure and the flow of TV programmes between nations*. Tampere, Finland: University of Tampere.

Wells, C. (1987). *The UN, UNESCO, and the politics of knowledge*. London: Macmillan.

Weaver, D. H., Wilhoit, G. C., Stevenson, R. L., Shaw, D. L., & Cole, R. (1980). *The news of the world in four major wire services*. Prepared for inclusion in the final report of the "foreign images" project undertaken by members of the International Association for Mass Communication Research for UNESCO.

Winseck, D. (1995). *The shifting context of international communication: Possibilities for a New World Information and Communication Order*. Unit 21 of the M.A. in mass communications. Leicester, UK: University of Leicester, Centre for Mass Communications Research.

4

Mediated War, Peace, and Global Civil Society

THOMAS L. JACOBSON
WON YONG JANG
State University of New York at Buffalo

The "war to end all wars" ended over 80 years ago, but little that has occurred since that time can be taken to suggest that warlike activity has diminished. And little on the horizon encourages optimism regarding prospects for its ending anytime soon. World War I gave way to the second world war, and that gave way to the Cold War. The Cold War has, in turn, given way to a conflagration of regional conflicts. As World War I was gearing up, it was the massive scale of the effort and the interdependency of multiple alliances that suggested to some that this war might finally make the world safe. Today, there is no such dramatic event upon which hopes might be hung.

Yet the hope for peace endures. For some, of late, the process of globalization suggests a basis for hope beyond mere hope. On one hand, peace seems to be in the interest of economic "self-interest." Advances in communication and transportation have leveraged eco-

nomic development into an increased global interdependence of a new kind. This economic interdependence values stability. On the other hand, there is an emerging global civil society that might be able to bring a growing public opinion in favor of peace to bear upon the foreign policies of otherwise warlike nations.

This chapter addresses relationships among media, prospects for peace, and this emerging global civil society. The likelihood that media will help to promote the peace is an open question. Certainly, the global media are often associated with the notion of a global public sphere. This alone might encourage peace, if coverage of democratic struggles encourages democratic culture worldwide. However, it is possible that the media promote war and violence. Profits encourage privately held mass media to feature sensational stories that contain graphic and often gratuitous violence. And the lowest-common-denominator principle in news-writing produces stories that oversimplify events to the point of being substantially misleading. Or perhaps the media are somehow neutral.

But what does peace require, in addition to communication? Certainly, communication in a global public sphere alone is not sufficient. Civil society in the Lockean tradition is a society of property-bearing citizens whose association is free from control by the state. What has recently been referred to as the public sphere is a process specifically of communication among citizens in civil society about matters of public concern, leading to public opinion. But this opinion is of no consequence unless it is fed into mechanisms of a democratically managed government. This is where it assumes legitimate power. Democratic power circulates thus: Public opinion legitimates administrative institutions that serve the public, including the public's interest in peace and safety.

At the global level today, a global civil society and accompanying public sphere might be evolving. And this global society's opinion might be in favor of peace. However, the state, or state surrogate, that is required to pursue and enact this peace does not exist. Or to put it another way, without the first three estates of government, of what value is a fourth journalistic estate? Ultimately, questions about global media performance, peace prospects, and global civil society refer to questions of global governance.

For this reason, this chapter addresses the emergence of global civil society, war, peace, and media in relation to prospects for global governance. Immanuel Kant's political writings represent a touchstone for contemporary discussions on the pacifying effects of the rule of law. Kant assumed that peace cannot exist merely as a disembodied ideal, but can exist only as a product of institutions designed to settle disputes by means other than violence. These are the institutions of self-governance and the administration of justice. And as the rule of law keeps the peace in nation-states, it is said, global peace will require some form of global law.

These discussions generally take the form of a constructive critique of Kant, including suggestions designed to remedy those of his ideas that are dated or otherwise inadequate. Specific neo-Kantian proposals for global legal and governmental systems vary in the degree of centralization recommended, in the specific role of a global public sphere, and in many other ways. And in total they are incomplete. Yet they nevertheless indicate the kinds of issues that one must entertain if one hopes for media, peace, war, and civil society in the long run.

The first section in this chapter reviews research in order to identify major trends in news coverage of war and peace during the post–Cold War period. This provides some indication of contemporary media behavior and offers a necessary springboard for speculation about future possibilities. The second section reviews recent discussions concerning the emergence of a global public sphere and its relation to peace and global governance. The key here is Kant's treatment of the possibility of a global confederation of peaceable democratic nations, or cosmopolitan democracy. The third section returns to the matter of trends in news coverage of war and peace, and it reviews them in the context of discussions about cosmopolitan democracy. A summary and concluding section suggest directions for future research.

We conclude with the argument that normative theories of the press must be advanced at the global level and must be developed in association with a theory of global democracy. For it is only in the context of such a framework as this that the behavior of the media with regard to war, peace, and civil society can be evaluated.

NEWS COVERAGE
OF WAR AND PEACE

If one looks to empirical research on relations among war, peace, media, and civil society, the pickings are slim. Most studies of news coverage, for example, examine war rather than peace coverage, and few of these address the more general question of civil society. Nevertheless, news coverage research does reveal some important characteristics of media behavior. Here we review war and peace news coverage, focusing on the post–Vietnam era and especially the post–Cold War period, after 1989. Literature on the relation between the press and foreign policy is also addressed.

War Coverage

The impact of the Vietnam experience, on both news media and American consciousness generally, is still debated publicly as well as in scholarly circles. But it cannot be ignored. Some argue that the media never did confront the true causes of the war. Others argue that the media were slow coming around but eventually recognized the horror of the war for what it was and fortified the resolve of American leadership to stop it. Still others have argued that the media somehow lost the war for America.

The final truth of this matter is not at issue here, but a few widely shared things can be said about the impact of this debate on news media following the war. First, the Vietnam experience made both the military and policy-making bodies of the United States more cautious about foreign adventures. Engagements

followed subsequently, in Grenada, Panama, the Persian Gulf, and elsewhere. But such engagements have been accompanied by expressions of the need for clearly defined goals and exit strategies. And the media, too, have become cautionary, regularly raising warning flags about being drawn into "another Vietnam."

A second thing that can be said about the Vietnam experience is that it illustrated the impact of technological evolution on news reporting. Portable cameras and satellite communications brought the war into American living rooms. Americans had learned of previous wars more through the printed word than the camera, despite newsreels and Edward R. Murrow's acclaimed radio reports during World War II. After Vietnam, many commentators believed that the horror of war would now be brought graphically into America's living rooms.

This latter predication has not yet been born out. Even while reporting technology improved, the technology of warfare has progressed to the point that America is now able to conduct many military operations with relatively little threat to its own troops. New technologies, rather than communicating the horrors of war, have themselves become news.

The Gulf War's laser-guided bombs were favored footage on both CNN and network news broadcasts. And audiences have been treated to near live footage including cockpit communication among strike pilots. Griffin and Lee (1995) studied Gulf War–related pictures appearing in *Time, Newsweek,* and *U.S. News & World Report* and found that images tended to deal with military technology. More generally, Hallin and Gitlin (1993) argue that media presented the war as an expression of technological skill. Thus, recent war news has not conveyed more horrible violence, because technological evolution is itself complex.

Other developments have also affected war reporting subsequent to the Vietnam War. The Vietnam War made the military mindful of the impact of war coverage on public opinion and hence on war policy. As a result, the military has changed its methods of managing reporter pools. In the days and hours leading up to the U.S. invasion of Grenada, the Department of Defense misdirected news organizations, resulting in their late arrival to the theatre of operations (Servaes, 1991). In Panama, news organizations were promised military helicopter transport to the theatre in time to witness the operation from its beginning. However, this transport arrived too late to film most of the action. And in the Gulf War, as is well known, reporters were prevented from traveling independently and forced into highly controlled military debriefing and press conference meetings. The military's new approach to news media has badly blunted the potential impact of war reporting on public perceptions.

Technology and access aside, how well have the news media performed in covering recent wars? The Gulf War is the single most thoroughly studied case in the post-Vietnam era (Allen, O'Loughlin, Jasperson, & Sullivan, 1994; Bennett & Paletz, 1994; Denton, 1993; Iyengar and Simon, 1993; Kaid et al., 1994; Mowlana, Gerbner, & Schiller, 1992).

The vast preponderance of studies indicates that news coverage of this war portrayed the conflict in a manner supportive of parochial interests and of war. Kellner (1992) argues that television news failed to adequately inform the public. Instead, it transmitted, promoted, and legitimized the U.S. government's Gulf War policy. It acted as a mouthpiece for the Bush administration rather than illuminating the complexities of America's foreign policy history in the region. LaMay, FitzSimon, and Sahadieds (1991) note that newspaper editorials reflected government perspectives

and expressed little dissent in connection with any aspect of the war.

This tendency has been found in numerous studies. Although there were some differences in coverage among local, national, commercial, and public media, the pattern generally obtains across all major media outlets (Peer & Chestnut, 1995; Reese & Buckalew, 1995; Vincent, 2000). And this kind of bias toward government policy is not limited to American media. Media in most countries seem to operate in a similar manner, including Greece, Norway, Sweden, the United Kingdom, and Serbia (Nohrstedt, Kaitatzi-Whitlock, Ottosen, & Riegert, 2000); Israel (Liebes, 1992); and Canada (Garon, 1996; Kirton, 1993). Nor has it been limited to Gulf War coverage. Thussu (2000) examined CNN coverage of NATO's bombing of Yugoslavia in March-June 1999 and argues that "television pictures tended to follow the news agenda set up by the U.S. military" (p. 345).

In short, there is a disconcerting uniformity of bias in war reporting globally. The news media do not provide the information required for citizens to have a clear view of events and their causes. Rather, coverage tends to follow national policy perspectives. This bias results partly from military management of news media, partly from the inclination of news media to pander to fascination with technology, and partly from the influence of standard news values that tend to simplify events.

Peace Coverage

During the Cold War, news media regularly covered disarmament negotiations and agreements among major powers (Bruck, 1989; Dorman, Manoff, & Weeks, 1988; Gamson & Stuart, 1992). More recently, the origins of war and the conditions of peace have broadened.

One reason for this change is geopolitical. Changes in the global balance of power during the post–Cold War period have led to an increase in the number of conflicts worldwide. The loosening of Cold War pressures and alliances has allowed many Third World states and movements to use military options more freely. Thus, peace refers not only to peace among major powers but also to a range of civil wars and regional conflicts. And this same loosening of geopolitical pressures allows the United States more latitude in intervening. Shaw (1996) notes, "In the 1990s the U.S.-led bloc of Western states has started to act, with U.N. legitimation, like a global state intervening to regulate political and military conflicts across the world" (p. 5).

As a result, the number of peace-related interventions and enforcement operations has increased dramatically over the past decade. Jakobsen (1996) notes that "the U.N. launched only one enforcement operation between 1945 and 1990, i.e., Korea 1950" (p. 205). After the Cold War, these proliferated, including actions in Kuwait, Liberia, northern Iraq, Somalia, Rwanda, and Haiti. Peace movements worldwide have also grown. This creates a new environment for peace work in the post-Cold War era.

Another reason for change in conditions related to war and peace results from growing awareness within the global public sphere of a connection between war and poverty. Poverty itself is a persistent cause of conflict within nations. It creates tensions, which if accompanied by other conditions can lead to civil war (Wolf, 2000). And due to the increasing interdependence among economies, poverty is in part an outcome of economic relations among countries. Covering peace adequately would require reporting on general social and economic conditions that lead to war, including structural economic conditions at the international as well as national levels.

Yet neither the increase in state interventions on behalf of peace nor the new determinations of poverty have led to a concomitant growth in amounts of peace reporting. Peace coverage itself characteristically lacks news value. Shinar (2000) notes that war provides

> good visuals, focuses on heroism and conflict, and emphasizes the emotional rather than the rational. . . . By contrast, peace discourse, that typically features "talking heads," ceremonial setups and gestures, press conferences, and airport scenes, has less news value. . . . International journalism history underscores the preference of war-oriented framing. (p. 91)

Some studies of peace reporting indicate, for this reason, the problems faced by the peace movement in attempting to mobilize coverage of their activities (Gitlin, 1980; Glasgow University Media Group, 1985; Hackett, 1991; Ryan, 1991; Small, 1987; Stone, 1989).

This is not to say that there is no peace reporting. The most common coverage of peace efforts is found in reports on regional peace negotiations. This includes coverage, for example, of the Israeli-Palestinian situation (Wolfsfeld, 1997a, 1997b) and the Irish peace process (McLaughlin & Miller, 1996). And researchers have begun to connect peace with media behavior more generally. One collection of articles has been devoted to the idea that peace and media coverage of war and peace must be understood in connection with culture (Roach, 1993). The Toda Peace Institute has supported a number of studies related to media and the conditions required for peace (Tehranian & Tehranian, 1992; Tehranian, 1999).

Nevertheless, in general, media coverage of peace-related activities falls far short of what is required to actually foster peace. Peace reporting is spotty because it is unlikely to gather audiences.

Public Opinion and Foreign Policy

One additional consideration that should be taken into account when reviewing war and peace coverage in the context of global civil society concerns public opinion. Do coverage patterns of war and peace reflect public interests? If a vigorous global public sphere is to emerge, then press reports must represent public opinion accurately to government, as well as to the public itself.

The relevance of media coverage to foreign policy is a question that has been a subject of serious concern at least since Bernard Cohen's book *The Press and Foreign Policy* (1963). In this highly influential work, Cohen argued that the opinion of the public at large did not, and should not, bear greatly on the foreign-policy-making apparatus. More recently, due in part to debates over the impact of Vietnam War coverage, and more recently to the global omnipresence of CNN, there is speculation that the public may have more impact on foreign policy today than it did previously. Media coverage can shine a light on trouble spots such as Haiti, Bosnia, Kosovo, Rwanda, and Somalia, helping bring about foreign policy action where it would not otherwise have been forthcoming.

One hypothesis offered here concerns a so-called CNN effect (Carruthers, 2000; Livingston, 1997; Robinson, 1999, 2000a; Strobel, 1997). Thussu (2000) argues that "CNN has become a particularly significant news outlet in times of international crisis" (p. 349). Skeptics argue that the so-called effect is an illusion and that CNN's coverage itself is derivative of other causes (Jakobsen, 2000). A compromise perspective splits the difference. Robinson (2000b) proposes a "media-policy interaction model" in which media influence government policy only when policy is uncertain and media advocate a clear course of action.

Of course, the relevance of the CNN effect to democratic self-governance depends on the extent to which the media, in this case CNN, reflect public opinion. Herman and Chomsky (1988) have prominently argued that parochial patterns in news coverage represent interests of government elites. Others agree: Hallin (1994) argues that "the media play a relatively passive role and generally reinforce official power to manage public opinion" (p. 11). Some analysts find that the media represent neither government nor public interests but rather their own, corporate media, interests. Sobel (1998) found in a study of the Bosnia conflict that media coverage stressed opposition to humanitarian intervention, despite the fact that a majority of the polls showed support for it.

At the very best, the situation regarding the relation between public opinion and coverage of war and peace is complicated. As Shaw (1996) observes, "governments often act on calculations about how coverage will affect public opinion, and media do not only report but also attempt to mobilize and represent opinion" (p. 7).

In sum, the literature on war and peace news coverage reveals much about contemporary press behavior, even if the nexus of peace, media, and civil society is understudied. Media coverage of war is biased toward narrow national interests. Peace coverage is partial and fragmented. And coverage may be worsening. In the United States, at least, the military has improved its press management skills to the detriment of quality reporting. And foreign business news coverage is growing, whereas coverage of other foreign news beats is declining (Herbers & McCartney, 1999; Strupp, 2000). Nevertheless, it appears that the media may be affecting foreign policy somewhat more today than they did a few decades ago. And this would be to the positive, if the media were accurate and reflected public opinion.

THE EMERGENCE OF GLOBAL CIVIL SOCIETY

It is against this backdrop that globalization proceeds. It proceeds in the growing interdependence of national economies, the growing power of multilateral financial and commercial institutions, the increasingly dense web of global professional associations, the ever more rapid flows of cultural products, and other developments.

It is clear that something is happening. A related research literature is growing rapidly. But definitions of globalization vary widely. Robertson (1992) refers to globalization as a matter of consciousness: "Globalization refers both to the compression of the world and the intensification of consciousness of the world as a whole" (p. 8). For McGrew (1992), social space is key, with globalization implying a "complex condition, one in which patterns of human interaction, interconnectedness and awareness are reconstituting the world as a single social space" (p. 65).

And the emergence of a global civil society has been identified as part of globalization (Braman & Sreberny-Mohammadi, 1996). As noted, the idea of civil society descends from a number of sources, John Locke's formula being prominent among them. The idea of a public sphere has been most prominently argued, of late, by Jürgen Habermas (1962/ 1989). The public sphere refers to a figurative space in which private citizens discuss matters of public concern. In literal terms, this space can be coffee houses, public squares, or mass media. The key point is that this public discussion represents the ultimate court of appeal in democratic society. The globalization thesis suggests that a global public sphere may be evolving, where private citizens of many countries are concerned about matters of global public concern. There is some question, however, whether such a global public sphere exists, or if it does exist, whether it will be

allowed to grow. The corporatization of media, represented above all by concentration of ownership, is resulting in counter pressures that threaten to replace public communication with commercial communication.

A strict definition is not at issue for the purposes of our analysis here. But to consider global civil society in relation to war, peace, and media, a few definitional issues must be addressed. To focus on the social and communicative elements, that is, those related to civil society and a public sphere, at least two levels of analysis must be considered. One of these is the individuals whose needs and rights are ultimately at issue in the globalization processes. The other is the organizations through which these individuals associate for purposes of deliberation and expression.

In relation to individuals and globalization, the largest literature addresses identity and global hybridization. Appadurai (1996), for one, emphasizes the role of modern communications, transportation, and migration patterns in creating large populations around the world whose identities attach in part to adopted lands, in part to original homelands, and in part are newly emerging global cosmopolitan identities. At least some empirical studies are being conducted. Norris (1999) has analyzed data from the World Values Surveys conducted in the early to mid-1990s and found that a significant number of individuals now think of themselves as members of a global community. Notably, she also finds that this effect is markedly generational. Global identity is experienced more by younger generations, which suggests that change is under way and can be expected to increase.

A literature on globalization and organizations focuses on the activities of nongovernmental organizations (NGOs), international governmental organizations (IGOs), and international nongovernmental organizations (INGOs). The political role of these organizations—which we will call NGOs—

has by all accounts increased dramatically in the past 25 years (Fernando & Heston, 1997; McCormick, 1999). Estimates differ, but it is safe to assume that tens of thousands of NGOs worldwide are currently covering a multitude of concerns including basic human rights, economic justice, environmental protection, labor conditions, and the rights of women and minorities, in addition to disarmament and peace.

These NGOs influence forums that are traditionally dominated by state actors. They facilitate informed participation in policy processes at both the national and international levels. Serra (1996) argues that these NGOs have indeed become important actors in world politics, referring to "communicative functions in constructing a global public sphere" (p. 222). Rotberg and Weiss (1996) argue that the role of NGOs in expanding policy debate beyond the nation-state is key in the development of a global civil society. Falk (1987) argues that new social movements and their companion NGOs are leading the way toward a more egalitarian and socially just international community.

So, both at the individual and organizational levels, there does seem to be some kind of global civil society evolving. And this civil society includes peace among its concerns not only in terms of organizations dedicated to peace advocacy, strictly speaking. Human rights work overlaps with peace advocacy insofar as rights need protection in relation to civil wars, war crimes, and other kinds of violence. Economic justice for the Third World overlaps with peace efforts insofar as basic economic and social security is a prerequisite for peace and stability. Advocacy for women's rights overlaps with peace efforts insofar as male socialization engenders dominance behaviors and a predisposition toward resolution of difference by force.

It is notable that the activities of these organizations have grown largely without the benefit of media publicity. Certainly, the larger and more successful NGOs have become media savvy and work to use the media effectively for their own purposes. However, with the possible exceptions of Amnesty International and Greenpeace, the large increase in the number of NGOs and their members has taken place outside of both public awareness and media coverage. This growth may be due in part, at least during the late 1980 and 1990s, to evolution in global computer networks (Norris, 2001; Ricci, 1998).

Before turning from the emergence of a global civil society to other matters, it is worth noting here that the call for a New World Information and Communication Order (NWICO) during the 1970s advocated the same issues now treated under the rubric of global civil society, media, and peace. This can be recalled simply by reference to the full name of the 1978 Mass Media Declaration that was adopted by the United Nations Educational, Scientific and Cultural Organization (UNESCO) in response to the NWICO movement, that is, the *Declaration on Fundamental Principles Concerning the Contribution of the Mass Media to Strengthening Peace and International Understanding, to the Promotion of Human Rights and to Countering Racialism, Apartheid and Incitement to War* (UNESCO, 1979). More specifically, demands for a balanced flow of information and the right to communicate were advocated in the spirit of creating a global public sphere serving not just those having the ability to pay for information but all the world's populations. The NWICO was explicitly oriented toward a global culture of peace (Becker, 1982).

THE GLOBAL RELEVANCE OF GLOBAL DEMOCRATIC THEORY

It is clear that individual identities are evolving a global dimension and that a growing number of organizations now devote their energies to social and political rights within the context of globalization. But to what end? A global public opinion requires a flow of information that is free and substantially more balanced than it is today. In addition, even if a vigorous global public opinion develops it has no target, no authoritative global institution to petition. International governmental organizations do exist, notably the European Union and the United Nations. But these are powerless in the face of opposition from major powers.

The weakness of contemporary international organizations should not obscure completely the progressive fact of their simple existence. The European Union needs to make its operations more transparent. The United Nations needs to be made more representative. And the story of the NWICO indicates how leery powerful governments can be about progressive globalization agendas (Giffard, 1989). These organizations are not yet responsive to truly universal needs, but they do provide in principle for service in scores of social sectors including health, education, science, culture, labor, and so on.

The existence of such mechanisms and organizations is evidence that global governance is not so much a pipe dream as a work in progress (Frederick, 1993). And a number of questions follow from this. How can the contribution of these imperfect institutions to peace be improved? What kinds of new or modified institutions can advance the cause of peace more effectively? What role can the media play, and in what way can international institutions evolve?

Such questions have earned a renewed interest in contemporary political philosophy. One important discussion started in the 1990s as geopolitical conditions changed and peace and human rights movements evolved. This discussion addresses precisely the conjunction of peace, global governance, and communica-tion (Bohman & Lutz-Bachmann, 1997; Falk, 1995). The reason for this convergence of concerns is connected with the thought of Kant. His political writings were devoted to the argument that the rule of law, based in a universal morality, would make it possible for nation-states to jointly pursue peace (Reiss, 1970). These writings have been key in recent political theorizing about global democracy.

Kant's concern was the "horror of violence" and the damage to peace and security committed by the "heinous waging of war." He sought a "perpetual peace" among morally oriented nations. The mechanism through which this condition would be attained was a federation of nations, actually a confederation. Under his confederal system, countries would retain their sovereignty and participate voluntarily in a system of rights. Representing a universal morality, these rights would embody a rule of law among participating states and thus also represent the pacifying effects of the rule of law.

Though voluntary, this system would be more binding than the existing system of international law, and be characterized as "cosmopolitanism." Kant expected this cosmopolitan system to emerge in an evolutionary fashion, for three reasons: (1) the peaceful character of republics, which consists in their moral character; (2) the power of international trade to forge cooperation through self-interest; and (3) the operations of a political public sphere, which he saw as a public reliance on the unbiased opinion of the community of philosophers. He explained away the improbability of these conditions actually leading to a peaceable confederation by reference to a hidden "purpose of nature." This hidden purpose comprised the expression of reason in connection with the conditions of self-interest among states.

Much in his system requires revision. For one example, the idea of a hidden purpose of nature propelling the evolution of a confederation is no longer defensible philosophically. Contemporary debate addresses possible approaches to revising or updating Kant's system in such a manner that his basic analysis of the pacifying effects of law can be recovered in a contemporary form.

One revision concerns the suitability of a voluntary federation of nations for accomplishing peace. Habermas (1998) argues that Kant's voluntary federation is too weak to effect peace. He proposes a binding system of cosmopolitan law with powers of enforcement to protect the interests of individuals globally.

Another commonly debated revision concerns today's global stratification of states. Today's Third World countries did not exist during Kant's time. Under contemporary conditions, a model of global peace must anticipate not only the cessation of wars, as addressed by Kant, but also the conditions, such as civil war and other disturbances, that make enduring peace less likely. This includes distributive justice on a global level.

And finally, Kant's teleological account of historical evolution toward a global cosmopolitan system of peace based on a hidden purpose of nature must be replaced by a more fallible and nuanced account of historical change.

David Held has taken up this philosophical discussion in relation to contemporary democratic theory. His book *Democracy and the Global Order* (1995) presents an argument for cosmopolitan democracy, based on Kant but systematically updated in relation to contemporary conditions. He argues that cosmopolitan democracy is needed to attend to issues such as environmental protection, for one, where individual nations alone cannot solve global problems. It is also needed because the global forces constraining national governments are constraining democracy *within* nation-states as well. Democratic governments must be refigured to incorporate global-level mechanisms, or else freedom within states will suffer.

Held points out that the idea of a level of government above the nation-state is not entirely strange. Pressure toward consolidation of political systems is what led to the formation of nation-states in the first place, beginning in the late 16th century. The states that resulted were multitiered, including local, regional, and national governments. Citizenship itself became multitiered, with specific rights and obligations attached to these various levels of government. Global democratic mechanisms will add one more layer.

Held, too, proposes a confederal approach to global institutions, in which participation is voluntary. And the media play an instrumental role in an emerging global public sphere. We will not review his particular formulation in detail, for it is not at issue here. Rather, Held's study is one example of globally oriented democratic theory that provides the kind of conceptual framework necessary to more fully examine relations among global civil society, media, war, and peace.

Even these theoretical discussions are still new, and many questions are open as is indicated by debate over suitable revisions of Kant's proposal. How binding could and should a confederation be? Should individuals receive protection directly from cosmopolitan law, or only through the mechanisms of national law? What, if any, indications in recent history point to the possibility of cosmopolitanism? Perhaps the most daunting question faces the variety of economic, political, and social forces arrayed against any reasonable prospects for democratic global governance in the short, or even the medium, term.

But we shall leave these many, and focus on one question concerning the role of global media in whatever might take place. Combining the above discussions on the growth of a global public sphere and a loosely Kantian model of the evolution of a global confederation of states based on the pacifying effects of law, what role might media play?

COSMOPOLITAN DEMOCRACY AND THE GLOBAL PUBLIC SPHERE

A compelling argument in this regard has been advanced by James Bohman (1997), and it previews an important role for a global sphere. The problem he addresses concerns the likelihood that Kant's global federation might possibly evolve, or more accurately, the likelihood that it won't evolve, at least in the short run. He recognizes, on one hand, that a strong global system of positive law is not likely to appear anytime soon, for that would require nation-states to relinquish a considerable amount of their sovereignty. On the other hand, a weak system lacking enforcement provisions is more likely to be achievable, but it would not be able to guarantee peace and the protection of individual rights globally.

Bohman proposes that the weak and strong approaches can be combined, for a weak confederation will perform an important function in creating the conditions necessary for a subsequent stronger confederation. He is referring here to the role of a global public sphere. The function of an intermediate, weak confederation, "is to create the institutional conditions necessary for a cosmopolitan public sphere and for the international civil society" (Bohman, 1997, p. 180).

A strong federation cannot simply be legislated and built as an empty legal structure. For laws that have a normative binding power sufficient to engender lawful behavior can exist only within a prior cultural value system that is commensurate with that behavior. From a discursive point of view, this is to say that a structure of law and policy requires legitimation by those who are affected, and this can be

accomplished only through deliberation in a public sphere in which cultural preferences are negotiated fairly and over time. "A federation of nations is not enough for peace. Peace is achieved by something that emerges within such a federation: the cosmopolitan public sphere" (Bohman, 1997, p. 181). Government does not create a public sphere. Rather, a public sphere creates government, whether nationally or globally.

In developing his analysis. Bohman reconstructs Kant's propositions regarding public opinion, or "publicity," and elaborates them in contemporary conditions. He refers here, for example, to the public sphere as a spaceless mechanism through which problems and issues circulate, as in Giddens's (1990) account of globalization. Most important, he emphasizes the importance of a tolerance for difference:

> World citizenship ought not to be simply a matter of all the peoples of the world finally coming to have enough similar beliefs and goals to enter into a common republic; rather, it should be a matter of achieving the conditions under which a plurality of persons can inhabit a common public space. (Bohman, 1997, p. 185)

Of course, this is not a practical proposal. Rather, it takes the form of a normative theory of global democracy, with regard to the necessary communicative processes. Bohman is well aware of the difficulties that the evolution of such a sphere faces, including commercialization of global media. But as normative theory, this analysis is not political, strictly speaking, and therefore does not bear the burden of projecting what is immediately possible. The aim, rather, is to provide an account of a possible relationship between communication and peace. In this account, the global media will have to facilitate a public sphere in which difference, stratification among countries, and power can be discussed in connection with global citizen interests. And the outcomes of discussions in this sphere must be fed into systems of global governance that evolve over time to more effectively advocate for peace.

CONCLUSION

In addressing the media in relation to war, peace, and civil society, this chapter has covered both empirical research and normative political theory. Empirical studies of news coverage indicate that war coverage tends to be biased toward nationalistic interests. Perhaps this is understandable, but it means that coverage is accurate neither in terms of so-called objectivity nor in terms of fairness to multiple viewpoints. It matters not whether this bias represents the interests of average citizens or of elites. In either case, the outcome for a global public sphere is biased reporting. The plurality of voices might provide enough variety from which to choose, but such reporting does not represent anyone's ideal of journalistic practice.

In the case of peace, research indicates that peace-related processes often lack the news values required to attract media attention. Peace treaties and negotiations do command considerable attention. However, the underlying causes for conflict and the requirements of peace are generally overlooked. The number of international organizations and movements dedicated to disarmament, peace, and human rights have grown dramatically over recent decades, but coverage of their activities has not grown concomitantly.

The relation of the media to war and peace is not only a function of the quality of news coverage. Regardless of quality, the media can and sometimes do affect foreign policy. Foreign policy has historically been made with little if any input from the citizenry. However, it is widely felt that the mass media influence on the policy-making process has increased since the Vietnam War. The hypothesis of a CNN effect may overstate the influence, but the growing interest among governments in "public diplomacy" indicates that public opinion cannot be ignored entirely, either inside or outside national borders (Bleifuss, 2000; Gill, 1999). Government efforts to massage public opinion are on the increase.

All this suggests that a fully functioning global public sphere has a steep hill to climb. War and peace reporting appears from a global perspective to be a cacophony of nationalistic debates. A global civil society is growing in the sense that individual identities are increasingly global, and globally oriented voluntary organizations are multiplying. However, the media will apparently do little to help this society codify its opinions. Thus, for the time being, a proto-civil society is served by only a proto-public sphere. The question is whether they will evolve past this stage.

Recent developments in political theory addressing the question of global democracy suggest that this should be no surprise. Even casual reflection suggests that global institutions will be required to serve a global public interested in protecting a common heritage, improving life conditions for the world's poor, and promoting the security that peace requires. Yet the studies required as preparation for building such institutions, or modifying existing institutions, have barely started. This is aside from the practical matters of global power today.

Bohman's argument suggests both a reasonable basis for hope and a useful direction for productive research. Institutions that serve to protect human rights, minimize conflict, and promote peace cannot be built out of whole cloth. If a strong confederation is ever to evolve, it will of necessity be proceeded by a weaker confederation. Here a public sphere could serve discursively to spread universalistic values, respect for difference, and understanding of how institutions can serve the respect of difference through the observance of laws and policies designed to protect all. The specific nature of the media and their potential role in relation to evolving international institutions require study in this context.

As Bohman argues, a weak federation and suitable accompanying public sphere is not dramatically different from what exists today. Modern democracies have evolved institutions designed to do these things already, albeit imperfectly. On a global scale difference is magnified. But there is no reason why difference cannot be productively engaged on this scale. Power as always is sought in service of the interest of particular minorities, but the existence of democratic government testifies to the existence more generally of mechanisms for harnessing power legitimately for the benefit of all.

This makes global civil society and peace a project in which the media would need to serve, in the future, as they have always represented themselves ideally, as a fourth estate, now on a global level. The nature and role of this global fourth estate might be very similar to the now traditional ideals of a libertarian press, perhaps with more emphasis on difference and with mechanisms to somehow make real the "socially responsible" press asked for by the Hutchins Commission (Bates, 1995). Or perhaps there would need to be some more fundamental changes. If global government evolves in a less centralized form than have national governments, then the press might function somehow differently.

In the American school of journalism, this kind of question has traditionally been addressed through normative press theory. The signal statement on this subject was Siebert, Peterson, and Schramm's book, *Four Theories of the Press* (1956). The book is dated in a number of ways today (Nerone, 1995). It is dated due in part to its own success. It iden-

tified with clarity weaknesses in the libertarian model and called for the counterbalance of a socially responsible press. Yet this call has gone entirely unheeded. Another analysis is required. Another way the book has become dated results from its implicit cultural context. The book assumed cultural and political values reflecting an idealized form of American society, and in today's increasingly global environment the work appears somewhat parochial.

Nevertheless, the book characterized notable forms of press-state relations. Press-state relations remain of central importance today at the national level, and they will be increasingly important at the global level. On this note, our review of research and theory concerning war, peace, media, and civil society suggests the following: Normative press theory is required that moves from the parochial paradigm of national governments to a global paradigm. This kind of project should be undertaken again, at a global level. The conditions are different. More cultures are involved, more languages, different business cultures and political systems, all within a single global system. Yet the basic issues are the same. What form shall government take? And what form shall media take in relation to government?

REFERENCES

Allen, B., O'Loughlin, P., Jasperson, A., & Sullivan, J. L. (1994). The media and the Gulf War: Framing, priming and the spiral of silence. *Polity, 27*(2), 255-284.

Appadurai, A. (1996). *Modernity at large: Cultural dimensions of globalization.* Minneapolis: University of Minnesota Press.

Bates, S. (1995). Realigning journalism with democracy: The Hutchins Commission, its times, and ours. Washington, DC: Annenberg Washington Program in Communications Policy Studies of Northwestern University.

Becker, J. (1982). Communication and peace: The empirical and theoretical relations between two categories in social science. *Journal of Peace Research, 19*(3), 227-240.

Bennett, W. L., & Paletz, D. L. (1994). *Taken by storm: The media, public opinion, and U.S. foreign policy in the Gulf War.* Chicago and London: University of Chicago Press.

Bleifuss, J. (2000, March 20). Ready, aim, inform. *In These Times,* pp. 2-3.

Bohman, J. (1997). The public spheres of the world citizen. In J. Bohman & M. Lutz-Bachmann (Eds.), *Perpetual peace: Essays on Kant's cosmopolitan ideal* (pp. 179-200). Cambridge: MIT Press.

Bohman, J., & Lutz-Bachmann, M. (Eds.). (1997). *Perpetual peace: Essays on Kant's cosmopolitan ideal.* Cambridge: MIT Press.

Braman, S., & Sreberny-Mohammadi, A. (Eds.). (1996). *Globalization, communication, and transnational civil society.* Cresskill, NJ: Hampton.

Bruck, P. A. (1989). Strategies for peace, strategies for news research. *Journal of Communication, 39*(1), 108-129.

Carruthers, S. L. (2000). *The media at war.* London: Macmillan.

Cohen, B. (1963). *The press and foreign policy.* Princeton, NJ: Princeton University Press.

Denton, R. E., Jr. (Ed.). (1993). *The media and the Persian Gulf War.* Westport, CT: Praeger.

Dorman, W., Manoff, R. K., & Weeks, J. (1988). *American press coverage of U.S.-Soviet relations, the Soviet Union, nuclear weapons, arms control, and national security: A bibliography.* New York: Center for War, Peace, and the News Media.

Falk, R. (1987). The global promise of social movements: Explorations at the edge of time. *Alternatives, 12,* 173.

Falk, R. (1995). *On humane governance: Toward a new global politics.* University Park: University of Pennsylvania Press.

Fernando, J. L., & Heston, A. W. (1997). Introduction: NGOs between states, markets, and civil society. *The Annals of the American Academy of Political and Social Science, 554,* 8-20.

Frederick, H. (1993). Communication, peace, and international law. In C. Roach (Ed.), *Communication and culture in war and peace* (pp. 216-251). Newbury Park, CA: Sage.

Gamson, W. A., & Stuart, D. (1992). Media discourse as a symbolic contest: The bomb in political cartoons. *Sociological Forum, 7,* 55-86.

Garon, L. (1996). A case study of functional subjectivity in media coverage: The Gulf War on TV. *Canadian Journal of Communication, 21*(3), 317-337.

Giddens, A. (1990). *The consequences of modernity.* Stanford, CA: Stanford University Press.

Giffard, C. (1989). *UNESCO and the media.* New York: Longman.

Gill, B. (1999). Limited engagement. *Foreign Affairs, 78*(4), 65-76.

Gitlin, T. (1980). *The whole world is watching.* Berkeley: University of California Press.

Glasgow University Media Group. (1985). *War and peace news.* Philadelphia: Open University Press.

Griffin, M., & Lee, J. (1995). Picturing the Gulf War: Constructing an image of war in *Time, Newsweek,* and *U.S. News & World Report. Journalism and Mass Communication Quarterly, 72*(4), 813-825.

Habermas, J. (1989). *The structural transformation of the public sphere: An inquiry into a category of Bourgeois society* (T. Burger & F. Lawrence, Trans.). Cambridge: MIT Press. (Original work published 1962)

Habermas, J. (1998). Kant's idea of perpetual peace: At two hundred years' historical remove. In J. Habermas, *The inclusion of the other* (pp. 165-202). Cambridge: MIT Press.

Hackett, R. (1991). *News and dissent: The press and politics of peace in Canada.* Norwood, NJ: Ablex.

Hallin, D. C. (1994). *We keep America on top of the world: Television journalism and the public sphere.* London: Routledge.

Hallin, D. C., & Gitlin, T. (1993). Agon and ritual: The Gulf War as popular culture and as television drama. *Political Communication, 10*(4), 411-424.

Held, D. (1995). *Democracy and the global order: From the modern state to cosmopolitan governance.* Stanford, CA: Stanford University Press.

Herbers, J., & McCartney, J. (1999). The new Washington merry-go-round. *American Journalism Review, 21*(3), 50.

Herman, E. S., & Chomsky, N. (1988). *Manufacturing consent: The political economy of the mass media.* New York: Pantheon.

Iyengar, S., & Simon, A. (1993). News coverage of the Gulf crisis and public opinion. *Communication Research, 20*(3), 365-383.

Jakobsen, P. V. (1996). National interest, humanitarianism or CNN: What triggers UN peace enforcement after the Cold War? *Journal of Peace Research, 33*(2), 205-215.

Jakobsen, P. V. (2000). Focus on the CNN effect misses the point: The real media impact on conflict management is invisible and indirect. *Journal of Peace Research, 37*(2), 131-143.

Kaid, L. L., Myrick, R., Chanslor, M., Roper, C., Hovind, M., & Trivoulidis, N. (1994). CNN's Americanization of the Gulf War: An analysis of media, technology and storytelling. In T. A. McCain & L. Shyles (Eds.), *The 1000 hour war: Communication in the Gulf.* Westport, CT: Greenwood.

Kellner, D. (1992). *The Persian Gulf TV war.* Boulder, CO: Westview.

Kirton, J. (1993). National mythology and media coverage: Mobilizing consent for Canada's War in the Gulf. *Political Communication, 10*(4), 425-441.

LaMay, C., FitzSimon, M., & Sahadieds, J. (1991). *The media at war: The press and the Persian Gulf conflict.* New York: Gannett Foundation.

Liebes, T. (1992). Our war/their war: Comparing the "Intifadeh" and the Gulf War on U.S. and Israeli television. *Critical Studies in Mass Communication, 9*(1), 44-55.

Livingston, S. (1997). *Clarifying the CNN effect: An examination of media effects according to type of military intervention* (Harvard Research Paper R-18). Cambridge, MA: Harvard University, Joan Shorenstein Barone Center on the Press, Politics and Public Policy.

McCormick, J. (1999). The role of environmental NGOs in international regimes. In J. Norman & R. S. Axelrod (Eds.), *The global environment: Institutions, law, and policy* (pp. 52-71). Washington, DC: CQ Press.

McGrew, T. (1992). A global society? In S. Hall, D. Held, & T. McGrew (Eds.), *Modernity and its futures* (pp. 62-102). Cambridge, UK: Polity.

McLaughlin, G., & Miller, D. (1996). The media politics of the Irish peace process. *Harvard International Journal of Press/Politics, 1*(4), 116-134.

Mowlana, H., Gerbner, G., & Schiller, H. I. (1992). *Triumph of the image: The media's war in the Persian Gulf—A global perspective.* Boulder, CO: Westview.

Nerone, J. C. (1995). *Last rights: Revisiting four theories of the press.* Urbana: University of Illinois Press.

Norris, P. (1999). Global governance & cosmopolitan citizens. In J. S. Nye, Jr. & E. C. Kamarck (Eds.), *Democracy.com? Governance in a networked world.* Hollis, NH: Hollis Publishing.

Norris, P. (2001). Democratic divide? The impact of the Internet on parliaments worldwide. In P. Norris (Ed.), *Digital divide? Civic engagement, information poverty and the Internet worldwide.* Cambridge, UK: Cambridge University Press.

Nohrstedt, S. A., Kaitatzi-Whitlock, S., Ottosen, R., & Riegert, K. (2000). From the Persian Gulf to Kosovo—War journalism and propaganda. *European Journal of Communication, 15*(3), 383-404.

Peer, L., & Chestnut, B. (1995). Deciphering media independence: The Gulf War debate in television and newspaper news. *Political Communication, 12*(1), 81-95.

Reese, S. D., & Buckalew, B. (1995). The militarism of local television: The routine framing of the Persian Gulf War. *Critical Studies in Mass Communication, 12*(1), 40-59.

Reiss, H. (Ed.). (1970). *Kant's political writings.* Cambridge, UK: Cambridge University Press.

Ricci, A. (1998). Towards a systematic study of Internet based political and social communication in Europe. *Telematics and Informatics, 15*(3), 135-161.

Roach, C. (Ed.). (1993). *Communication and culture in war and peace.* Newbury Park, CA: Sage.

Robertson, R. (1992). *Globalization: Social theory and global change.* London: Sage.

Robinson, P. (1999). The CNN effect: Can the news media drive foreign policy? *Review of International Studies, 25,* 301-309.

Robinson, P. (2000a). The news media and intervention: Triggering the use of air power during humanitarian crises. *European Journal of Communication, 15*(3), 405-414.

Robinson, P. (2000b). The policy-media interaction model: Measuring media power during humanitarian crisis. *Journal of Peace Research, 37*(5), 613-633.

Rotberg, R., & Weiss, T. (Eds.). (1996). *From massacres to genocide.* Cambridge, MA: World Peace Foundation.

Ryan, C. (1991). *Prime time activism.* Boston: South End.

Serra, S. (1996). Multinationals of solidarity international civil society and the killing of street children in Brazil. In S. Braman & A. Sreberny-Mohammadi (Eds.), *Globalization, communication, and transnational civil society* (pp. 219-241). Cresskill, NJ: Hampton.

Servaes, J. (1991, October). Was Grenada a testcase for the disinformation war? *Media Development* [Special issue], pp. 41-44.

Shaw, M. (1996). *Civil society and media in global crises: Representing distant violence.* London and New York: Pinter.

Shinar, D. (2000). Media diplomacy and "peace talk": The Middle East and Northern Ireland. *Gazette, 62*(2), 83-97.

Siebert, F. S., Peterson, T., & Schramm, W. (1956). *Four theories of the press: The authoritarian, libertarian, social responsibility and Soviet communist concepts of what the press should be and do.* Urbana: University of Illinois Press.

Small, M. (1987). Influencing the decision-makers: The Vietnam experience. *Journal of Peace Research, 24*(2), 185-198.

Sobel, R. (1998). Portraying American public opinion toward the Bosnia crisis. *Harvard International Journal of Press/Politics, 3*(2), 16-33.

Stone, S. (1989). The peace movement and Toronto newspapers. *Canadian Journal of Communication, 14*(1), 57-69.

Strobel, W. (1997). *Late breaking foreign policy.* Washington, DC: United States Institute of Peace.

Strupp, J. (2000, March 13). More windows on the world. *Editor & Publisher,* pp. 26-27.

Tehranian, K., & Tehranian, M. (Eds.). (1992). *Restructuring for world peace: On the threshold of the twenty-first century.* Cresskill, NJ: Hampton.

Tehranian, M. (1999). *Worlds apart: Human security and global governance.* Honolulu, HI: Toda Institute for Global Peace and Policy Research.

Thussu, D. K. (2000). Legitimizing "humanitarian intervention"? CNN, NATO and the Kosovo crisis. *European Journal of Communication, 15*(3), 345-362.

Vincent, R. C. (2000). A narrative analysis of U.S. press coverage of Slobadan Milosevic and the Serbs in Kosovo. *European Journal of Communication, 15*(3), 321-344.

United Nations Educational, Scientific and Cultural Organization. (1979). *Declaration on fundamental principles concerning the contribution of the mass media to strengthening peace and international understanding, to the promotion of human rights and to countering racialism, apartheid and incitement to war* (Adopted at the 20th session of UNESCO's General Conference, November, 22, 1978). Paris: Author.

Wolf, M. (2000, December 27). How civil war plagues the poor. *Financial Times,* p. 11.

Wolfsfeld, G. (1997a). Fair weather friends: The varying role of the news media in the Arab-Israeli peace process. *Political Communication, 14*(1), 29-48.

Wolfsfeld, G. (1997b). Promoting peace through the news media: Some initial lessons from the Oslo peace process. *Harvard International Journal of Press/Politics, 2*(4), 52-70.

5

Transnational Advertising

K. VISWANATH
National Cancer Institute

LIREN BENJAMIN ZENG
Mount Royal College

In 1999, concomitant with the World Trade Organization (WTO) meetings in Seattle, United States, a number of events in opposition to the WTO occurred—protests, marches, press conferences, and teach-ins—the intensity of which was a surprise to many observers in the United States and the world. Simultaneously, a doctored photograph made its way through the Internet showing the Seattle Police in riot gear facing an angry crowd of protesters. Underneath it was a caption: "Just do it. Run like hell" with the omnipresent symbol, the Nike "swoosh."

How an obscure athletic shoe company from the northwestern United States has come to become a symbol of cultural imperialism, labor exploitation, celebration of athletic suprem-

acy, unbridled freedom, and limitless possibilities is a tale in itself and a topic of controversy. What is less debated, however, is the universal appeal and recognition of the Nike symbol and the central role played by advertising in making this arguably the most widely recognized logo in the world.

From Asia to Africa, Latin America to North America, through the steppes of Russia to the foggy islands in the Atlantic, advertising, along with financial capital, has become a central arm in promoting what has now come to be called globalization. If financial capital is the fuel that fired the engine of transnational corporations (TNCs), transnational advertising is the fire that lights the path toward capitalism and consumption.

AUTHORS' NOTE: The views expressed in this chapter are those of the authors and not of the National Cancer Institute.

Figure 5.1. Photo That Circulated on the Internet After the Seattle Protest Against the World Trade Organization

The dismantling of economic barriers through various trade agreements such as the WTO, European common market integration, and the North American Free Trade Agreement (NAFTA) is prodded by modern means of communication through transnational communication corporations (TCCs) whose base of sustenance is transnational advertising. It is little wonder then that in 2000, transnational advertising agencies (TNAAs) conducted business worth $235.5 billion, larger than the gross national product (GNP) of several countries. In the United States alone, billings for the year 2000 amounted to $138.6 billion. The importance of transnational advertising is further enhanced by the entry of interactive commerce, which drove the gross income of U.S. advertising agencies by more than 50% (Endicott, 2000). Transnational advertising is truly global with operations spread all over the world including China, yet inspired by leadership from the United States, the leading advertising market in the world.

Transnational advertising continues to play a critical role in the worldwide drive toward media deregulation, privatization, and globalization, deserving appropriate scholarly and public policy scrutiny.

Given this sketchy overview, the study of transnational advertising is essential to any discussion and study of international and intercultural communication. This chapter will review some of the major themes in transnational advertising that were extant in the literature over the past 25 years, identify the ideological debates and positions of actors involved in the debate, review the limited empirical evidence informing the debates, and end with a call for a systematic research agenda to pursue a research program.[1]

Defining Transnational Advertising

This chapter proposes to take a very broad and catholic definition of advertising. Advertising textbooks focus on paid forms of communication with an intent to persuade. Here is a sample of definitions:

> Advertising is nonpersonal communication of information, usually paid for and usually persuasive in nature, about products (goods and services) or ideas by identified sponsors through various media. (Arens & Bov'ee, 1994, p. 6)

> Advertising is paid nonpersonal communication from an identified sponsor using mass media to persuade or influence an audience. (Wells, Burnett, & Moriarty, 1992, p. 10)

Although it cannot be denied that advertising is a paid form of communication to promote ideas, goods, and services, we find these sample definitions limiting in some respects. Advertising does promote goods and services, but it also promotes particular worldviews and ideologies that define the parameters of how one might look at things, whom one should emulate, and what one must aspire to. That is, it has a social control function (Viswanath & Demers, 1999). The effects of advertising go beyond individuals and their consumption to an impact on the larger social institutions, such as the economy, media, and cultural establishments. Furthermore, the effects are not only direct but also latent to the extent that transnational advertising affects behaviors, practices, and formats of media and cultural institutions.

In summary, in our view,

> Advertising is the promotion of an ideological worldview with the direct intent to influence individuals but with the latent consequences on institutions and cultures with often explicit and sometimes implicit sponsorship by commercial institutions.[2]

By extension, transnational advertising may be defined as the establishment, practice, and study of consequences of advertising across nation-states.

Transnational Advertising and Transnational Media

If the transnational corporations received their legal authority and protection from the General Agreement on Tariffs and Trade (GATT) and the WTO, their intellectual authority and legitimacy is promoted by the transnational communication corporations, specifically, transnational advertising agencies. The global conglomeration and consolidation of TCCs, through vertical integration that has occurred since the 1980s and 1990s, are expected to increase synergies among the various divisions of the media organizations leading to operational efficiencies and profitability (Gershon, 1997). Furthermore, establishment in foreign locations and strategic alliances with foreign corporations may allow cost efficiencies and provide a global audience for its products making a critical difference in profitability of the media firms.

Given this situation, the contemporary TCC is a conglomeration of companies and divisions that both produce content and allow for the distribution of that content. Owning book publishing companies, movie and television studios, recording studios, and contracts with talent facilitates content production; owning magazines, newspapers, and cable and satellite television systems facilitates distribution.

This last point is significant as media companies built alliances across the world to cobble together a global audience reach that makes mockery of national borders. They have aggressively sought to expand their empires through a combination of partnerships or outright ownership accelerating media development in many markets of the world

(Demers, 1999; Herman & McChesney, 1997).

As media development accelerates, a significant communication policy issue is how to finance the development and the operations of the media. Many nations are opting to rely on the private sector to subsidize their media systems. This shift in reliance from audience either through circulation or licensing to advertising could have a profound impact on the media and their behaviors. Program production and distribution require a scale of investment, capital, and infrastructure that could be borne only by the largest of organizations, thus giving an incentive for conglomeration and concentration in the interest of deriving economies of scale. The medium that attracts advertising is usually able to mount marketing and promotional efforts, leaving the small media at a competitive disadvantage.

There is likely to be considerable pressure on the media to offer programming fare that could attract audiences that are desirable, that is, audiences with discretionary income that will allow them to buy the products advertised in the media. This is not unlike the British experience where the press focused on more sensational and lurid fare to attract large audiences in 19th-century Britain (Curran, 1979). More instructive is Curran's observation that advertising volume increased but went mostly to the "established middle-class newspapers."

Historical Overview

The beginnings of transnational advertising, as is the case with much else in the field of international communication, could be traced back to the rise in the dominance of the United States in the global economy, politics, and communication in the post-World War II period (Fejes, 1980; Mattelart, 1979; So, 1990).[3] A confluence of at least three signifi-

cant factors is said to have been responsible for the rise of advertising: an economic and technological boom that emerged out of the war economy, the increase in the production of consumer goods, and last, the rise of television as a medium of information and entertainment (Janus, 1980a).[4]

At the same time, there has been increasing transnationalization of the U.S. economy when American companies began investing abroad financed by large domestic profits. To increase their market share, they shifted their strategy from production to marketing. Major clients of ad agencies such as General Motors and Standard Oil opened branches abroad and persuaded their agencies also to do the same. Apparently, the well-defined advertising agency-client relationship and the agency-medium relationship that evolved in the United States was nonexistent in the international arena in the 1950s when advertising was expanding in the United States. As the American manufacturers expanded abroad, they were forced to contract with local agencies as few American advertising agencies had offices overseas. The lack of standardization was a critical problem as the agencies had to contend with inconsistency in quality, execution of campaigns, and contracts and accounting procedures (Janus, 1980b). Furthermore, market and audience research were virtually nonexistent, leaving out the possibility of assessing campaign exposure and effect. The lack of standardization in campaign planning, execution, and practice internationally left American manufacturers to rely on domestic media, particularly magazines with high international circulation.

This was the principal force underlying the expansion of American advertising agencies abroad, that is, at the behest of their domestic clients who were wary of problems in advertising abroad (Janus, 1980a). The decades of the 1960s and 1970s were a watershed for American advertising industry as it started expanding abroad rapidly. American agencies had a decided advantage because of their expertise, resources, and technology (Janus, 1980b; Janus & Roncagliolo, 1979). Higher growth rates, greater profits, and lower costs from foreign operations further fueled the international expansion (Fejes, 1980; Janus, 1980a). This era also coincided with the development of communication systems, a requisite for advertising, in many parts of the world. Thus began a fruitful nexus between transnational manufacturers, advertising agencies, and local and transnational media. It also began the era of the global consumer who could be reached with a standardized campaign.[5]

If the 1960s and 1970s were decades of global expansion, the decades of the 1980s and 1990s were characterized by the increasing penetration of TNCs into developing countries and the consolidation of advertising agencies in different parts of the world. The driving force behind the consolidation and penetration is the development of new communication technologies. With New York, Tokyo, London, and Paris serving as centers, the 1980s and 1990s saw the emergence of advertising conglomerates with different agency brands operating under each.

TRANSNATIONAL ADVERTISING: A MACRO-LEVEL ANALYSIS

Political Economy of Transnational Advertising

An understanding of the contemporary structure and scope of transnational advertising must be discussed in the context of contemporary structure of global trade in capital and goods. International financial institutions such as the International Monetary Fund (IMF), the International Bank for Reconstruction and Development (commonly known as the World Bank), and global trade regimes

such as the WTO and NAFTA have set into motion an inexorable trend of globalization facilitating the establishment and operations of TNCs. Global movement of capital and goods was further facilitated and accelerated by the development of new communication technologies that had at least the following significant consequences:

- Communication allows for more efficient coordination of activities in far-flung organizations, leading to greater centralization and control (Demers, 1996).

- Communication technology made time and space less important and facilitated the evolution of markets (Gershon, 1997).

- More germane to this topic, it became *the* critical engine in the emergence and establishment of genuine TCCs.

The TNC, and especially the TCC, is arguably the primary institution driving global trade, often indirectly, sometimes directly influencing the economic policies of nations (Gershon, 1997).

Regulation of Transnational Advertising

Although the international political economy provides the context, such factors as the political philosophy of the state, dominant religion of the country, and legal and statutory bodies, among others, enable one to understand how advertising is regulated. Regulation, formal or informal, may cover such subjects as products that could or could not be advertised, advertising content, media that could be used in preparation of the materials, and taxation (Mueller, 1996). Mueller (1996), in an extensive discussion of regulation, suggests that there is considerable variation in both the nature and the mechanisms of regulation of advertising. Religion or the institutions of religion could, for example, find certain content offensive or threatening, which might constrain the approach one might take in campaigns. The laws regulating such advertising undoubtedly reflect the influence or social power of these sectors in that nation-state.

The role of the state and the relative autonomy it enjoys vis-à-vis other institutions have been a subject of long-standing contention in the social sciences. Questions for the future may study the extent to which the state could influence, regulate, and even restrict advertising; the efficacy of such regulation; and the likely consequences of regulation. The state could restrict advertising within its sovereign territory, but may hold no leverage when attempting to control advertising coming in from other countries. The current pace of movement of goods and ideas across national borders makes regulation of any content including advertising by a single nation-state challenging. International or supranational bodies are hence venturing into the arena of regulation: the various bodies of the United Nations, the European Union, and inter-country agreements, among others. For example, the World Health Organization could be expected to play an increasingly important role in the advertising of tobacco products in the future. Issues that will attract attention are likely to include the type of products, advertising content, protection of vulnerable groups such as children, ownership of data, and information and data privacy.

THE TRANSNATIONAL ADVERTISING AGENCY: NATURE OF THE ORGANIZATION

The forces of globalization of capital and development of technologies have also affected the contemporary structure of TNAAs. A typical transnational agency is an agglomeration of a number of brand advertising agencies under a parent or holding company, offering an array of services, including creative and marketing strategy, media buying, and consumer intelligence. This includes message testing and evaluation and public and strategic communication services, including public relations (Endicott, 2000). Lately, they have forged alliances with, if not outright purchases of, interactive service agencies, hoping to reap the expected windfalls of a wired economy. The transformation of a mere advertising agency into a consumer intelligence organization is now well on its way.

Specialization in one large conglomerate ideally should create synergy in operations and provide a one-stop shop for a client. For example, in 2000, the largest such group, Omnicom, acquired more than 20 agencies, whereas the second largest group, the Interpublic Group of Companies, bought up 30 agencies (Endicott, 2000). Such merger and acquisition activity, at least in theory, allows organizations to offer a wide array of services and "expand their billing base" according to the annual report of the industry magazine, *Advertising Age*.

Thus, the TNAA, with its global reach, scope, and execution, has successfully influenced and shaped content, format, and style of the media all over the world. It is a singular organization connecting the global manufacturers with global consumers through the global media. Yet, unlike a typical TNC or a TCC, an advertising conglomerate faces a number of challenges in addition to the ones that are faced by a TCC. Gershon (1997) identifies a few of them: overestimation of synergies, financial viability, and client conflicts.

As is the case with transnational media corporations, the optimistic assumptions that hoped for synergies are yet to be completely realized. In addition to organizational turf wars, employee resistance, and reluctance to share creative concepts, problems also arise in the areas of media buying. Clients are reluctant to subsidize the media buys of their competitors, and there is active resistance by the powerful media conglomerates to any packaging deals that could be to their disadvantage. Furthermore, clients have become increasingly nervous over the potential conflict that could emerge when different agencies with accounts that compete with each other are brought together under one conglomerate.

Although the advertising business itself is booming, a reflection of the strength of the larger global market economy, traditional business models that drove the industry are increasingly being challenged on different fronts—changing technologies particularly the arrival of the Internet, compensation packages, competing alternative means of communications, and client conflicts. The future of the conglomerates and what shape they are likely to take given these challenges could be a topic for future empirical inquiry.

Social Science Measurements and the Transnational Advertising Agency

The significant contribution of the audience measurement techniques to the functioning of a TNAA cannot be underestimated. Global market and public opinion research organizations such as Nielsen, Gallup, and Harris International among many others not only have emerged but have grown enormously over the past decade and are major business enterprises in themselves. For example, in 1998 alone, the top 10 research companies earned more than $5.4 billion, out of which $2.8 billion was earned outside the United States. The top-ranked research company AC Neilsen conducts business operations in more than 100 countries and earned more than $1 billion outside the United States in 1998.

Their use of sophisticated social science techniques for audience research provided the appropriate tools for the agencies to serve their clients efficiently thus strengthening their importance. The expense of the services and the requirement of sophistication acquired through training and infrastructure give the transnational agency a distinct competitive edge over a local or domestic agency.

Export of Professionalism

Increasing transnationalization of advertising poses a challenge in understanding the impact on the diffusion of professionalism and occupational practices of communication practitioners. Although there are several surveys of practitioners on their views on advertising and on some practices in regard to message construction (standardization vs. localization), our review revealed few if any systematic, empirical studies that focus on professionalism. Furthermore, fewer have meaningful theoretical or analytical frameworks to explain the findings.

Golding (1979) provides a powerful analytical framework by identifying three mechanisms through which professionalism could be exported: institutional transfer, education and training, and informal diffusion.

The first mechanism, institutional transfer, is clearly the dominant outcome of the current trend in transnational advertising. For example, data reported by the advertising industry trade magazine, *Advertising Age,* suggest that some of the major advertisers in the "top 10 global ad markets," the United States, Japan, the United Kingdom, Germany, France, Brazil, Italy, Australia, Canada, and South Korea, are mostly TNCs. Another example is that Procter & Gamble and the automobile company General Motors, along with Philip Morris and Ford Motors, remain among the top-ranked advertisers in the top 10 markets.[6] Similarly, in some of the largest countries in the world, the top-ranked agencies have multinational tie-ups.

It is evident from this brief review that institutional transfer has been a singular feature of the contemporary expansion of advertising into global markets. What remains to be assessed is the amount of education and training that is being provided with transnational connection and how working in the larger agencies along with foreign linkages is leading to informal socialization.

Advertising Practices: Issues and Debates

Transnational advertising is a complex phenomenon involving international clients and their local subsidiaries, TNAAs and local collaborators/branches, and cultural and legal norms that vary across nations and regulatory institutions. Amid this complexity, TNCs strive to formulate and implement their marketing and communication strategies, aiming for some "uniform advertising concept" (Vardar, 1992).

Several tools and models, some based on theories such as hierarchies of effects (Ray, 1973), with different names and terms such as CAPP (continuous advertising planning program), 4Cs (cross-cultural consumer characterization), and DAGMAR (defining advertising goals for measured advertising results), and segmentation strategies such as VALS (values and lifestyles) and AIO (activities, interests, and opinions), among others, are used by the agencies to make their advertising communications more effective (Vardar, 1992).

Who Controls: Centralization Versus Decentralization

One issue of interest that relates to the practice of TNAAs and TNCs is the locus of control over decisions on strategies and execu-

tion of advertising campaigns. TNCs with branches in different parts of the world may centralize all functions including campaign planning, creative strategy, media selection, and sales promotion in the place where they are headquartered in an attempt to exercise complete control over their campaigns. As Mueller (1996) avers, centralization is also correlated with *standardization* where a company may adopt a more uniform worldwide advertising campaign strategy (see next section). Although this approach enables the company to stay on the message and maintain uniformity in image, it is not without its weaknesses: insensitivity to the local market and cultural conditions and lack of an ability to react quickly to changing market conditions.

On the other side of the coin, decentralization is where TNCs may allow local agencies sufficient autonomy in planning and execution of campaigns with attendant advantages of local cultural sensitivies, flexibility to react to changing market conditions, and local expertise. A disadvantage is that companies may lack a uniform brand image and there may be considerable unevenness in the quality of campaigns throughout the world.

It is understandable that some firms may attempt to maintain a balance between the two approaches, sometimes using *pattern advertising* where the creative and message strategy is done centrally, but the execution is left to the local branches (Mueller, 1996). This dilemma of centralization versus decentralization in management is directly related to the creative strategy and involves a major debate in transnational advertising: standardization versus localization.

The Debate on Standardization Versus Localization

One major debate that occupied the attention of advertising practitioners and scholars alike is often phrased as "localization versus standardization," referring to the dilemmas of TNCs whether to tailor the advertising messages to local cultures or not (Elinder, 1965; Fatt, 1967; Harris & Attour, 2000; Hite & Fraser, 1988; Levitt, 1983; Ricks, Arpan, & Fu, 1974, among others). The major issues will be reviewed briefly and critically.[7]

Although no clear definitions of these terms exist, standardization refers to an advertiser's practice that uses almost similar brand image, strategy, and format across different markets of the world. The assumption underlying this approach is that there are certain universal commonalities among the peoples of the world and that the differences among nations are superficial and do not warrant distinctive marketing and advertising approaches. Despite their cultural differences, the basic physiological and psychological needs of the consumer worldwide are similar and can be targeted by the same appeals. Last, with the improvement in communication infrastructure and growing commonality in cultures and tastes in media and the arts, similar appeals of persuasion should work worldwide. Several advantages, simplification in decision making, easier execution of strategy, consistent brand image, and economies of scale are assumed to accrue from standardization.

Localization is when the advertisers change the models, background, language, and appeal to take into consideration local cultural sensitivities and tastes. The proponents of this approach point out that there exist barriers of tastes, cultures, language, and literacy and variations in laws, regulation, and media infrastructure that warrant distinct approaches in different markets. Localization is purportedly helpful in avoiding blunders and gaffes that may go against local norms and cultures, identifying differences among prospects in what product attributes they value, and in accounting for differences in tastes, local communications, and legislation.

It is clear that if the standardization side of the argument were to prevail, the implication is that only certain agencies that have worldwide presence could be capable of executing advertising strategies in contrast to a localization argument that calls for expertise from local markets. Furthermore, standardization raises questions about the very existence of the idea of market segmentation that assumes that consumers are heterogeneous and that different audience segments require different approaches.

Given the economic and political implications of this debate, it is of little surprise that several scholars have examined both the advertisements and the views of advertisers on this topic. Yet, despite the overwhelming attention the topic has received in scholarly circles, there is a lack of empirical data (Hornik, 1980). Oftentimes, anecdotes (Onkvisit & Shaw, 1999) and logical and theoretical arguments (Taylor, Miracle, & Chang, 1994) are used to speculate whether to standardize or localize.

Agrawal (1995) traces a four-decade history of the debate, identifying the major arguments from the 1950s through the 1980s. The assumptions in earlier years, the decade of the 1950s and before, were based on age-old, often insulting stereotypes rather than on logical, theoretical deductions and favored localized approach to transnational advertising. The decade of the 1960s, when advertising agencies began expanding abroad, saw some empirical studies examining the basis of earlier assumptions and tilted toward standardization given the inherent advantage of cost savings. At the same time, there was greater sensitivity to the possible barriers in a universal approach to advertising. Further research and an effort to identify factors that influence standardization or localization characterized the decade of the 1970s. With globalization occurring at a more rapid pace, and with the expansion of new communication technologies and media across the nations of the world, the enthusiasm for standardization increased in the 1980s.

The consensus of the 1990s in the literature seemed to be that standardization and localization should not be viewed as a dichotomy, but rather a continuum and practiced with sensitivity. Transnational corporations should not use purely standardized or localized ads as the decision is contingent on many factors including the nature of the product, the audience, and the market conditions.

For practitioners, this debate is of immediate and practical interest. In general, the review by Onkvisit and Shaw (1987) suggests that standardization and localization could be viewed along a continuum where most TNCs used an approach that balances both (Jain, 1989). For example, a survey of more than 400 *Fortune* 500 companies by Hite and Fraser (1988) showed that a majority of the companies used a combination of standardized and localized advertising strategies. Given the increasing globalization and popularity of global brands such as Nike and Coca-Cola, one hypothesis to test in the future is whether standardization may become more common.

In summary, the brief review suggests that answers to this issue depend on three broad groups of factors: characteristics of the product (Harris & Attour, 2000), consumers, and market conditions (Agrawal, 1995; Hite & Fraser, 1988; Onkvisit & Shaw, 1987). It is nonetheless surprising that little of this research draws from the literature in communication. For example, a number of assumptions and considerations are questionable and lead to several research questions that remain to be addressed:

- To what extent are media use and exposure patterns and tastes similar and different across different audience subgroups?

- Are there variations within and among nations? For example, research on cosmopo-

lites versus localities in the literature suggests that the differences among groups within a nation are more profound than among groups across nations.[8]

Even in marketing, this has long been recognized in the form of the "intermarket segment concept" where scholars have suggested that people in urban areas of many countries in the world are more similar to each other than to their rural counterparts (Jain, 1989).

- Along the same lines, one might question the impact of increasing penetration of TCCs and increasing convergence in tastes and media programming among certain groups of the world.

- What about advertising and media effects? Recent literature suggests that media have differential effects on audience subgroups (Bryant & Zilmann, 1994; Viswanath & Demers, 1999). In advertising, too, differences in consumer characteristics and advertising practices are shown by a large amount of empirical evidence to be different. If indeed there are differences among the audiences, the very core assumption of the standardization-localization debate is questionable, thus making the issue moot.

- Last, the issue of validity comes up in measuring standardization. Standardization has been conceptualized as anything from just commonality in creative or media strategy to complete and wholesale transfer of messages created in one place to the rest of the world. It is more fruitful to conceptualize standardization in degrees and assess its utility based on such a measure (Onkvisit & Shaw, 1999). Harris and Attour (2000) offer the provocative idea of developing an advertising standardization index (SI) and report, based on their pilot study, that there is a high degree of standardization globally. They also are cautious enough to attribute their figures to the possible type of products they studied. What their study suggests is a need for more careful and critical examination of the debate to broaden the empirical bases of interpretation.

MESSAGE SYSTEM ANALYSIS

The large body of empirical work in transnational advertising defies easy classification. Most transnational advertising message and effects studies center on the theme of culture. Therefore, in transnational advertising, a lot of effort is devoted to identifying the cultural themes, values, and appeals. Culture and advertising are appropriately brought together here to the extent that culture is a key contextual independent variable that could influence advertising strategies, appeals, and audience behavior (Clark, 1990).[9] Almost all the studies in the literature showed that there are differences among the consumers in what they value among product attributes, their media exposure, and behavior patterns, values, and attitudes (Caffyn & Rogers, 1970; Hornik, 1980; Onkvisit & Shaw, 1987, among others). That is, whatever commonalities might exist are overshadowed by variations in local market and cultural conditions.

We will briefly summarize the work on advertising messages, possibly the most thoroughly examined area of transnational advertising, often using the method of content analysis (Samiee & Jeong, 1994):

- Appeals are used in the advertisements to attract attention or interest consumers and/or to influence their feelings toward the product, service, or cause (Belch & Belch, 1993). It is not surprising to learn from the empirical studies that advertisers use appeals that are salient to a given culture (Belk, Bryce, & Pollay, 1985), which is also taken into consideration when packaging, positioning, promoting, and distributing the product. Furthermore, the type of appeals used in one culture may or may not be used in another culture in the interest of maintaining cultural

proximity in appeals and advertising construction (Chirapravati, 1996; Frith & Wesson, 1991; Mueller, 1992; Pernia, 1996; Taylor et al., 1994).

- The amount of informational cues in advertising could also vary with ads depending on the culture. Certain cultures rely more on nonverbal cues compared with others, which, in turn, influences the way the message is constructed and the amount of information presented in the ad. For example, Krishna, Chuang, and Axinn (1997) report that local brand advertising on Taiwanese TV relies on much fewer informational cues compared with global brands to account for the difference in cultures.

- The images of women in advertising has been an area of long-standing interest in advertising and, more recently, in transnational advertising. Some scholars, based on the assumption that advertising reflects social reality, attempted to map the differences and similarities of advertising appeals with depiction of women in society of different ethos (e.g., Gilly, 1988) or chart the changing trend in a specific culture (e.g., Cheng, 1997; Kang, 1993). Others have argued that sustained depiction of women (usually stereotypical and negative) in advertising creates an ideology that "naturalizes" the hegemony of one section of the population over another (e.g., Goffman, 1979), and the export of these formats in advertising is an indicator of the transfer of media professionalism (e.g., Balasubramanian, 1999; Griffin, Viswanath, & Schwartz, 1994).

TRANSNATIONAL ADVERTISING: SOCIAL AND INDIVIDUAL IMPACT

To do justice to the debate on the social effects of transnational advertising on international politics and culture requires nothing less than a book-length treatment that is beyond the scope of this chapter. A brief overview of the issues, however, will provide the flavor of the critique as well as an idea on the nature of issues that require more systematic and appropriate treatment elsewhere.

From its very beginnings, advertising has been a subject of intense scrutiny both for acts of commission and omission.[10] The votaries of advertising start with the assumption that the consumer is "rational" and uses advertising to acquire information on products and matches his or her needs with available products in the marketplace. That is, advertising is seen as the medium that educates the consumer by offering product information. A consequence is that advertising results in market efficiency, an assumption informed by classical liberal economic theory, thus implying that marketing and advertising are essential ingredients in the makeup of a market economy (Leiss, Kline, & Jhally, 1986).

The critics, on the other hand, contend that advertising is a wasteful expenditure contributing to the creation of wants and needs whose satisfaction is of limited value and may even be harmful to the larger society (Ewen, 1976; Galbraith, 1958, 1967). Advertising manipulates audience needs and wants by changing and associating simple consumer goods with attributes that are desirable or made to be desirable (Ewen, 1976; Packard, 1957). Advertising or "publicity" in the words of Berger (1972) creates envy and dissatisfaction leading to an attempt to abate the dissonance through consumption. Ultimately, it is a "distorted mirror" that is an agent of control and manipulation creating false consciousness and a dysfunctional distraction from real issues (Pollay, 1986; Williamson, 1978).

This critique of advertising practices, and the institution of advertising itself, has been extended to the realm of transnational advertising drawing on theoretical views informed by modernization and dependency approaches.[11]

From a modernization perspective, advertising helps in subsidizing the development and maintenance of private sector mass media and inducing "modernizing"—consumption-oriented values. Dependency scholars, on the other hand, argue that such factors as foreign aid, trade, TNCs, and multinational lending institutions foster Third World economic and cultural dependency on the industrialized world, posing a threat to Third World nations' cultural and political sovereignty. Of particular relevance are the writings of a number of scholars who assayed the potential of TCCs, particularly TNAAs (Nordenstreng & Schiller, 1993; Schiller, 1976, 1979, 1989), and their role in shaping the worldviews of Third World citizenry. Their focus was on the penetration of Western ideologies, culture, and communication media and is usually discussed under the broad topic of media or cultural imperialism (Lee, 1979; Straubaar, 1991). Based on the work of communication scholars working in this tradition of media imperialism, one might posit three broad consequences of transnational advertising:

P1: Transnational advertising poses a threat to the economic and cultural sovereignty of the nations.

Advertising influences the mass media impelling them to offer programming that attracts the audience that is desirable to the advertisers, a factor that contributes to changes in the communication policies and media behaviors of nations as detailed earlier in the chapter. Because few countries in the world have the capacity to produce content, especially television programming, many nations are compelled to rely on a small core group of exporters leading to greater cultural homogenization (Janus, 1980b; Janus & Roncagliolo, 1979; Siune & Hulton, 1998; Tsirulnikov, 1996).[12] Nation-states are thus caught in a bind being forced to import programming from abroad to retain their audience, yet potentially opening themselves to the erosion of their cultural autonomy and uniqueness.

P2: Transnational advertising leads to a promotion of consumption-oriented values thus displacing and misplacing national priorities. *✓*

Transnational advertising, it is argued, carries with it a message that is ideologically laden, promoting consumption-oriented lifestyles, values, worldviews, and life's priorities, which is necessary for the market expansion of TNCs (Schiller, 1979). Commercialized local mass media whose major source of income is TNCs, says Schiller (1979), reproduce the superstructure of dependency by transmitting consumerism from the center to the periphery. This process of imbalance in the flow was justified under the principle of free-market economy always favorable to advanced industrialized countries. The result of this structural situation was, in Schiller's view, the intensification of economic and cultural dependency and led to the underdevelopment of Third World nations.

Others have questioned the promotion of consumer goods such as soft drinks, tobacco, cosmetics, and expensive products such as automobiles and electronics in Latin American nations (Janus & Roncagliolo, 1979). A demand for and consumption of such products may have two consequences, they suggest. First, such an artificially induced demand could influence the national priorities distracting the state from meeting more basic human needs such as food and clothing. Second, the goods that are usually promoted through advertising are generally unaffordable, requiring a considerable shift in resources of a family to satisfy the demand. The failure to satisfy the demand could lead to discontentment at the individual level and instability at the societal level.

P3: Advertising alters the programming functions of media compelling them to attract audiences. *✓*

What is the empirical evidence we have so far? The work by the Euromedia group shows that even public broadcast systems have adopted a mixed model increasing their number of channels and offerings and the nature of their programming to compete with their private sector counterparts (McQuail & Siune, 1998; Siune & Hulten, 1998; Siune & Truetzschler, 1992). Both domestic and imported fare have increased as a result of increase in the number of channels—a phenomenon also experienced in Russia (Tsirulnikov, 1996).

Thus, the effect of advertising on media is subtler, consequential, and indirect. Advertising exercises a form of social control through its focus on programming fare that attracts audiences who are consumers and on programming that is noncontroversial so as not to distract the audience from its message. The question remains whether advertising subsidy leads to a decrease in variety of programs and limits diversity as is often assumed by the critics. As audience measurement techniques and lifestyle analyses become more sophisticated, advertisers seek more target-specific programming that reaches a well-defined audience and an environment that suits their message. This need of the advertiser, combined with the larger trend toward complexity and specialization in the society and the development of communication technologies that increase channel capacity, offers the potential for a more diverse array of programming for specialized audiences.

The impact of commercialization and advertising on media structure, organization, and program formats is possibly one of the most profound questions of our times. As an increasing number of countries continue to opt for more advertising-dependent media, scholars are required to answer normative as well as empirical questions that can inform the communication policy of the nation-state. Some questions that deserve to be studied include the following:

- What is the relative contribution of transnational advertising and commercialization on local communication policies?

- To what extent are "good values" of a media system affected by advertising and are made vulnerable (Blumler, 1992)?[13]

- Will advertising contribute to or take away from specialization and diversity in traditional and new media?

Despite the practical and policy-relevant nature of the answers to these questions, surprisingly little research is being carried out.

These propositions and the assumptions therein deserve closer empirical attention from scholars and policymakers alike. Although some evidence exists to support aspects of the hypotheses, much else remains unverified and undocumented. This remains an area ripe for investigation.

The Glamour-Communication Industry Complex

An extensive review of both scholarly and popular writing on advertising revolves around the issue of social control. It is suggested that advertising, as reviewed earlier, makes explicit what is acceptable and desirable and sells its ideas by fostering discontent among its target audience.[14] Whatever the merits or empirical bases of this argument, the impact of media and advertising lies in its ubiquity and consonance.[15] Its pervasive presence either directly through explicit advertising or indirectly through commercial sponsorship ensures a sufficient level of exposure that

few audiences can ever escape. In addition, thoughtfully strategized, specifically targeted, carefully crafted, deliberately constructed, and vigorously implemented campaigns are made only stronger because they carry the same theme through different media. Last, some media environments are considered more fertile for intended effects than other media, which results in the specific medium shaping itself in a way that is attractive to the advertisers and their prospects.

These propositions are more applicable in the case of gender advertising, that is, advertising portrayals of women's roles and body images. An extensive corpus of work analyzing the images of women in advertising, and some empirical work on the effects of these images on women, has developed. Our review of this work suggests that these studies must be put in the appropriate context of the political economy of the institutions that generate these images. In the case of gender advertising, it is instructive to explore the nexus of the relationship between the glamour and communication industries, a glamour-communication industry complex, and the impact of this mutually beneficial relationship on the intended and unintended audience.

The glamour industry includes fashion apparel and personal care items including cosmetics, fragrances, and toiletries. The media that appear to enjoy special patronage are women's magazines, which appear to focus predominantly on sex, relationships, and fashion tips. Advertising agencies are the principal link between the magazine industry and the glamour industry. Glamour product manufacturers have extensive advertising budgets and appear to spread their largesse primarily on the magazine industry. Furthermore, glamour knows no boundaries and appears to treat the world as its market. Although specific figures are hard to come by, some numbers are instructive:

- In 1998, for example, the three cosmetic manufacturers of Revlon, L'Oreal, and Estée Lauder, for whom the figures are available, spent a combined $1.658 billion on advertising in the United States alone.

- 58% of the advertising media budget of the apparel industry in 1998 was spent on consumer magazines, and it is reasonable to assume that they are fashion magazines. Almost 48% of the cosmetic and beauty aids media budget was spent on consumer magazines. Network TV garnered the next largest share.

- Recently, the chief executive of Avon announced that Avon is doubling its transnational advertising spending to $100 million covering at least 25 markets around the world (Linnett, 2000).

Spending on marketing communications need not be limited to paid advertising but might include promotions and sponsorship, which, in turn, have a healthy impact on the corporate sales and profits. For example, a *Business Week* report states that the recent wins in beauty pageants by women from India have resulted in a boom in the cosmetics, fitness, and cosmetic surgery industries there. The Indian market for beauty products, driven by women who are influenced by imported programming and advertising, is reportedly worth $1.5 billion. The rate of growth at 20% a year is twice that of the United States and Europe.

Given this symbiotic relationship between the communication industries of mass media (especially women's magazines) and advertising, on the one hand, and the glamour industry, on the other, it is time to analyze the impact of this nexus on message construction, media content, and the target audience. Some evidence of discrete aspects of this chain exists. For example, a plethora of studies have documented the stereotypical portrayals of women, particularly in women's magazines

(Goffman, 1979; Griffin et al., 1994; Millum, 1975; Williamson, 1978, among many others). A program of research by Viswanath and colleagues suggests that stereotypical portrayals of women (especially in body size and shape) are particularly prevalent in women's magazines. Furthermore, there appears to be a greater convergence of this imagery over time and across national boundaries (Heinonen, 2000; Ogilvy, Simmonds, Urbano, & Viswanath, 1997; Simmonds, Urbano, Ogilvy, & Viswanath, 1997; Viswanath & Balasubramanian, 2000). The impact of this sustained imagery on body images and worldviews appears to be promoting dissatisfaction over their body images among the women, though much evidence so far is either from experiments or nonrandom, limited-sample surveys. The effects of these images at the macro level, although anecdotal, point to a fruitful area of examination. What these anecdotes point to is the potential shift in the very conception of beauty as is evident from the following quote from a top executive of a multinational firm: "The Indian woman no longer compares herself to other Indians. She uses the international concept of beauty" (*Business Week*, June 19, 2000, p. 68).

The foregoing is a sketchy review of one significant area of future research in transnational advertising, the role of the glamour-communication industry complex on perceptions of beauty and how the definition of beauty is changing over time as a result of globalization and commercialization.

Country-of-Origin Effect

Most buyers, according to this line of research, have some opinions and images about the quality of products and services from different countries. For example, the Marlboro Western cowboy image, Mc-

Donald's as a symbol of American consumption habits, the service efficiency in the United States, quality of perfume from France, pasta from Italy, and electronic products from Japan are some of the typical images and opinions held about different countries. Such country-of-origin (COO) perceptions, it is hypothesized, influence the way target audiences react to advertising messages and can also be used in market segmentation to customize messages and in marketing mix (Johansson, 1993; Parameswaran & Pisharodi, 1994).

Mueller (1996) cites a study that investigated the COO effect in consumers from 20 countries. The study found that consumers generally consider products from Japan, Germany, and the United States to be of the highest quality and Spain, China, and Taiwan to be of the lowest quality.

The studies examining the COO effect are not without problems because the images themselves are culturally laden and the selection of the countries is somewhat arbitrary and is based on convenience. No wonder several discrepancies of COO effects have been reported in the literature.

DISCUSSION AND CONCLUSIONS

The foregoing review may seem extensive and imply that we know a lot about transnational advertising. Indeed, the literature on the evolution of advertising and impact of its messages on some audiences at some times is well documented. Much more, however, remains to be investigated.

From the point of view of practitioners and advertising scholars, it is still unclear what kinds of appeals work under what conditions with what audience, though we know something. For example, as some have averred, it is empirically questionable to make cross-

cultural comparisons as is being done in many studies without being aware of the problems that such comparisons may pose. It is apparent from the literature that there is often a greater variance among population groups within nations than groups across nations. That is, it is reasonable to make problematic the units of population for comparisons. This becomes even more critical as new communication technologies will make it even easier to span national borders.

Another critical challenge for students of transnational advertising is the emergence of the Internet and the World Wide Web. The estimates of actual Web users remain purely speculative, though it is clear that the WWW and E-commerce on the WWW are undermining traditional business and regulatory models. Several points are worth mentioning in this context. Business, government, and the academy are engaged in discussions on how to subsidize and maintain the network, and advertising is already a reliable source of subsidy for some. Recent corporate mergers of global actors such as America Online (AOL) and Time Warner, whose base for sustenance will be advertising, point to the importance of integration of new and old media. Last, transnational advertising on the WWW poses significant challenges to the regulatory models currently in practice in all the countries. Yet it remains to be seen how transnational advertising influences and is influenced by the development of such new communication technologies—the Internet and satellite and cable television—and is a fruitful area for future research.

Students of postindustrial societies have focused on the increasing importance of the service sector, which is characterized by production of knowledge and information (Bell, 1973). Benjamin Barber (1996) argued that postmodern societies are rooted in information, entertainment, and lifestyles that blur the distinctions between soft and hard goods. One might also add that as we emerge into an era of consumer cultures, the distinction between advertising, promotion, and sponsorship becomes almost meaningless, and the line between entertainment, education, and publicity often questionable. What we are witnessing is an era that clearly builds on synergies between sports, celebrity, entertainment, and advertising, and the promotion of products, ideas, appeals, customs, and practices that at one time were restricted to national borders. The precise impact of this phenomenon on society, culture, and politics remains unclear. To imagine a world without advertising makes for an interesting parlor game but is a distraction from a more thorough, systematic examination of a phenomenon, a commercial art form that spans borders, cultures, and generations.

NOTES

1. The literature is replete with several terms used when discussing advertising spanning national boundaries: transnational advertising, global advertising, multinational advertising, and international advertising, among others. We will use the term *transnational advertising*, which incorporates both cross-national and cross-cultural advertising.

Jones (2000, pp. 22-23) offers cogent definitions of each of these terms. For example, he defines *global advertising* as advertising of global brands and *international advertising* as advertising from another country, or the international dimension of advertising agency business. He goes on to define *multinational advertising* as advertising of multinational brands (less commonly found than global brands) and *multidomestic advertising* as advertising of the same brand in a number of different countries but at different stages of brand development in each of these countries. He defines *transnational advertising* as "advertising in a more participatory, decentralized manner," with input from consumers and agency personnel (p. 22).

We feel that all these terms are too restrictive and descriptive and do not capture the overall role of advertising, including the promotion of goods and services through paid communications, but also the communication and promotion of ideologies. See our definition in the Defining Transnational Advertising section.

2. By identifying advertising as a part of the capitalist system and with the statement that advertising intends to influence ideological worldviews, we are not implying anything negative or positive about transnational advertising. We feel that advertising could be functional and/or dysfunctional depending on one's ideology, power position, and expectations.

3. For a more detailed explication on the emergence of the dominance of the United States and the role of social science, see So (1990).

4. In fact, Janus (1980a) characterizes the role of television as that of a "super salesman" (p. 290).

5. The issue of whether standardized campaigns are more efficacious than localized ones has been of tremendous interest to scholars and practitioners alike and will be discussed later in the chapter.

6. The data can be found at the Web site http://adage.com/dataplace/index.html.

7. For a more extensive review, particularly from a marketing point of view, see Onkvisit and Shaw (1987), Agrawal (1995), and Jain (1989).

8. In fact, the argument of dependency scholars in international communication has been precisely aimed at in this issue. That is, the globalization and economic linkages among the "triple alliance" work to the advantage of the transnational elite rather than the local populace.

9. It is little wonder, then, that some have used the term cross-cultural advertising instead of transnational advertising (e.g., Samiee & Jeong, 1994).

10. For a more elaborate treatment both in support of and in opposition to advertising, see the useful review by Leiss, Kline, and Jhally (1986), especially pages 13-42.

11. Lack of space constrains us from a detailed explication of these two approaches. For more extensive reviews and critiques of these and other

"theories of development," see Lee (1979) and So (1990).

12. The market leaders in program exports include the United States and, to an extent, Mexico, Brazil, the United Kingdom, and France.

13. Blumler (1992) argues that increasing commercialization makes certain values of a public broadcasting system vulnerable. The values that could be eroded include the quality and diversity of programs and their ability to satisfy different audiences, the extent to which the programming reflects different cultures as well as the culture of the nation-state, independence of the producers, and civic communication.

14. As defined earlier in the chapter, social control is what determines the boundaries of what is acceptable and unacceptable, what is to be valued or not to be valued, with an aim to influence a community member's behavior either directly or indirectly (Viswanath & Demers, 1999). Although there are several agencies that perform the control function, including education, religion, and family, mass media are the primary agents in contemporary times (Galbraith, 1958; Gerbner, 1998; Tichenor, Donohue, & Olien, 1980; Viswanath & Demers, 1999). It was not clearly referred to as such, but Schiller's terms such as the "mind managers" imply such a role for the media, especially advertising. Other writings that either explicitly or implicitly imply the control function for advertising include Janus (1980a), Leiss, Kline, and Jhally (1986), and Schudson (1984) among many others.

15. Two major propositions in mass communication, "the spiral of silence" hypothesis proposed by Noelle-Neumann (1973) and the "cultivation" hypothesis proposed by Gerbner, Gross, Morgan, and Signorielli (1982), both suggest that media effects are stronger precisely because of the ubiquity of the media and consonance in their messages.

REFERENCES

Agrawal, M. (1995). Review of a 40-year debate in transnational advertising. *International Marketing Review, 12*(1), 26-48.

Arens, W. F., & Bov'ee, C. L. (1994). *Contemporary advertising* (5th ed.). Burr Ridge, IL: Irwin.

Balasubramanian, K. (1999). *The impact of globalization of media on media images: A study of Indian media images between 1987 and 1997.* Unpublished master's thesis, The Ohio State University, Columbus.

Barber, B. R. (1996). *Jihad vs. McWorld: How globalism and tribalism are reshaping the world.* New York: Ballantine.

Belch, G. E. , & Belch, M. A. (1993). *Introduction to advertising and promotion: An integrated marketing communication perspective.* Homewood, IL: Irwin.

Belk, R., Bryce, W. J., & Pollay, R. W. (1985). Advertising themes and cultural values: A comparison of U.S. and Japanese advertising. In K. C. Mun & T. C. Chan (Eds.), *Proceedings of the inaugural meeting of the Southeast Asia region* (pp. 11-20). Hong Kong: Academy of International Business.

Bell, D. (1973). *The coming of post-industrial society: A venture in social forecasting.* New York: Basic Books.

Berger, J. (1972). *Ways of seeing.* London: Penguin.

Blumler, J. G. (1992). *Television and the public interest.* London: Sage.

Bryant, J., & Zilmann, D. (1994). *Media effects: Advances in theory and research.* Hillsdale, NJ: Lawrence Erlbaum.

Caffyn, J., & Rogers, N. (1970). British reactions to TV commercials. *Journal of Marketing Research, 10,* 21-27.

Cheng, H. (1997). "Holding up half of the sky?" A sociocultural comparison of gender-role portrayals in Chinese and U.S. advertising. *International Journal of Advertising, 16,* 295-319.

Chirapravati, M. L. V. (1996). The blossoming of advertising in Thailand. In K. T. Frith (Ed.), *Advertising in Asia: Communication, culture and consumption* (pp. 223-240). Ames: Iowa State University Press.

Clark, T. (1990, October). International marketing and national character: A review and proposal for an integrative theory. *Journal of Marketing, 54,* 66-79.

Curran, J. (1979). Capitalism and the control of press. In J. Curran, M. Gurevitch, & J. Woollacott (Eds.), *Mass communication and society* (pp. 195-230). Beverly Hills, CA: Sage.

Demers, D. P. (1996). *The menace of the corporate newspaper: Fact or fiction.* Ames: Iowa State University Press.

Demers, D. (1999). *Global media: Menace or messiah?* Cresskill, NJ: Hampton.

Elinder, E. (1965). How international can European advertising be? *Journal of Marketing, 29*(2), 7-11.

Endicott, C. (2000, April 24). 56th annual agency report: At agencies, a growth year for the ages. *Advertising Age,* p. S1.

Ewen, S. (1976). *Captains of consciousness.* New York: McGraw-Hill.

Fatt, A. C. (1967). The danger of "local" transnational advertising. *Journal of Marketing, 31*(1), 60-62.

Fejes, F. (1980). The growth of multinational advertising agencies in Latin America. *Journal of Communication, 30*(4), 36-49.

Frith, K. T., & Wesson, D. (1991). A comparison of cultural values in British and American print advertising: A study of magazines. *Journalism Quarterly, 68*(1-2), 216-230.

Galbraith, J. K. (1958). *The affluent society.* Boston: Houghton Mifflin.

Galbraith, J. K. (1967). *The new industrial states.* Boston: Houghton Mifflin.

Gerbner, G. (1998). Cultivation analysis: An overview. *Mass Communication and Society, 1,* 175-194.

Gerbner, G., Gross, L., Morgan, M., & Signorielli, N. (1982). Charting the mainstream: Television's contributions to political orientations. *Journal of Communication, 32*(2), 100-127.

Gershon, R. A. (1997). *The transnational media corporation: Global messages and free market competition.* Mahwah, NJ: Lawrence Erlbaum.

Gilly, M. C. (1988). Sex roles in advertising: A comparison of television advertisements in Australia, Mexico, and the United States. *Journal of Marketing, 52*(2), 75-85.

Goffman, E. (1979). *Gender advertisements.* New York: Harper Torchbooks.

Golding, P. (1979). Media professionalism in the Third World: The transfer of an ideology. In J. Curran, M. Gurevitch, & J. Woollacott (Eds.), *Mass communication and society* (pp. 291-308). Beverly Hills, CA: Sage.

Griffin, M., Viswanath, K., & Schwartz, D. (1994). Gender advertising in the U.S. and India: Exporting cultural stereotypes. *Media, Culture & Society, 16,* 487-507.

Harris, G., & Attour, S. (2000). The practice of multinational corporations and advertising standardization. In S. O. Monye (Ed.), *The handbook of international marketing communications.* Malden, MA: Blackwell.

Heinonen, J. (2000). *Societal diversity: A comparative analysis of American and Finnish women's magazines.* Unpublished honors thesis, The Ohio State University, Columbus.

Herman, E. S., & McChesney, R. (1997). *The global media: New missionaries of global capitalism.* London and Washington, DC: Cassell.

Hite, R., & Fraser, C. (1988). Transnational advertising strategies of multinational corporations. *Journal of Advertising Research, 28*(4), 9-17.

Hornik, J. (1980). Comparative evaluation of international vs. national advertising strategies. *Columbia Journal of World Business, 15*(1), 36-45.

Jain, S. C. (1989, January). Standardization of international marketing strategy: Some research hypotheses. *Journal of Marketing, 53,* 70-79.

Janus, N. (1980a). Advertising and the mass media in the era of the global corporation. In E. McAnany, J. Schnitman, & N. Janus (Eds.), *Communication and social structure: Critical studies in mass media research.* New York: Praeger.

Janus, N. (1980b). Advertising and the mass media: Transnational link between production and consumption. *Media, Culture & Society, 3,* 13-23.

Janus, N., & Roncagliolo, R. (1979). Advertising, mass media and dependency. *Development Dialogue, 1,* 81-97.

Johansson, J. K. (1993). Missing a strategic opportunity: Managers' denial of country-of-origin effects. In N. Papadopoulos & L. A. Heslop (Eds.), *Product-country images: Impact and role in international marketing* (pp. 77-86). New York: International Business Press.

Jones, J. P. (2000). *International advertising: Realities and myths.* Thousand Oaks, CA: Sage.

Kang, M. E. (1993). *Images of women in magazine advertisements: 1979 and 1991.* Unpublished master's thesis, The Ohio State University, Columbus.

Krishna, V., Chuang, R., & Axinn, C. (1997). Global versus local advertising in Taiwan. *Gazette, 59*(3), 224-233.

Lee, C. C. (1979). *Media imperialism reconsidered.* Beverly Hills, CA: Sage.

Leiss, W., Kline, S., & Jhally, S. (1986). *Social communication in advertising: Persons, products and images of well-being.* Toronto, Ontario: Methuen.

Levitt, T. (1983). The globalization of markets. *Harvard Business Review, 61*(3), 92-102.

Linnett, R. (2000, June 19). Avon's calling beyond in-house; marketer hears at least one pitch; expects to spend $100 mil on ads. *Advertising Age.*

Mattelart, A. (1979). *Multinational corporations and the control of culture.* Atlantic Highlands, NJ: Humanities Press.

McQuail, D., & Siune, K. (1986). *New media politics: Comparative perspectives in Western Europe.* London: Sage.

McQuail, D., & Siune, K. (Eds.). (1998). *Media policy.* London: Sage.

Millum, T. (1975). *Images of women: Advertising in women's magazines.* London: D. McKay.

Mueller, B. (1992). Standardization vs. specialization: An examination of Westernization in Japanese advertising. *Journal of Advertising Research, 32*(1), 15-24.

Mueller, B. (1996). *Transnational advertising: Communicating across cultures.* New York: Wadsworth.

Noelle-Neumann, E. (1973). Return to the concept of the powerful mass media. *Studies of Broadcasting, 9,* 67-112.

Nordenstreng, K., & Schiller, H. I. (1993). *Beyond national sovereignty: International communication in the 1990s.* Norwood, NJ: Ablex.

Ogilvy, C., Simmonds, B., Urbano, K., & Viswanath, K. (1997, June). *In the eye of the beholder? Advertising, body image and the definition of "beauty."* Paper presented at the 11th annual Visual Communication Conference, Jackson Hole, WY.

Onkvisit, S., & Shaw, J. J. (1987). Standardized international advertising: A review and critical evaluation of the theoretical and empirical evidence. *Columbia Journal of World Business, 22*(3), 43-55.

Onkvisit, S., & Shaw, J. J. (1999). Standardized transnational advertising: Some research issues and implications. *Journal of Advertising Research, 39*(6), 19-24.

Packard, V. (1957). *The hidden persuaders.* New York: D. McKay.

Parameswaran, R., & Pisharodi, R. M. (1994). Facets of country of origin image: An empirical assessment. *Journal of Advertising, 23*(1), 43-56.

Pernia, E. (1996). Advertising in the Philippines: Communication, culture and consumption. In K. T. Frith (Ed.), *Advertising in Asia: Communication, culture and consumption* (pp. 189-222). Ames: Iowa State University Press.

Pollay, R. W. (1986, April). The distorted mirror: Reflections on the unintended consequences of advertising. *Journal of Marketing, 50,* 18-36.

Ray, M. L. (1973). Marketing communication and the hierarchy of effects. In P. Clarke (Ed.), *New models for mass communication research* (pp. 137-162). Beverly Hills, CA: Sage.

Ricks, D. A., Arpan, J. S., & Fu, M. Y. (1974). Pitfalls in advertising overseas. *Journal of Advertising Research, 14*(6), 47-51.

Samiee, S., & Jeong, I. (1994). Cross-cultural research in advertising: An assessment of methodologies. *Journal of the Academy of Marketing Science, 22*(3), 205-217.

Schiller, H. I. (1976). *Communication and cultural domination.* White Plains, NY: International Arts and Sciences Press.

Schiller, H. I. (1979). Transnational media and national development. In K. Nordenstreng & H. I. Schiller (Eds.), *National sovereignty and international communication* (pp. 21-32). Norwood, NJ: Ablex.

Schiller, H. I. (1989). *Culture, Inc.: The corporate takeover of American expression.* New York: Oxford University Press.

Schudson, M. (1984). *Advertising: The uneasy persuasion.* New York: Basic Books.

Simmonds, B., Urbano, K., Ogilvy, C., & Viswanath, K. (1997, July-August). *Black and white: Differences in body images in advertisements for African-American and white women.* Paper presented at the annual conference of the

Association for Education in Journalism and Mass Communication, Chicago.

Siune, K., & Hulten, O. (1998). Does public broadcasting have a future? In D. McQuail & K. Siune (Eds.), *Media policy* (pp. 23-37). London: Sage.

Siune, K., & Truetzschler, W. (Eds.). (1992). *Dynamics of media politics: Broadcasts and electronic media in Western Europe.* London: Sage.

So, A. Y. (1990). *Social change and development: Modernization, dependency, and world-system theories.* Newbury Park, CA: Sage.

Straubhaar, J. D. (1991). Beyond media imperialism: Asymmetrical interdependence and cultural proximity. *Critical Studies in Mass Communication, 8,* 39-59.

Taylor, C. R., Miracle, G. E., & Chang, K. Y. (1994). The difficulty of standardizing transnational advertising: Some propositions and evidence from Japanese, Korean, and U.S. television advertising. In B. G. Englis (Ed.), *Global and multinational advertising* (pp. 171-191). Hillsdale, NJ: Lawrence Erlbaum.

Tichenor, P. J., Donohue, G. A., & Olien, C. N. (1980). *Community conflict and the press.* Beverly Hills, CA: Sage.

Tsirulnikov, M. Y. (1996). *Influence of the broadcasting subsidy on a variety of the broadcasting programming in Russia.* Master's thesis, The Ohio State University, Columbus.

Vardar, N. (1992). *Global advertising: Rhyme or reason?* London: Paul Chapman.

Viswanath, K., & Balasubramanian, K. (2000, April). *Advertising, body images and implications for public health: A comparative analysis of American and Indian women's magazines.* Paper presented at the annual Kentucky Conference on Health Communication, University of Kentucky, Lexington.

Viswanath, K., & Demers, D. (1999). Mass media from a macrosocial perspective. In D. Demers & K. Viswanath (Eds.), *Mass media, social control and social change: A macrosocial perspective* (pp. 3-28). Ames: Iowa State University Press.

Wells, W., Burnett, J., & Moriarty, S. (1992). *Advertising: Principles and practice* (2nd ed.). Englewood Cliffs, NJ: Prentice Hall.

Williamson, J. (1978). *Decoding advertisements: Ideology and meaning in advertising.* London: Marion Boyars.

6

Differing Traditions of Research on International Media Influence

BELLA MODY
ANSELM LEE
Michigan State University

Legend has it that a kindly fourth-century priest called Nicholas who lived in what is present-day Turkey was the original Santa Claus. One of Nicholas's claims to global fame was donating wedding dowries to brides whose families could not afford them. Varied hybrids of Santa Claus have evolved in localities all over the world over the past 17 centuries. We know that even before the invention of the printing press that democratized literacy, empires and states had been in contact with each other through a range of means of transport and communication: the horse and camel that carried the invading army, the ship and canon that facilitated intercontinental trade and colonizations, the telegraph that enabled recent expansion.

In the 1950s, political scientist Daniel Lerner (1958) maintained that the mass media could be used as powerful international multi-pliers of knowledge and attitudes for the modernization of former colonies. Benedict Anderson (1983) identified unintended ways in which print media might have facilitated the spread of nationalism. Anthropologist Arjun Appadurai (1996) argued that daily programs of fantasy and reality in electronic media allow audiences to imagine and remake themselves, facilitating a distinct rupture toward a world beyond nation-states. Herbert Schiller (1989) continued to underline the expansion rather than rupture of the profit-making world business system that old and new technologies support.

The practice of communication by individuals and institutions is instrumental and goal directed. This chapter introduces five research traditions organized around the following foci: psychological warfare and propaganda, modernization and diffusion of innovations, political economy of culture, quantifiable effects of media on audiences, and audience reception within particular cultural contexts. Each section presents the contextual conditions that gave rise to the research, exemplary research questions, research methods, findings, and implications for conceptualizations of media power.

PSYCHOLOGICAL WARFARE AND PROPAGANDA

Lerner and Nelson (1977) see the story of communication research beginning with the study of propaganda, in particular with the 1927 publication of Harold Dwight Lasswell's *Propaganda Technique in the World War*. This book about World War I is the source of what became the foundational research question in the field of communication: Who says what to whom with what effect. Psychological warfare and propaganda by both sides in World War I were the basis for Lasswell's case study of the enemy's political communication strategies. Simpson (1994) cites studies that showed how World War I propaganda projects often exaggerated both the enemy and Allied images to stir up soldiers and the public. The Allied victory was attributed in part by national governments to exposure to the persuasive power of propaganda. Content analyses and case studies were the dominant research methods. Surveys of propaganda impacts on audiences were not in use in World War I (1914-1918), and access to audiences for propaganda research was even more limited than it is today.

Shils and Janowitz's (1948) World War II study of Allied propaganda impact on the German Army's effectiveness in combat found German troops indifferent to Allied leaflets and radio broadcasts. Effects were limited by interpersonal discussion with friends after message transmission, consistent with what

Lazarsfeld and his students were discovering in their voting and consumption studies since the 1940s. Thus, psychologists (e.g., Hovland, Janis) in the United States focused on *how* to use these media that had limited effects so they had the most persuasive power.

Many of the founders in the field of communication and institutes of communication in the United States were a product of World War II government funding for propaganda (see Simpson, 1994, and McDowell, Chapter 16 in this volume). Some Cold War studies conducted for the U.S. government were subsequently published, frequently with a change in the names of concepts. Individuals funded by U.S. government propaganda initiatives included Wilbur Schramm, Paul Lazarsfeld, Hadley Cantril, Irving Janus, Ithiel de Sola Pool, Morris Janowitz, Daniel Lerner, Alex Inkeles, Herbert Marcuse, and Nathan Maccoby. Many of them worked at research institutes that were generously funded by U.S. government propaganda research, for example, Lazarsfeld's Bureau of Applied Social Research at Columbia University, Cantril's International Institute for Social Research at Princeton University (better known for its study of the invasion from Mars/*War of the Worlds* CBS radio drama rather than for its intelligence gathering in France, Italy, the Soviet Union, Brazil, the Dominican Republic, Egypt, India, Nigeria, the Philippines, and Poland), and the Center for International Studies at Massachusetts Institute of Technology (MIT) associated with Lerner and Pool. Given that U.S. military, intelligence, and propaganda agencies provided the large majority of research funding for the field during the 1945-1955 decade when U.S. communication study was developing into a distinct field, it is also not surprising that the research focuses on ambitious change-oriented goals rather than the predominant reinforcement effect that Lazarsfeld's Bureau of Applied Social Research found in its U.S. studies.

"Propaganda" was transformed into the more sophisticated art of "public diplomacy" at Tufts University in 1965 (Manheim, 1994). Lectures and essays around the theme of public diplomacy were funded by the Bernays Foundation and included some familiar names from the psychological warfare era, namely, Daniel Lerner and Lloyd Free. Lloyd Free was a former Roosevelt administration secret agent and a collaborator with Hadley Cantril at Princeton University. In this new era, the target audience became the domestic public (see Jacobson & Jang, Chapter 19 in this volume); image management strategies included hosting global media events such as the Olympics and U.N. summit meetings. Taylor (1997) shows how government use of strategic public communication in international affairs has evolved since 1945. Beyond nation-states, the client who commissions campaigns is frequently the private firm, foreign and domestic, seeking to influence U.S. (and other) governments through the for-profit message design and news analysis skills of advertising agencies. The issue was not whether media were powerful or not, but how to use these instruments "strategically," for whatever they could do.

Although there was no evidence to prove that international media-based propaganda had direct or strong effects on beliefs, attitudes, and behavior in the two world wars or more recently, annual World Radio-TV handbooks show many governments and nongovernmental religious organizations continue to expand their transmissions and Web site development. This may be due to popular beliefs that open access to the media led to disenchantment with U.S. performance in Vietnam and that Western broadcasts expedited the collapse of communism in Eastern Europe and the Soviet Union. Continued funding of external propaganda in the United States may be also due to influential political lobbies, for example, Cuban Americans who want to embarrass Castro through Radio Marti and TV Marti (Alexandre, 1992; Nichols, 1996). The politics of representation, image, identity, and discourse is undoubtedly central (see Manheim, 1994; Wilkins, Chapter 29 in this volume).

Audience research on international public diplomacy in the past decade has been done in house and subcontracted out to private firms, sometimes to interview exiles from and travelers to countries where access is limited. Scholarship continues to consist of case studies of government and private sector information programs (e.g., Grunig, 1993), how the military and executive branch manipulate the domestic public through strategic use of the media to support their foreign policy positions, and how news shapes public opinion and policymakers (e.g., Bennett & Paletz, 1995; Herman, 1993; Malek, 1997; Sobel, 1993). The U.S. CIA has expressed concern about the unusual nature of conflicts in the 21st century; departments of the military (e.g., the Marine Corps Warfighting Lab) have invited media research aimed at addressing nontraditional problems (e.g., terrorism over unequal resources, population growth, and ethnic animosities) (*Commerce Business Daily,* 2000).

Former psychological warriors of World War II vintage also used U.S. government funds to win the hearts and minds of developing countries for the United States (and against the Soviet Union) through media appeals to Western-style modernization. The subsequent transnational expansion of Anglo-American media firms and their continuing lead in news and entertainment exports lessened the need for government propaganda initiatives. Gerald M. Mayer (1947) of MGM pictures is supposed to have said there has never been a more effective salesman for American products in foreign countries than the American motion picture. Thus, the political economy tradition (presented later) considered the transnational media system as a commercial propaganda tool that transmitted Anglo-American ideas and cultural values; the topic of research therefore became the sources or owners of media systems.

MODERNIZATION AND DIFFUSION

This section describes two decades of international communication research activity that began in the late 1950s in the United States. Researchers recommended that media power should now be harnessed to serve other practical areas of U.S. foreign policy, namely, attracting developing countries to the Western bloc and away from the Soviet Union in the Cold War. Thus, MIT political scientists moved from the rhetoric of political propaganda to the rhetoric of modernization to save developing countries from communism. By diffusing Western scientific ideas, sociologist Everett M. Rogers showed that media could be part of MIT professor Walter Rostow's (1960) "non-Communist Manifesto" at crucial stages of economic growth. Western innovations selected for diffusion (e.g., chemical fertilizers) in developing countries jumped national borders through scientists and subject specialists in foreign aid agencies such as the U.S. Agency for International Development (USAID), intergovernmental organizations such as the Food and Agriculture Organization of the United Nations, private foundations such as Rockefeller, and developing country government bureaucrats.

The foreign policy agenda of the United States, the national loyalty of its psychological warfare researchers, their previous contacts with the military and propaganda agencies, and professorial jobs in U.S. universities that reward external grant money now led academic entrepreneurs to media and modernization research in support of U.S. global ambi-

tions (see Simpson, 1994, and chapters in this volume by McDowell, Melkote, and Waisbord). *The Passing of Traditional Society: Modernizing the Middle East* by Daniel Lerner (1958) was to the communication and development field what Lasswell's *Propaganda* was to psychological warfare. Samarajiwa's (1987) historical and contextual research was the first to disclose that Lerner's book was based on Voice of America (VOA) radio audience research conducted in the Middle East by the Bureau of Applied Social Research at Columbia University where he worked before joining MIT. The original data collection was conducted at the request of the Office of International Broadcasting (of the U.S. Department of State), evaluating the performance of the VOA radio services in seven countries. The interviews used a standard questionnaire developed and pretested in Greece. The questionnaire had 120 questions on media use, media comparison, feelings about foreign countries (especially the United States, Britain, and the Soviet Union to evaluate the effectiveness of the VOA, the BBC, and Radio Moscow), psychological characteristics of respondents, and personal data. Data categorizing the psychological characteristics of individual respondents into *moderns, transitionals,* and *traditionals* were central to the model of modernization that Lerner developed for his book. The transitionals were recommended targets for U.S. modernization projects, combinations of propaganda, economic development aid, and counterinsurgency. Because social mobility was the distinguishing characteristic of industrially advanced societies, Lerner focused on the role of media to inject empathy into personalities to increase their psychic mobility. The post hoc society-level model specified the proportion of urbanization in a nation that would lead to economic and political participation with the help of literacy and mass media exposure. The causal links were strictly correlational. The data were individual level and were collected at one point in time, whereas we now know the obstacles to societal change are frequently structural (economic, political, cultural), historical (colonial and precolonial), and external to a nation. Lerner's model gave media the power to change traditional personalities into socially mobile empathetic ones, a strong relationship that was not consistent with the "limited effects" paradigm of media effects established by domestic U.S. projects on voting and consumption researched at the Bureau of Applied Social Research at Columbia University.

Written at the request of the United Nations Educational, Scientific and Cultural Organization (UNESCO), which was dominated by U.S. journalists who saw the free flow of information as guardian against authoritarian governments, Wilbur Schramm's *Mass Media and National Development* (1964) expanded into new application areas when he wrote, "No one who has seen modern communication brought to traditional villages could ever doubt its potency" (p. 20). He summarized case studies of media use in Asia, Africa, the Middle East, and Latin America to show the conditions under which media could be used to promote national development. He then illustrated the role of media in four essential sectors: agriculture, health, literacy, and formal education. This very readable book (that incidentally quoted several psychological warfare studies under their sanitized names such as *Communication in Africa* by Leonard Doob), was written with broad nontechnical strokes for policymakers. National leaders were told populations of 1,000 people should have 20 TVs, 50 radios, and 10 newspapers.

In 1962, Rogers's *Diffusion of Innovations* exported U.S. studies on how innovations spread through media and opinion leaders to developing countries. This book (now in its fourth revised and expanded 1995 edition) is the most cited in the field of communication.

(See the Melkote chapter in this volume for details). The book catalogs more than 5,000 studies as testimony to the wide applicability of the diffusion process across disciplines. The first edition of the book led to many UNESCO-financed and USAID-financed diffusion studies in developing countries. Scholarships were granted by international funding agencies for developing country students to study toward doctoral degrees in communication with Rogers, at Michigan State University initially and then at his subsequent places of work. Fifteen years and many attempts at diffusion later, when few modernization and development indicators had been reached, Rogers, Schramm, and Lerner indicted the development paradigm. Rogers published his postmortem and the analyses of former students (e.g., Beltran, Bordenave, Ascroft) and others (including this author) in a special volume of the journal *Communication Research*; the demand was so great that it was also published as a stand-alone Sage Publications monograph (Rogers, 1976). New media systems had been established in many countries, he reported, but little development followed by any standard.

Lerner, Schramm, and Rogers were not specialists in Third World development: They did not trace the root causes of underdevelopment/maldevelopment to precolonial interrupted growth, economic and technological stagnation under colonial rule, or to class, religious, ethnic, and gender hierarchies. The diffusion model found that early adopters were younger men with education and income; this was reinforcing business as usual rather than supporting change through a more equitable flow of information: To those who had youth, education, and capital, the media-energized diffusion process gave more know-how. Western innovations selected for diffusion did not address the reason why up to one third of the people in Asia, Africa, the Caribbean, and Latin America did not have basic levels of food, clothing, and shelter. The top-down diffusion of inappropriate solutions from the West to the capital owners and rulers of developing countries and from them to their working classes did not recognize the need for diffusion of information on grassroots problems and grassroots solutions from the bottom up and horizontally. The third edition of *Diffusion* did present an exchange-convergence definition of communication rather than a one-way transmission definition, but the case still needs to be made on how media with limited power are able to address deep-rooted causes of differences in beliefs and behavior such as the unequal distribution of land or the inferior status of women. If the diffusion process is supposed to take off where media channels leave off and interpersonal channels are mobilized, perhaps the community level is where more research and development communication implementation is needed. (See the discussion on participation in the Huesca and Melkote chapters.)

An assessment by Schramm and Lerner (1976) of what communication applications had achieved in terms of national development applications from the mid-1960s to mid-1970s involved researchers from all over the world. The agreement seemed to be that the top-down development model was wrong and that a new bottom-up participatory development paradigm was needed. Funded by the World Association for Christian Communication, Hartman, Patil, and Dighe (1989) found that where there was evidence of mass communication as a factor in change, it is normally subsidiary to word-of-mouth communication. Those few who are directly exposed to the media did influence others but within their caste, class, age, and sex-stratified reference groups. Over a decade later, little had changed for the majority of the world's population, who live in developing countries. Normative research to develop a different communication model has been conducted by another generation of researchers (Jacobson & Servaes, 1999; see the chapters by Huesca and Melkote in this volume) but with levels of funding much lower than in the anticommunism era.

This section has sought to show how linking media as instruments of modernization to the foreign policy agenda of the United States made the media appear more powerful than the limited effects research of the 1940s justified. Although the fine print in much of the modernization literature was qualified, the broad brush strokes addressed to policymakers led to big expectations of media as basic information diffusion infrastructure. Little wonder, then, that researchers trained in the politics and economics of power chose to investigate the institutional and structural aspects of these media that were entrusted with stopping the spread of communism.

POLITICAL ECONOMY OF CULTURE

Political economy focuses on the centrality of economics to politics (i.e., power), culture, and society rather than only limiting economics to supply and demand equilibrium. Thus, a political economy approach is more multidimensional than mainstream economics. This political economy tradition of global media research followed on the heels of grand claims of media potency to modernize individuals in the developing world in the U.S. image (as against the Soviet image). It was initiated by social scientists trained to work at the macro level who felt it was important to focus on *which forces* decide what is said and how it is said through these much-touted tools (channels and programs). They thus took a few steps back from prevailing research on what is said (content analysis) with what effects (audience research). Not funded by any government or corporation, this research questions

and to whom?

ownership, industry structure, and flows that were ceteris paribus conditions in the effects tradition. They have been criticized for not studying the power structure within developing societies consisting of domestic capital and the state and how it was complicit in the nation's domination.

Latin neighbors of the United States (e.g., Pasquali of Venezuela) were the first to identify the dependency of their television and press content on the media and culture of the United States as part of their region's general economic dependency. Herbert Schiller (1969) argued that this cultural dependency was not accidental: U.S. media and media products were used around the world to support the American empire that came into existence after World War II. Using secondary data collected by government, industry, and private organizations, Wells (1972) illustrated the extent to which Latin American broadcasting systems had been influenced by the U.S. government and corporations. Prompted by developing countries that were not aligned with the Soviet or U.S. bloc, UNESCO funded Nordenstreng and Varis (1974) and later Varis (1984) to document changes in international television traffic over time; these studies provided part of the basis for UNESCO's move from a free flow of information (from a few sources) position to a campaign for a fair and balanced international New World Information and Communication Order (see Boyd-Barrett, Chapter 18 in this volume). The MacBride report (International Commission for the Study of Communication Problems, 1980) documented unbalanced flows of information in many media. Defining the skewed flow as part of long-standing cultural imperialism, Schiller (1976, p. 9) urged study of society and class levels of analysis in his recommendation that we study the "sum of the processes by which a society is brought into the modern world system and how its dominating stratum is attracted, pressured, forced

into shaping social institutions to correspond to, or even to promote, the values and structures of the dominant center of the system." Philip Elliott and Peter Golding (1974) studied the Western dominance of international news flows, especially the flow of news between Britain and African countries; they concluded that the international media system was one mechanism by which developing countries were brought within the purview of Western capitalism. Dorfman and Mattelart's classic *How to Read Donald Duck* (1975) revealed how the transmission of ideology took place through the transmission of cultural products. Given the unidirectional flow of media products, and the dominance of source countries such as the United States, the United Kingdom, France, West Germany, and Russia, Oliver Boyd-Barrett (1977) urged that the unit of analysis should be the international system rather than the national when studying media "imperialism" (referring to the unequal balance of power resources between states). Media imperialism may be said to exist when "the ownership, structure, distribution or content of the media in any one country singly or together is subject to substantial external pressures from the media interests of any other country or countries without proportionate reciprocation of influence by the country so affected" (Boyd-Barrett, 1977, p. 117). Boyd-Barrett goes on to theorize how different aspects of media in other countries were formed as a result of U.S. media influence: the shape of their channels (e.g., daily transmissions, one-way), the industrial and financial model (e.g., vertical integration, the star system), organizational practices (e.g., objectivity, production values), and most visibly, the market penetration of media content. Mattelart (1979) analyzed the emergence of private transnational corporations in electronics, aerospace, book publishing, education, the printed press, film, TV, and advertising that now played a political role in international communication. The 1980 MacBride report documented imbalances in several areas of communication. The International Telecommunication Union's Maitland Commission report (1984) found imbalances in telephony availability around the world that matched imbalances in news and entertainment media.

Sussman and Lent (1991) edited developing country national and regional case studies (the Philippines, the Caribbean, sub-Saharan Africa, Mexico, Malaysia, Brazil, India, and Singapore) to show the political economy of communication that cut across nation-states. The Reagan-Thatcher alliance recommended that developing countries open up their state-owned telecommunications operators to investment and competition from private capital, foreign and domestic, and introduce competition (Mody, Bauer, & Straubhaar, 1995). Major mergers and buyouts made the transnational media corporation a salient feature of the economic landscape in the 1980s and 1990s (Gershon, 1997). Herman and McChesney (1997) profiled the strategies of the largest media transnational corporations in the historical context of the global market system, and how telegraphy, film, and shortwave radio lead up to television. They showed how convergence between distribution systems, the spread of deregulatory policies, and the corporate consolidation of global advertising within a few agencies had given U.S. firms who lead the cultural industries even greater power. Inagaki's (2000) analysis of foreign direct investment by telecommunications companies reveals not only the transfer of domestic assets to foreign private corporations but also intensified economic ties between foreign telecom firms that jointly invest, similar to the news and entertainment providers who do not go it alone. Instead of promoting competition, deregulation is leading to transnational consolidation of owner-

ship and control among the 14 largest telecommunications transnational corporations.

Mainstream economists argued that U.S. dominance of the global media market was the natural logic of this business rather than the result of any intent to be imperial or destructive of other civilizations. Explanations for U.S. dominance included the role of the U.S. government in promoting its exports (e.g., films, TV shows, potash) through collusionary legal cartels and trade promotion, the large U.S. domestic market (in terms of gross national product and numbers of TV sets), larger production budgets, production in English for the largest market in the world, and vertical integration of the Hollywood majors who control production and distribution and can hence set export prices lower than U.S. exhibition or production costs. The development and export successes of national media industries in some countries (e.g., Brazil, Mexico) led Straubhaar (1991) to propose a national classificatory continuum called asymmetrical interdependence to reflect the range between complete national dependence to dominant interdependence. Sinclair (1996) provides compelling evidence from Brazil and Mexico of Tunstall's (1977) perception that regional centers would develop, although the United States continues as the single largest exporter. Mowlana (1997) introduced a four-factor model of international information flows consisting of hardware, software, production, and distribution. Control of the distribution process was the most important index of the way in which power is distributed in a communication system. Dependency on the outside system occurred when there was a lack of control in one or more elements. Mowlana and Wilson (1990, pp. 91-93) used this model to explain the right to communicate, message costs, structural changes, product differentiation, media domination, cultural pluralism, and the role of the state. Building on a lifetime of writing and policy advocacy on the impossibility of cultural autonomy in an increasingly corporate global village, Hamelink (1994) identified four interrelated trends of digitization, consolidation, deregulation, and globalization against a background of the history of world communication.

The agent of global economic expansion has historically been private capital. Since the origins of capitalism in the city-states of Western Europe and their exploration of trade routes in search of gold, spices, cotton, and silk, capitalism has been a globally mobile system. Present-day cultural globalization or "complex interconnections between societies, cultures and individuals worldwide" (Tomlinson, 1991, p. 170) did not emerge out of the clear blue sky one fine day in the mid-1980s; it was the effect of the Thatcher-Reagan International Monetary Fund-World Bank initiatives on deregulation and its export that enabled Western capital to mobilize again in search of more profitable overseas investment opportunities. The pattern of the economic expansion of capital at the turn of the 20th century was skewed toward profits and was globally unequal just as it was in the colonial era: Not all countries were/are equal recipients of foreign direct investment and trade. Implicit and complicit in this recent wave of foreign capital expansion are the enabling telecommunication and cultural industries of advertising, entertainment, and news, for-profit businesses themselves. Dan Schiller (1999) calls the Internet-enabled expansion and intensification (into education and entertainment sectors) of economic activity *digital capitalism*. Cultural industries from North America and Western Europe have expanded into potentially profit-making markets (upper-income and then mass) on other continents; cultural industries in other parts of the world (e.g., Latin America, Hong Kong) have expanded into culturally proximate geolinguistic markets (Sinclair, 1996;

Straubhaar, 1991); the United States is expected to continue to lead well into the future. Meers and Bittereyst (1999) have shown that the contradictory flow of Latin American *telenovelas* into parts of Europe were limited in time and scope. The Brazilian superstar Xuxa has not been able to cross cultural linguistic markets. Nevertheless, having penetrated boundaries and national protectionist walls for economic reasons, the Thatcher-Reagan wave of deregulation and economic globalization have enabled the flow of some cultural products between some national and subnational groups between and within countries that did not happen before. Cultural globalization is not universal; it shares some patterns with the flows of other economic products while it has some other unique elements. The entering cultural product or service is localized and domesticated to expand beyond elite markets to mass audiences over time; the global-local nexus produces a hybrid that retains its extranational strengths but acquires local appeal, for example, various translations of television program formats described in Moran (1998); MTV's use of multilingual DJs, and Western musicians' borrowings from Africa, the Caribbean, and Asia. Some (e.g., Robertson, 1992) have called the present phase of the historically continuous process of interaction and hybrid development that followed economic globalization *glocalization,* after the Japanese recommendation that their businesses adapt to local conditions to be more successful in penetrating new markets. The global product might be available for certain "upper class" markets, and the *glocal* product might be for mass markets. Thussu (2000) highlights Zee TV, India's first private satellite TV Hindi-language channel, as a prime example of cultural hybridity. The images are flexibly Indian and Western; the struggle is between the past and modern values that are generally individualistic, consumption oriented, and consonant with the capitalist form of economic organization. Whether this greater rural penetration of modern capitalism through televised advertising (and entertainment to attract viewers to it) leads to the kind of disjuncture and difference in the cultural mediascapes (Appadurai, 1990) of small-town India worth celebrating remains to be seen. Barber (1995) sees global capitalism (McWorld) leading to resistance from fundamentalist parts of religious groups (Jihad), both laying siege to the democratic nation-state.

The political economy research area found strong evidence at the societal, media organization, and program levels of dominant flows of cultural products. The consequences for audiences of these cultural flows is the topic of research presented in the next section: When cultural channels and products flow from one part of the world to localities in the rest of the world in response to commercial as against state initiatives as in the world wars, do they have more power on audiences than Shils and Janowitz found in 1948? Do profit-making media programs and channels homogenize the rest of the world in the image of their parent societies, do they promote individualism and consumption basic to private profit-maximization irrespective of local ethnic origins, or are effects ambivalent and contingent because the channels and programs themselves are nationally footloose local-global alliances and individual readers/viewers bring different frames of reference (age, class, gender, ethnicity, religion, language, occupation) to the medium?

EFFECTS ON THE AUDIENCE OF DOMINANT MEDIA SOURCES

This section presents the work of communication researchers who were trained to quantify audience effects caused by a message stimulus. Their scholarly inheritance included findings of selective audience influences; the importance of audience interest and social categories (gender, socioeconomic status, religion, rural-urban residence) in qualifying media power, uses, and gratifications; the role of interpersonal influence; the principal media effect of reinforcement and hence predictions of "limited effects" since Lazarsfeld, Berelson, and Gaudet (1948) and Katz and Lazarsfeld (1955); and the disappointing results of the modernization applications of the 1960s-1970s. Boyd-Barrett (1998) repeated that the main effect of generic media imperialism was the exclusion of other voices as sources of news and entertainment and not particular predictable effects on audience attitudes and beliefs. Sinclair (1990) claimed that the major influence of Western imports was on media institutions in the rest of the world that adopted the U.S. advertising-supported model of programming for the largest audience. But Schiller (1969), Beltran (1976), and Mattelart (1979) did express concern about effects on audiences of media dominated by some sources. In their minds, the media must have seemed to have power if Lerner had been funded to study how media could change personalities in developing countries and diffusion researchers had been funded to use media to spread innovations based on Western science and technology.

There is no overarching conceptualization of international media influence on individuals that problematizes the border crossing. To generalize or develop probabilities, an input-output model or a typology of categories and contingent conditions is needed classifying sources (state/market), messages (public interest or corporate, global or glocal, news or entertainment), media (radio vs. TV vs. multimedia), levels of effects (on the state, on media institutions, on program plans, on genres, on audience reinforcement of traditional community, on community processes such as conversation, on consumption and individualism or both), and audience categorization (class, gender, age, urban-rural) to guide international effects research. Research on media effects on individuals across national boundaries has also ignored previous research on media effects on individuals within a nation, for example, 1940s research within the United States. This lack of conceptualization of the border and the neglect of literature on individual effects within the United States has often led to one-shot empirical data collection investigations in different countries since the 1970s, for example, in Argentina, Australia, Belize, Canada, China, Hong Kong, Korea, Iceland, the Philippines, Singapore, and Turkey. Space limitations do not allow us to reference each study. Pingree and Hawkins (1980), Weiman (1984), Oliveira (1986), and Chaffee (1992) did report findings consistent with a media imperialism hypothesis; others did not. These studies have not amounted to much as predicted by Fejes (1981), who advocated prior development of a theoretical framework that prioritized questions and issues. In addition, we have very few field experiments in international communication that compare randomly selected experimental and control groups because we cannot control media availability and audience exposure very well. One exception is a natural experiment: Shortly after the Canadian government introduced television to the Algonkian Indians, Granzberg (1982) reported that television disrupted their traditional ways of living. There was more fighting among children and increased consumption of packaged foods, and children of native Canadians who were heavy viewers were more likely to consider white Canadians as role models. A review of literature in the first edition of the *Handbook of International and Intercultural Communication* by Yaple and Korzenny (1989) found that media effects on individuals across national and cultural groups were small, detectable, and varied according to audience selectivity, context, and culture. Elasmar and Hunter's (1996) quantitative meta-analysis of previous studies found that the effect of foreign TV varied across studies and effects investigated and was probably weak. This is consistent with what we have been able to quantitatively measure *within the United States* since Katz and Lazarsfeld identified selective effects in their 1940s studies: The effects of television on individuals are not uniform; they depend on interaction between the characteristics and goals of the viewer, the content of what is watched, and the medium. The viewer's level of understanding, knowledge, motivation, personality, attitudes, and purposes for viewing affect how content is used and understood (Huston et al., 1992). Salwen's (1991) review of media effects literature with reference to cultural imperialism urged that micro-level audience data be integrated with macro-level political and economic theories, but no framework was offered. Duane Varan (1998) advocates a cultural erosion metaphor that promises to bring together the media effects tradition, political economy, and cultural studies to address the lack of cumulative knowledge. The first author and doctoral students (Kingsley, Rampoldi-Hnilo, & Mody, 1999) attempted to culturally complicate and embed television reception by also surveying the influence of particulars such as urban-rural location, language, and gender on adolescent television preferences and impacts in India rather than focus on national universals and generalizations. We found higher preferences for foreign TV shows in the big city rather than in the small town in a study of high school students in one south Indian state. Cultural proximity dictated program preferences in the small town but not in the big city consistent with Straubhaar (1997). Similarly, urban size was a significant predictor of preference for foreign brands advertised on television.

A break from the theoretically derived hypothesis testing for particular processes (e.g., consumer socialization) or effects (e.g., desensitizing attitudes to violence, sex) is seen in the open-ended focus groups on the cross-cultural reception of the television program *Dallas* conducted by Katz and Liebes (1985) (of limited media effects, active audience findings fame) and Liebes and Katz (1990). Their qualitative method solicited emic views on interpretations of particular programs. This interpretive turn taught them that differences in the reception of *Dallas* between subcultures and nations were so complex that the socio-psychological effects question had become almost impossible to study.

The next section presents studies that have investigated foreign media and program influences in the cultural studies tradition. The theoretical question is how viewers interpret media and programs within particular time-and-place cultural contexts. Knowledge gained from these studies is consistent with the social constructionist paradigm: Findings are contextual, partial, and subject to improvement rather than tending toward universal and general laws.

AUDIENCE RECEPTION STUDIES

Since Morley's (1980) study of how British TV viewers belonging to different classes interpreted the program *Nationwide*, new ways of studying how audiences make sense of media have been evolving in cultural studies distinct from both the effects tradition and the sole emphasis on semiotic textual analysis that had dominated cultural studies. The impetus for cultural studies to move beyond analysis of the program or text to audiences came from Hall (1980), who framed the distinction between the message and what the audience gets out of it in terms of the encoder's "preferred" meaning and the meaning

that viewers negotiate for themselves at the time of decoding. Ang (1985) wrote about the popularity of *Dallas* in the Netherlands, partly based on 42 responses to a magazine ad she placed. She concluded that women watched because they enjoyed watching the show and that the production of pleasure and meaning was in the process of viewing, the program-viewer communication interaction. The neglect of the context of viewer lives and the power of transnational media scheduling, promotion, and related industry issues has been criticized by political economists (e.g., Schiller, 1989). Since then, the focus has moved to knowledge of the everyday cultural, political, and historical life of viewers within which context the medium is one input. How the media are received varies, depending on the local situation. The goal is not to develop parsimonious theories that explain commonalities in the communication process across countries but to inductively build cultural knowledge from the ground up on the micro-politics of how audiences make meaning out of media consumption in their everyday routines.

Although the initial focus was on audience interpretation (decoding, dialogue, negotiation, and contestation of the text or media program) in terms of ethnicity and gender, researchers in this tradition have recognized the need but have been slower to address class differences. The largest number of reception and textual analyses have been conducted in Brazil on the telenovelas. The proliferation of media and media programs across national boundaries (e.g., satellite TV, *Dallas*) and the migration of subcultural groups to foreign locales have led to several national studies (e.g., Norway, Trinidad, Egypt, India, Germany, Australia) on reasons for the global popularity. Lull (1988) has edited a compendium of ethnographic analyses of how world families watch television. Ang (1989) is at pains to explain that what makes the cultural studies perspective unique is its <u>understanding of how audience viewing and meaning making are constrained and qualified by the structures of power in the life of viewers that is not of their own making</u>. It may appear that the understanding of an active audience and the reality of viewing as a social activity are common to the media effects tradition and to cultural studies. Cultural studies' use of focus groups and ethnographic observation notwithstanding, Ang maintains that <u>the mainstream media effects tradition</u> (e.g., Liebes & Katz, 1990) <u>does not present the act of viewing as a cultural struggle between different meanings</u>. Whether and how economic, political, and cultural struggles at the point of reception are investigated in the increasing number of cultural studies that try to investigate reasons for the near-global popularity of some genres and some TV shows (e.g., *Dallas, Dynasty,* Latin American telenovelas) will be of great interest to international communication researchers. Distinct perspectives from developing country researchers (e.g., Adra, 1996; Garcia Canclini, 1995; Manuel, 1993; Martín Barbero, 1993; Monteiro & Jayasankar, 2000; Sampedro, 1998) and on students/ diasporic immigrants from developing countries (Cunningham & Jacka, 1994; Gillespie, 1995; Sinclair, Pookong, Fox, & Yue, 2000) are increasing.

SUMMING UP

This chapter has divided research on media influence in international communication into five chronological and frequently overlapping traditions. During the first and second world wars, the nature of media influence on the audience was conceptualized as simple, direct, powerful, and linear. Research focused on content and audience effects. Consistent with U.S. domestic research in mass communication, this stimulus-response

perspective on media effects should have been replaced by a limited effects research tradition in the international arena that saw the media's role as reinforcing preexisting conceptions. But the U.S. foreign policy agenda needed tools to keep developing countries out of the Soviet bloc. Cold War academics among U.S. communication researchers had stepped into the breach before, and they were willing and able to contribute media ammunition to the national political agenda once again. From the end of the 1950s, researchers were funded by the U.S. federal government and U.S.-influenced U.N. agencies to do research in developing countries on how to prevent the spread of communism through the promotion of Western innovations and modernization. Given that propaganda, diffusion, and modernization had been funded to promote the U.S. anticommunist international agenda by harnessing the power of the media, a third group of researchers who were profoundly critical of power, its sources, and uses began to take notice at the end of the 1960s: Political economists <u>researched the source</u> <u>and message in media programs to investigate</u> <u>what was being advocated, by whom, and in</u> whose political and economic interest. <u>They</u> <u>feared that media and Hollywood commer-</u> <u>cial movies were synchronizing foreign cul-</u> <u>tures for market expansion.</u> They analyzed issues such as media ownership, industry structure, program flows, and content. The last section focuses on studies of audience reception that grew from within the British cultural studies tradition in the 1980s. The focus has been on media as one input affecting identity formation within a complex of cultural forces. The field has advanced from simple linear didactic models to complex ways of analyzing media influence at many levels.

The individual traditions of research on international media influence have showed inadequate and polemical reviews of the Other's literatures to score points and put down colleagues. There was no larger conceptual vision of what the influence of media internationally might be, in terms of the whole. Partial conceptualizations of the process and differences in estimates of media effect underscore the socially constructed (i.e., subjective, partial, needing improvement) nature of the research. Research funding sources differed. The basic paradigms of research (mainstream positivist/postpositivist as against critical) varied in terms of the goal of the inquiry and its application area, the nature of knowledge sought, and the values and ethics of the researchers. Although the effects researchers wanted to verify hypotheses to establish generalizations or probabilities in the positivist tradition, the aim of inquiry for political economists was praxis, the transformation of all inequitable structures (e.g., national, class, capital, ethnicity, gender) that constrain humans across the world.

We close with two recommended areas of research and one area for praxis. First, we need to think historically about the diverse origins and motivations of the motley opposition to cultural imperialism among researchers. What influence did this have? Bedfellows ranged from early proponents of cultural imperialism who fine-tuned their positions to focus on dominance of the capitalist system of production through congenial regional production centers and hybrid genres, to developing country nationals offended at the thought that their cultures were conceived as easy pushovers, to U.S. loyalists who did not perceive their modern-day liege as a cultural bully or want it to be perceived as such, to true believers in the market system. A second area for research is interpersonal communication at the point of international (or domestic for that matter) media reception. Rather than beginning with international media content (in this case) and seeing how people make sense of it when it touches ground, it is time to begin from the bottom up, with needs and issues that concern the everyday lives of different groups. We need to observe how and where individuals and groups seek what kinds of information to actively grapple with their own challenges, from Ang's (1996) "living room" to Morley's "sitting room" to public wells in villages. Rather than focus on the top-down diffusion of innovative solutions of interest to a private business or a state, let us begin disinterestedly to focus on the role of individuals and groups and the part played by communication media, if any, in distinct situations of power in different parts of the world. A new version of *Personal Influence: The Part Played by People in the Flow of Mass Communication* (Katz & Lazarsfeld, 1955) is long overdue, specific to a range of power contexts. One question relevant to this chapter might be how the different "locals" around the world interact with manifestations of the "global" in a range of sectors from politics to technology to culture.

The third and final suggestion is in the area of academic praxis and organization. The characteristics of this enterprise over the past 75 years since Lasswell (1927) seem to be similar to bigoted, blindfolded zealots groping for the proverbial elephant, finding only a part of it (e.g., the tail), and belligerently refusing to acknowledge the existence of the rest of its body (e.g., media firms, states as senders, messages as ideological, viewers as citizens) and those who study these different parts of the whole because they do not use the same research methods. Some might maintain that if an effect cannot be measured in a particular way, it does not exist. Holier-than-thou sniping against the distinct terminology and research methods of effects researchers, cultural studies researchers, and political economy researchers of media institutions continues in many university departments that have not succeeded in expelling the Other(s).

Attempts to understand the whole "media ele-phant" in all its "morphing" convergences (e.g., the Internet) and consolidations (e.g., AOL-Time Warner) require the efforts of dif-ferent specializations interested in the study of media in society. University departments that continue to be sites of 21st-century crusades to hound out infidels who do not quantify (or qualify) need to revise their constructions of scholarship and research. Every academic cen-ter needs to constantly re-vision more sensi-tive constructions of each medium and each message and become educated about alterna-tive ways of doing research on other parts of the media elephant. Rather than trying to blindly imitate political science, psychology, sociology, or economics, the study of inter-national communication (and communication in general) needs to take the best from all sources and imagine a new agenda for current political-technological-cultural space-time.

REFERENCES

Adra, N. (1996). The "Other" as viewer: Reception of Western and Arab televised representations in rural Yemen. In P. I. Crawford & S. B. Hafsteinsson (Eds.), *The construction of the viewer*. Højbjerg, Denmark: Intervention Press.

Alexandre, L. (1992). Television Marti: Electronic invasion in the post-Cold War. *Media, Culture & Society, 14*, 523-540.

Anderson, B. (1983). *Imagined communities: Re-flections on the origin and spread of nationalism*. London: Verso.

Ang, I. (1985). *Watching* Dallas. London: Methuen.

Ang, I. (1989). Wanted: Audiences, on the politics of empirical audience studies. In E. Seiter, H. Borchers, G. Kreutzner, & E.-M. Warth (Eds.), *Remote control: Television, audiences, and cultural power*. London and New York: Routledge.

Ang, I. (1996). *Living room wars*. New York: Routledge.

Appadurai, A. (1990). Disjuncture and difference in the global cultural economy. *Public Culture, 2*(2).

Appadurai, A. (1996). *Modernity at large: Cultural dimensions of globalization*. St. Paul: University of Minnesota Press.

Barber, B. R. (1995). *Jihad vs. McWorld*. New York: Times Books.

Beltran, L. R. (1976). Alien promises, objects and methods in Latin American communication re-search. In E. M. Rogers (Ed.), *Communication and development: Critical perspectives* (pp. 15-42). Beverly Hills, CA: Sage.

Bennett, W. L., & Paletz, D. (Eds.). (1995). *Taken by storm: The media, public opinion and U.S. foreign policy in the Gulf War*. Chicago: Univer-sity of Chicago Press.

Boyd-Barrett, O. (1977). Media imperialism: To-wards an international framework for the analy-sis of media systems. In J. Curran, M. Gurevitch, & J. Woollacott (Eds.), *Mass communication and society* (pp. 174-195). London: Edward Arnold.

Boyd-Barrett, O. (1998). Media imperialism re-formulated. In D. K. Thussu (Ed.), *Electronic empires: Global media and local resistance* (pp. 157-176). London: Edward Arnold.

Chaffee, S. (1992). Search for change: Survey stud-ies of international media effects. In F. Korzenny & S. TingToomey (Eds.), *Mass media effects across cultures*. Newbury Park, CA: Sage.

Commerce Business Daily. (2000, February 18). Emerging threats and opportunities. SOL M67854-00-R-2070.

Cunningham, S., & Jacka, E. (1994). Neighborly relations? Cross-cultural reception analysis and Australian soaps in Britain. *Cultural Studies, 8*(3), 509-526.

Dorfman, A., & Mattelart, A. (1975). *How to read Donald Duck: Imperialist ideology in the Disney comics*. New York: International General.

Elasmar, M. G., & Hunter, J. E. (1996). The impact of foreign TV on a domestic audience: A meta-analysis. In B. R. Burleson (Ed.), *Communica-tion yearbook 20* (pp. 47-69). Thousand Oaks, CA: Sage.

Elliott, P., & Golding, P. (1974). Mass communi-cation and social change: The imagery of development and the development of imagery. In E. De Kadt & G. Williams (Eds.), *Sociology and development* (pp. 229-254). London: Tavistock.

Fejes, F. (1981). Media imperialism: An assessment. *Media, Culture & Society, 3*, 281-289.

Garcia Canclini, N. (1995). *Hybrid cultures*. Minneapolis: University of Minnesota Press.

Gershon, R. A. (1997). *The transnational media corporation: Global messages and free market competition*. Mahwah, NJ: Lawrence Erlbaum.

Gillespie, M. (1995). *Television, ethnicity and cultural change*. London: Routledge.

Granzberg, G. (1982). Television as storyteller: The Algonkian Indians of central Canada. *Journal of Communication, 32*(1), 43-52.

Grunig, J. E. (1993, Summer). Public relations and international affairs: Effects, ethics. *Journal of International Affairs*.

Hall, S. (1980). Encoding/decoding. In S. Hall, D. Hobson, A. Lowe, & P. Willis (Eds.), *Culture, media, language: Working papers in cultural studies, 1972-1979*. London: Hutchison.

Hamelink, C. J. (1994). *Trends in world communication: On disempowerment and self-empowerment*. Penang, Malaysia: Southbound.

Hartman, P., Patil, B. R., & Dighe, A. (1989). *The mass media and village life*. New Delhi: Sage.

Herman, E. S. (1993, Summer). The media's role in U.S. foreign policy. *Journal of International Affairs*.

Herman, E. S., & McChesney, R. W. (1997). *The global media*. London: Cassell.

Huston, A. C., Donnerstein, E., Fairchild, H., Feshback, N. D., Katz, P. A., Murray, J. P., Rubenstein, E. I., Wilcox, B. L., & Zuckerman, D. (1992). *Big world, small screen*. Lincoln: University of Nebraska Press.

Inagaki, N. (2000, June). *Joint foreign direct investment: The economic linkage among transnational telecommunication companies*. Paper presented at the annual meeting of the International Communication Association, Acapulco, Mexico.

International Commission for the Study of Communication Problems. (1980). *Many voices, one world: Toward a new, more just and more efficient world information and communication order*. Paris: UNESCO.

Jacobson, T., & Servaes, J. (Eds.). (1999). *Theoretical approaches to participatory communication*. Cresskill, NJ: Hampton.

Katz, E., & Lazarsfeld, P. (1955). *Personal influence: The part played by people in the flow of mass communication*. Glencoe, IL: Free Press.

Katz, E., & Liebes, T. (1985). Mutual aid in decoding *Dallas*: Preliminary notes from a cross-cultural study. In P. Drummond & R. Paterson (Eds.), *Television in transition* (pp. 187-198). London: British Film Institute.

Kingsley, C., Rampoldi-Hnilo, L., & Mody, B. (1999, May). *The influence of location, language and gender on adolescent television viewing preferences and impacts in India*. Paper presented at the annual meeting of the International Communication Association, San Francisco.

Lasswell, H. D. (1927). *Propaganda technique in the world war*. New York: Knopf.

Lazarsfeld, P., Berelson, B., & Gaudet, H. (1948). *The people's choice*. New York: Columbia University Press.

Lerner, D. (1958). *The passing of traditional society: Modernizing the Middle East*. Glencoe, IL: Free Press.

Lerner, D., & Nelson, L. (1977). *Communication research—A half century appraisal*. Honolulu: University Press of Hawaii.

Liebes, T., & Katz, E. (1990). *The export of meaning: Cross-cultural readings of Dallas*. New York: Oxford University Press.

Lull, J. (1988). *World families watch television*. Newbury Park, CA: Sage.

Maitland, D. (1984). *The missing link*. Geneva: International Telecommunication Union.

Malek, A. (1997). *News media and foreign relations: A multi-faceted perspective*. Norwood, NJ: Ablex.

Manheim, J. B. (1994). *Strategic public diplomacy and American foreign policy: The evolution of influence*. New York: Oxford University Press.

Manuel, P. (1993). *Cassette culture: Popular music and technology in north India*. Chicago: University of Chicago Press.

Martín Barbero, J. (1993). *Communication, culture and hegemony: From the media to mediations*. London: Sage.

Mattelart, A. (1979). *Multinational corporations and the control of culture: The ideological apparatuses of imperialism*. Sussex, UK: Harvester.

Mayer, G. M. (1947). American motion pictures in world trade. *The Annals of the American Academy of Political and Social Science, 254*, 31-36.

Meers, P., & Biltereyst, D. (1999, May). *The international telenovela debate and the contra flow argument: A reappraisal and a case study*. Paper presented at the annual meeting of the International Communication Association, San Francisco.

Mody, B., Bauer, J. M., & Straubhaar, J. D. (Eds.). (1995). *Telecommunications politics: Ownership and control of the information highway in developing countries*. Mahwah, NJ: Lawrence Erlbaum.

Monteiro, A., & Jayasankar, K. P. (2000). Between the normal and the imaginary: The spectator-self, the other and satellite television in India. In I. Hagen & J. Wasko (Eds.), *Consuming audiences? Production and reception in media research* (pp. 301-321). Cresskill, NJ: Hampton.

Moran, A. (1998). *Copycat television*. Luton, UK: University of Luton Press.

Morley, D. (1980). *The "nationwide" audience: Structure and decoding*. London: British Film Institute.

Mowlana, H. (1997). *Global information and world communication: New frontiers in international relations* (2nd ed.). London: Sage.

Mowlana, H., & Wilson, L. J. (1990). *The passing of modernity: Communication and the transformation of society*. New York: Longman.

Nichols, J. S. (1996). Effects of international propaganda on U.S.-Cuban relations. In R. R. Cole (Ed.), *Communication in Latin America* (pp. 77-103). Wilmington, DE: SR Books.

Nordenstreng, K., & Varis, T. (1974). *Television traffic—A one way street? A survey and analysis of the international flow of television programme material*. Paris: UNESCO.

Oliveira, O. S. (1986). Satellite television and dependency: An empirical approach. *Gazette, 36*, 127-145.

Pingree, S., & Hawkins, R. (1980). U.S. programs on Australian television: The cultivation effect. *Journal of Communication, 31*(1), 97-105.

Robertson, R. (1992). *Glocalization*. London: Sage.

Rogers, E. M. (Ed.). (1976). *Communication and development: Critical perspectives*. Beverly Hills, CA: Sage.

Rogers, E. M. (1995). *Diffusion of innovations* (Rev. 4th ed.). New York: Free Press.

Rostow, W. W. (1960). *The stages of economic growth: A non-Communist Manifesto*. Cambridge, UK: Cambridge University Press.

Salwen, M. (1991). Cultural imperialism: A media effects approach. *Critical Studies in Mass Communication, 8*(1), 29-38.

Samarajiwa, R. (1987). The murky beginnings of the communication and development field: Voice of America and "The passing of traditional society." In N. Jayaweera & S. Amunugama (Eds.), *Rethinking development communication*. Singapore: Asian Mass Communication Research and Information Centre.

Sampedro, V. (1998). Grounding the displaced: Local media reception in a transnational context. *Journal of Communication, 48*(2), 125-143.

Schiller, D. (1999). *Digital capitalism*. Cambridge: MIT Press.

Schiller, H. I. (1969). *Mass communications and American empire*. New York: A. M. Kelley.

Schiller, H. I. (1976). *Communication and cultural domination*. White Plains, NY: International Arts and Sciences Press.

Schiller, H. I. (1989). *Culture, Inc.: The corporate takeover of public expression*. New York: Oxford University Press.

Schramm, W. L. (1964). *Mass media and national development: The role of information in the developing countries*. Stanford, CA: Stanford University Press.

Schramm, W., & Lerner, D. (Eds.). (1976). *Communication and change, the last ten years—And the next*. Honolulu: University Press of Hawaii.

Shils, E. A., & Janowitz, M. (1948). Cohesion and disintegration in the Wehrmacht in World War II. *Public Opinion Quarterly, 12*.

Simpson, C. (1994). *Science of coercion: Communication research and psychological warfare 1945-1960*. New York: Oxford University Press.

Sinclair, J. (1990). Spanish language TV in the U.S. *Studies in Latin American Popular Culture, 9,* 39-63.

Sinclair, J. (1996). Mexico, Brazil and the Latin world. In E. Jacka, J. Sinclair, & S. Cunningham (Eds.), *New patterns in global television.* Oxford, UK: Oxford University Press.

Sinclair, J., Pookong, K., Fox, J., & Yue, A. (2000). Diasporic identities. In I. Hagen & J. Wasko (Eds.), *Consuming audiences? Production and reception in media research.* Cresskill, NJ: Hampton.

Sobel, R. (Ed.). (1993). *Public opinion in U.S. foreign policy: The controversy over contra aid.* Lanham, MD: Rowman & Littlefield.

Straubhaar, J. (1991). Beyond media imperialism: Asymmetrical interdependence and cultural proximity. *Critical Studies in Mass Communication, 8,* 39-59.

Straubhaar, J. (1997). Distinguishing the global, regional and national levels of world television. In A. Sreberny-Mohammadi, D. Winseck, J. McKenna, & O. Boyd-Barrett (Eds.), *Media in global context: A reader.* London: Edward Arnold.

Sussman, G., & Lent, J. A. (Eds.). (1991). *Transnational communications: Wiring the Third World.* Newbury Park, CA: Sage.

Taylor, P. (1997). *Global communications, international affairs, and the media since 1945.* London: Routledge.

Thussu, D. K. (2000). *International communication: Continuity and change.* London: Edward Arnold.

Tomlinson, J. (1991). *Cultural imperialism.* Baltimore: Johns Hopkins University Press.

Tunstall, J. (1977). *The media are American: Anglo-American media in the world.* London: Constable.

Varan, D. (1998). The cultural erosion metaphor and the transnational impact of media systems. *Journal of Communication, 48*(2), 58-86.

Varis, T. (1984). The international flow of television programs. *Journal of Communication, 34*(1), 143-152.

Weiman, G. (1984). Images of life in America: The impact of American TV in Israel. *International Journal of Intercultural Relations, 8,* 185-197.

Yaple, R., & Korzenny, F. (1989). Electronic mass media effects across cultures. In M. K. Asante & W. B. Gudykunst (Eds.), *Handbook of international and intercultural communication* (pp. 295-317). Newbury Park, CA: Sage.

Wells, A. (1972). *Picture-tube imperialism? The impact of U.S. television in Latin America.* Maryknoll, NY: Orbis.

7

From the Modern to the Postmodern

The Future of Global Communications Theory and Research in a Pandemonic Age

SANDRA BRAMAN
University of Alabama

International communication theory and research historically have done well with those subjects that characterize modernity, such as the nation-state and "the fact." Today, however, it is the postmodern condition within which communication takes place—a condition also known as the information society, for many of the critical features of postmodernity are the effects of the use of new information technologies. Under either designation, international communication theory and research must respond to circumstances qualitatively and quantitatively different from those of the past. The current environment may be described as "pandemonic," following Hookway (1999), because it is ubiquitously filled with information that makes things happen in ways that are often invisible, incomprehensible, and/or beyond human control— "demonic" in the classic sense of nonhuman agency, and "pan" because this agency is everywhere. This chapter reviews international communication theory and research as they have dealt with key features of modernity—the nation-state, the fact, the universal, and power. Each of these elements must now be reconsidered.

THE NATION-STATE

The geopolitical form of modernity was the combination of bureaucratic and cultural elements that came to be known as the nation-state (Greenfeld, 1992; Held, 1989). International communication historically has been oriented almost exclusively around nation-states, looking at differences between what happens within them (comparative studies) and at flows of communications between them (international communication).

International communication, like the field of communication itself, has largely been a product of the U.S. higher education system in the 20th century. From World War II on, however, the vast expansion of the reach and impact of that system exposed the ideas it produced to profound questioning and criticism from other societies around the world (Wallerstein, 1996). Important work by largely Western European sociologists enriches and in some cases underlies international communication theory, but it is one of the important markers of the turn of the 21st century that theory has itself become internationalized. Increasingly, major works in the field are being written by scholars outside the United States, such as recent works on public opinion by Shamir and Shamir (2000) from Israel and by Splichal (1999) from Slovenia. Although in the past work that drew together theories from the United States and Europe with those from elsewhere often cast one perspective within the context of a second, as when Mowlana and Wilson (1990) examined development communication within the context of Islamic philosophy and practice, in the future the most important work will be based on genuine theoretical syntheses of ideas from around the world of the type modeled by Lull (2000) and Mattelart (1994).

Theories from outside international communication should also be useful. Melucci (1996), for example, provides an alternative approach to understanding political communication across cultures with his emphasis on identity issues as the crux of contemporary social movements. Theories of turbulence and chaos in international relations (Rosenau, 1990) should provide some relief for those seeking to find generalizations in what may well be ephemeral, and perhaps random, conditions. Network economists (Antonelli, 1992) argue for the use of new units of analysis, such as long-term projects carried out by multiply interdependent entities, as most valid and useful in today's environment. Ethnic and family ties have been identified as structural forces in their own right as manifested in international trade and other types of international information flows (Iyer & Shapiro, 1999). Non-state actors, such as regions (Blanco & van den Bulck, 1995), transnational corporations (Dezalay & Garth, 1996), and nongovernmental organizations (NGOs) (Waterman, 1990), replace or complement the nation-state as site, subject, and agent in global communication studies. Increasingly, statelike communities are defined virtually rather than geographically (Arquila & Ronfeldt, 1996; Gopnik, 1996).

Such "cascading" interdependence (Rosenau, 1984) demands that those studying global communication move beyond dependency theory. Constructivism (Adler, 1997) provides one means of doing so, focusing on the impact of today's global information infrastructure on all aspects of international relations (Singh & Rosenau, 2001). Other work that starts from the position that borders between nation-states today are often not bright lines but rather zones that may be populated by millions of people with well-developed and unique cultures of their own is beginning to appear (Lull, 1997). Within such zones, individual identity is no longer a question of citizenship but rather of ethnicity and/or hybridity (Mouffe, 1992).

The nation-state as the unit of analysis also provided a logic and justification for comparative studies. Media systems have been compared along several dimensions, including ownership patterns, organizational structures, regulatory systems, content trends, and reception. The example of comparisons of normative press-state relations—the ways in which a media system and a government interact with mutual effect—demonstrates the limits of such comparative work. The Cold War–era typology known as the "four theories of the press" (Siebert, Peterson, & Schramm, 1956) distinguishes among types of media systems according to where they lie on a spectrum from complete government control (totalitarian or communist) to democratic, with the notion of a press that operates in terms of "social responsibility" lying in between. This model reeks of its geopolitical origins (Simpson, 1994); for decades now—even in North America, and even before the dissolution of the Soviet Union—although the theory has been taught, in many cases this was done with the caveat that the theory doesn't actually apply to the contemporary situation. A wide-ranging critique of this approach appeared in *Last Rights* (Nerone, 1995). The task today, however, is to come up with an alternative typology of media systems that is comprehensive and complex enough to be able to cope with the great variety of media systems currently in existence and emerging. Chan (1997) offers one such alternative typology based on his analyses of media systems in Asian countries.

A further concomitant of the focus on the nation-state is that each is a place between which communications flow. International communication theory historically has done a good job of looking at the nature and impact of communications flows on large populations, examining both mass media content as it affects society and political communications as it affects nation-states. Conceptualization of these flows has become more complex and has come to encompass not only flows of content but also those of infrastructure, audiences, genres, and knowledge structures (Appadurai, 1990; Braman, Shah, & Fair, 2000).

Those studying international communication have focused exclusively on flows between humans. In the future, however, there will be an increasing need to take into account communications between humans and computers—distinguishing between communication with databases, programs, intelligent agents, and avatars—as well as those communications between computers that never involve humans at all. Not only do these other types of flows comprise an ever-larger proportion of global information flows (Tele-Geography, 2000), but they are also increasingly significant as structural forces for human society (Lessig, 1999). Indeed, the argument has been made that the nation-state itself might be best understood as an information processor (Richards, 1993).

THE FACT

The narrative forms of modernity were defined by their relationship to the fact, what is known as "facticity." Fiction, for example, defines itself as *not* being fact, whereas journalists, on the other hand, claim the news they present *is*. Issues raised by facticity are important to the study of global communication today in a number of ways.

The unbundling of different types of information resources, the ways in which value is added to them, and the means by which property rights can be asserted over them have been among the most notable features of the information economy that had appeared by the close of the 20th century. This was just the point of the debate over the New World Information and Communication Order (NWICO), which concerned the right and ability of developing nations to control flows of information about themselves, whether via journalism or satellite surveillance. The question of ownership and control over facts is also at the heart of data privacy issues, first addressed by the Organization for Economic Cooperation and Development (OECD) in the 1970s. Already at that point Europe and the United States were diverging in the degrees to which they protected the privacy of individuals about whom data had been gathered for commercial, administrative, and other purposes with significant impacts on international trade. And as the two types of informational meta-technologies—biotechnology and digital information technology—themselves converge, political and legal struggles over each have implications that apply to the other. Work has begun on the ways in which this will shape the context and content of global communication (Braman, 2001).

There are three ways in which debates over how a fact is determined in the first place appeared as issues with which international communication theorists had to deal. First, debates over the relative accuracy of the procedures used by "objective" and "new" journalism parallel those over the procedures of social science: "Objective" *New York Times*-style journalists attempt to mimic the natural sciences in the collection and presentation of narrowly defined, or "thin," facts derived exclusively from official institutional sources presented in data form without contextualization, and what became known as "new" journalists in the 1960s seek to provide richer, or "thick," facts derived from a wider variety of types of sources presented in narrative form contextualized as fully as possible. Journalists working from the two different perspectives on the same story can produce radically different versions of reality, with deep significance for the quality and effects of reportage on political and cultural affairs in the international environment (Braman, 1985). Second, claims of the kind of dependency asserted by those calling for a New World Information and Communication Order (NWICO) have been challenged on factual grounds also having to do with the nature of the procedures by which facts are produced (Cioffi-Revilla & Merritt, 1982). And third, it appears that fact and fiction are translated and received in different ways (Biltereyst, 1992;

Cohen & Roeh, 1992). Whereas the first two issues mentioned here deal with differences in how facticity is produced, the sets of questions pursued by this last group of researchers concern the reception of facticity.

Although modernity was characterized by optimism regarding the possibility of coming to know the "facts" of social life, another characteristic of postmodernity is that this confidence is waning or lost. One factor contributing to this loss of confidence is yet another consequence of the state-centrism of social theory: Beck (1992) has powerfully argued that societies are failing to track much environmental damage and the causal chains leading to it because it is beyond the geographic and time horizons of the state's statistical perceptual mechanisms. Although international agreements that push toward ever greater "transparency" (Florini, 2000) across geopolitical boundaries yield the perception that there is greater knowledge, international communication theory and research in the future will also need to acknowledge and deal with situations in which it is difficult to determine the facts at all.

THE UNIVERSAL

The epistemological ground of modernity was found in the universal, the notion that there are eternal laws discoverable by science. As applied to the social sciences, this universalism led to an assumption that the social structures being studied were stable or, if changing, developed only in linear, predictable, and inevitable ways. Today, however, social conditions are undergoing rapid and seemingly constant change. Thus, theory and research must deal with the ways in which social structures come about and are transformed. Downing (1996) has drawn our attention to the difference between the two approaches as played out in international communication; he found that the assumption of stability in communications systems in the theories he had used for decades in research around the world severely limited the utility of those ideas for understanding the societies of the former Soviet Union in the 1990s. The emergence of the postmodern condition has implications for the study of international communication because it draws attention to the role of communications in the transformation of societies, affects how the relationships between communications and society are understood from a systems perspective, and raises into visibility "the local" in the context of "the global."

The oldest strand of work in international communication that dealt with social change is in the area of development communication, or planned social change. Beginning in the 1950s, early approaches assumed a singular and one-way progression from an agricultural to an industrial society, from the premodern to the modern, and from the nondemocratic to the democratic. Most of this work also assumed that development would be exogenously driven—that is, that a society farther along the development path would facilitate change in those societies "running behind." More recent work, however, has suggested there may be a multiplicity of ways in which societies may choose or find themselves adapting to changing global conditions in ways satisfying and appropriate to their own cultures and values (Servaes, 1986). Increasingly, it is acknowledged that this may be done most successfully when development is endogenously driven—that is, when members of a society determine their own directions for change in what is called "participatory development" (White, Nair, & Ascroft, 1994). And a far more complex picture is being given of the ways in which interactions among societies at different stages of development and following different types of development paths influence each other, including what is being learned by the most "developed" societies from those historically perceived as underdeveloped (Braman, 2001). The past couple of decades have also seen increasing attention to the study of the role of communications in societies undergoing unplanned change driven by geopolitical shifts, such as in the former Soviet Union, eastern and central Europe (Jakubowicz, 1990) and Hong Kong (Chan & Lee, 1991).

Although these different ways of understanding the role of communications in planned and unplanned social change have rarely been cast in terms of systems theory, they are ripe for doing so. Systems theory, or cybernetics, was one of the intellectual products of World War II, and in its first decades of development—coincident with the first decades of development communication work—focused on stable systems structures for which change was problematic and examined single systems in isolation. Only two thinkers took a systems approach to development during this period (Mewes, 1971; Myrdal, 1956), and neither had much impact on thinking or practice in international communication. More recently, systems theory, now referred to as second-order cybernetics or complex adaptive systems theory, has come to take a more complex view of systems as healthy when undergoing often necessary transformations, and as always operating within a larger universe of multiply interacting systems at the same, infra-, and supralevels. Krippendorff (1987) has begun the work of applying second-order cybernetics to the study of the role of communications in societies undergoing planned and unplanned change, but a great deal of both theory and research needs to be done in this area.

Views of globalization that focus on singular causality, homogenization of effect, and the need to focus on the general rather than the particular (Featherstone, 1990) are another way in which modern interest in the universal has been expressed in international communication. Today, however, many argue that both causality (Abbate, 1999) and the effects of globalization are multiple, diverse, and differ from place to place (Enzensberger, 1992). The most important direction in which this thinking has led has been in the study of the local and particular in contrast to the universal and the global (Borgmann, 1999; Entrikin, 1991). Indeed, a new sense of the local *as* the global emerged in the 1960s (Ang, 1998). The global and the local are understood to compete with each other in the orientation of production (Thorbecke, 1992), appeals for markets (Cunningham & Jacka, 1996), content provision (Boyd-Barrett, 1998), and definition of class (Parameswaran, 1997; Wallerstein, 1990). Taxation (Goolsbee, 2000) and control over intellectual property rights (Sell, 1995) are among the techniques by which nation-states seek to pursue their individual objectives within an increasingly globalized environment. Struggles over memory and archival systems are particularly important arenas in which success of the global and general can cause destruction of the local and particular (Greaves, 1994). Meyrowitz (1994) uses the term saturation to describe such a situation, but Hannerz (1997) argues in response that in today's environment there is gradually unfolding maturation of multiply layered understandings as global culture is mediated via the different frames of the market, the nation-state, everyday life, and social movements. Meanwhile, the global is made local through consumption (Maxwell, 1996), infrastructure (Star & Ruhleder, 1996), and the design of specific artifacts (Tice, 1995).

Both spatial and symbolic approaches have been used to locate the site of the local. Among spatial approaches, a number of scholars look to the body (Featherstone, Hepworth, & Turner, 1991), whereas others argue that the body itself is now so infected with the machine —whether mechanical or computational— that it is best referred to as "cyborg," itself a challenge to the nation-state because it is deterritorialized (Beller, 1996). The home is now studied as a site in which the global and the local meet (Silverstone & Hirsch, 1992), in part because media use in the home is a means of leaving. Cities have gained in importance in the study of global communication, culture, and information: The notion of a "world city" appeared as early as the beginning of the 1980s (Abu-Lughod, 1992), and approaches to study of the city now include those that look at urban centers as command and control sites for the intermeshing of global financial, production, and distribution systems (Sassen, 1991); as economic engines because they are dense in information resources (Lash & Urry, 1993); as serving global functions because of their cultural creativity (Amin, 1997); as edges, or links between nodes, rather than nodes themselves (Garreau, 1992); and as symbolic sites altogether (Jasen-Verbeke, 1998).

The most influential approach to symbolic constructions of the local was launched by Anderson's (1983) analysis of the nation-state as an "imagined community." The local is seen as the site of specific knowledge or information, and therefore of power (Geertz, 1983). Place as a site of information and as discourse appears in usages such as the notion of a "European information area" that has replaced "European audiovisual space" in European policy discourse (Schlesinger, 1997). Individual identity is also seen as a site in which globalization forces are expressed today. As Elkins (1997) notes, in today's environment each individual is in effect a community of the communities in which each voluntarily chooses to participate. Hybridity—*uma cultura mulata* in Brazil (Canevacci, 1992)—is a new type of identity formation characterized by a greater degree of openness and acceptance of internal splits. Bhabha (1993) argues that hybrid identities are a form of political resistance, a notion supported by Sakamoto (1996) when he describes its first appearance in Japan during the Meiji Restoration of the mid-19th century at a time when that government deliberately took up study of the West as a means of protecting Japanese culture. Nardi and O'Day (2000) suggest that the intersection between global and local knowledge be viewed as the information ecology unique to each person. The growth of indigenous voices and media in global communication has further strengthened appreciation of the local as symbolically defined (e.g., Ginsburg, 1994).

"Authenticity" tells you whether or not you're "there" (Ning, 1999), whether you go to it, as in tourism (Chang & Holt, 1991), or bring it to you in the home or the museum (Errington, 1994). Multiple typologies of authenticity distinguish among sources of the perception of authenticity—whether it is authenticity of the self, experience, other persons, or objects—as well as among degrees of simulation versus verisimilitude (Wang, 1999). As Clifford (1997) notes, every appropriation of culture, including the sense of authenticity, reveals a specific historical narration that can vary from those of accumulation and preservation to those of redistribution and decay.

Although movement in and of itself was a characteristic of modernity important to understanding communication (Bachmair, 1991), the local has now become detached from physical space as a result of the movement of populations who carry with them a symbolic space but leave behind the geographic and of the ubiquitous diffusion of the information infrastructure. Over the past 30 years, migration has emerged as a major social force as the numbers of people in movement have vastly grown and their composition has shifted (Castles, 1998). Even directionality

has changed: In Europe, countries that for centuries had been sending out migrants are now receiving them, and even Japan is opening itself to migrants from poorer countries in Asia and South America to satisfy its labor needs. As a result, most of the world's developed countries are now diverse, multiethnic societies (Massey, et al., 1993). Traditional types of migrant press continue to thrive, sometimes serving migrant populations with new demographics such as those of the Hong Kong "yacht immigrants" in Canada (So & Lee, 1995). Migrant populations produce content of their own as well; Austrian artist Ingo Gunther conceives of this population as the citizenry of a nation-state of its own. Ultimately, the local today is an effect of "viscosity" (Hookway, 1999), what Amin (1997) describes as sites of fixities of tradition and continuity within a globalized environment of transformation.

Hookway (1999) describes individual uses of the global information infrastructure today as producing "predatory locales." These interactions and transactions are local because they always occur at a specific time and place, but are predatory because each now triggers actions within global human and nonhuman systems. Because such predatory locales are ubiquitous globally, and because the interactions they trigger are carried out by the nonhuman agents of software, Hookway describes today's environment as pandemonic. One is "acquired" by becoming visible to a system, whether of marketing or other surveillance interests. The predatory locale can emerge via mass media experiences as well as individual transactions: Canevacci (1992) details the ways in which the Brazilian *telenovela* has abandoned traditional audience research in favor of using what he describes as an "anthropology" of visual communication in which the telenovela "emits" a participant observer from its flexible production center in response to every changing nuance of the environment. This can have a powerful effect, as when telenovelas used speech from the barrios when those voices were silenced, thus educating the middle class and serving as a force for democracy.

POWER

Much of the study of international communication is about power—either how to exercise it or complaining about its exercise by others. Throughout the period of modernity, however, conceptualizations of power grew more complex and power itself came to be understood as multiple. One of the characteristics of postmodernity is that a new form of power has come to be dominant both in itself and as it has affected the exercise of other forms of power long available. Political scientists and communication scholars studying the conditions of modernity explored instrumental power (control over the material world), structural power (control over rules and institutions), and symbolic power (control over ideas); postmodern attention has turned in addition to the study of genetic power (control over the informational bases of materials, rules and institutions, and ideas). Too, historically the distinction between power in its actual state (as exercised) and its potential state (power allegedly available for use) has been important; today power in its virtual state (forms of power that do not yet exist but that can be brought into being using extant knowledge and skills) is now increasingly important. Because information and information technologies are critical to power in its genetic form and in its virtual state, these shifts in the nature of power and the ways in which it is conceptualized are fundamental to the study of global information, communication, and culture (Braman, 1995).

The earliest form of power to be recognized as such was clearly instrumental power; power is generally equated with physical control over a territory and its population. War is perhaps the ultimate in the actual exercise of instrumental power. The impact of new information technologies on the tools and practices of war has stimulated a reconsideration of the role of such technologies throughout history in weaponry (Dandeker, 1990; de Landa, 1991; Macksey, 1989) and in the command and control systems that determine how weapons will be used (Dandeker, 1990; Dudley, 1991; Keegan, 1987). Both have grown more sophisticated; weapons today are increasingly "smart" and the U.S. military, taking advantage of developments in biotechnology, is currently pursuing co-design of weapons and the humans who will use them. These developments both illustrate the intertwining of various forms of power and identify a research agenda for those working to build international communication theory in the future and to operationalize that theory in practice. Historically not a topic for those in communications, weapons and their support systems today are critical participants in the production and flows of information globally.

The history of modernity is one of the ever-greater articulation of structural forms of power via the elaboration of legal and regulatory systems and of the bureaucracies that enact them—the power to decide how things are done. Structural power has been the subject of those in international communication largely through critiques of the effects of flows, as in explorations of dependency caused by media, or cultural, imperialism (Schiller, 1991). From this perspective, the entire debate about NWICO should be understood as an examination of and struggle over the structural effects of the global communication system, as are analyses of the political effect of international communication flows such as those of the telephone (Cioffi-Revilla, Merritt, & Zinnes, 1987). Studies of the geopolitical effects of the building of the global information infrastructure, such as Headrick's (1990) history of the telegraph and telephone systems from the middle of the 19th to the middle of the 20th centuries, highlight the role of communications systems in producing and reproducing structural power. Diplomacy is the communications hinge between structural and symbolic power: Diplomatic communication takes place within a rigidly defined and formal system of roles and rules established early in the 19th century as a means by which nation-states officially communicate with each other (Korzenny & Ting-Toomey, 1990; van Dinh, 1987). The interdependence of today's global system discussed above and the increasingly important roles of non-state—and therefore non-diplomatic—political communications, whether via terrorism, NGOs, or other routes, provide theoretical and research challenges that are new.

Symbolic power has been an important topic in international communication research that has examined propaganda (Taylor, 1995) and the role of the press in geopolitical relations (classically explored by Cohen, 1963) as well as rhetoric in formal political speech (Hinds & Windt, 1991). The role of international communication in the exercise of symbolic power is not always publicly evident; Schlesinger and Kinzer (1982), for example, provide a detailed history of the way in which the use of public relations behind the scenes in Central America shaped political developments there in ways that served U.S.-based interests. Anderson (1983) and Calhoun (1991) elaborate on the relations between structural and symbolic power and their geopolitical effect.

The study of the role of international communication in the exercise of genetic power has just begun. De Landa (1991) is moving in this direction when he notes that intelligence agencies have moved away from pure information collection toward the use of simulacra as a means of substituting for actual information. Foucault's notion of governmentality as extending to relations within the self, what he refers to as the microphysics of power, is also a precursor of this notion (Burchell, Gordon, & Miller, 1991), as is Nye's (1990) notion of "soft" power, Rabinow's (1992) concept of "bio" power, and Strange's (1996) explorations of the ways in which power is diffused today. Several ways of thinking about the impact of informationally based genetic power in international relations are introduced by the authors in the Singh and Rosenau (in press) collection. Deleuze and Guattari (1997) and Virilio (Der Derian, 1998) push the metaphoric bounds of such arguments theoretically. The level of analytic detail achieved by Lessig (1999) in his analysis of the informational bases of control within the U.S. system, however, has not yet been seen for the international arena. This is a critically important area for future work in the study of global communication, information, and culture.

Though historically power in its virtual state was trivial compared with its importance in its actual and potential states because the pace of innovation was so slow, the use of new information technologies has reversed this relationship. The U.S. defense establishment maximizes the utility of the virtual in its current approach to information gathering. Rather than identifying specific subjects of surveillance interest and arraying them about a sensor, today the National Security Agency takes as its model of information-gathering the panspectron. Multiple sensors are arrayed around all bodies so that information is gathered about everyone, all the time, launching analysis of specific information when triggered by a particular question (De Landa,

1991). This, too, exacerbates the pandemonic nature of the environment.

INTERNATIONAL COMMUNICATION IN A PANDEMONIC ENVIRONMENT

In the end, developments in each of these areas complement, exacerbate, and extend those in the others. The institutions by which facticity has been determined have essentially been those certified by the nation-state, for whom the insistence on the universal and appearance of stability have been useful tools for the assertion of power by individual states. Theory about and research into the details of international communication have historically accepted these terms and focused on the modern questions they framed about the nature of flows of information, communication, and culture around the globe.

In the postmodern condition, however, facticity has come to be understood as culturally rich in addition to being empirically grounded, and thus determined by social interactions in organizational and communal forms beyond those of the nation-state. Such forms—those of the family, ethnicity, community, NGOs, and transnational and multinational corporations—compete and work with the nation-state not only in determination of facticity but in the exercise of other forms of power. The dominant forms of power in the contemporary environment are those that deal with the informational bases of materials, rules and institutions, and ideas—that is, with identity. The local, the site in which identity is grounded, has itself become mobile.

With this, international communication theory and research return to where they started, in Jeremy Bentham's almost simultaneous coinage of the words *panopticon* and *international*. The panopticon, like the pan-

orama of the same era, offered the sense of omniscience that was critical to modern exercises of power. In the panopticon, exemplified by modern prisons, the observer rotates in order to see all, whereas in the panorama, predecessor to film, the observer remains still and that which is being observed moves past the line of vision. In both cases, power is exercised by an observer at the center of a system in which those being surveilled are arrayed about, specifically selected, and arranged for observation.

Under the postmodern conditions of the panspectron, within a pandemonic environment, a new definition of information has emerged. As recently as a decade ago, the range of definitions of information in use fell into a typology in which they were distinguished from each other by the breadth and complexity of the social structure to which the definition was intended to refer and to the amount of power granted information in itself; the typology included information as a resource, as a commodity, as perception of pattern (or as knowledge structures), and as a constitutive force in society (Braman, 1989/1996). In the pandemonic environment, information is also an agent.

International communication theory in the past has dealt with the problems raised by modernity—how communications systems interact with nation-states; effects of flows of information, communication, and culture between them; and what happens to the fact. It has begun to deal with the transformations that have brought about the postmodern conditions of the information society, primarily in the analysis of globalization and, now, the local. Analyses of hybrid identities, border communities, and mobile or virtual populations are important explorations of the impact of global communication not interpretable within a solely state-centric frame. A number of specific areas in which theoretical and conceptual development are needed to understand contemporary communications processes and their effects have been identified throughout this chapter. Premier among them may be the need to understand the impact of information flows when information is not a conduit of agency but the agent itself.

REFERENCES

Abbate, J. (1999). *Inventing the Internet.* Cambridge: MIT Press.

Abu-Lughod, J. L. (1992). Communication and the metropolis: Spatial drift and the reconstitution of control. *Asian Journal of Communication, 2*(3), 12-30.

Adler, E. (1997). Seizing the middle ground: Constructivism in world politics. *European Journal of International Relations, 3*(3), 319-364.

Amin, A. (1997). Placing globalization. *Theory, Culture & Society, 14*(2), 123-137.

Anderson, B. R. (1983). *Imagined communities: Reflections on the origin and spread of nationalism.* London: Verso Editions.

Ang, I. (1998). Doing cultural studies at the crossroads: Local/global negotiations. *European Journal of Cultural Studies, 1*(1), 13-32.

Antonelli, C. (Ed.). (1992). *The economics of information networks.* Amsterdam: North-Holland.

Appadurai, A. (1990). Disjuncture and difference in the global cultural economy. *Theory, Culture & Society, 7,* 295-310.

Arquila, J., & Ronfeldt, D. (1996). *Advent of netwar.* Santa Monica, CA: RAND.

Bachmair, B. (1991). From the motor-car to television: Cultural-historical arguments on the meaning of mobility for communication. *Media, Culture & Society, 13,* 521-533.

Beck, U. (1992). *Risk society: Toward a new modernity* (M. Potter, Trans.). London: Sage.

Beller, J. L. (1996). Desiring the involuntary: Machinic assemblage and transnationalism in Deleuze and *Robocop 2.* In R. Wilson & W. Dissanayake (Eds.), *Global/local: Cultural production and the transnational imaginary* (pp. 193-218). Durham, NC: Duke University Press.

Bhabha, H. K. (1993). *The location of culture.* New York: Routledge.

Biltereyst, D. (1992). Language and culture as ultimate barriers? An analysis of the circulation, consumption and popularity of fiction in small European countries. *European Journal of Communication, 7*(4), 517-540.

Blanco, V. S., & van den Bulck, J. (1995). Regions versus states and cultures in the EC media policy debate. *Media, Culture & Society, 17,* 239-251.

Borgmann, A. (1999). *Holding on to reality: The nature of information at the turn of the millennium.* Chicago: University of Chicago Press.

Boyd-Barrett, O. (1998). Media imperialism reformulated. In D. K. Thussu (Ed.), *Electronic empires: Global media and local resistance* (pp. 157-176). London: Edward Arnold.

Braman, S. (1985). The "facts" of El Salvador according to objective and new journalism. *Journal of Communication Inquiry, 13*(2), 75-96.

Braman, S. (1995). Horizons of the state: Information policy and power. *Journal of Communication, 45*(4), 4-24.

Braman, S. (1996). Defining information: An approach for policy-makers. In D. M. Lamberton (Ed.), *The economics of communication and information* (pp. 3-12). London: Edward Elgar. (Reprinted from *Telecommunications Policy, 13*(3), 233-242, 1989)

Braman, S. (in press). Informational meta-technologies and international relations: The case of biotechnologies. In J. P. Singh & J. Rosenau (Eds.), *Information technologies and global politics: The changing scope of power and governance.* Albany: State University of New York Press.

Braman, S. (2001). Reinventing policy technologies: South African decision-making for the information infrastructure. In S. Burton, A. Leach, & C. Stilwell (Eds.), *Superhighway or footpath? Knowledge, information and development* (pp. 3-10). Durban, South Africa: University of Natal-Pietermaritzsburg.

Braman, S., Shah, H., & Fair, J. E. (2000). "We are all natives now": An overview of international and development communication research. In W. B. Gudykunst (Ed.), *Communication yearbook 24* (pp. 160-186). Thousand Oaks, CA: Sage.

Burchell, G., Gordon, C., & Miller, P. (Eds.). (1991). *The Foucault effect: Studies in governmentality*. Chicago: University of Chicago Press.

Calhoun, C. (1991). Large-scale social integration and the transformation of everyday life. In P. Bourdieu & J. S. Coleman (Eds.), *Social theory for a changing society* (pp. 95-120). Boulder, CO: Westview.

Canevacci, M. (1992). Image accumulation and cultural syncretism. *Theory, Culture & Society, 9*(3), 95-110.

Castles, S. (1998). New migrations in the Asia-Pacific region: A force for social and political change. *International Social Science Journal, 50*(2), 215-228.

Chan, J. M. (1997). National responses and accessibility to STAR TV in Asia. In A. Sreberny-Mohammadi, D. Winseck, J. McKenna, & O. Boyd-Barrett (Eds.), *Media in global context: A reader* (pp. 94-106). London: Edward Arnold.

Chan, J. M., & Lee, C.-C. (1991). *Mass media and political transition: The Hong Kong press in China's orbit*. New York: Guilford.

Chang, H.-C., & Holt, R. (1991). Tourism as consciousness of struggle: Cultural representations of Taiwan. *Critical Studies in Mass Communication, 8*(1), 102-118.

Cioffi-Revilla, C., & Merritt, R. L. (1982). Communication research and the new world information order. *Journal of International Affairs, 35*(2), 225-245.

Cioffi-Revilla, C., Merritt, R. L., & Zinnes, D. A. (Eds.). (1987). *Communication and interaction in global politics*. Newbury Park, CA: Sage.

Clifford, J. (1997). *Routes: Travel and translation in the late twentieth century*. Cambridge, MA: Harvard University Press.

Cohen, B. C. (1963). *The press and foreign policy*. Princeton, NJ: Princeton University Press.

Cohen, A. A., & Roeh, I. (1992). When fiction and news cross over the border: Notes on differential readings and effects. In F. Korzenny & S. Ting-Toomey (Eds.), *Mass media effects across cultures* (pp. 23-34). Newbury Park, CA: Sage.

Cunningham, S., & Jacka, E. (1996). The role of television in Australia's "paradigm shift" to Asia. *Media, Culture & Society, 18,* 619-637.

Dandeker, C. (1990). *Surveillance, power and modernity: Bureaucracy and discipline from 1700 to the present day*. New York: St. Martin's.

De Landa, M. (1991). *War in the age of intelligent machines*. New York: Zone.

Deleuze, G., & Guattari, F. (1997). *Nomadology: The war machine*. New York: Autonomedia.

Der Derian, J. (Ed.). (1998). *The Virilio reader*. Oxford, UK: Basil Blackwell.

Dezalay, Y., & Garth, B. G. (1996). *Dealing in virtue: International commercial arbitration and the construction of a transnational legal order*. Chicago: University of Chicago Press.

Downing, J. D. H. (1996). *Internationalizing media theory: Transition, power, culture—Reflections on media in Russia, Poland and Hungary 1980-95*. London: Sage.

Dudley, L. M. (1991). *The word and the sword: How techniques of information and violence have shaped our world*. Cambridge, MA: Blackwell.

Elkins, D. J. (1997). Globalization, telecommunication, and virtual ethnic communities. *International Political Science Review, 18*(2), 139-152.

Entrikin, J. N. (1991). *The betweenness of place: Towards a geography of modernity*. Baltimore, MD: Johns Hopkins University Press.

Enzensberger, H. M. (1992). *Mediocrity and delusion: Collected diversions* (M. Chalmers, Trans.). New York: Verso.

Errington, S. (1994). What became of authentic primitive art? *Cultural Anthropology, 9*(2), 201-227.

Featherstone, M. (Ed.). (1990). *Global culture: Nationalism, globalization and modernity*. London: Sage.

Featherstone, M., Hepworth, M., & Turner, B. S. (Eds.). (1991). *The body: Social process and cultural theory*. Newbury Park, CA: Sage.

Florini, A. M. (2000, March). *The politics of transparency*. Paper presented at the annual meeting of the International Studies Association, Los Angeles.

Garreau, J. (1992). *Edge city: Life on the new frontier*. New York: Doubleday.

Geertz, C. (1983). *Local knowledge: Further essays in interpretive anthropology*. New York: Basic Books.

Ginsburg, F. (1994). Embedded aesthetics: Creating a discursive space for indigenous media. *Cultural Anthropology, 9*(3), 365-383.

Goolsbee, A. (2000). In a world without borders: The impact of taxes on Internet commerce. *Quarterly Journal of Economics, 115*(2), 561-577.

Gopnik, A. (1996, March 18). The virtual bishop. *New Yorker,* pp. 59-63.

Greaves, T. (Ed.). (1994). *Intellectual property rights for indigenous peoples: A sourcebook.* Oklahoma City, OK: Society for Applied Anthropology.

Greenfeld, L. (1992). *Nationalism: Five roads to modernity.* Cambridge, MA: Harvard University Press.

Hannerz, U. (1997). Notes on the global ecumene. In A. Sreberny-Mohammadi, D. Winseck, J. McKenna, & O. Boyd-Barrett (Eds.), *Media in global context: A reader* (pp. 11-18). London: Edward Arnold.

Headrick, D. R. (1990). *The invisible weapon: Telecommunications and international relations, 1851-1945.* New York: Oxford University Press.

Held, D. (1989). *Political theory and the modern state: Essays on state, power, and democracy.* Stanford, CA: Stanford University Press.

Hinds, L. B., & Windt, T. O., Jr. (1991). *The Cold War as rhetoric: The beginnings, 1945-1950.* New York: Praeger.

Hookway, B. (1999). *Pandemonium: The rise of predatory locales in the postwar world.* Princeton, UK: Princeton Architectural Press.

Iyer, G. R., & Shapiro, J. M. (1999). Ethnic entrepreneurial and marketing systems: Implications for the global economy. *Journal of International Marketing, 7*(4), 83-111.

Jakubowicz, K. (1990). Musical chairs? The three public spheres of Poland. *Media, Culture & Society, 12,* 195-212.

Jasen-Verbeke, M. (1998). Tourismification of historical cities. *Annals of Tourism Research, 25*(3), 739-742.

Keegan, J. (1987). *The mask of command.* New York: Elisabeth Sifton Books, Viking.

Korzenny, F., & Ting-Toomey, S. (Eds.). (1990). *Communicating for peace: Diplomacy and negotiation.* Newbury Park, CA: Sage.

Krippendorff, K. (1987). Paradigms for communication and development with emphasis on autopoiesis. In D. L. Kincaid (Ed.), *Communication theory: Eastern and Western perspectives* (pp. 189-208). San Diego, CA: Academic Press.

Lash, S., & Urry, J. (1993). *Economies of signs and space.* London: Sage.

Lessig, L. (1999). *Code and other laws of cyberspace.* New York: Basic Books.

Lull, J. (1997). Hybrids, fronts, borders: The challenge of cultural analysis in Mexico. *Cultural Studies, 1*(3), 405-418.

Lull, J. (2000). *Media, communication, culture.* New York: Columbia University Press.

Macksey, K. (1989). *For want of a nail: The impact on war of logistics and communications.* London: Brassey's.

Massey, D. S., Arango, J., Hugo, G., Kouaouci, A., Pellegrino, A., & Taylor, J. E. (1993). Theories of international migration: A review and appraisal. *Population and Development Review, 19*(3), 431-466.

Mattelart, A. (1994). *Mapping world communication: War, progress, culture* (S. Emanuel & J. A. Cohen, Trans.). Minneapolis: University of Minnesota Press.

Maxwell, R. (1996). Out of kindness and into difference: The value of global market research. *Media, Culture & Society, 18,* 105-126.

Melucci, A. (1996). *Challenging codes: Collective action in the information age.* Cambridge, UK: Cambridge University Press.

Mewes, W. (1971). *Cybernetic energy strategy.* Frankfurt, Germany: Mewes Systems.

Meyrowitz, J. (1994). *No sense of place: The impact of electronic media on social behavior.* New York: Oxford University Press.

Mouffe, C. (Ed.). (1992). *Dimensions of radical democracy: Pluralism, citizenship, community.* London and New York: Verso.

Mowlana, H., & Wilson, L. J. (1990). *The passing of modernity: Communication and the transformation of society.* New York: Longman.

Myrdal, G. (1956). *Development and underdevelopment: A note on the mechanism of national and international economic inequality.* Cairo, Egypt: Rod El Farag.

Nardi, B. A., & O'Day, V. L. (2000). *Information ecologies: Using technology with heart.* Cambridge: MIT Press.

Nerone, J. (Ed.). (1995). *Last rights: Revisiting four theories of the press.* Urbana: University of Illinois Press.

Ning, W. (1999). Rethinking authenticity in tourism research. *Annals of Tourism Research, 26*(2), 349-370.

Nye, J. S., Jr. (1990). *Bound to lead: The changing nature of American power.* New York: Basic Books.

Parameswaran, R. E. (1997). Colonial interventions and the postcolonial situation in India: The English language, mass media and the articulation of class. *Gazette, 59*(1), 21-41.

Richards, T. (1993). *The imperial archive: Knowledge and the fantasy of empire.* New York: Verso.

Rosenau, J. N. (1984). A pre-theory revisited? World politics in an era of cascading interdependence. *International Studies Quarterly, 28*(3), 245-306.

Rosenau, J. N. (1990). *Turbulence in world politics: A theory of change and continuity.* Princeton, NJ: Princeton University Press.

Rabinow, P. (1992). Artificiality and enlightenment: From sociobiology to biosociality. In J. Crary & S. Kwinter (Eds.), *Incorporations* (pp. 234-252). New York: Zone.

Sakamoto, R. (1996). Hybridity and the creation of colonialist discourse. *Theory, Culture & Society, 13*(3), 113-128.

Sassen, S. (1991). *The global city: New York, London, Tokyo.* Princeton, NJ: Princeton University Press.

Schiller, H. I. (1991). Not yet the post-imperialist era. *Critical Studies in Mass Communication, 8*(1), 13-28.

Schlesinger, P. (1997). From cultural defence to political culture: Media, politics and collective identity in the European Union. *Media, Culture & Society, 19,* 369-391.

Schlesinger, S. C., & Kinzer, S. (1982). *Bitter fruit: The untold story of the American coup in Guatemala.* Garden City, NY: Doubleday.

Sell, S. K. (1995). Intellectual property protection and antitrust in the developing world: Crisis, coercion, and choice. *International Organization, 49*(2), 315-349.

Servaes, J. (1986). Development theory and communication policy: Power to the people! *European Journal of Communication, 1*(2), 203-230.

Shamir, J., & Shamir, M. (2000). *The anatomy of public opinion.* Ann Arbor: University of Michigan Press.

Siebert, F. S., Peterson, T., & Schramm, W. (1956). *Four theories of the press: The authoritarian, libertarian, social responsibility and Soviet communist concepts of what the press should be and do.* Urbana: University of Illinois Press.

Silverstone, R., & Hirsch, E. (Eds.). (1992). *Consuming technologies: Media and information in domestic spaces.* London: Routledge.

Simpson, C. (1994). *Science of coercion.* New York: Oxford University Press.

Singh, J. P., & Rosenau, J. (Eds.). (in press). *Information technologies and global politics: The changing scope of power and governance.* Albany: State University of New York Press.

So, C. Y. K., & Lee, A. Y. L. (1995). Tapping "yacht immigrants": Overseas editions of Hong Kong newspapers as econo-cultural spin-off. *Asian Journal of Communication, 5*(2), 122-141.

Splichal, S. (1999). *Public opinion: Developments and controversies in the 21st century.* New York: Rowman & Littlefield.

Star, S. L., & Ruhleder, K. (1996). Steps toward an ecology of infrastructure: Design and access for large information spaces. *Information Systems Research, 7*(1), 111-134.

Strange, S. (1996). *The retreat of the state: The diffusion of power in the world economy.* New York: Cambridge University Press.

Taylor, P. M. (1995). *Munitions of the mind: A history of propaganda from the ancient world to the present era.* Manchester, UK, and New York: Manchester University Press.

TeleGeography. (2000). *Hubs & spokes: A telegeography Internet reader.* Washington, DC: Author.

Thorbecke, E. (1992). *The anatomy of agricultural product markets and transactions in developing countries.* Washington, DC: Institute for Policy Reform.

Tice, K. E. (1995). *Kuna crafts, gender, and the global economy.* Austin: University of Texas Press.

van Dinh, T. (1987). *Communication and diplomacy in a changing world.* Norwood, NJ: Ablex.

Wallerstein, I. (1990). Culture as the ideological battleground of the modern world-system. In M. Featherstone (Ed.), *Global culture: Nationalism, globalization and modernity* (pp. 31-55). London: Sage.

Wallerstein, I. (1996). *Open the social sciences: Report of the Gulbenkian Commission on the restructuring of the social sciences.* Stanford, CA: Stanford University Press.

Wang, N. (1999). Rethinking authenticity in tourism research. *Annals of Tourism Research, 26*(2), 349-370.

Waterman, P. (1990). Reconceptualizing the democratization of international communication. *International Social Science Journal, 42*(1), 77-92.

White, S. A., Nair, K. S., & Ascroft, J. (Eds.). (1994). *Participatory communication: Working for change and development.* Thousand Oaks, CA: Sage.

PART II

Development Communication

Introduction

Bella Mody

Communication technologies have been used as strategic interventions for the development of former colonies in Asia, Africa, Latin America, and the Caribbean since their advocacy by Lerner (1958). The seven chapters in this section address 40-odd years of research on communication. Development (variously defined) has been historically conceptualized as an international rather than an internal domestic issue for several reasons by different groups. First, European colonization created many aspects of the pathology of underdevelopment (Rodney, 1974). Second, a particular kind of complementary growth (in economic and political terms) was seen by each power bloc as part of its own global ambitions in the Cold War. Third, the expansion of U.S. businesses after World War II continued to require international sources of raw materials,

labor, and markets just like European expansion after the 16th century did.

After the Great Depression and the failure of markets, governments of newly independent states and their advisers in international governmental organizations such as the World Bank saw national development as a state responsibility. The complex challenges of the development project, the inability of governments to meet the challenge, and the privatization push from Reagan and Thatcher to enable their firms to expand into previously impermeable state-monopolized foreign markets have swung the pendulum in the direction of marketplace solutions to national development.

Lerner felt that the need was to modernize traditional societies; he recommended the use of media as a tool to create Western empathic personality types as a step toward his goal. (See chapters by Melkote, Waisbord, and Singh.) Transnational businesses see communication technology as the central nervous system of global business management, and the means of demand creation. Thus, whether development was conceived as the end product of strategic state-initiated interventions or the result of market forces left to themselves, media play a major role.

How, then, have the roles of media been studied? The earliest researchers (e.g., Wilbur Schramm) were not disinterested scholars looking to discover generalizations and probabilities about communication processes and effects in technologically less advanced societies in the positivist paradigm. They were technology promoters (see the Singh chapter). They focused on influencing the actions of the state (see the Waisbord chapter). Their objective initially was to improve the penetration of media (e.g., the number of radios per 1,000 population) much as Internet promoters do today. When research showed that mere access to communication technology was not enough, attention switched to the content that media carried: It was thought that the messages were not having the impact that advertising is supposed to have because they were not designed on the basis of audience/market research like ads were (see the chapter by Snyder). Analyses of development failures also indicated that communities needed to set their own agendas (see the Melkote chapter). This reality combined with a focus on formative research for message design led to recognition that communication as essentially dialogic could not be designed except in the participatory mode (see the chapter by Huesca). Rogers's (1995) diffusion of innovations found that development possibilities started where communication media left off: Interpersonal processes were crucial influences on whether and when audiences tried an innovation. Small-group discussion and action

groups followed media exposure in some communication for development projects, for example, rural radio forums (Jamison & McAnany, 1978). The Satellite Instructional Television Experiment in India made explicit provision for program utilization activity in villages to follow up on transmissions.

A distinct tradition of research emerged that questioned the bona fides of the power structure rather than the technology, that is, which international bank or national agency decided what kind of development would take place. This was a macro-level conceptualization of the first few steps in Lasswell's (1927) question: Who said what? The political economy approach asked why: Why were particular goals set and not others? Were these goals public-interested or control and dominance oriented? What cultural and political baggage did technology bring with it from the distinct foreign society in which it was imagined and constructed? Critical contextual national and project-level frameworks (e.g., Mody, 1983) and case studies (e.g., Sussman & Lent, 1991; Urey, 1995) followed.

The ethnographic turn in the social sciences has opened up additional ways of analyzing development (Crush, 1995; Escobar, 1995) and communication for development (Waters, 2000). The new areas draw attention to discourse, power, and praxis. They are addressed centrally in the Wilkins chapter. The discourse of modernization is addressed in the Melkote chapter. The Mody and Lee chapter in Part III, in the discussion on reception studies, briefly addresses the ethnographic turn. Ethnographies of how decoders interpret television programs and why particular genres (e.g., *telenovelas*) have become popular across several countries are increasing; we hope future studies will include implications for the development process.

This part of the book on development communication opens with a theoretical reprise by Srinivas Melkote in Chapter 8. He concludes with suggestions about more appropriate approaches for technologically less advanced societies. Sociologist Silvio Waisbord describes the changing role of the state in Chapter 9. He also tries to understand neglect of this force in communication and development research. Communication researcher Leslie Snyder in Chapter 10 analyzes communication campaigns, which are a major strategy in doing development communication. Her chapter may be considered the authoritative update of Hornik (1988). Political scientist J. P. Singh in Chapter 11 does us a great service by reviewing the literature and presenting dominant and alternative positions on communication technology over the past 50 years. Young scholars will find his table capturing the main elements of the half-century in communication and development invaluable. Communication scholar Robert Huesca in Chapter 12 reminds us of the key elements in the call to participatory research from Latin America in his review of the conceptual directions that have been emphasized and neglected over time. He concludes that the future of this normative ideal faces serious practical and conceptual impediments. Communication researcher Leslie Steeves in Chapter 13 draws on feminist theory and feminist scholarship in development studies and communication studies through an examination of three overlapping traditions: information delivery for economic gain, collective resistance, and spiritual awakening and empowerment. Communication researcher Karin Gwinn Wilkins in Chapter 14 ably wraps up the development communication part of the handbook by pointing us to a future research agenda characterized by *communication about development* or its discourse. She shows how analyzing the assumptions of texts, speeches, and practice by project funders and implementers can tell us how certain situations are framed as problematic and particular approaches to resolution are legitimized (and not others).

This historical analytical approach to the field was chosen to ensure that we learn from those who have gone before as we construct our conceptualizations of how communication can support national development, social change, and social resistance in this new millennium. Our chapters on communication and development fittingly give voice to natives of former colonies in Asia, Latin America, and North America; they work toward a balance of men and women scholars. This part of the book is the richer for scholars in sociology and political science who have shared their insights here.

REFERENCES

Crush, J. (1995). Introduction: Imagining development. In J. Crush (Ed.), *Power of development* (pp. 1-23). London: Routledge.

Escobar, A. (1995). *Encountering development*. Princeton, NJ: Princeton University Press.

Hornik, R. C. (1988). *Development communication: Information, agriculture, and nutrition in the Third World*. New York: Longman.

Jamison, D., & McAnany, E. (1978). *Radio for education and development*. Beverly Hills, CA: Sage.

Lasswell, H. D. (1927). *Propaganda technique in the world war*. New York: Knopf.

Lerner, D. (1958). *The passing of traditional society: Modernizing the Middle East*. Glencoe, IL: Free Press.

Mody, B. (1983). First World technologies in Third World contexts. In E. M. Rogers (Ed.), *Communication technology in the U.S. and Western Europe* (pp. 134-149). Norwood, NJ: Ablex.

Rodney, W. (1974). *How Europe underdeveloped Africa*. Washington, DC: Howard University Press.

Rogers, E. M. (1995). *Diffusion of innovations* (4th ed.). New York: Free Press.

Sussman, G., & Lent, J. A. (Eds.). (1991). *Transnational communications: Wiring the Third World*. Newbury Park, CA: Sage.

Urey, G. (1995). Infrastructure for global financial integration: The role of the World Bank. In B. Mody, J. M. Bauer, & J. D. Straubhaar (Eds.), *Telecommunications politics: Ownership and control of the information highway in developing countries*. Mahwah, NJ: Lawrence Erlbaum.

Waters, J. (2000). Power and praxis in development communication: Discourse and method. In K. G. Wilkins (Ed.), *Redeveloping communication for social change* (pp. 89-102). Lanham, MD: Rowman & Littlefield.

8

Theories of Development Communication

SRINIVAS R. MELKOTE
Bowling Green State University

This chapter explores the scholarship and practice of communication for development and empowerment in the Third World. The exercise of explicating theories, concepts, and methodologies in development communication presents unique challenges. This exploration requires an understanding of key concepts and how these meanings compare and contrast with how they have been used and defined by others during different historical settings. The overarching concepts in this field are *communication, modernization, development, participation,* and *empowerment.* Combinations of these terms have yielded additional concepts and accompanying controversies. Thus, terminology has been problematic within the rubric of development communication and related areas and has varied significantly from text to text and one context to another. The distinction made between *development communication* and *development support communication* constitutes one such

example. Development means different things to different scholars and practitioners. Therefore, the theory and practice of development communication cannot be meaningfully discussed without defining development as well as communication. Though the importance of defining development is obvious, relatively few studies of development communication bother to do so. In a recent meta-analysis, Fair and Shah (1997) looked at nearly 140 studies of communication and development and found that only about a third conceptualized development. Where definitions are provided, understandings about it vary. Though most would agree that development means improving the living conditions of society, there has been much debate on just what constitute improved living conditions and how they should be achieved.

The definition and boundaries of all these overlapping interdisciplinary areas have become even more fluid and nebulous in the past decade. The end of the Cold War in the early 1990s, alongside greater polarization along ethnic, religious, and nationalistic lines, increased transnationalization, increased information flow and influence, and a growing consciousness of marginalized groups and diminished resources have challenged and changed the issues and questions.

Over the years, there have been at least four perspectives or ways of thinking about and practicing development. The first is *modernization* that is based on neoclassical economic theory and promoting and supporting capitalistic economic development. This perspective assumes that the Western model of economic growth is applicable elsewhere and that the introduction of modern technologies is important in development. *Critical* perspectives constitute a second way of thinking about development. These perspectives challenge the economic and cultural expansionism and imperialism of modernization; they argue for a political and economic restructuring to produce a more even distribution of rewards and resources between and within societies. *Liberation* or *monastic* perspectives constitute the third area of scholarship and practice. These perspectives derive largely from liberation theology (Freire, 1970), which prioritize personal and communal liberation from oppression as the keys to self-reliance, which is seen as the goal of development. The fourth concept is *empowerment*. This construct is mentioned frequently in the communication and development literature of the 1990s, but terms, exemplars, levels of analysis, and outcomes have not been fully explicated. In addition, empowerment cannot be understood without first defining *power*. As such, this concept introduces the concepts of power and control in development theory and practice.

The theory and practice of development communication as described and analyzed in this chapter reflect varied underlying views about communication, development, and empowerment. Development communication scholars and practitioners still tend to be split between those who view communication as an organizational delivery system and those who view communication more broadly, as inseparable from culture and from all facets of social change. This orientation rests on certain assumptions consistent with divisions in views on development, empowerment, and development communication.

In this chapter, I attempt to provide an analysis of the theories used in communication for development (see Melkote & Steeves, 2001). First, I describe the discourse on modernization and the historical and conceptual biases introduced and reinforced by this discourse. The earlier communication theories inherited from the modernization paradigm and their institutional and context-related biases will be discussed in this section. Second, I describe and critique the theories in communication for development. I conclude by looking at the contemporary social and political situations in the developing countries that are characterized by unequal power relationships and structural inequities. I suggest communication approaches that better fit the contemporary challenges in Third World societies.

THE PARADIGM OF MODERNIZATION

Among the most powerful paradigms to originate after World War II, with enormous social, cultural, and economic consequences for the Third World, was that of modernization. Modernization, an operational artifact of the concept "development," was based on liberal political theory and was therefore grounded in the grand project of the Enlightenment, namely, reasoning, rationality, objectivity, and other philosophical principles of Western science. In modernization theories, the definition of a modern nation resembled Western industrialized nations in all areas of society, including political and economic behavior and institutions, attitudes toward technology and science, and cultural mores. The economic model that grounded modernization theories was the *neoclassical* approach that had served as the basis for Western economies. The dominant paradigm was mainly concerned with economic growth as measured by gross national product (GNP) rates and encouragement of all factors and institutions that accelerated and maintained high growth in areas such as capital-intensive industrialization and technology with private ownership of factors of production, free trade, and the principle of laissez-faire.

The modernization paradigm emerged not only from economic theory but also from social evolutionary theory. At the macro level, theories applied Darwin's ideas to the process of modernization of human societies. The theories of social evolution influenced and gave rise to important concepts in the sociology of development such as, for example, the various bipolar theories of modernization. In these theories, the universal stages in the earlier theories of social evolution were reduced to ideal-typical extremes: gemeinschaft versus gesellschaft, traditional versus modern societies, and so forth. The Third World nations were usually described as traditional, whereas the industrialized nations of the West signified the modern counterpart. The advanced Western nations had a wide range of systemic autonomy, that is, their capacity to cope with a range of social, cultural, technological, and economic issues in the process of social change. The Third World nations, on the other hand, lacking the higher differentiation of roles and institutions, the evolutionary universals, and other qualitative sociological characteristics of industrial societies, were limited in their capacity to cope with problems or crises or even master their environment. At

the micro level, theories on individual psychological attributes stressed that attitudinal and value changes among individuals were prerequisites to the creation of a modern society. Scholars such as McClelland (1967), Lerner (1958), Inkeles (1966), and Rogers (1969) described certain value-normative complexes that were responsible for the modernization of individuals in the West and that the individuals in the Third World were lacking. These scholars posited that modernization of the Third World was dependent on changing the character of individuals living there to resemble more closely the attitudinal and value characteristics of people in Western Europe and North America.

Modernization theories provided the epistemological foundation for the initial theories in communication for development. This led to the inheritance of historical and institutional biases emanating from propaganda research conducted in the United States between the two world wars. During this period, the mass communication media were viewed as powerful instruments that could be successfully used to manipulate people's opinions and attitudes, and thereby their behaviors, in a relatively short period of time. The institutional bias involved in this research has been carefully analyzed and revealed by scholars (Glander, 2000; Simpson, 1994). Simpson (1994) reveals the social, political, and economic context to the powerful effects research. In particular, he points out the support and funding that this research received from powerful sponsors such as the U.S. government, Army, Air Force, and the CIA; the active professional links that academicians maintained with the above groups; and importantly, the one dominant view of media effects that was propagated to the exclusion of other, nonmainstream, views—a dominant view that was also very supportive of the then U.S. foreign policy. This bias of powerful effects of the media was incorporated in development communication theories during the 1950s and 1960s. Thus, the initial biases set the norm for the field that was not necessarily appropriate for the socioeconomic and cultural conditions that existed in Asia, Africa, the Caribbean, or Latin America. To complicate matters, young researchers from developing countries were being taken to the United States under the PL 480 Program (a food aid program) to be trained in the American mold.

Starting in the 1970s, there were serious criticisms leveled at the propositions of the modernization paradigm, especially by scholars from Latin America and Asia. They contended that the development process in the Third World countries did not fit the assumptions implicit in the modernization paradigm. The paradigm worked better as a description of social change in Western Europe and North America than as a predictor of change in developing countries. The neoclassical economic model that suggested a *trickle-down* approach to development benefits started losing credibility in the 1970s. The worldwide recession of the 1980s and the neoliberal economic reforms in the Third World countries left them even further behind. The criticisms of the sociology of development models were directed at the abstractness of the social theories, the ahistorical nature of the propositions, and incorrect nature of development indicators that constituted the "evolutionary universals" proposed by scholars such as Parsons (1964). In addition, the value-enactment models of McClelland (1967), Hagen (1962), Inkeles and Smith (1974), Lerner (1958), Rogers (1969), and others were criticized for their ethnocentrism and for neglecting to account for the influence of structural constraints on individual action and enterprise. The modernization paradigm was further criticized for its negative view of culture, especially religious culture, for its patriarchal biases, and for its androcentrism. In the mainstream view, cultural traditions had to be destroyed if the

Third World nations and peoples wanted to modernize. This notion no longer had overt supporters, though modernization processes still function to destroy, appropriate, or absorb indigenous traditions. Neo-Marxist scholars criticized many of the tenets of the modernization paradigm. To them, underdevelopment was not a process distinctly different from development. In fact, they constituted two facets of the same process. The *development of underdevelopment* (Frank, 1969) in Third World nations was and is related to the economic development of Western Europe and North America.

Below, I summarize some of the overt and covert biases of the dominant paradigm and its discourse. The list is not exhaustive, but rather should be seen as a start in the deconstruction of the dominant paradigm:

- Rationality and progress are synonymous with economic rationality and growth as articulated by the economic and political elite in the North, by multilateral organizations controlled by such elite, state bureaucrats, and by vested interests in the South (Braidotti, Charkiewicz, Hausler, & Wierninga, 1994).

- A higher and higher standard of living as quantified by indicators such as per capita income, per capita consumption of resources, and GNP constitutes a key goal. The bias is not necessarily the "well-being" of an individual or community that would include the material and nonmaterial aspects of life, but "well-having" that denotes maximum material consumption (Latouche, 1992).

- The dominant discourse aided by the positivistic scientific method has claimed to speak the "truth" about development. Thus, assumptions and images of modernity and progress as exported from the industrialized West have been uncritically accepted by the leaders of many recipient countries (Foucault, 1980). These assumptions frequently have overruled other analyses, such as folk-scientific descriptions of nature (Alvares, 1992).

- The prior histories of developing countries have been considered irrelevant to the enterprise of modernization. Communities have been stripped of their histories and cultures and a technocratic plan has been constructed for their future (Crush, 1995). Thus, objects of development are treated in a historical vacuum that precludes any analysis of previous initiatives and their harmful effects (Mitchell, 1995).

- Development concepts, initiatives, and their presumed benefits have been guided by master geographies constructed by the dominant states and institutions. Thus, notions such as the Third World, Oriental, African, and North-South have become stereotypes. Third World countries or poorer enclaves within them are incorrectly viewed as net receivers of development assistance (Hewitt, 1995).

- There is a strong biological metaphor in development discourse. *Entwicklung* or the process of social evolution was considered similar to the phylogenic changes in a biological organism. Over time, ontogeny imitated the irreversible and linear stages of phylogeny.

- The irrelevance of history leads to social problems that are interpreted as occurring naturally rather than as outcomes of politics, mismanagement, corruption, greed, or the exercise of power (Escobar, 1995; Wilkins, 1999). "Natural" hazards such as famine and drought, for example, are not regarded as possible outcomes of policy failure, failures of research paradigms, or the crises of capitalist modernization ventures (Crush, 1995; Hewitt, 1995).

In essence, positivistic science has claimed to be the final arbiter of truth. As the Enlightenment values that undergird science are consistent with those of modern political-economic systems, science and scientific discourse, economics, and politics constitute mutually reinforcing systems. Thus, modern states, bureaucrats, elite in positions of power, and scientist-technocrats using science have taken over the responsibility of deciding what is truth and what is not. Poststructuralists such as Foucault (1980) have posited that as a servant of the state, science has been used not just to explain reality but to produce, control, and normalize. The process of normalization reduces heterogeneity by homogenizing individual feelings, desires, and actions.

THEORIES IN COMMUNICATION FOR DEVELOPMENT

The theories in communication for development may be categorized under two heads: those that fall within the dominant paradigm of modernization that I have discussed above and an alternative paradigm that has been put forward as a desirable alternative to the overly prescriptive and top-down model of modernization (see Rifkin, 1996). The first family of theories comprises communication and modernization theory, the diffusion of innovations theory, social marketing approach, and entertainment-education strategies. Within the second family, approaches such as the participatory action research model and empowerment are included.

Theories and Interventions Within the Dominant Paradigm of Modernization

Communication and modernization theory. In communication and modernization theory, communication was more than just an interplay between the source and receiver. It served as a complex system fulfilling certain social functions. Thus, the mass media came to serve as agents and indices of modernization in the Third World countries. Besides this macro-level analysis of the role of mass media, researchers also drew on communication effects research and on models describing social-psychological characteristics of individuals that were considered necessary for a successful transition from a traditional to a modern society.

Daniel Lerner's *The Passing of Traditional Society* (1958) illustrates the major ideas of the early mass media and modernization approach. Lerner identified and explained a psychological pattern in individuals that was both required and reinforced by the modern society: a mobile personality. This person was equipped with a high capacity for identification with new aspects of his or her environment and internalized the new demands made by the larger society. In other words, this person had a high degree of empathy, the capacity to see oneself in the other person's situation. Lerner stated that empathy fulfilled two important tasks. First, it enabled the person to operate efficiently in the modern society, which was constantly changing. Second, it was an indispensable skill for individuals wanting to move out of their traditional settings. The second element in Lerner's model was the mass media. They performed a special function: By exposing individuals to new people, ideas, and attitudes, they accelerated the process of modernization. Thus, the mass media were important agents of modernization. People in the Third World could expand their empathy by exposure to the mass media, which showed them new places, behavior, and cultures. In short, the mass media had the potential of blowing the winds of modernization into isolated traditional communities and replacing the structure of life, values, and behavior with ones seen in modern Western society.

The powerful role of the mass media in modernization was clearly implied in Lerner's (1958) and Schramm's (1964) research and many other studies in the 1950s and the 1960s. These studies complemented the postulates of the dominant paradigm of development. Mass media were the vehicles for transferring new ideas and models from the West to the Third World and from urban areas to rural countryside. Importantly, they were entrusted with the task of preparing individuals in developing nations for a rapid social change by establishing a "climate of modernization." The mass media were thought to have a powerful and direct influence on individuals. Thus, the bullet theory model of mass media effects seemed to hold in the Third World countries in the 1950s and 1960s, even though this model had been discarded earlier in North America (Mody, 2000). The strength of the mass media lay in their one-way, top-down, simultaneous and wide dissemination. They were considered as "magic multipliers" of development benefits in Third World nations. Administrators, researchers, and field workers sincerely believed in the great power of mass media as harbingers of modernizing influences. Therefore, information was considered the missing link in the development chain.

Diffusion of innovations theory. While scholars and policymakers were making macro-level arguments and funding experiments on the role of the media in supporting modernization, diffusion of innovations theory gradually evolved as the local-level framework to guide communications planning for modernization. Diffusion of innovations also had important theoretical links with communication effects research. The emphasis was on particular communication effects: the ability of media messages and opinion leaders to create knowledge of new practices and ideas and persuade the target to adopt the exogenously introduced innovations.

The diffusion of innovations approach is rooted in the postulates and implicit assumptions of exogenous change theory. The notion of exogenously induced change permeates assumptions of fundamental concepts in diffusion research. The earliest definition of development was "a type of social change in which new ideas are introduced into a social system in order to produce higher per capita incomes and levels of living through more modern production methods and improved social organization" (Rogers, 1969, p. 18). The necessary route for the change from a traditional to a modern person was understood as the communication and acceptance of new ideas from sources external to the social system (Fjes, 1976).

Everett M. Rogers, whose work has been central in this area, identified the following main elements in any analysis of diffusion of an idea or innovation: (1) the *innovation,* (2) its *communication* through certain *channels,* (3) among members of a *social system,* (4) over *time* (Rogers, 1971). Adoption was defined as the process through which the individual arrived at the decision to adopt or reject the innovation from the time he or she first became aware of it. The five stages were awareness, interest, evaluation, trial, and adoption. Diffusion studies indicated a great difference among the adopter groups in terms of their personal characteristics, media behavior, and position in the social structure. The relatively early adopters were usually younger, had a higher social status, had more favorable financial status, engaged in more specialized operations, and were equipped with greater mental abilities than later adopters. In terms of communication behavior, earlier adopters used more mass media and cosmopolite information sources. Also, the social relations of earlier adopters were more cosmopolite than for later categories, and the earlier adopters had more opinion leadership characteristics.

In sum, the diffusion of innovations research established the importance of communication in the modernization process at the local level. In the dominant paradigm, communication was visualized as the link through which exogenous ideas entered the local communities. Diffusion of innovations then emphasized the nature and role of communication in facilitating further dissemination within local communities. Thus, diffusion of innovations studies documented the impact of communication (interpersonal and mass media) on the change from a traditional to a modern way of life.

Social marketing approach. Over time, diffusion theory alone proved inadequate as a guide to communications planning in development campaigns. The diffusion concepts are imprecise, and the diffusion model does not sufficiently account for recipient feedback, which is crucial to campaign success. Communication efforts both in First World and Third World contexts have increasingly turned to science-based commercial marketing strategies to disseminate ideas to promote social causes, a process called *social marketing.* Examples in the First World include campaigns to discourage tobacco smoking, encourage use of auto seat belts, stop drinking and driving, promote healthful diets, discourage teen sex (or encourage safe sex), and prevent HIV/AIDS and other sexually transmitted diseases. In the Third World context, the major themes have included family planning, equal status for women, responsible sexual relationships, adult literacy, responsible parenthood, and HIV/AIDS prevention and control.

Until the early 1970s, communication models in family planning or other health-related areas reinforced the active source and passive receiver stereotypes. Communication campaigns used one-way, top-down, source-to-receiver transmission models with the belief that effects would occur autonomously once

Table 8.1   Stage Theories in Behavior Change

Stage Models	Hierarchy of Effects	Source
Social psychology	cognition-attitude-behavior change	Hovland, Lumsdaine, and Sheffield (1949)
Diffusion of innovations	awareness-interest-evaluation-trial-adoption	Rogers (1962)
	knowledge-persuasion-decision-implementation-confirmation	Rogers (1995)
Marketing and advertising	attention-interest-comprehension-impact-attitude-sales	Palda (1966)
Social marketing	cognition-action-behavior-values	Kotler (1984)
Psychotherapy	precontemplation-contemplation-preparation-action-maintenance	Prochaska, DiClemente, and Norcross (1992)

the target received the message (Rogers, 1973). Opinion leaders, change agents, and mass media outlets such as the radio were used to transmit persuasive messages. The assumption in these strategies was that knowledge was the missing link in the adoption and use of the service or product. The incorporation of social marketing techniques in the 1970s emphasized the challenges of changing the values and knowledge as well as behavior patterns of the receivers. Social marketing has introduced several new concepts in the dissemination of ideas and services: *audience segmentation, market research, product development, incentives,* and *facilitation* to maximize the target group's response (Kotler, 1984). Social marketers take a holistic view of the process by emphasizing the four Ps in the marketing chain: product, pricing, placement, and promotion.

Since the 1990s, the Population Communication Services (PCS), aided by the U.S. Agency for International Development (USAID), has adopted a strategic communication framework to overcome past weaknesses in family planning communication. Strategic communication describes an operational framework that incorporates the concepts of

social marketing and behavior change models in the design, execution, and evaluation of communication strategies intended to influence behavior change. The concepts of audience research, market segmentation, product development, incentives, and promotion are contributions from social marketing research applied to strategic family planning communication. In addition, the communication process itself has evolved into a convergence model where participants create and share information in order to reach a mutual understanding. This orientation, then, pulls in formative research procedures such as focus groups, audience surveys, and pretesting of messages into communication research in family planning (Piotrow, Kincaid, Rimon, & Rinehart, 1997). Stage models in several disciplines such as social psychology, marketing, rural sociology, and psychotherapy identified a series of steps that an individual would pass through from first awareness to adoption. This hierarchy of effects in behavior change indicated a similar step process in family planning communication. Some of the most frequently used stage models of behavior change used in family planning are listed in Table 8.1.

The stage theories represent behavior change as a sequence of steps with intermediate goals. These dictate that the communication process should also be a stage process needing different messages and approaches at each step of the behavior change process.

Entertainment-education strategies. In mass communication theory, the minimal effects hypothesis was gradually losing its appeal by the early 1970s (Lowery & DeFleur, 1995). Since the early 1940s, research testing this hypothesis had showed that mass media were not particularly effective in changing opinions and attitudes of the audience members. However, new research in the area of agenda setting showed that the mass media were very effective in increasing the cognition levels of audiences of salient events and thus serving as important agents of surveillance (Shaw & McCombs, 1974). Another area of research labeled as the uses and gratifications perspective (Blumer & Katz, 1974) put the focus on an active audience member as opposed to the passive receiver stereotype depicted in the minimal effects theories. In the uses and gratifications model, audience members actively selected media products to satisfy a range of needs: new information, entertainment, news, relaxation, and more. This research showed that audiences were actively selecting radio and television programs to gratify their perceived needs. A parallel development in the Third World has been the trend toward increasing commercialization and privatization of television and radio channels. These concomitant developments have provided a fertile ground for the growth and popularity of entertainment-education programs. In this approach, educational content is embedded in entertainment programs in media such as the radio, television, records, videos, and folk theater.

Singhal and Rogers (1999) point out that entertainment-education programs either directly or indirectly facilitate social change. At the individual level, they influence awareness, attention, and behavior toward a socially desirable objective, and at the larger, community level, they serve as an agenda setter or influence public and policy initiatives in a socially desirable direction. Entertainment-education programs represent a unique kind of social marketing where pro-social ideas are marketed within media products. Results show primarily cognitive changes, though some changes have been recorded that require behavior and value shifts. Modeling theory, self-efficacy, and para-social interaction models have been used to predict and explain the hierarchy of effects produced by these media programs.

Approaches Within an Alternative Paradigm for Social Change

This is an appropriate juncture to examine the changes in the notion of development and directed social change. The earliest descriptions of development were technologically deterministic and centered on quantifiable indicators such as the GNP. They stressed industrialization and economic growth while ignoring other human and nontechnological factors. The ferment in the field of development communication in the 1970s broadened the definitions to include growth with equity, provision of basic needs, meaningful employment, and rich and varied interpersonal relationships. Descriptions of directed change also incorporated the protection of the environment and native cultures. At present, the definitions tend to be qualitative and pluralistic. In this chapter, I see development as a process that should provide people with access to appropriate and sustainable opportunities to improve their lives and lives of others in their communities. This definition provides a segue to a comprehensive discussion of concepts and approaches that have attempted to provide people with credible opportunities to define their idea of development and construct approaches to achieving them.

An approach that has found wide support in the past 20 years has been the participatory approach to communication and development. Attempts at operationalization of the term *participation* range from those that reflect the dominant paradigm—the participation-as-a-means approach—to those that genuinely represent the case for a context-based paradigm—the participation-as-an-end approach (Ascroft & Masilela, 1989). The participation-as-an-end approach has received support from many scholars and administrators (Díaz Bordenave, 1989; Kothari, 1984). They argue that participation must be recognized as a basic human right. It should be accepted and supported as an end in itself and not for its results. The need to think, express oneself, belong to a group, be recognized as a person, be appreciated and respected, and have some say in crucial decisions affecting one's life are as essential to the development of an individual as eating, drinking, and sleeping (Díaz Bordenave, 1989). And participation in meaningful activities is the vehicle through which the needs described above are fulfilled.

Many scholars and practitioners over the past two decades have favored active participation of the people at the grassroots. On the surface, these signaled a positive departure from the earlier overly top-down and prescriptive approaches. However, the structure of elite domination was not disturbed as the participation that was expected was often directed by the sources and change agents. Although the people were induced to participate in self-help activities, the basic solutions to local problems had already been selected by the external development agencies. Critics argued that true participation should encourage social and political action by the people at all levels. The goal of participation efforts should be to facilitate *conscientization* of marginalized people globally of unequal social, political, and spatial structures in their societies. It is through conscientization and collective action that they perceive their needs, identify constraints to addressing these needs, and plan to overcome problems (Freire, 1970).

The term *participatory communication* has been frequently misunderstood and misused. Participation has been defined and operationalized in many ways: from pseudo participation to genuine efforts at generating participatory decision making (Ascroft & Masilela, 1989; Díaz Bordenave, 1989; Freire, 1970; White, 1994). There is a great deal of confusion about the outcomes desired and a contradiction between exemplars (or best practices) and phenomena of interest (or outcomes). Although the practice of participatory communication has stressed collaboration between the people and experts, a co-equal knowledge-sharing between the people and experts, and a local context and cultural proximity, the outcome in most cases has not been true empowerment of the people, but the attainment of some indicator of development as articulated in the modernization paradigm. Thus, participatory approaches have been encouraged, though the design and control of messages and development agendas usually have remained with the experts. Also, issues of power and control by the authorities, structures of dependency, and power inequities have not been addressed adequately within Third World settings (Wilkins, 1999). Thus, most of the participatory approaches have been essentially old wine in new bottles.

This postmodernist deconstruction of the participatory development paradigm puts the focus squarely on the contemporary power relations in society and the structures of inequities that they create and strengthen. For "real" social change for individuals and groups

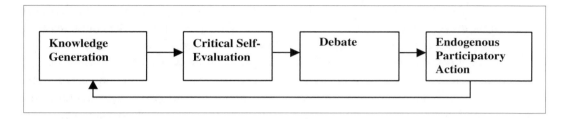

Figure 8.1. Praxis in Participatory Action Research

trapped in the margins, the search is for development communication models and analytical tools that can address and overcome these systemic barriers. Two areas/concepts that look fruitful in this endeavor are participatory action research (PAR) and empowerment strategies.

Participatory action research. PAR encompasses an experiential methodology. In this process, the people on their own develop methods of consciousness-raising of their existential situation; the knowledge that is generated or resuscitated is by collective and democratic means; and this is followed by reflection and critical self-evaluation, leading to endogenous participatory social action (see Figure 8.1). This in essence forms the praxis.

PAR has emerged as a forceful methodology-cum-action approach, principally as a reaction to the degradation of the economic and social conditions of poor and marginalized groups. PAR is dedicated to resuscitating both the power of marginalized people and their popular knowledge. The knowledge that PAR attempts to generate is specific, local, non-Western, and nonpositivist. Importantly, it is used to initiate collaborative social action to empower local knowledge and wrest social power inherent in knowledge away from the privileged (Friesen, 1999).

Domination of the poor and marginalized comes about in at least three ways: (1) control over the means of material production, (2) control over the means of knowledge pro-

duction, and (3) control over power that legitimizes the relative worth and utility of different espistemologies/knowledges (Rahman, 1991). Those who have social power will legitimize their knowledge and techniques of knowledge generation as superior. Critical scholars have shown how local narratives, popular knowledge, cultural meanings, and social arrangements have been devalued in the dominant development discourse. Nearly all of the knowledge of the oppressed and the marginalized has been disqualified as inadequate and unscientific by the dominant forces (Foucault, 1980). As long as there are inequalities in knowledge relations between different sections of a society, there will be inequities in the relations of material production. Therefore, in PAR an important objective to achieve the liberation of the poor and the oppressed is to recapture their knowledge and narratives. Thus, the basic ideology of PAR is that endogenous efforts and local leaders will play the leading role in social transformation using their own praxis. The PAR approach, then, by resuscitating and elevating popular knowledge, attempts to create a counterdiscourse, disrupts the position of development as articulated by the dominant discourse as problematic, causes a crisis in authority, and creates a space for marginalized groups to influence social change (White, 1999).

Empowerment. Much work has been done on empowerment in fields such as community organization, education, and community psychology, and we may do well by borrowing and adapting these concepts to development support communication. Although empowerment as a construct has a set of core ideas, it may be defined at different levels—individual, organization, and community—and operationalized in different contexts (Rowlands, 1998). Several working definitions of empowerment are available. However, given the nature of our work, which can be described as directed social change, and given the power inequities in societies that are posited as the major impediments to achieving meaningful change, it is important that the working definitions be linked directly to the building and exercise of social power (Speer & Hughey, 1995).

The following definitions and descriptions of the term *empowerment* are useful. According to Fawcett et al. (1984), "Community empowerment is the process of increasing control by groups over consequences that are important to their members and to others in the broader community" (p. 679). Rappaport (1987) describes empowerment as "a psychological sense of personal control or influence and a concern with actual social influence, political power, and legal rights. It is a multilevel construct applicable to individual citizens as well as to organizations and neighborhoods; it suggests the study of people in context" (p. 121). Another definition describes empowerment as "an intentional, ongoing process centered in the local community, involving mutual respect, critical reflection, caring and group participation, through which people lacking an equal share of valued resources gain greater access to and control over those resources" (Cornell Empowerment Group, 1989, p. 2). In summary, empowerment is the "manifestation of social power at individual, organizational, and community levels of analysis" (Speer & Hughey, 1995, p. 730).

The construct of empowerment has been mentioned quite often in the communication for development literature, but the terms, exemplars, levels of analysis, and outcomes have not been thoroughly explicated. Table 8.2 attempts to articulate elements for a conceptual framework of development support communication that is informed by the goals of the empowerment model. The concept of empowerment is heuristic in understanding the complex constraints in directed social change. It clarifies the empowerment-oriented outcomes and provides a useful niche for development communication.

Comparison of Development Communication Theories and Approaches

Table 8.2 provides a framework to compare the theories under the modernization paradigm with approaches under the empowerment model on several criteria. The phenomena of interest in the two approaches are vastly different and so are the underlying beliefs. The bias in the diffusion of innovations and social marketing approaches has been to favor exogenous ideas and innovations over the local. In the absence of active local people participation, such exogenously introduced changes most often result in social engineering by the government or the elite. In addition, the diffusion and social marketing approaches have been criticized for their pro-innovation bias and victim blame hypotheses. Although social marketing theoretically begins with a thorough analysis of local needs, campaigns have often been largely top-down with individual receivers treated as objects or targets for persuasion and change.

The differences are stark when it comes to the communication models used. The empowerment model puts the focus on a symmetrical

Table 8.2   Comparison of Development Communication Theories and Approaches in the
Modernization and Empowerment Frameworks

	Development Communication in the Modernization Framework[a]	Development Communication in the Empowerment Framework[b]
Phenomenon of interest/goal	National and regional development, people development, community improvement	Empowerment of people, social justice, building capacity and equity
Belief	Underdevelopment due to economic, political, cultural, geographic, and individual inadequacies; due to lack of power and control on the part of the existence of a single standard (as articulated by diversity of standards	Underdevelopment due to lack of access to economic, political, and cultural resources; underdevelopment people; experts)
Bias	Cultural insensitivity, environmentally unsustainable, standardization; change directed by external sources and ideas; deterministic process toward a predetermined end dictated by an external agency; pro-innovation bias; individual as locus of change and blame; victim blame hypotheses	Cultural proximity; ecological, diversity of standards; change directed and controlled by endogenous sources and ideas; open-ended and ongoing process of change; system blame hypotheses; group or community is paramount
Context	Macro and micro settings; very little interest in local cultures or power relationships and structural impediments in host society	Local and community settings; cognizant of formidable power inequities and systemic constraints
Level of analysis	Nation, region, individual	Individual, group or organization, community
Role of change agent	Expert, benefactor, nonparticipant	Collaborator, facilitator, participant, advocate for individuals and communities, risk taker, activist
Communication model	Linear, top-down, transmission of information using big mass media; media treated as independent variables with direct and powerful effects; pro-source bias; asymmetrical relationship (subject-object)	Nonlinear, participatory; used to convey information as well as build organizations; increased use of small media, traditional media, group as well as interpersonal communication; media treated as dependent variables; communication used for transaction, negotiation, understanding and not for powerful effects of a source; symmetrical relationship (subject-subject); horizontal flows
Type of research	Usually quantitative (surveys); some use of focus groups; contextual or evaluation research	Quantitative and qualitative; longitudinal studies; labor-intensive participatory action research
Exemplars mutual	Prevention of underdevelopment; remedy through/by experts; blame the victim; individual adjustment to a dominant norm; use of mass media to spread standardized messages and entertainment; messages that are preachy, prescriptive, and/or persuasive	Activate social support systems, social networks, help, and self-help activities; participation of all actors; empower community narratives; facilitate critical awareness; facilitate community and organizational power; communication used to strengthen interpersonal relationships
Outcomes desired	Modernization; economic growth; political development; infrastructure development; change in people's attitudes and behavior toward modernization objectives	Increased access of all citizens to material, psychological, cultural, and informational resources; honing of individual and group competence, leadership skills, useful life, and communication skills at the local level; honing of critical awareness skills; empowered local organizations and communities

a. Diffusion of innovations, social marketing, entertainment-education.
b. Participatory action research, empowerment strategies

relationship between relevant actors with all communication participants treated as subject-subject rather than the subject-object relationship found in the diffusion and social marketing approaches. Also, given its focus on the unequal power dynamics in societies, empowerment requires more than just information delivery and diffusion of technical innovations. The objective of development communication professionals is to work with the individuals and communities at the grassroots so that they eventually may enter and participate meaningfully in the political and economic processes in their communities/societies. This calls for grassroots organizing (Kaye, 1990) and communicative social action on the part of the poor, women, minorities, and others who have been consistently and increasingly marginalized in the process of social change. The implication for development communication, then, is a reconceptualization of its role. Greater importance will need to be placed on the organizational value of communication and the role of communicative efforts in empowering citizens.

It became increasingly clear in Asia and in Latin America that socioeconomic structural constraints greatly diminished the power of the mass media in overcoming problems of development. Far from being independent variables in the change process, the mass media were themselves affected by extraneous factors such as power imbalances and other structural and systemic barriers within societies. The dominant paradigm, with its exaggerated emphasis on the individual blame causal hypotheses regarding underdevelopment, obfuscated the social structural, political, and institutional constraints acting against individuals' efforts to change. Furthermore, what sets empowerment apart from the models informed by the modernization paradigm is that the locus of control in this process rests with the individuals or groups involved and not with the experts, the development com-

munication professionals, or the sponsoring organizations. Although the professionals may have a role to play in designing intervention strategies, they are not the key actors. The key players are the people handling their problems in local settings and learning and honing their competencies in the concrete experiences of their existential realities.

CONCLUSION

Today, the poststructuralism and postmodernism embraced by leading theorists challenge universal truths and our notions of objective social reality. Epistemological plurality is the favored outcome in these approaches, which also assume that language actively constructs (vs. merely conveys) meaning and that it is more valuable to discover representational meaning than to find explanations. At the same time, political economists, socialist feminists, and others with Marxist leanings have cautioned against going too far in rejecting theories and methods of the social sciences to the neglect of real material structures that also—along with ideological factors—contribute to social inequalities, as well as to progressive change (e.g., Barrett, 1999). For development communication, the combined effect of all these trends has been to encourage the acceptance of multiple meanings, symbolic rationality (or irrationality), cultural specificity, change through human agency, communicative action and structuration, deconstruction of dominant ideology of power, and the strengthening of critical consciousness among the people in a community (Jacobson & Kolluri, 1999; Servaes, 1999; Tehranian, 1994).

In general, the intellectual ferment in the humanities and social sciences (with ethical, practical, and philosophical implications) has increasingly favored participatory approaches in development communication, as appropriate for each unique context. Some of the assumptions that undergird the ferment include the following:

1. The scientific method and the knowledge that it has generated are value laden reflecting the economic-political-cultural contexts involved. In general, there is a suspicion of logocentric views. One major area of criticism relates to notions of objectivity and causality.

2. As all knowledge systems and the scientific method are value biased, the accumulation of "objective" knowledge by such methods is a futile exercise. Universally valid explanations are nothing more than probabilistic explanations that have finite range and scope limitations (Jacobson, 1993).

3. Given the oppression of large groups of people—women; the poor; ethnic, racial, and linguistic minorities; refugees; and other marginalized people—ethical and practical concerns should take precedence in social science over principles of objectivity and detachment.

4. Therefore, the goal of research should be the liberation of the oppressed rather than the generation of objective generalizations (Servaes & Arnst, 1999) or the search for the ultimate truth, which is only a mirage.

5. Research, then, should be problem solving, "involved, relevant and activist, not afraid to tackle problems, take positions, or intercede on behalf of certain interests and intrude on the state of nature" (Rosenau, 1992, p. 173).

The basic premise guiding theory and practice in development communication (as articulated in the modernization paradigm) has been the notion that human societies are just and fair in their distribution of resources to individuals and groups within them and that all people, with some effort and help, can achieve the benefits that societies have to offer. Thus, as articulated in the dominant paradigm of development, if an individual or group does not possess "desirable" attitudes, opinions, behaviors, or other attributes, or does not participate effectively in a society's affairs, it is the individual who is deficient and thus needs to be taught skills and provided help. The earlier development communication models have accepted such a victim blame hypothesis. However, large sections of the population in the Third World continue to be impoverished and lack access to necessities that would make a qualitative improvement in their lives. The reality of the social and political situation in most developing countries is such that the urban and rural poor, women, and other people at the grassroots are entrapped in a dependency situation in highly stratified and unequal social and economic structures.

It is usually futile and may be unethical for communications and human service professionals to help solve minor and/or immediate problems while ignoring the systemic barriers erected by societies that permit or perpetuate inequalities among citizens. Certainly, sustainable change is not possible unless crucial problems in human societies such as the lack of economic and social power among individuals at the grassroots are addressed. More than 25 years ago, Latin American communication scholars such as Beltran (1976) and Díaz Bordenave (1976), among others, observed the oppressive social, political, and economic structures that exist in developing countries and that constitute barriers to progressive social change. Yet most of the models and strategies that followed have failed to address directly these constraints. Individuals are impoverished or sick or often are slow to adopt useful practices, not because they lack knowledge or reason, but because they do not have access to appropriate or sustainable opportunities to improve their lives. This is an issue of power. Unless scholars and practitioners are willing to recognize this and act on it, our work will be either ineffective or superficial, functioning as temporary band-aids for far larger problems. If development support communication (DSC) is to continue to play an effective role in social change processes, researchers and practitioners must address fundamental problems of unequal power relations.

The choice, then, for development communicators is to increasingly use the empowering theories and models discussed in this chapter and to devise even more appropriate communication models and analytical tools that can address and overcome these systemic barriers.

REFERENCES

Alvares, C. (1992). Science. In W. Sachs (Ed.), *Development dictionary* (pp. 219-232). London: Zed.

Ascroft, J., & Masilela, S. (1989, February). *From top-down to co-equal communication.* Paper presented at the seminar Participation: A Key Concept in Communication for Change and Development, Pune, India.

Barrett, M. (1999). *Imagination in theory: Essays on writing and culture.* Cambridge, UK: Polity.

Beltran, L. R. S. (1976). Alien premises, objects, and methods in Latin American communication research. In E. M. Rogers (Ed.), *Communication and development: Critical perspectives* (pp. 15-42). Beverly Hills, CA: Sage.

Blumer, J., & Katz, E. (1974). *The uses of mass communication: Current perspectives on gratifications research.* Beverly Hills, CA: Sage.

Braidotti, R., Charkiewicz, E., Hausler, S., & Wieringa, S. (1994). *Women, the environment and sustainable development.* London: Zed.

Cornell Empowerment Group. (1989). Empowerment and family support. *Networking Bulletin, 1*(2), 1-23.

Crush, J. (1995). Introduction: Imagining development. In J. Crush (Ed.), *Power of development* (pp. 1-23). London: Routledge.

Díaz Bordenave, J. (1976). Communication of agricultural innovations in Latin America: The need for new models. In E. M. Rogers (Ed.), *Communication and development: Critical perspectives* (pp. 43-62). Beverly Hills, CA: Sage.

Díaz Bordenave, J. (1989, February). *Participative communication as a part of the building of a participative society.* Paper presented at the seminar Participation: A Key Concept in Communication for Change and Development, Pune, India.

Escobar, A. (1995). *Encountering development: The making and unmaking of the Third World.* Princeton, NJ: Princeton University Press.

Fair, J. E., & Shah, H. (1997). Continuities and discontinuities in communication and development research since 1958. *Journal of International Communication, 46*(2), 3-23.

Fawcett, S. B., Paine-Andrews, A., Francisco, V. T., Schultz, J. A., Richter, K. P., Lewis, R. K., Williams, E. L., Harris, K. J., Berkley, J. Y., Fisher, J. L., & Lopez, C. M. (1995). Using empowerment theory in collaborative partnerships for community health and development. *American Journal of Community Psychology, 23*(5), 677-697.

Fjes, F. (1976). *Communications and development.* Unpublished paper, University of Illinois, Urbana-Champaign, College of Communications.

Foucault, M. (1980). *Power/knowledge.* New York: Pantheon.

Frank, A. G. (1969). *Latin America: Underdevelopment or revolution.* New York: Monthly Review Press.

Freire, P. (1970). *Pedagogy of the oppressed.* New York: Seabury.

Friesen, E. (1999). Exploring the links between structuration theory and participatory action research. In T. Jacobson & J. Servaes (Eds.), *Theoretical approaches to participatory communication* (pp. 281-308). Cresskill, NJ: Hampton.

Glander, T. (2000). *Origins of mass communications research during the American Cold War.* Mahwah, NJ: Lawrence Erlbaum.

Hagen, E. E. (1962). *On the theory of social change.* Homewood, IL: Dorsey.

Hewitt, K. (1995). Sustainable disasters? In J. Crush (Ed.), *Power of development* (pp. 115-128). London: Routledge.

Hovland, C. I., Lumsdaine, A. A., & Sheffield, F. D. (1949). *Experiments in mass communication.* New York: John Wiley.

Inkeles, A. (1966). The modernization of man. In M. Weiner (Ed.), *Modernization: The dynamics of growth* (pp. 138-150). New York: Basic Books.

Inkeles, A., & Smith, D. H. (1974). *Becoming modern: Individual change in six developing countries.* Cambridge, MA: Harvard University Press.

Jacobson, T. L. (1993). A pragmatist account of participatory communication research for national development. *Communication Theory, 3*(3), 214-230.

Jacobson, T. L., & Kolluri, S. (1999). Participatory communication as communicative action. In T. Jacobson & J. Servaes (Eds.), *Theoretical approaches to participatory communication* (pp. 265-280). Cresskill, NJ: Hampton.

Kaye, G. (1990). A community organizer's perspective on citizen participation research and the researcher-practitioner partnership. *American Journal of Community Psychology, 18*(1), 151-157.

Kothari, R. (1984). Communications for alternative development: Towards a paradigm. *Development Dialogue,* pp. 1-2.

Kotler, P. (1984). Social marketing of health behavior. In L. W. Frederiksen, L. J. Solomon, & K. A. Brehony (Eds.), *Marketing health behavior* (pp. 23-39). New York: Plenum.

Latouche, S. (1992). Standard of living. In W. Sachs (Ed.), *Development dictionary* (pp. 250-263). London: Zed.

Lerner, D. (1958). *The passing of traditional society: Modernizing the Middle East.* Glencoe, IL: Free Press.

Lowery, S., & DeFleur, M. L. (1995). *Milestones in mass communication research* (3rd ed.). New York: Longman.

McClelland, D. C. (1967). *The achieving society.* New York: Free Press.

Melkote, S., & Steeves, H. L. (2001). *Communication for development in the Third World: Theory and practice for empowerment* (2nd ed.). New Delhi: Sage.

Mitchell, T. (1995). The object of development. In J. Crush (Ed.), *Power of development* (pp. 129-157). London: Routledge.

Mody, B. (2000). The contexts of power and the power of the media. In K. Wilkins (Ed.), *Redeveloping communication for social change* (pp. 185-196). New York: Rowman & Littlefield.

Palda, K. S. (1966). The hypothesis of a hierarchy of effects: A partial evaluation. *Journal of Marketing Research, 3,* 13-24.

Parsons, T. (1964). Evolutionary universals in society. *American Sociological Review, 29*(3), 339-357.

Piotrow, P. T., Kincaid, D. L., Rimon, J. G., II, & Rinehart, W. (1997). *Health communication: Lessons from family planning and reproductive health.* Westport, CT: Praeger.

Prochaska, J. O., DiClemente, C. C., & Norcross, J. C. (1992). In search of how people change: Applications to addictive behaviors. *American Psychologist, 47*(9), 1102-1114.

Rahman, M. A. (1991). The theoretical standpoint of PAR. In O. Fals-Borda & M. A. Rahman (Eds.), *Action and knowledge: Breaking the monopoly with participatory action research* (pp. 13-23). New York: Apex.

Rappaport, J. (1987). Terms of empowerment/exemplars of prevention: Toward a theory for community psychology. *American Journal of Community Psychology, 15*(2), 121-144.

Rifkin, S. B. (1996). Paradigms lost: Toward a new understanding of community participation in health programmes. *Acta Tropica, 61,* 79-92.

Rogers, E. M. (1962). *Diffusion of innovations.* New York: Free Press.

Rogers, E. M. (1969). *Modernization among peasants.* New York: Holt, Rinehart & Winston.

Rogers, E. M. (1973). *Communication strategies for family planning.* New York: Free Press.

Rogers, E. M. (1995). *Diffusion of innovations* (4th ed.). New York: Free Press.

Rogers, E. M. (with Shoemaker, F. F.) (1971). *Communication of innovations: A cross-cultural approach.* New York: Free Press.

Rosenau, P. V. (1992). *Post-modernism and the social sciences.* Princeton, NJ: Princeton University Press.

Rowlands, J. (1998). *Questioning empowerment, working with women in Honduras.* London: Oxfam.

Schramm, W. L. (1964). *Mass media and national development: The role of information in the developing countries.* Stanford, CA: Stanford University Press.

Servaes, J. (1999). *Communication for development: One world, multiple cultures.* Cresskill, NJ: Hampton.

Servaes, J., & Arnst, R. (1999). Principles of participatory communication research: Its strengths (!) and weaknesses (?). In T. Jacobson & J. Servaes (Eds.), *Theoretical approaches to participatory communication* (pp. 107-130). Cresskill, NJ: Hampton.

Shaw, D. L., & McCombs, M. E. (1974). *The emergence of American political issues: The agenda-setting function of the press.* St. Paul, MN: West.

Simpson, C. (1994). *Science of coercion: Communication research and psychological warfare 1945-1960.* New York: Oxford University Press.

Singhal, A., & Rogers, E. M. (1999). *Entertainment-education: A communication strategy for social change.* Mahwah, NJ: Lawrence Erlbaum.

Speer, P. W., & Hughey, J. (1995). Community organizing: An ecological route to empowerment and power. *American Journal of Community Psychology, 23*(5), 729-748.

Tehranian, M. (1994). Communication and development. In D. Crowley & D. Mitchell (Eds.), *Communication theory today* (pp. 274-306). Stanford, CA: Stanford University Press.

White, K. (1999). The importance of sensitivity to culture in development work. In T. Jacobson & J. Servaes (Eds.), *Theoretical approaches to participatory communication* (pp. 17-50). Cresskill, NJ: Hampton.

White, S. A. (1994). Introduction: The concept of participation. In S. A. White, K. S. Nair, & J. Ascroft (Eds.), *Participatory communication: Working for change and development* (pp. 15-32). New Delhi: Sage.

Wilkins, K. G. (1999). Development discourse on gender and communication in strategies for social change. *Journal of Communication, 49*(1), 46-68.

9

State, Development, and Communication

SILVIO WAISBORD
Rutgers University

The state remains one of the most elusive concepts in the social sciences (Held, 1989; Hoffman, 1995; Offe, 1996; Smith, 1986). In the past few decades, renewed intellectual interest in the subject has not put this matter to rest, but rather has revealed the persistent difficulty in reaching even a minimal, widely accepted definition. Normative and theoretical differences exclude the possibility of reaching a common definition. Continuous interest in the state has not helped to dissipate the existing confusion. Recent studies on the state and globalization have muddled the definition waters even further. Arguments about globalization as responsible for the withering of the state are far from agreeing on what becomes eroded and what remains, precisely because of the different conceptions of the state.

Despite the considerable attention it still attracts from diverse academic quarters, little is agreed on beyond the fact that the state is a political unit with rule-making powers existing within geographical boundaries. What is unique about the state? What is characteristic of certain forms of state? What elements are essential for a state to be a state? How successful does a particular state need to be for it to be called a state? These are some of the complicated questions that still lack single answers.

This chapter reviews the place of the state in studies of communication and development. Once the darling of development projects, the state has fallen from grace in recent decades. The state was conceived as the agent of socioeconomic change in the Third World. With the ascendancy of free-market princi-

AUTHOR'S NOTE: I am grateful to peer reviewers Robert Huesca and Karin Wilkins for their valuable comments and suggestions. Thanks to Bella Mody for superb guidance and direction.

ples under the influence of the Washington consensus coupled with the checkered (if not dismal) record of state-centered experiences in the Third World (see Scott, 1998), however, the idea that the state should have important functions in programs for development has lost much of its past luster. Whereas during the postwar years, Keynesian and socialist programs saw the "developmental" state as the best solution to lift Third World countries out of underdevelopment, today the dominant perspective is, if not outright anti-statist, definitely suspicious of the state. Kohli and Shue's (1994) conclusion that Third World states have been dominant in the control of resources and decision but not very effective in promoting change represents a sentiment shared among lending institutions, policymakers, and academics. Much of the recent development theory and programs have moved toward a more grassroots approach that puts nongovernmental organizations and civic associations at the center of current initiatives. Also, a host of institutions have supported development programs inspired in free-market thinking. This shift toward a "scale-down," "small is beautiful" approach has been responsible for diminishing interest in the state as an analytical category and as a central actor in development programs.

In the first section of this chapter, I argue that the state remained a blindspot in the modernization literature in the 1950s and 1960s. In subsequent studies, the state is present, but has rarely been at the forefront of the analysis. The articulation of state and communication appears in the literature in regards to three central functions of states: sovereignty, rule making, and citizenship. None of the major theoretical approaches in the field of communication and development, however, has placed the state at the center of the analysis. This is the subject of the second section. My argument is that although the role of the state has diminished in studies and in development

initiatives, the state remains important both in terms of analytical relevance and programs. Analytically, states are still able to exert a significant impact on communication issues notwithstanding the impact of globalization. Positions that brush aside the significance of the state amid globalizing dynamics need to be reevaluated by considering the strengths and weaknesses of contemporary states. States also remain important for development initiatives. Despite anti-statism in recent development thinking, program planners and officials actually still work closely with governments. Government and nongovernment agencies may think globally and promote to act locally, but between the global and the local, states continue to be important units in the design and application of development programs.

MODERNIZATION AND THE STATE

Although the postwar development literature in the social sciences paid particular attention to the state, it is remarkable that the founding writings in the field of development communication practically ignored it. It could be argued that the state absorbed the attention of political scientists and sociologists of development for obvious disciplinary reasons. Classic texts in both disciplines conceived the state as a primary unit of analysis. There were also empirical reasons why the state was at the center of political and sociological studies of development. In the postwar years, Western scholars were especially intrigued by the political turbulence in non-Western countries and sought to understand its causes and prospects. The maintenance of political order in the Third World was a topic that squarely fit within political science and sociology. A study of political order required an understanding of the characteristics of the state and the prospects of state formation in those regions of the world. These concerns were also prominent in the Cold War agenda of Western policymakers and clearly influenced the research agenda of area studies in the social sciences. The rise of nationalistic elites in the postcolonial Third World combined with the popularity of state-centered development models also accounted for why the state occupied a central position in both academic and policy analyses.

What is remarkable is that the subject of state and political order did not fall outside the theoretical premises and interests of communication scholars. Communication was not an intellectual enterprise clearly separated from political science and sociology. Early communication studies straddled both politics and sociology. Within both disciplines, communication shared theoretical frameworks and research questions (Peters, 1999). The study of development communication was no different. The same conceptual frameworks informed the interests of communication scholars, particularly among those who founded the field of development communication. The first generation of "development communication" scholars such as Daniel Lerner and Wilbur Schramm shared the conceptual premises of the modernization paradigm with political scientists and sociologists of development. They subscribed to the same theoretical framework. They were also intrigued and perplexed by the question of underdevelopment. They were interested in answering the same question, namely, "Under which conditions could underdeveloped countries become more like Western countries?"

What is striking is that the state looms in their writings but it was not a focal point. Consider Daniel Lerner's *The Passing of Traditional Society* (1958), a book that defined the boundaries of the debate in international communication for decades to come. The state is omnipresent in his study as well as in his case

studies, but it is never closely examined from a communication perspective. Lerner's well-known argument is that modernization requires psychological changes and that the media can serve as an engine for this transformation. Through the media's capacity to disseminate modern beliefs, changes in individual attitudes and behavior are possible. In this way, Third World societies could "become modern," to paraphrase the title of Alex Inkeles and David Smith's (1974) book, another major study in the modernization tradition. Yet Lerner's premises and research questions make the state invisible in his analysis. He fails to put the state toward the center of his analysis, largely because of the underlying epistemological premises. Besides actual data, Lerner also carried the premises of psychological warfare research into his work in communication and development (see Samarajiwa, 1987), namely, making the individual, rather than collective actors, the unit of analysis. In contrast to society-centered approaches taken by political scientists and sociologists who studied postwar development at the same time, Lerner offers a picture of societies as the aggregation of individuals and their characteristics. No wonder, then, that given the premises, Lerner proposes psychological and cultural changes (rather than political) to overcome underdevelopment. It is not that Lerner is completely oblivious to politics; in fact, he spends considerable attention dissecting the agitated politics in the Middle East during the postwar years. He is not interested in making a political argument. By making psychology the variable that explains present conditions and the factor capable of lifting societies out of underdevelopment, Lerner minimizes the role of politics. Modern politics are implicitly understood as a by-product of individual characteristics. Politics do not explain why some countries are "traditional" and others are "modern." Nor do politics play any role in making possible "the passing" from one society to the next. When politics are irrelevant to understanding the causes of underdevelopment, it is not surprising that the state as a political institution is ignored.

What is even more remarkable is that all of the regimes that Lerner examined in his six-country sample subscribed to the state-led modernization programs so in vogue in the developing world in the postwar period. Even within the theoretical boundaries of his analysis, the state arguably performed an important role in making "modernization" possible. For example, Lerner's mention that Ataturk's modernizing ambitions were expanding access to media in Turkey indicates the relevance of the state in the dissemination of information. By aspiring to put radios within the reach of the population, Lerner argues, Ataturk's goal was to build political legitimacy rather than to expand worldviews, and ultimately, he argues, about making citizens "psychologically mobile." Yet Ataturk was not alone in envisioning the mass media as agents of legitimization in the building of a modern state. Egypt's Nasser and numerous other leaders of the time attest to the prominence of state-led models in the use of the mass media in the developing world.

States had a crucial role in the planning and implementation of development programs carried out in the 1950s and 1960s under the supervision and support of international agencies. Improvements in transportation, sanitation, health, and energy, which profoundly changed Third World societies, featured governments that somewhat crystallized then in vogue ideals about welfare states. The 1950s, unlike the 1990s, were a time of contagious optimism globally about the ability and appropriateness of the state to carry out a number of tasks. Lerner identifies the weighty presence of the state in the societies he discusses, but he does not take the next analytical step. His analysis could have presented a more detailed account of the role of the state in development communication. One of the consequences of this absence is that he skirts the question of the role that states play in the introduction of media technologies. Lerner focuses his analysis on why the media can teach modernity rather than with the fact that many Third World governments introduced media technologies to unify nations, to create political consensus, and to drum up support (Singhal & Sthapitanonda, 1996). Certainly, the media could have had, from his view, unintended consequences by exposing populations to "modern" cultures and attitudes, but this does not neglect that, particularly autocratic states, had other goals in mind for the media.

By focusing solely on the media as both the generator of and requirement for a modern society, Lerner fails to address the issue that politics, not development, motivated the engagement of the media in the developing world. Contrary to the conclusions he draws, the cases he examines suggest that the media were conceived of as agencies for political domination and acted as tribunes for political confrontation in the fractious politics of the Middle East. More than obvious instruments of modernization, the media seem, in Lerner's account, central institutions in the process of state building and political struggle in the postwar years. Public communications, to use Lerner's terminology, were, ostensibly, channels for a vast array of warring interests in the prolonged construction of modern states.

It is notable that the question of power and media in the Middle East underlies all cases but it is not at the forefront, precisely because Lerner's interest lay elsewhere. There is much value to the criticism made by dependency scholars that modernization theorists refused to consider power, and specifically power inequalities in the global scene, in understanding communication issues in Third World countries. Reading Lerner, however, one is impressed by his interest in internal political developments. Moreover, he correctly identifies new forms of political domination that the media make possible. A number of issues that are at the core of the state are present in Lerner's analysis: the participation of the military in the process of state building after colonialism, the difficulty of cobbling together unified nations out of a mosaic of languages and religions, the emergence of nationalism after the collapse of European empires in the region, the role of the mass media in the rise of charismatic leaderships, and the formation of revolutionary states in newly independent societies. Lerner does recognize these issues but does so almost in passing, as if he needs to acknowledge them in order to arrive at his major argument about the connection between media and modernization.

His detailed portrayal of political instability in the Middle East coexists with a simplistic and optimistic diagnosis according to which media development will bring about fundamental changes. Nowhere does he explain his argument that media consumption and dramatic changes in attitudes can almost magically solve the deep-seated problems that he identifies in the Middle East. He does not address head-on whether those countries can effectively construct nation-states, although he does provide sufficient evidence of the difficulties they would encounter achieving this. The reason for this is that Lerner is concerned with modernization rather than with power, and with cultural transition from traditional to modern societies instead of how power functions in these societies. For this reason, he fails to discuss the articulation of states and communications in the developing world.

More than his theoretical premises, what prevents Lerner from seeing the state is his assumption that psychology and culture are the prime movers, the Archimedian points of development. In his view, once psychological traits and cultures change, the basis of traditional societies collapses. Media consumption

brings about those fundamental changes that amount to the coming of a modern society. This shortsightedness could not be attributed to the fact that Lerner wears modernization blinders or to his focus on individual psychology, but to the lack of an examination of the linkages between communication and power.

Lerner and Schramm's *Communication and Change in the Developing Countries* (1967), in contrast, hints at some important questions related to state and communication. Among these they discuss the relevance of communication policy in developing countries and the role of communication in nation building, particularly as used by authoritarian regimes in the Third World.[1] In later writings, Lerner seems more sensitive to the role of states in development communication. In examining the situation of development communication in Asia, he notes that government expenditures are central to development and that "quasi Marxist regimes often are seen as more damaging to develop communication than military regimes" (Lerner, 1972, p. 15). But the analysis stops short of providing an in-depth examination of such differences. A deeper examination of these issues could have been useful for fleshing out the differences among Third World states in adopting and implementing media development policies. The authors' overriding concern, however, remains how the media can produce empathy and spread modern attitudes (see Schramm & Lerner, 1976).

Although modernization theorists have been criticized for putting emphasis on the nation-state as the unit of analysis, they did not take the state seriously enough. Scholars have charged them with prioritizing the nation-state at the expense of ignoring larger global dynamics in understanding the role of communications in development (Golding, 1974; Halloran, 1981; Mowlana, 1997). Despite this, they failed to closely examine the nation-state. Even in subsequent studies within the modernization paradigm, such as "diffusion of innovations" research as well as education-entertainment and health promotion projects, the state is missing. The reason for this absence is that these studies assume that the problems of development are mainly informational (rather than political) problems. There is no room for considering the state, or politics more broadly, because the premise is that the obstacles to development are individual attitudes and cultures. Why should the state be examined if the premise is that a lack of information underlies social problems? Why should the state be analytically relevant if solutions are assumed to consist of persuasion strategies?

In summary, the state received scarce attention from the "dominant paradigm" in development communication. The fact that the work of scholars in the modernization tradition has been mainly rooted in psychosocial premises accounts for why the state was largely absent. The study of the state required a concern with the question of power and a sensitivity to political-institutional issues. It was only with the emergence of a critical perspective in development communication in the 1960s that the state became more important as an analytical preoccupation.

ALTERNATIVE AND CRITICAL PERSPECTIVES

By critical perspectives in development communication, I refer to dependency and alternative/participatory theories. Although both coincided in criticizing the modernization paradigm on several points, they differed in many aspects that are important to understanding how they approached the state. The dependency model drew from Marxist and structuralist theories, and it offered a macro, political-economic approach to the study of

development communication. The alternative paradigm proposed a bottom-up approach that emphasized the development of critical consciousness and collective mobilization at the local level. The work of Paulo Freire (1970) was particularly influential. Based on his work in northeastern Brazil in the 1960s, Freire challenged dominant conceptions of development communication, particularly as applied to literacy training. He argued that development programs had failed to educate small farmers because they were interested in persuading them about the benefits of adopting certain innovations. Development programs tried to domesticate foreign concepts, to feed information, to force local populations to accept Western ideas and practices without asking how such practices fit existing cultures. The underlying premise of such programs was an authoritarian conception of communication that stood against the essence of communication understood as community interaction and education. Freire offered the concept of liberating education that conceived communication as dialogue and participation. The goal of communication should be *conscientization*, which Freire defined as free dialogue that prioritized cultural identity, trust, and commitment. His approach has been called "dialogical pedagogy," which defined equity in distribution and active grassroots participation as central principles. Communication should provide a sense of ownership to participants through sharing and reconstructing experiences.

Certainly, shades of Marxist thinking are present among different strands of the alternative paradigm. In fact, radical movements in the 1960s and 1970s gave original impetus to much of the thinking and action strategies that became identified with the alternative paradigm. In contrast to dependency theories, the alternative paradigm put the emphasis on politics and culture (rather than economics), on bottom-up (rather than top-down) development initiatives, and on diverse strategies that a myriad of social actors need to put into practice to redress conditions of inequality.

These theoretical differences are important to understand why the dependency and alternative paradigms have examined different dimensions of the state. Whereas dependency analysts focused on the state as the guarantor of capitalist relations of development/underdevelopment and, alternately, as the engine for development in Third World countries, the alternative paradigm shifted attention to grassroots, community-level issues. Simultaneously, this shift in development thinking from state-led models to strategies driven by private business and nongovernmental organizations also accounts for the relative absence of the state in current analyses about development communication.

There is a notable irony in the theoretical progression in the field of development communication: Modernization theories, which along the lines of then prevalent approaches in international relations understood the world as a state-centric system, paid little attention to the state. In contrast, critical theories, which adopted a globalist perspective, showed more interest in the state. For example, Herbert Schiller (1976) argued that "national states exist and impinge on the 'pure' workings of the world system" (p. 5). Modernization theorists could never have given a similar assessment not only because of lack of attention to global dynamics, but also because they failed to pay attention to the state.

HOW TO THINK ABOUT THE STATE IN DEVELOPMENT COMMUNICATION

To analyze how critical theorists have examined the state, it is necessary to keep in mind that the state is multidimensional. It would be impossible within the limits of this chapter to do justice to the enormous literature on the many dimensions that pertain to the state (Jessop, 1990; Mann, 1990). Much has been written on what is characteristic of the state, regardless of its incarnations across history and geography. For the purposes of this chapter, however, it will suffice to mention the main dimensions of the state that have been identified in the literature: violence, territory, sovereignty, constitutionality (rule making), impersonal power, bureaucracy, legitimacy, citizenship, and taxation (Pierson, 1996). The state has appeared in studies that examine communication/media processes in relation to three issues that are at the core of the state: sovereignty, rule making, and citizenship.

Sovereignty

As with the term *the state* itself, *sovereignty* is also a problematic and ambiguous concept. Sovereignty is premised on two notions/dimensions: Externally, states are central actors in the global scene, and internally, states are the supreme, uncontested authorities within a given spatial jurisdiction. International laws grant states the right to have exclusive power within their territories, establish the principle of noninterference, and give states equal participation in global decision making. More specifically, sovereignty can also refer to the capacity of states to rule without intrusion within a certain territory in regard to political, military, economic, legal, and communication affairs. Sovereignty also assumes the undivided and absolute power of states in the geographical space that they claim to rule. Based on sovereignty rights, states are the legitimate powers to control politics, economics, and culture within defined boundaries.

Although sovereignty is commonly associated with a physical, spatial dimension, the intangible spaces of communication are part of claims to sovereignty as well. Communication sovereignty, then, refers to the claim of states to exercise authority over the flow of ideas, information, and cultures inside their territories. In this sense, states have been endowed with the mission of monitoring and securing communication sovereignty. The ability of the state to exercise this authority is based on the rights of the people to self-determination. Ideally, the state achieves this authority through a variety of means: control of media systems, censorship of media content, restrictions on the entrance of foreign interests, legislation in regard to linguistic and religious matters, domestic intelligence and propaganda, and the making and remaking of national cultures.

The actual success of states to effectively maintain sovereignty, however, should not be confused with the *claim* of modern states to exercise sovereignty. Sovereignty assumes that other states and organizations do not undermine a state's ability to make autonomous decisions regarding political, economic, military, and communication matters. In reality, however, state interdependency has flied in the face of the legal definition of sovereignty. States have historically been linked in multiple ways, making sovereignty a principle rather than a concrete reality. Much of the recent discussion about globalization has focused on the idea that a number of recent developments have contributed to the inexorable erosion of state sovereignty (Camilleri & Falk, 1992; Viotti & Kauppi, 1993). Stateless forces continue to challenge state sovereignty: Cross-border flows of capital and information, the global capacity of military superpowers, and international agreements and treaties are some of the recent developments that have rendered sovereignty difficult or, in some cases, virtually impossible. The demise of national economies at the expense of global capital and free-market principles, the subjection of military forces to global designs, and the collapse of barriers to information trade worldwide have put sovereignty in history's dustbin. Some authors have even suggested the end of the nation-state (Ohmae, 1995).

In light of these developments, some authors prefer to talk about a limited notion of sovereignty given a growing number of factors (e.g., international agreements and laws) that restrict the capacity of states to rule autonomously. Not only do a considerable number of states in developing countries lack the power to enforce sovereignty rights in certain arenas (from ecological to financial), but they are at the same time subject to the designs and intervention of the international community.

Dependency theorists have emphatically argued that there is a gap between the ideal and the reality of sovereignty. For them, the difficulties that states have historically experienced in securing hermetically closed communication and information borders suggested that sovereignty was a claim more than an actual achievement. Cees Hamelink (1993) writes, "The concern about the integrity of national sovereignty emerged with the aggressive proliferation of Western technology and cultural products that began in the 1950s and accelerated throughout the 1960s" (p. 371). As the argument goes, the spread of information technologies coupled with laissez-faire media policies has compromised information sovereignty. The ideology of free flow of information championed by the U.S. government is conducive to the weakening of information sovereignty worldwide. For its critics, this ideology serves to justify U.S. global information interests that are antithetical to the needs and goals of sovereign states.

This dynamic has been particularly evident in the Third World. The widespread dissemination of Western information in developing countries—in the form of advertising, entertainment, and news—was evidence that information sovereignty was impossible. The notions of "media/cultural imperialism" (Boyd-Barrett, 1977) and "cultural synchronization" (Hamelink, 1983) described the crumbling of information sovereignty due to Western domination in communication and media. It was not just a matter of the West "influencing" other cultures but also of it imposing its values on other societies (Schiller, 1976). This situation also attests to the domination of transnational corporations over national communication sovereignty. The plight of information sovereignty is not just a matter of Western cultures dominating global communication environments but also one of private interests eclipsing states in the production and distribution of information. These types of concerns about information sovereignty were prominent in the New World Information and Communication Order debates in which critics of U.S. policies adamantly defended the position of noninterference as the backbone of sovereignty (Vincent, Nordenstreng, & Traber, 1999).

The development of satellite technologies backed by U.S.-promoted "open skies" policies further complicated the prospects for information sovereignty (Hudson, 1990). Western control of remote sensing satellites contradicted the principle of sovereignty rights. In the 1970s, this situation made Third World political elites anxious about foreign control of vital economic resources and security secrets, and it fueled national satellite projects. Many countries under military regimes at that time were plunged in a race to develop home-grown satellite technologies. Their goals were not only ostensibly military but also educational and directed at nation building. In this sense, satellite technologies were viewed as useful instruments for national

and geographical integration and for propagandistic goals (Mody, 1987).

In the 1980s, nonmilitary uses of satellites further undermined the ability of states to maintain information sovereignty. As a result, a vast number of businesses and institutions gained control of information directly related to states' functions. Western governments and businesses increasingly gained access to information about other states' economies, finances, defense, and resources (Liftin, 1999). In this way, satellite technologies contributed to the global commercialization of the airwaves and promoted the penetration of Western ideas into the sovereign communicative space of Third World countries.

Although plenty of evidence can be found in support for this argument, one can question to what extent the concept of sovereignty has ever been truly attainable. As Robert Holton (1998) points out, there has been no golden age of sovereignty "when states possessed some kind of absolute control over their territory and the movement of resources, people, and cultural influences across their borders" (p. 83). Even before globalization gained momentum in the post-Cold War years, sovereignty was a principle, rather than a reality, underlying global relations. More than having ushered in a completely new situation, globalization has exacerbated the impossibility of total sovereignty. One could argue that communication sovereignty has never been possible, even in the West. For cultural imperialism theorists, the relations of global domination exclude the possibility that communication sovereignty is possible in the South because Western powers undercut the ability of Third World states to exercise sovereignty. The problem with this perspective, however, is that it assumes a static model of cultural purity that neglects the fluid, open-ended nature of the process of cultural formation. Arguably, multiple influences, not solely the prowess of

Western media conglomerates, shape communicative spaces contained within the political
boundaries of any state. Cultural histories
show that contacts between states and societies have been continuous through history
both in the North and in the South. This intangible nature of communication and culture
has made it difficult to control where and
when they flow.

It is hard to minimize the overwhelming
influence of Western media in the communica-
tion/information space of developing countries and the unequal relations in the traffic of
information/cultural goods between the core
and the periphery. But has communication
sovereignty ever been possible? This is not an
issue unique to the Third World, nor is it a
problem that began when communication
technologies made cross-border transmissions
of information possible. The flimsy foundation for information sovereignty, instead,
seems characteristic of the relation between
state and culture/information. Even authoritarian regimes that were determined to control information flows and patrol cultural
borders had a mixed record when it came
to exercising communication sovereignty.
Whereas maintaining economic sovereignty
seems chimerical amid today's globalized
financial and trade systems, and preserving
political sovereignty seems all but impossible
as global laws and social movements prevail
over the principle of noninterference and self-
determination, keeping airtight communication boundaries seems an equally unattainable
goal. This even more so considering that
despite globalization, the traffic of goods and
people may be stopped at border checkpoints;
stopping information flows, however, presents a more formidable challenge. As Hirst
and Thompson (1995) write, "States remain
'sovereign,' not in the sense that they are all-
powerful or omnicompetent within their territories, but because they police the borders of

a territory and . . . the state may have less control over ideas, but it remains a controller of
its borders and the movement of people across
them" (pp. 420, 431).

Rule Making

Studies of development communication
have also paid attention to states in terms of
rule making. Rule making refers to the system
of governance, that is, the laws and institutions that uphold a given political order.
Studies about media legislation under different political regimes, and the influence of public and private groups on media and information policy, have tackled this dimension of the
state. In this regard, one of the main issues of
contention has been the role of the state as
both actor in and arena for media policy. In a
globalized context, are states powerful or
weak qua rule makers?

Dependency arguments have posited the
idea that the dynamics of the global media
have eroded the rule-making capacity of the
state. One of the central points in the "media
imperialism" tradition is that Western powers have successfully exported their media
institutions worldwide, and this facilitated
their global expansion (Boyd-Barrett, 1982).
Media legislation around the world reflected
the prominent presence of the West. Domestic
legislation favoring foreign capitalist interests
reproduced relations of dependency (Sussman
& Lent, 1991). Corporate control of information undercut the decision-making capacity of
governments (Herman & McChesney, 1997;
Schiller, 1981).

Globalization studies have taken this point
further, arguing that global dynamics have
completely overridden domestic politics.
States cannot make policy by keeping global
forces at a distance. In the 1980s, the shift
from protectionist and government-regulated

policies to laissez-faire and market policies patently reflects the weakness of states as rule makers. Globalization has eviscerated the power of states, reducing them to mere instruments of policies that support the interests of global capital and the U.S. government. Media legislation worldwide increasingly reflects the steamrolling dynamics of global capital and the loss of state autonomy, with governments adopting market policies in broadcasting and telecommunications worldwide. As a consequence of market reform programs coupled with the intense pressure of global media moguls, states have enacted legislation that favors private interests.

An alternative view suggests that states cannot be discounted as rule-making institutions in communication issues. This view appears in a number of recent studies about media policies that implicitly assume that the state remains a "power center" (Garnham, 1986). Globalization has challenged but not obliterated the state (see Morris & Waisbord, 2001). The risk is to overlook, as Thomas Jacobson (1994) writes, "the power of the State to negotiate in international trade agreements, to establish national economic priorities, to employ force in its own interests, and the effects these uses of power have on local possibilities" (p. 72). This perspective invites us to bring the state to the forefront of the analysis while recognizing the relevance of global dynamics.

States are neither unified actors nor obedient soldiers in the service of global media capital. Against traditionally Marxist accounts of the state underlying dependency analyses, neoinstitutional perspectives suggest a view of states as arenas where different groups vie to shape policy making. States comprise a complex set of institutions crossed by internal contradictions and tensions (Servaes, 1999). If states lack a single logic, can we argue that they diligently follow decisions made in corporate boardrooms? Pressured by various groups (e.g., religious organizations, unions, intellectuals, and domestic businesses), many governments continue to enforce protectionist policies to halt the flood of Western media products. Domestic businesses do not necessarily rally behind globalization policies: Some may support the elimination of restrictions on foreign capital hoping to form alliances with well-heeled foreign partners; others, instead, may prefer to keep regulations in place to fend off larger competitors. The politics of "cultural defense" in countries as diverse as Brazil, Canada, France, Iran, and Korea suggest that not all states have rushed to align themselves with global actors (Grantham, 2000; Mohammadi, 1997). Certainly, protectionist policies have failed to create pristine media landscapes that are free from global influences. Video piracy, the influx of satellite television, and the Internet, among other developments, allow global media content to vault over policy barriers. Some domestic actors whose interests are different from those of global corporations do not submissively surrender to globalization, however. If they wield sufficient power, they are able to influence government media policy making to advance political, economic, and cultural goals.

Global forces are not the only threats to information democracy in developing countries. In addition, privatization and media monopolies, government bureaucracies, and the so-called information state also threaten public access to information (Sreberny-Mohammadi, 1984). Political economists generalize the argument that runaway *conglomerization* is the most formidable adversary to information democracy worldwide. This argument is too general to provide a nuanced understanding of the situation in the Third World. It is hard to dispute that the global forces of commerce undercut democratic efforts. This position, however, has two problems. First, it omits the fact that, particularly in countries with small and impoverished media markets, states have historically wielded more power than markets (see Reeves, 1993). In postcolonial Africa and Asia, one-party states have been enemies of media pluralism and, in the name of national unification, have often shut down critical media organizations (Barnett, 1997). In Latin America, there is a long history of military regimes that have tightly controlled the media and censored any manifestation of dissent (Waisbord, 1995). Globalization does have negative impacts, but it introduces changes with potential contributions to dismantling repressive structures (see Ronning & Kupe, 2000; Sreberny-Mohammadi, 2000). Second, political economists do not offer analytical tools that are sensitive to political changes in capitalist societies. Because they assume that any change within capitalism leaves corporate structures untouched, they conclude that liberal democracies make little difference in redressing information inequalities. The analysis, however, needs to take into consideration the consequences of media policies under different political regimes. The form of the state is not inconsequential. Whether a state is authoritarian or liberal-democratic cannot be dismissed as a superficial difference on the grounds that either state fails to demolish capitalism.

Consider the case of social movements that animated hopes for media democratization in several regions of the world. The energy of civic movements during the transition years in Asia, Eastern Europe, and Latin America was reflected in the optimism of writings about alternative media, a point to which I return in the next section. There is plenty of evidence that the rapid consolidation of business interests allied with pro-market governments shattered early hopes. From a distance, this seems to unequivocally confirm the dynamics of media globalization. A closer analysis shows, however, that other processes have also taken place. In some countries, the elimination of censorship laws, the passing of legislation to protect journalists, the incipient strength of media transparency initiatives, the support for indigenous media production, or the legalization of community radio indicates the possibility that not all is lost for democratic causes amid globalization (see Waisbord, 2000). None of those developments could have been conceivable during authoritarian rule: They directly undermined the intentions of dictators to control information flows with a tight grip. No need to wax romantic about these changes, however. Many civilian governments have shown an inclination to dismiss media democracy as a nagging problem and to resort to a vast array of legal (and violent) instruments to punish critical media.

Because states remain important as rule makers in the face of globalization, they can enforce policies that redress inequality in the access to information or, conversely, that favor concentrated interests. Globalization undercuts the model of the state as media owner and operator, but this does not imply the complete disappearance of states as rule makers. Not all states have reacted identically to globalization pressures: Some have readily caved in to market demands, whereas others have tried to harness global forces without totally dismantling protectionist policies. Globalization sets up structural contexts, but states make choices according to the resolution of internal conflicts and the weight of different domestic actors (Horwitz, 2001).

Finally, domestic politics and states also shape the nature of globalization (Hirst & Thompson, 1996; Palan, 1999). It could be argued that globalizing policies actually require strong states as policymakers that not only adopt legislation advocated by global media industries but also effectively regulate media markets. States fulfill a crucial role in the restructuring of communications markets worldwide. States are the actors that ultimately pass and enforce (or fail to) laws that regulate capital investments and the workings of telecommunication and media industries (Mody, Bauer, & Straubhaar, 1995; Petrazzini, 1995). Regardless of actual goals and accomplishments, the state remains a political authority with power to decide the structure of information and media markets.

Citizenship

Studies of communication and development have also examined the state as a space for citizenship. Participatory theorists have put citizenship at the center of development communication. For them, development is understood fundamentally as participation, and communication refers to activities to achieve that goal. Against the idea that development should consist of transmission of information, as proposed by early modernization scholars, they argue that development requires community participation to improve the quality of life.

Participation is a confusing concept, as authors have noted (Narula & Pearce, 1986; Servaes, Jacobson, & White, 1996). There seems to be agreement among participatory theorists, however, that participation equals development. In their view, development initiatives need to strive for self-reliance and self-management, that is, the ability of communities to take control over decisions that affect their lives. In this sense, communication needs to be understood as dialogue among citizens toward development.

Given these theoretical premises, it is not surprising that participatory approaches offer a critical perspective of the state. The state is seen as distant and remote, a set of institutions dominated by elites in isolation from communities, the incarnation of verticalism and centralism. In other words, the state is the antithesis of development. States represent top-down communication vis-à-vis bottom-up initiatives. States represent the persistence of political hierarchies and the obstacles for development. For participatory theorists, state officials have historically been fearful of political participation and have tried to manipulate citizens through government-controlled institutions. Moreover, many state-centered development experiences have a questionable record in terms of redressing social inequalities and improving general conditions. They were ineffective in propelling social change by ignoring local expectations, needs, and conditions. They had temporary success as long as official presence, supported by international funds, remained. Once funds dried up and state agencies pulled out, such initiatives died out, leaving conditions of underdevelopment untouched as well as negative experiences in communities. In sum, state-centered programs failed to promote sustainable development.

The anti-statist perspective found in participatory approaches also reflects the authoritarian record of most Third World states. The struggle for democracy in the 1980s and 1990s clearly articulated this view, holding the state (and its controlling interests) responsible for poverty and oppression. This represented an important shift in the conceptualization of the state in development communication. Against early views that advocated state intervention in planning and organization of development programs, participatory theorists stress the centrality of popular participation and the need to be sensitive to local experiences (Servaes, 1999). For the latter, true participation means the existence of mechanisms of self-government and empowerment for citizens. At best, the state can do a limited amount of work within strategies of self-sustained development (Narula & Pearce, 1986). Some authors warn, however, that although community participation is desirable, it is naïve to ignore the role of the state (Midgley, 1986).

Against state-centric perspectives of development communication and citizenship, participatory approaches counteroffer a community-centered view. In the same spirit of communitarian positions, they question the legitimacy of the nation-state in claiming to represent diverse political and cultural identities and to provide effective mechanisms for democratic action. Contra state-led projects of citizens' mobilization, which characterized states in developing countries in the 1950s, they propose decentralized, grassroots programs as effective alternatives for participation. Whereas media citizenship referred in the past to passive media exposure and state-led national integration, community media projects are offered as examples of decentralized citizenship. Community video, radio, and television are illustrations of a model of citizenship that is critical of both statist and diffusionist perspectives (Atwood & McAnany, 1986; Huesca & Dervin, 1994; Reyes Matta, 1983). Opposed to a paternalistic model of participation, such projects offer spaces for citizens to express opinions and experiences and become truly involved in the affairs of their communities (Díaz Bordenave, 1994). They also illustrate an important shift: From being limited to passive reception of information, citizenship is understood as the sharing and production of information among community members.

Participatory theorists also criticize the model of state-based citizenship for offering an inadequate view of participation in the contemporary world. They argue that it is too narrow to comprehend and account for problems that exceed the boundaries of states. The environment, human rights, women's issues, armed conflicts, health crises, and the situation of refugees are examples of global problems that go beyond state limits and require global participation. Global social movements challenge traditional conceptions of citizenship grounded in the nation-state (Cohen & Rai, 2000). Nation-states are too big to deal with problems at the community level, and too small to confront global issues. National citizenship, then, is insufficient. The model is also obsolete, they argue, because it belongs to a time when nation-states were central units in the world system. The emergence of global social movements and the prominent role of global institutions and nongovernmental organizations patently attest to the limitations of state-centric citizenship. Such arguments render an accurate picture of important developments in recent decades that question the limits of national citizenship. But despite the relevance of global, post-state citizenship, it is important to keep in mind that political membership continues to be tied to states. Citizenship is still territorialized and grounded in laws that rule over a given political geography. States continue to monopolize citizenship rights, even though international agreements assign individuals with membership rights in a global community.

CONCLUSIONS

This chapter has examined how the literature on development communication has dealt with the state in regard to issues of sovereignty, rule making, and citizenship. Attention to the state has fluctuated according to shifts in the fields of communication and development at large, and in the agenda of international development organizations.

It is not surprising, then, that globalization studies, in emphasizing transnational dynamics, have belittled the contemporary relevance of the state. The reason for this is twofold. The first reason is conceptual: Globalization theorists explicitly criticize and reject a state-centered perspective on the basis that it is inadequate to understand current dynamics that go well beyond the nation-state (Sklair, 1991). If we focus on the state, they warn, we lose perspective of whirlwind global dynamics. The second reason is empirical: For them, the state is passé, moribund, a relic of Modernity. Arjun Appadurai's (1996) statement echoes widespread conclusions in the field of development communication:

> I have come to be convinced that the nation-state, as a complex modern political form, is on its last legs. . . . Nation-states, as units in a complex interactive system, are not very likely to be the long-term arbiters of the relationship between globality and modernity. (p. 19)

In abandoning the economy, politics, and culture to the market, the state has surrendered some of its essential functions. What remains of the modern state are oversized police and military apparatuses in charge of controlling the violence and insurrection that grow out of the poverty and unemployment that the hurricane of globalization leaves in its path (see Bauman, 1998).

States, however, are more than institutions that effectively monopolize (or fail to control) the legitimate means of violence. With the ascent of neoliberalism, the politics of privatization, liberalization, and deregulation of media markets have tilted the balance in favor of markets. It is premature to issue death certificates on the state, however. Yet states have not been sitting idle, waiting for the next global tsunami to sweep everything away. Subject to different pressures, some states have been busy trying to protect media industries, to shut off ideas considered damaging to "national cultures," to suppress internal dissent, to retain policy control over media markets, and to control domestic public opinion. This reality of states is hardly the image of the despondent, elderly institution wasting time away in a rocking chair waiting for the funeral car. Truly, globalization weakens states in

terms of cultural sovereignty, rule makers, and as containers of citizenship. Globalization saturates cultural spaces that states claim as their own, influences media policy making, and opens spaces for new forms of participation and citizenship. Depending on whether the state is the object of affection or hate, the impact of globalization on the state can be deemed positive or negative. Strange bedfellows celebrate and mourn the weakening or the survival of the state. Globalization partisans and postmodernists cheer the passing away of the state; in contrast, cultural nationalists and anti-neoliberal activists lament the dreadful effects of globalization on it.

My intention is neither to pass judgment on the merits of states in development programs nor to recommend adopting a statist orientation at the expense of a global perspective. Critics have offered convincing arguments for why state-centered projects have failed and for why nation-states should not be central units of study à la modernization theory. Rather, my interest is to call attention to the need to maintain a bifocal approach that considers the multifaceted relationship between states and globalization in studies of communication and development. The state is not the force to be reckoned with that it was in the early days of development programs, but it cannot be completely discounted for analytical or ideological reasons. What states do and cannot do, how they articulate domestic and global dynamics, how they shape globalization, and what they are able to achieve are questions that need to be disaggregated. Communication scholars should take cautiously economists' conclusion about the death of national economies in a globalized world or political scientists' assessment that Third World states had limited capacity in accomplishing a number of goals. Such conclusions only partially translate into communication studies. Because the efficacy of the state varies across issues and regions, generalizations about "strong" or "weak" states in regards to communication and development are of little help. Future studies need not only to be sensitive to these differences but also to address specific characteristics of states in different regions of the world. Why states are still politically and culturally salient amid globalizing media and cultural processes is a question that awaits further attention.

NOTE

1. Consider, for example, Karl Deutsch's (1966) landmark *Nationalism and Social Communication* as a successful attempt in the modernization tradition that, although it was not only concerned with developing countries, examined the relations between state and communication. Deutsch tackled the old sociological question, "What ties societies together after massive social changes?" How is unity possible in a world of difference? Whereas classic sociologists such as Durkheim, Marx, and Tonnies were intrigued by these questions in the context of European societies in the aftermath of the French and industrial revolutions, Deutsch was interested in the question of social order in postwar developing countries. His interest in the prospects of achieving order leads him to examine the functioning of power and establishing criteria for how power works. His view of power is state-centric. Effective power is concentrated in a set of effectively functioning structures. This idea resonates with a key tenet of modernization political theory as developed, for example, by political scientists David Easton and Samuel Huntington: the existence of an institutionalized state as a condition for political order. Toward achieving social cohesion, Deutsch writes, "the nation-state, it seems, is still the chief political instrument for getting things done" (p. 4). A modern, developed polity requires nation-states that are respected and obeyed by its subjects.

How do states get things done? It is here where communication systems play a vital role. Communication is central to the maintenance of political order and to the process of nation-state building. Political power needs information, and information is disseminated through communication networks, including mass media, educational institutions, libraries, railroads, and telephones. Only through communication can cultural differences that underlie social divisions be bridged. The lack of common cultural ties makes order, if not difficult, impossible, particularly in the context of developing countries. Against the backdrop of inequality and poverty, Deutsch affirms, the absence of commonness continuously fuels chaos. Besides economic growth, peaceful change and development require political-cultural integration. Because communication barriers keep people separated, communication, thus, needs to be part of the solution. Communication systems make integration possible by exposing populations to the same content. Central tenets of the modernization paradigm are unmistakable in Deutsch's analysis: Communication is seen as a top-down process, communication is equated with media systems, and despite some reservations, media exposure is believed to lead to cultural integration.

REFERENCES

Appadurai, A. (1996). *Modernity at large: Cultural dimensions of globalization*. Minnesota: University of Minneapolis Press.

Atwood, R., & McAnany, E. G. (Eds.). (1986). *Communication and Latin American society*. Madison: University of Wisconsin Press.

Barnett, T. (1997). States of the state and Third World. In P. Golding & P. Harris (Eds.), *Beyond cultural imperialism: Globalization, communication and the new international order* (pp. 25-48). London: Sage.

Bauman, Z. (1998). *Globalization: The human consequences*. New York: Columbia University Press.

Boyd-Barrett, O. (1977). Media imperialism: Towards an international framework for the analysis of media systems. In J. Curran, M. Gurevitch, & J. Woollacott (Eds.), *Mass communication and society* (pp. 116-135). London: Edward Arnold.

Boyd-Barrett, O. (1982). Cultural dependency and the mass media. In M. Gurevitch, T. Bennett, J. Curran, & J. Woollacott (Eds.), *Culture, society and the media* (pp. 174-195). London: Methuen.

Camilleri, J., & Falk, J. (1992). *The end of sovereignty? The politics of a shrinking and fragmenting world.* Aldershot, UK: Edward Elgar.

Cohen, R., & Rai, S. M. (Eds.). (2000). *Global social movements.* London: Athlone.

Deutsch, K. (1966). *Nationalism and social communication.* Cambridge: MIT Press.

Díaz Bordenave, J. (1994). Participative communication as a part of building the participative society. In S. A. White, K. S. Nair, & J. Ascroft (Eds.), *Participatory communication: Working for change and development.* Thousands Oaks, CA: Sage.

Freire, P. (1970). *Pedagogy of the oppressed.* New York: Continuum.

Garnham, N. (1986). *Capitalism and communication.* London: Sage.

Golding, P. (1974). Media role in national development: A critique of a theoretical orthodoxy. *Journal of Communication, 24*(3), 39-53.

Grantham, B. (2000). *Some big bourgeois brothel: Contexts for France's culture wars with Hollywood.* Luton, UK: University of Luton Press.

Halloran, J. (1981). The context of mass communication research. In E. McAnany, J. Schnitman, & N. Janus (Eds.), *Communication and social structure: Critical studies in media research* (pp. 21-57). New York: Praeger.

Hamelink, C. (1983). *Cultural autonomy in global communications: Planning national information policy.* New York: Longman.

Hamelink, C. (1993). Globalism and national sovereignty. In K. Nordenstreng & H. Schiller (Eds.), *Beyond national sovereignty: International communication in the 1990s* (pp. 371-393). Norwood, NJ: Ablex.

Held, D. (1989). *Political theory and the modern state.* Stanford, CA: Stanford University Press.

Herman, E. S., & McChesney, R. (1997). *The global media: The new missionaries of corporate capitalism.* London and Washington, DC: Cassell.

Hirst, P., & Thompson, G. (1995). Globalization and the future of the nation-state. *Economy and Society, 24*(3), 408-442.

Hirst, P., & Thompson, G. (1996). *Globalization in question: The international economy and the possibilities of governance.* Cambridge, UK: Polity.

Hoffman, J. (1995). *Beyond the state: An introductory critique.* Cambridge, UK: Polity.

Holton, R. J. (1998). *Globalization and the nation-state.* Basingstoke, UK: Macmillan.

Horwitz, R. (2001). "Negotiated liberalization": The politics of communication sector reform in South Africa. In N. Morris & S. Waisbord (Eds.), *Media and globalization: Why the state matters.* Lanham, MD: Rowman & Littlefield.

Hudson, H. (1990). *Communication satellites: Their development and impact.* London: Macmillan.

Huesca, R., & Dervin, B. (1994). Theory and practice in Latin American alternative communication research. *Journal of Communication, 44*(4), 53-73.

Inkeles, A., & Smith, D. (1974). *Becoming modern.* Cambridge, MA: Harvard University Press.

Jacobson, T. (1994). Modernization and postmodernization approaches. In S. A. White, K. S. Nair, & J. Ascroft (Eds.), *Participatory communication: Working for change and development* (pp. 60-75). Thousands Oaks, CA: Sage.

Jessop, B. (1990). *State theory: Putting the capitalist state in its place.* University Park: Pennsylvania State University Press.

Kohli, A., & Shue, V. (1994). State power and social forces: On political contention and accommodation in the Third World. In J. Migdal, A. Kohli, & V. Shue (Eds.), *State power and social forces: Domination and transformation in the Third World* (pp. 293-325). Cambridge, UK: Cambridge University Press.

Lerner, D. (1958). *The passing of traditional society: Modernizing the Middle East.* Glencoe, IL: Free Press.

Lerner, D. (1972). *Communication for development administration in Southeast Asia.* Cambridge: MIT Press.

Lerner, D., & Schramm, W. (Eds.). (1967). *Communication and change in the developing countries.* Honolulu, HI: East-West Center.

Liftin, K. (1999). The status of the statistical state: Satellites and the diffusion of epistemic sovereignty. *Global Society, 13*(1), 95-116.

Mann, M. (Ed.). (1990). *The rise and decline of the nation state.* Oxford and Cambridge, UK: Basil Blackwell.

Midgley, J. (Ed.). (1986). *Community participation, social development, and the state.* London: Methuen.

Mody, B. (1987). Contextual analysis of the adoption of a communication technology: The case of satellites in India. *Telematics and Informatics, 4*(2), 151-158.

Mody, B., Bauer, J. M., & Straubhaar, J. D. (1995). *Telecommunications politics: Ownership and control of the information highway in developing countries.* Mahwah, NJ: Lawrence Erlbaum.

Mohammadi, A. (1997). Communication and the globalization process in the developing world. In A. Mohammadi (Ed.), *International communication and globalization* (pp. 67-89). London: Sage.

Morris, N., & Waisbord, S. (2001). *Media and globalization: Why the state matters.* Lanham, MD: Rowman & Littlefield.

Mowlana, H. (1997). *Global information and world communication: New frontiers in international relations.* Thousand Oaks, CA: Sage.

Narula, U., & Pearce, W. B. (1986). *Development as communication: A perspective on India.* Carbondale: Southern Illinois University Press.

Offe, C. (1996). *Modernity and the state: East, West.* Cambridge: MIT Press.

Ohmae, K. (1995). *The end of the nation state.* New York: Free Press.

Palan, R. (1999). Recasting political authority globalization and the states. In R. D. Germain (Ed.), *Globalization and its critics* (pp. 139-163). New York: Macmillan.

Peters, J. D. (1999). *Speaking into the air: A history of the idea of communication.* Chicago: University of Chicago Press.

Petrazzini, B. A. (1995). *The political economy of telecommunications reform in developing countries.* Westport, CT: Praeger.

Pierson, C. (1996). *The modern state.* London: Routledge.

Reeves, G. (1993). *Communications and the "Third World."* London: Routledge.

Reyes Matta, F. (Ed.). (1983). *Comunicación alternativa y búsquedas democráticas* [Alternative communication and the search for democracy]. Mexico: Instituto Latinoamericano de Estudios Transnacionales/Fundación Friedrich Ebert.

Ronning, H., & Kupe, T. (2000). The dual legacy of democracy and authoritarianism: The media and the state in Zimbabwe. In J. Curran & M.-J. Park (Eds.), *De-Westernizing media studies* (pp. 157-177). London: Routledge.

Samarajiwa, R. (1987). The murky beginnings of the communication and development field: Voice of America and "The passing of traditional society." In N. Jayaweera & S. Amunugama (Eds.), *Rethinking development communication* (pp. 3-19). Singapore: Asian Mass Communication Research and Information Centre.

Schiller, H. I. (1976). *Communication and cultural domination.* White Plains, NY: International Arts and Sciences Press.

Schiller, H. I. (1981). *Who knows? Information in the age of the* Fortune 500. Norwood, NJ: Ablex.

Schramm, W., & Lerner, D. (Eds.). (1976). *Communication and change, the last ten years—And the next.* Honolulu: University Press of Hawaii.

Scott, J. C. (1998). *Seeing like a state: How certain schemes to improve the human condition have failed.* New Haven, CT, and London: Yale University Press.

Servaes, J. (1999). *Communication for development: One world, multiple cultures.* Cresskill, NJ: Hampton.

Servaes, J., Jacobson, T., & White, S. (Eds.). (1996). *Participatory communication for social change.* London: Sage.

Singhal, A., & Sthapitanonda, P. (1996). The role of communication in development: Lessons learned from a critique of the dominant, dependency, and alternative paradigms. *Journal of Development Communication, 7*(1), 10-25.

Sklair, L. (1991). *Sociology of the global system.* Baltimore: Johns Hopkins University Press.

Smith, A. D. (1986). State-making and nation-building. In J. A. Hall (Ed.), *States in history.* Oxford, UK: Basil Blackwell.

Sreberny-Mohammadi, A. (1984). *Communication and democracy: Directions in research. A report on a conference.* Leicester, UK: International Association for Media and Communication Research.

Sreberny-Mohammadi, A. (2000). Television, gender, and democratization in the Middle East. In J. Curran & M.-J. Park (Eds.), *De-Westernizing media studies* (pp. 63-78). London: Routledge.

Sussman, G., & Lent, J. A. (Eds.). (1991). *Transnational communications: Wiring the Third World.* Newbury Park, CA: Sage.

Vincent, R., Nordenstreng, K., & Traber, M. (Eds.). (1999). *Towards equity in global communication: MacBride update.* Cresskill, NJ: Hampton.

Viotti, P. R., & Kauppi, M. V. (1993). *International relations theory: Realism, pluralism, globalism.* New York: Macmillan.

Waisbord, S. (1995). Leviathan dreams: State and broadcasting in South America. *Communication Review,* p. 1.

Waisbord, S. (2000). *Watchdog journalism in South America: News, accountability and democracy.* New York: Columbia University Press.

10

Development Communication Campaigns

LESLIE B. SNYDER
University of Connecticut

Development campaigns exist within the context of other development efforts. There are two broad categories of communication activities used for social change: communication channel enhancement and information provision. Channel enhancement, or communication infrastructure development, includes (1) increased availability of communication technologies, (2) improving education and socialization of people in knowledge and communication skills, and (3) organizing networks of people and improving or creating new organizations to increase information flows. Information provision includes (1) communication campaigns, (2) popular culture messages, (3) curriculum and training programs, (4) advocacy with elites, and (5) development support among publics. Although communication campaigns are only one type of activity, more and more strategic communication plans are, in fact, combining different types of activities.

A *communication campaign* is an organized communication activity, directed at a particular audience, for a particular period of time, to achieve a particular goal. Development communication campaigns are conducted for the purpose of developing a country or a population. How development is defined has been a matter of much debate over time. As the goals of development and beliefs about how to affect development change, so do the role and practice of development campaigns.

HISTORY

Communication campaigns are part of an old democratic tradition, dating back to the ancient Athenians campaigning to end slavery (Paisley, 1981). The first mass media—printed texts—enabled people to conduct communication campaigns as a means of

167

social change, including the distribution of radical religious texts, pamphleteering for political independence in the American colony, and a smallpox inoculation campaign in the late 1700s (Paisley, 1981). In the 1800s, there were campaigns for legal reform of slavery, alcohol, and women's rights; religious revival campaigns (Miller, 1965); and missionary campaigns for social and religious reform. Muckraking journalists were encouraged to campaign for social reforms as a way to sell inexpensive papers. Environmental campaigns, led by charismatic citizens and directed at public opinion and legislators, pioneered with efforts to preserve New York City's fresh water supply by preserving land in upstate New York, followed by efforts to preserve Yosemite and Yellowstone in the west. By the beginning of the 1900s, governments, occasionally aided by advertisers and universities, began using campaigns domestically for their definition of social good, including antituberculosis efforts and sanitation campaigns, political propaganda, and recruitment during the world wars.

Development programs grew out of the beliefs in the 1950s that newly independent and other poor countries had great needs, governments could socially engineer better societies, and development assistance would be a way to politically influence other countries in the context of the Cold War and waning colonial ties. There was an optimism about the ease of success based on the implementation of the Marshall Plan rebuilding the infrastructure of postwar Europe, and a model of what constituted social and economic improvements based on American and European society, technologies, and industrialization termed *modernization* (Rostow, 1960). The groups involved in development include bilateral donors, such as the U.S. Agency for International Development (USAID), which channels assistance directly from one government to another; multilateral organizations that formed after World War II, such as the World Bank, regional and development banks, and various U.N. agencies; nongovernmental organizations such as Save the Children and Oxfam; and consulting organizations.

Development campaigns began in the 1960s. After an analysis in Turkey proposed that one of the key factors on the path to political development was the existence of mass media such as newspapers and radio (Lerner, 1958), a very influential communication scholar wrote a book initially for the United Nations Educational, Scientific and Cultural Organization (UNESCO) on the roles mass media can play in development (Schramm, 1962). By emphasizing how the media can act as a "magic multiplier" to rapidly spread information throughout a population, Schramm's book set the stage for the growth in development communication activities in the 1960s, particularly family planning campaigns, agriculture outreach, and improving communication infrastructure such as radio and telephones. Development campaigns also drew on the *diffusion of innovations* framework, which had shown some success in spreading new agriculture techniques and technologies to farmers in Canada and the United States through media and outreach workers (Rogers, 1962, 1995). Independently, some socialist countries ran massive *mobilization campaigns* as a national priority, organizing very large numbers of children and adults to promote the behavior, idea, or skill, such as literacy, birth control, new marriage laws, rat annihilation, building of latrines, or political ideology (e.g., Fagen, 1969; Hall, 1978; Liu, 1981), based on Soviet and Mexican literacy campaigns from the 1920s.

The results of development campaigns and other development activities from the "development decade"—the 1960s—were disappointing. Population growth remained high, campaigns widened knowledge and resource gaps between the wealthy and poor and men and women, projects ignored and sometimes threatened local cultures, dependency on industrialized nations and multinational corporations was increasing, and environmental degradation accelerated (Díaz Bordenave, 1976; Isbister, 1991; Melkote, 1991).

Alternative visions of development were offered in the 1970s, and development campaigns slowly responded. The Group of 77 developing countries in the United Nations pushed for a new world economic order to address international economic disparities; some in development circles promoted meeting basic human needs first rather than the bottom-line concern with national economic growth; and the poorest of the poor, women, and children became a greater concern. Budgets for health, education, and agriculture projects increased, as did spending by nonovernmental organizations. Campaigns became an important activity for an increasing number of health problems when the World Health Organization of the United Nations adopted the slogan "Health for All by the Year 2000" in the mid-1970s, shifting its emphasize to prevention and widespread reach. UNICEF (United Nations Children's Fund) helped set priorities with donor organizations for a few key interventions for children that could be promoted using communication campaigns: oral rehydration therapy to combat diarrheal diseases, immunizations, and malnutrition. A large heart disease prevention campaign in the United States (Stern, Farquhar, Maccoby, & Russell, 1976) also helped convinced USAID that health campaigns were a viable strategy for other health topics.

Ironically, as international donors funded more and more health campaigns in the 1980s, domestic spending on health decreased. National debts from the failed development decade compounded by the oil crises in the 1970s financially crippled many developing countries. To secure new loans from the World Bank with which to pay their debts, governments were forced to agree to harsh financial guidelines (structural adjustment), including decreased government spending on health, education, and food subsidies. Poverty persisted and grew worse in the 1980s in Africa and elsewhere.

Agricultural campaigns also waned in the 1980s. The World Bank emphasized agricultural pricing policies, and also promoted the training and visitation (T&V) system for agriculture extension programs, which depend on a cadre of trained extension agents engaged in face-to-face communication (Benor & Baxtor, 1984). In recent years, the U.N. Food and Agriculture Organization (FAO) has sponsored a few campaigns, primarily in forestry, animal health, nutrition, and irrigation.

By the late-1980s and into the 1990s, budgets for international development programs became tighter in many less developed nations. Although the per capita gross national product (GNP) of developed nations increased by $7,878 between 1990 and 1997, the level of per capita aid given to developing nations fell by $18 (UNICEF, 2000). Decisions about which countries receive loans, grants, and technical assistance are political; the end of the Cold War shifted some aid to the former Soviet Union and Eastern Europe, aid to post-Mao China increased to the point where it was the nation receiving the most international aid in 1998 (Organization for Economic Cooperation and Development [OECD], 2000), Egypt and Israel remain among the top five recipients since the Camp David Accords (OECD, 2000), and development aid to sub-Saharan Africa declined, except for aid to postapartheid South Africa, which increased.

Topics changed, too. AIDS campaigns were conducted in many countries following international recognition of the AIDS pandemic. Although U.S. funding for family planning campaigns decreased under President Reagan in the 1980s, it increased again in the 1990s. In the wake of international recognition of environmental degradation, USAID began funding environmental campaigns in the 1990s. Today, the development priorities of the World Bank, the United Nations, and OECD (an umbrella group for bilateral donors) are

1. Reduce extreme poverty

2. Universal primary education

3. Gender equality in education

4. Reduce infant and child mortality

5. Reduce maternal mortality

6. Universal access to reproductive health and contraceptives

7. Environmental regeneration and sustainable development (OECD, 2000)

The priorities suggest continued support for maternal and child health campaigns, family planning, and environmental campaigns.

Communication campaigns remain one strategy for development. Today, they are more likely to be concerned with health, family planning, AIDS, and the environment than with agriculture. Out of the critical 1970s and 1980s rose new, sometimes complementary, approaches to development communication campaigns. Each of these is reviewed in turn.

APPROACHES TO DEVELOPMENT CAMPAIGNS

Formative Research

Campaigns in the 1970s began conducting formative research to respond to criticisms that they were not responsive to the campaign audience (Mendelsohn, 1973). Formative research is research conducted during the plan-

ning stages of a campaign with the goal of creating a better campaign. Formative research can be used to help segment the audience into homogeneous groups, select the focus of the campaign, decide the content and tenor of messages, choose appropriate channels, and pretest messages and programs. It was popularized through its successful application to the creation of educational media, first by Children's Television Workshop's *Sesame Street* (Palmer, 1981), and then by a project in Nicaragua run to teach schoolchildren mathematics over the radio (Friend, Searle, & Suppes, 1980), and an educational satellite project in India aimed at poor rural farmers (Mody, 1978). Campaigns in the 1970s used formative research to promote oral rehydration solutions for children with diarrhea in Latin America and nutrition in Indonesia, among other topics.

Although formative research is an accepted practice, it is not always done when campaign planners believe they know their audience well, have materials already produced, or feel pressed for time or when media producers feel it is their right to maintain control over messages. Among 99 Ugandan organizations conducting AIDS campaigns, 63.8% of the organizations conducted at least some research prior to conducting the campaign, but 23.2% did not (another 13.2% did not provide any data on research) (Kiwanuka-Tondo & Snyder, in press). Pretesting was done by 67% of the organizations.

Social Marketing

In the 1970s, USAID and the World Bank began funding campaigns that borrowed heavily from commercial advertising and marketing techniques, termed *social marketing* by Kotler and Zaltman (1971). In one of the earlier applications, Robert Manoff, a former advertising professional, used media advertisements to promote a "superlimonada" in Nicaragua to combat dehydration caused by diarrheal diseases. Social marketing is broadly defined as "the application of commercial marketing technologies to the analysis, planning, execution, and evaluation of programs designed to influence the voluntary behavior of target audiences in order to improve their personal welfare and that of their society" (Andreasen, 1995, p. 7). In practice, social marketing activities include setting specific measurable goals and objectives for the campaign, targeting specific segments of the audience with communications designed for them, conducting formative research with the target audience and other important people, making sure that the target behavior or product is one that could be acceptable and appropriate for the audience, planning the mix of appropriate channels to use, pretesting messages with the target audiences to improve them before using them, monitoring the implementation of the campaign, and evaluating the results.

Social marketing strategies spread rapidly to health and family planning campaigns, largely through USAID and a bevy of contractors. A series of social marketing projects in the 1980s and 1990s on diarrheal diseases, immunizations, nutrition, family planning, and mosquito control using mass media and interpersonal communication was extended to environmental topics by the mid-1990s.

AIDS prevention programs rely heavily on social marketing campaigns to promote condom use and other protective behaviors; in 1998 the Joint United Nations Programme on HIV/AIDS (UNAIDS) social marketing programs working with Population Services International distributed almost 800 million condoms in more than 50 countries (UNAIDS, 2000). Condoms and other contraceptive technologies lend themselves very well to social marketing, because of the strong parallel between marketing a product and marketing a contraceptive. An analysis of 100 community-based HIV prevention campaigns in San Francisco in 1995 to 1997 run by 49 organizations found that 91% used a key principle of social marketing—targeted which people to reach (Dearing et al., 1996). Community-based organizations in Uganda could easily answer questions about the key concepts of target audiences, channels, and pretesting (Kiwanuka-Tondo & Snyder, 1999); unfortunately, they were not asked directly about social marketing as their approach.

The difference between large-donor social marketing campaigns and community-based campaigns appears to be in the strong commitment that the latter retain to individual outreach through outreach workers. In both San Francisco (Dearing et al., 1996) and Uganda (Kiwanuka-Tondo & Snyder, in press), organizations relied on outreach workers more heavily than on media, perhaps because many of the organizations grew out of a counseling or community organizing orientations, prior successes in interpersonal outreach, or perceived barriers to using media such as cost or lack of expertise.

Agricultural outreach might benefit from a greater emphasis on using strategic social marketing campaigns along with extension programs. FAO's current approach, called strategic extension communication (Contado, 1997), places new emphasis on formative research and pretesting, but still neglects targeting.

Thus, social marketing techniques have penetrated many health and environment development campaigns. Strategic planning, targeting, systematic research (formative evaluation, pretesting, monitoring, and summative evaluation), and coordination of multiple media are widespread in health campaigns (e.g., Mody, 1991). Done correctly, social marketing incorporates a sensitivity to audience needs in deciding what an intervention should promote and how to promote it. Problems arise when campaign planners target general populations, stick to predetermined communication channels, skip essential research steps, or ignore research findings about audience needs, preferences, and communication styles. Many campaigns are never evaluated, missing an opportunity for essential feedback. Finally, the strategic nature of social marketing and flexible definition has enabled the approach to incorporate communication activities that were not originally viewed as part of either marketing or social marketing. Some of these other approaches are treated in sections below.

Participatory Campaigns

When critics raised objections about the role of foreigners in development, some people began advocating participatory approaches to development, which aim to involve the affected people in the development process (Freire, 1973; Korten, 1980; Marthur, 1989; Nyerere, 1973). Development campaigns began slowly to incorporate various participatory elements. (See the chapter by Huesca in this volume.)

What counts as participation within campaigns varies widely. *Representative participation* approaches include contacting local leaders to gain their support for a program and creating advisory boards composed of local representatives. *Local expert participation* approaches include funding local organizations to conduct campaigns, creating partnerships with local organizations and creating campaigns together, or hiring locals on staff to participate in campaigns design, implementation, or evaluation. *Audience research participation* calls for conducting intensive research with members of the target audience prior to

designing a campaign, using the feedback to refine campaign goals, targets, messages, persuasion strategy, and channels. *Local outreach worker participation* builds on diffusion theory advice to choose communicators who are similar to (or homophilous with) the target audience by choosing members of the target group to be communicators (Rogers, 1995). To communicate directly with the target audience, outreach workers may establish a central location in which to talk to people, such as a clinic or storefront, or may attempt to contact people in their homes, in workplaces, on the street, or at public spaces such as eating establishments, town squares, transportation centers, or community wells. *Government agenda-setting participation* links people to the decision makers in government, by establishing means of communication, such as videos created by local people or town meetings (Williamson, 1991). For example, an environmental project in Nepal gave people video cameras to film evidence of problems and suggested solutions, and shared the video with government officials (Grieser, 2000).

A study of 99 organizations involved in AIDS communication campaigns in Uganda found that the greater the participation of the audience, the greater the participation of outreach workers, which led, in turn, to better message quality (Kiwanuka-Tondo & Snyder, in press). The vast majority (86%) of organizations allowed participation of the audience and outreach workers in at least one campaign activity other than outreach, such as design research, monitoring, evaluation, or message design. In addition, organizations that had a more focused overall goal on AIDS education, more staff with professional training, and greater financial resources were more likely to allow participation of the audience in the campaign.

Participatory approaches that strengthen local organizations, which is possible with representative, local experts, and government agenda setting participation, may increase sustainability for a program over time. Representative, local experts, local outreach worker participation may have the added benefit of convincing frustrated people that change is possible, even when a particular campaign is viewed as a failure. However, it is also possible that the impact on local organizations fades quickly, as competent personnel change jobs or emigrate, political leaders face new problems that alter their agendas, or budget crises in poor nations hinder continuation of projects (e.g., McDivitt, 1991).

Two promises of participatory approaches are that they empower the audience and are more democratic. However, whether the audience is empowered depends precisely on how participation takes place—conducting research with the target audience does not empower them, because the audience only has the power to make suggestions. The ultimate position of power is to have a member of the community head the team designing and implementing the campaign. Although it is not clear how often this happens in developing nations, it is apparently rare for campaigns working with the poor in the United States (Myrick, 1998). Another question is how many members of the audience need to participate to make a campaign participatory. Furthermore, audiences are rarely homogeneous, especially in areas with multiple ethnic groups. Campaigns trying to be participatory need to consciously seek out partnerships with all affected groups, including people of different ethnicities, genders, ages, education levels, classes, and potentially castes.

Thus, there are many different ways that campaigns get members of the target audience involved in campaign design, implementation, and evaluation. Participatory programs need to be clear on how much they intend to build local capacity for future campaigns, empower

new groups, involve greater numbers of people in decision making, and ensure involvement by all relevant groups.

Organizational Improvements

In the past 20 years, donor organizations, consultants, and campaign planners have paid more attention to organizational factors that can enhance or hinder campaign success. Campaign evaluations had suggested there were problems with leadership, training, and interagency coordination in development campaigns. There had been criticism of development efforts in general that employed more people from the donor country than the local country, which was perhaps truer at higher levels within organizations. Another relevant issue was whether the local nation had the ability to continue programs after the foreign project ended. It became clear that an important long-term strategy for development was building domestic capacity.

Staff development and training. One way in which development campaign assistance supports domestic institutions is to fund training for staff members. Training takes on different forms, including sponsoring staff attendance at short courses and workshops in the country or abroad, giving or helping to secure scholarships for targeted staff so that they may enroll in relevant degree programs domestically or abroad, and mentoring through pairing local staff with foreign counterparts. UNESCO supports regional communication educational institutions. Training staff members has been part of many campaigns, including family planning in Ghana, Bolivia, and Nepal (Piotrow, Kincaid, Rimon, & Rinehart, 1997); breastfeeding in Mexico and Cameroon (Brown, Neumann, Sanders-Smith, & Snyder, 1994); oral rehydration in Senegal

(Roberts et al., 1988); sexual abuse of children in Southeast Asia ("Sida Supports," 2000); rinderpest control in cattle in Africa (D'Huys, 1998); and natural resource protection in Nicaragua (Monroe & Chambers, 2000). Key elements of training can include establishing a client orientation (Hornik et al., 1992), techniques to conduct formative evaluation and pretesting, and persuasion theory.

Training probably helps—especially in countries with lower rates of education and less experience with communication campaigns—but data are scarce. There are organizations conducting campaigns that do not have any trained staff. By 1997 in Uganda, at least 62% of organizations conducting HIV prevention campaigns had at least one member of their staff who had been trained, but 16% had no trained staff (Kiwanuka-Tondo & Snyder, in press).

Campaign management. Much more attention has been paid to managerial issues in the past 20 years than in the first 20 years of development campaigns. Activities included management training, technical assistance on managerial issues from consultants, conducting process evaluations, and gaining a commitment to and capacity for research as a management tool. For example, a series of national campaigns on family health in Uganda decentralized budget management to give more power to the districts and included nongovernmental organizations in strategic planning sessions with government officials and consultants ("Uganda Communication," 1999). Note that although process evaluations can provide valuable feedback on the quality of campaign management, they are not widely distributed due to their sensitive nature, and opportunities for campaigns to learn from each other's experiences are limited.

There are limited data on how well efforts to improve campaign management have worked. One study did show the importance of frequent contact between campaign supervisors and outreach workers in campaign message quality (Kiwanuka-Tondo & Snyder, in press), indicating either that outreach workers are providing important feedback to the campaign supervisors about what the messages should be or that campaigns that have better messages pay more attention to their outreach workers.

Coordination with service delivery. The goal of many campaigns is to stimulate demand for services, including family planning clinics, health clinics, pharmacies, and agricultural extension. The services, in turn, may be responsible for further communication with the audience. One promising method to recruit people into services is a peer-network model (Broadhead, Heckathorn, Weaklrem, Anthony, Madray, Mills, & Hughes, 1998), which has not yet been applied in developing countries.

It is important that the service institution is ready for an increase in demand, otherwise the institution will lose credibility with the population. There needs to be sufficient staff to meet with the increase in client load and adequate supplies, such as drugs, fertilizer, or seeds. In practice, improvements to service delivery are often strategically planned to coincide with family planning campaigns (Ross & Mauldin, 1996). On the other hand, there are also examples of campaigns that felt pressure to begin communicating before the service delivery component was ready (Singhal & Rogers, 1999).

Coordinating multiple organizations. Prompted by scarce resources and greater numbers of organizations working on the same problem, it is increasingly common to see organizations jointly address an issue, such as AIDS, family planning, childhood immunizations, onchoceriasis treatment, and vitamin A deficiencies. Coordinating bodies and organizations are able to take a broader vision of problems, concentrate resources and expertise, provide complementary activities, and compare the effectiveness of activities in different places in order to improve the quality of future work.

Organizations can be joined through horizontal partnerships to share resources or coordinate outreach to different groups, vertical hierarchies, or combinations of both. Organizations bring differences in competence, commitment, political clout, coverage, and continuity (Piotrow et al., 1997). For example, the Population Communication Services project at Johns Hopkins University in the United States is funded by USAID with a budget of more than $20 million and has worked in more than 50 countries since 1982 with hundreds of government agencies, nongovernmental organizations, commercial firms, and other consulting organizations (Piotrow et al., 1997). Although one organization frequently serves as the leader in coordinating the efforts of all the partners, it is not necessarily the foreign organizations. Only a small portion of Population Communication Services activities were implementations of programs in which it took the lead (260 projects); the most common activities were technical assistance trips (1,400), followed by trainings (500) (Piotrow et al., 1997).

Sometimes groups create a new coordinating body to share information among campaign organizations, donors, research institutions, and the government. For example, in the mid-1990s, the Ugandan government formed an umbrella organization, the Uganda AIDS Commission, to oversee the 135 organizations working on HIV prevention. The organizations included multilateral and bilateral donors, international nongovernmental organizations, government organizations, national nongovernmental organizations, reli-

gious organizations, and community-based organizations (Kiwanuka-Tondo & Snyder, in press). This type of structure preserves the local autonomy while fostering interorganizational communication.

Thus, the ways in which campaigns attempt to build local capacity and improve organization of campaigns are through staff training, attention to management issues, coordinating campaigns with service delivery, and forming coalitions of multiple organizations to work on particular problems. Although development campaigns often pay attention to developing domestic capacity in campaign design, implementation, and evaluation, there are little data on how successful the efforts have been. Coordinating multiple organizations is an efficient way to deal with scarce resources for development campaigns.

Advocacy

Some campaigns use advocacy to change policies, rules, regulations, or laws rather than aim at behavior change. The main targets for advocacy campaigns are decision makers in governments and corporations, although many try to rally public support as well. Media advocacy gained greater recognition in the 1990s as an important tool for social change with the publication of a text (Wallack, Dorfman, Jernigan, & Themba, 1993). Health advocacy campaigns have targeted national and workplace breastfeeding policies, national immunization policies, women's rights, and birth control policies. Environmental advocacy campaigns have had success with land, water, and wetland use; chemical and waste disposal and recycling; nuclear energy; tax structures to reduce fuel consumption and encourage renewable energy sources; endangered species; and international wildlife trade practices. There have also been notorious applications, such as Kuwait spending $10.8 million with the firm Hill and Knowlton to lobby the U.S. government during the time period leading up to the Persian Gulf War (Manheim, 1994).

Advocacy campaigns draw on community organizing, civil disobedience, lobbying, and public relations. Specific activities may include attending meetings, providing tours of a facility to educate policymakers and the media, circulating petitions, organizing boycotts and letter-writing campaigns, demonstrating, creating media events, and sponsoring original research by experts in the field to provide evidence of the need for change or efficacy of the proposal. For example, a campaign to stop the building of a dam in India organized rallies, marches, and hunger strikes, and a campaign to preserve indigenous land management rights in Brazil organized and lobbied government officials (Pick, 1993).

Creative Formats for Campaign Messages

Using the mass media can be an efficient way to reach target audiences (Hornik, 1988). Although the practice of using short messages such as public service announcements is still common, campaigns have also used other media formats.

News and public relations formats. Some campaigns use the news media to increase community awareness and support for an issue by gaining the cooperation of media organizations for sustained coverage of a problem and solutions (Weinreich, 1999). For example, a USAID-funded project in El Salvador trained reporters to improve the quality of environmental reporting and sensitivity to environmental issues, resulting in hundreds of articles a year, an organization of environmental reporters, and annual awards (Hough & Day,

2000). The project also convinced a major newspaper to incorporate environmental themes into its Sunday supplement for children and sponsor contests, and the supplement was used as an educational tool in schools (Ignacio Mata, 2000).

Campaign activities can include events and using celebrities to get publicity. Philly Bongoloey Lutaaya, a popular Ugandan singer who began singing about his AIDS status in 1989, was credited with removing a taboo against public discussion of the disease. Events may be the main thrust of a campaign, such as LiveAid, a concert event in 1985 that raised $70 billion for family relief and development activities. More typically, campaigns combine events, such as health fairs, contests, and health days, with other communication activities. A program to sensitize people to others with mental handicaps was promoted to youth in India through poster contests, among other activities (Ojha, Gupta, Dhingra, & Menon, 1993). Immunization days are a key component of international efforts to eradicate polio, along with door-to-door outreach, providing adequate drug supplies, and surveillance systems. In Madagascar, the October 1999 polio vaccine days promoted using banners, radio spots, and community theater and successfully vaccinated 99% of all children under age 5 (U.S. Agency for International Development Combating Polio in Madagascar, 2000). Events may be particularly suited to mobilizing people to do a one-shot activity, such as immunizations, tree plantings, or making appointments with service providers.

Another promising format that has not yet been tried in development campaigns is behavioral journalism. Campaigns arrange interviews with real people to act as role models for an advocated behavior, and organize news media to use and perhaps produce the stories (McAlister, 1995). Behavioral journalism seems to have about the same or slightly worse success rate in the United States as other formats (Snyder & Hamilton, in press), but may be more cost-effective. Behavioral journalism has been used in the United States to promote health topics among minorities and other hard-to-reach populations on smoking cessation (Marín, Peres-Stable, Marín, & Hauck, 1994; McAlister et al., 1992), mammography (McAlister et al., 1995), and HIV prevention (Fishbein et al., 1996).

Entertainment-education formats. Using entertainment formats such as dramas, puppet shows, dance, operas, and songs to promote ideas is an old tradition around the world and has been used with increasing frequency in development campaigns. Proponents of folk media point out that the media are compatible with local values and habits, credible, and persuasive and often reach people who do not have access to electronic media (Dissanayake, 1977; Pratt, Silva-Barbeau, & Pratt, 1997). Danish development agencies have used community theater groups, for example, to spread knowledge of health and agriculture and educational skills (Royal Danish Ministry of Foreign Affairs, 2000). In places with wide mass media coverage, it may be best to use both folk and mass media or to use folk media formats on television or radio, because it is more efficient to use mass media than folk media.

Family planning and HIV prevention songs using commercially successful artists have been broadcast in Latin America, the Philippines, and Nigeria, often with supporting promotional activities such as radio and television spots featuring a hotline number (Piotrow et al., 1997; Singhal & Rogers, 1999).

It is also possible to use radio and television dramas within campaigns. The first documented use of a radio drama for development was a 1951 BBC program on agriculture and rural life, *The Archers,* which was followed by programs in Jamaica on mosquito eradication, family planning, and other development topics (Singhal & Rogers, 1999). Kenya also experimented with family planning radio drama in the 1970s. The U.S. television series *Sesame Street,* starting in 1969, promoted children's literacy and numeracy and has spread to 140 countries in 17 different languages.[1] Mexican *telenovelas* promoted literacy and family planning beginning in 1975, followed by a television drama *Hum Log* in India in 1984 (Singhal & Rogers, 1999), and an ongoing health television and radio drama in South Africa, *Soul City,* beginning in 1994.

Piotrow and colleagues (1997) summarize the key components of entertainment-education approaches as "research on audience preferences; strategic decisions on top-quality talent, scripting, and positioning of the issues to be covered; pretesting; media promotion; personal appearances; monitoring; and evaluation" (p. 81). Successful radio and television programs can continue for years, as in the case of *The Archers* and *Sesame Street,* lasting beyond a particular campaign.

In addition to creating original programs, campaigns can lobby producers to introduce relevant storylines into existing dramatic series (Montgomery, 1989). Although campaign planners have far less control over the content when they are not producing it themselves, the approach can be cheaper in nations with commercial media.

Multipronged Approaches

Another trend in the past 20 years is to use a multipronged approach—coordinating media efforts, interpersonal outreach, services, policies, training, and other activities as part of a strategic campaign plan. An international breastfeeding campaign sponsored by USAID in the 1990s combined training and networking for health professionals, change in national and hospital policies, improved university curricula for future health professionals, research to answer questions about specific recommendations in particular countries, conferences, enhanced support for outreach workers, and media messages (Brown et al., 1994). Family planning campaigns often combine a media campaign, outreach workers, improved service delivery, and changes in government policies (Ross & Mauldin, 1996). The incidence of the cattle disease rinderpest dropped from 18 infected African countries in 1983 to only 4 by 1995 after a campaign that combined radio listening groups, a video van, banners, and interpersonal outreach with mass vaccination and permanent marking of cattle, surveillance and disease reporting, and animal movement controls (D'Huys, 1998). Agriculture campaigns could combine media components with outreach and research through the training and visitation system (Kumuk & van Crowder, 1996).

Coordinating multiple activities may be easier under a broad definition of campaigns, such as that urged by the social marketing advocates (e.g., Andreasen, 1995). Under a narrow definition, only the media effort, some outreach, and other activities that are not part of a permanent program would be considered part of a campaign.

Persuasion Theory and Message Design

There have been more development campaigns drawing on persuasion theory in order to design more effective messages (Mody, 1991). Some of the most important theories have been the information processing model (McGuire, 1981), social learning theory (Bandura, 1986), the health belief model (Janz & Becker, 1984), the theory of reasoned action (Ajzen & Fishbein, 1980), the stages of behavior change model (Prochaska & DiClemente, 1983), and child development theories (reviewed in Austin, 1995), along with the earlier diffusion of innovations (Rogers, 1962, 1995) and Cartwright's (1949) emphasis on the relationships between cogni-

tion, motivation, and behavior for campaign success.

How campaigns work seems to depend on the type of behavior and context.

1. Campaigns can *provide information* that causes people to alter their reasoning, in the same way that formal education is expected to work, when (a) there is a recognized emergency, such as meningitis inoculations, where a majority of the population is willing to act on information of a new and imminent threat that is preventable; (b) new information is conveyed (Snyder & Hamilton, in press); or (c) there is a threat of enforcement of behavior by the police (Snyder & Hamilton, in press).

2. For topics where compliance is easy and seen as relatively trivial, such as brushing teeth or trying a new food, campaign messages can *provide simple positive associations with a new behavior.* People remember the positive association and act on it in the moment when they have environmental cues, an interpersonal request, or new opportunity for trial (Ray, 1975). The process may become more thoughtful over time, after people have tried the behavior once (Chaffee & Roser, 1986).

3. Campaigns may *remind people of motivations they already have* to change their behavior, so they change sooner (Hornik & McAnany, 1999). Other contextual factors, such as changes in policies or services, may have helped provide motivations for change.

4. Campaigns may *teach the skills* people need to change their behavior—such as how to quit smoking—thereby enabling it (Bandura, 1986).

5. Over a long period of time, campaigns may *influence values* embedded within

interpersonal networks, organizations, and social cultures, so that people come to see the values promoted in the campaigns as dominant, change their own values, and eventually change their behaviors to be consistent (Hornik & McAnany, 1999). Campaigns can build on community coherence, as in the case of a Fijian smoking cessation campaign (Groth-Marnat, Leslie, & Renneker, 1996). Value change seems to underlay work on the entertainment-education approach.

6. Campaigns may *alter patterns of communication and confer legitimacy on sources of information,* such as by expanding the role of traditional birth attendants into teaching about infant health, or urging parents to talk to their children about AIDS.

Unfortunately, many campaigns in developing nations do not pay attention to the psychology of behavior change. They seem to assume that providing information is enough to convince people to change their behavior. These campaigns would benefit from more theoretically based message design. Evaluations, too, provide better feedback when they can test which aspects of the theoretical persuasion process succeeded; simple knowledge-attitude-practices (KAP) studies, a legacy of early family planning campaigns, provide far less feedback.

EFFECTIVENESS OF CAMPAIGNS

Despite the long history of communication campaigns, only a limited number of studies have examined their comparative effectiveness, using quantitative methods. In the United States, mediated health campaigns have small but real short-term effects, with an average increase of 7 to 10 percentage points in the desired behavior, slightly larger for campaigns that promote the commencement of a new behavior (12%) and less for campaigns that promote cessation of a behavior (5%) or prevention (4%) (Snyder et al., in press). A meta-analysis of mostly European media interventions with time-series data found a positive effect, especially for immunization campaigns (Grilli, Freemantle, Minozzi, Domenighetti, & Finer, 1999). Clinical outreach effects in the United States may be slightly superior to media campaigns, although the evidence from meta-analyses is mixed (Snyder et al., in press).

The results may be similar in developing nations. A meta-analysis of 16 family planning programs in developing countries from 1964 to 1987 found an average increase of 8 percentage points in couples practicing a family planning behavior (converted here from a reported effect size of $r = .08$, $SE = .28$; Bauman, 1997). The programs in the Bauman (1997) meta-analysis had all been evaluated using true experimental designs (random assignment to conditions), and activities included mailings, home visits, outreach workers, improved counseling, and group education. More recent evaluations of family planning campaigns show increases of 3 percentage points each for new users in Bolivia (Valente, Poppe, & Payne Merritt, 1996) and Turkey (Piotrow et al., 1997). A Bangladesh interpersonal family planning campaign improved the work of outreach workers by promoting small group discussions, and it found a 6% increase in married women using modern contraceptives (Piotrow et al., 1997). An analysis of the effectiveness of media campaigns to promote family planning in developing countries concludes that short-term campaigns can cause more people to go to clinics for family planning services (Hornik & McAnany, 1999).

A review of 10 USAID-funded child survival campaigns in different countries (Hornik et al., 1992) found some very positive effects and other campaigns with very small or null effects. Vaccination levels increased 12 percentage points on average, greater in areas with low initial rates and longer campaigns (up to 18 months). Vitamin A distribution increased 16 percentage points among those who live near health centers. Breastfeeding increased 19 percentage points among those who gave birth at home or in a public hospital, as opposed to a private hospital. The results for oral rehydration therapy were mixed, averaging 14 percentage points in three countries with significant gains, but 2% or less in three others. In Jordan, there was a 4 percentage point increase in the number of infants introduced to solid foods at the recommended age. There were no gains beyond preexisting trends for family planning services in Peru. The results suggest that at least some campaigns in developing countries can be successful and that the conditions for success depend greatly on the behavior and context.

Campaigns that use the entertainment-education approach in combination with other activities vary from 0.5% to 11% change. A radio drama in Zimbabwe was credited with increasing male family planning accepters by 0.5% points (Piotrow et al., 1997), and a radio drama in The Gambia caused a gain of 11% in men and women using a modern method of contraceptives (Valente, Kim, Lettenmaier, Glass, & Dibba, 1994). The Tanzanian drama increased family planning by 11% (computed from Table 7.3, Singhal & Rogers, 1999). Many studies show that audiences strongly identify with the stories in the dramas and talk about them with family, friends, and neighbors (Makekar, 1993; McAnany & Lapastina, 1994; Singhal & Rogers, 1999).

There is some evidence that the entertainment-education approach may be cost-effective. Costs for a Zimbabwe radio drama for male family planning were $2.41 per new user (Piotrow et al., 1997), and a Tanzanian campaign cost $1 per adopter of family planning and $0.10 per adopter of HIV prevention (Singhal & Rogers, 1999). However, there is a lack of data on the cost-effectiveness of other types of interventions with which to compare.

Analyses of trend data suggest that many problems have declined since development programs have focused on them, but there is no way to separate the impact of communication campaigns from other development activities and from other influences. A comparison of contraceptive prevalence rates in 17 countries between 1970 and 1996 found an average rise of 38%, or 2.7% per year (computed from Table 1.1, columns 2 and 3, in Piotrow et al., 1997). Uganda's rates of new AIDS cases stabilized and dropped after that country's coordinated efforts and much spending (*AIDS Analysis Africa*, 1997). Bangladesh had a 25% reduction in child mortality in the 1990s after many organizations were involved in immunization, oral rehydration, and pneumonia campaigns, as well as sanitation and education improvements, microcredit for women, and better access to health care and social services (*A Better World for All*, 2000). World immunization rates of children under five years old rose from around 30% in 1981 to 80% in 1996 (World Health Organization, 1996), and child mortality dropped 20% between 1985 and 1999 (*Budget Justification FY 2001*, 2000).

Last, note that exposure to campaign messages may be a problem. Because greater exposure leads to greater effects (Kiragu, Galiwango, Mulira, & Sekatawa, 1996, reported in Piotrow et al., 1997; Snyder & Hamilton, in press), a failure to reach people severely limits the possibility of the campaign changing behavior. In the United States, media campaigns have an average reach of 40% (Snyder & Hamilton, in press). Unfortunately, the average reach of developing campaigns is not known, and it most certainly varies by type of channels used and the extent of media competition/monopoly. Some development campaigns have shown very high rates of exposure, as in a campaign in Kenya that reached 83% (Kekevolo et al., 1996, cited in Piotrow et al., 1997). The figures for radio dramas in developing countries were similar to U.S. media campaigns: 40% of the population listened regularly to a Kenyan radio drama, *Ushikwapo Shikimana*; 40% listened to a Jamaican radio drama, *Nasebury Street*; and 55% ever listened to a Tanzanian drama, *Twende na Wakati,* but only 6% listened to an Indian drama, *Tinka Tinka Sukh* (Singhal & Rogers, 1999).

Thus, development campaigns, in conjunction with other development activities, appear to have small effects, perhaps ranging from 3 to 14 percentage point changes. Some topics that have been covered by many campaigns over the years have shown population-level changes, but there is no way to be certain that any of the changes were due to communication campaigns and not some other factors. As the library of good evaluation studies grows, it will be possible to conduct meta-analyses of development campaign effects.

ISSUES FOR THE FUTURE

Universal Evaluation

It is likely that only a small fraction of the development campaigns conducted every year are systematically evaluated. For example, only 11% of AIDS campaigns in Uganda knew how many people their campaign reached, let alone how many changed their behaviors (Kiwanuka-Tondo & Snyder, in press). Therefore, much information about which campaign approaches really work is lost. Health education offices and community organiza-

tions are often satisfied with an accounting of the number of the activities, media messages, and print materials produced, as if the creation of a message automatically results in audience members changing their behaviors (Yun, Govinder, & Mody, 2001). Evaluation research can also provide an opportunity to test underlying assumptions about the models of psychological and social change. Finally, evaluation documents provide a format to share results and lessons with others, thereby furthering collective knowledge about campaigns.

Cost-effectiveness studies in particular are needed to compare different campaign approaches and campaigns with other development approaches. For example, a study of a peer network model of outreach found that it was vastly more cost-effective than traditional outreach workers in AIDS prevention behavior among IV drug users in the United States (Broadhead, et al., 1998).

Choices Between Poverty-Reduction Programs and Campaigns

Gaps between the rich and the poor within and between nations are growing (UNICEF, 2000), prompting the United Nations to declare 1997 to 2006 the "First U.N. Decade to Eradicate Poverty." Because poverty is at the root of many of the problems in developing nations addressed by campaigns (e.g., World Bank, 2000/2001; Yun et al., 2001), analyses need to be conducted on the comparative effectiveness, cost-effectiveness, and duration of effects of poverty-eradication projects versus development campaigns for different types of problems. All of the parties involved in campaigns need to make decisions about allocations of scarce resources from a position of knowledge about the opportunity costs of not spending resources on other problems or in another way.

Capacity Building

It remains important for international and national funders to build local capacity to address new problems in the future, such as through community organizing, coalition building, training, curricula reform, and creation of new communication infrastructure. Often, international or domestic pressures to have an immediate impact on a problem can force campaigns to focus on immediate results, even when capacity-building activities were planned, as happened in a breastfeeding campaign in Jordan (McDivitt, 1991).

Sustainability and Culture

After many campaigns, behavior gains have evaporated over time, such as family planning in Iran (Rogers, 1973), vasectomy promotion in Guatemala (Bertrand, Santiso, Linder, & Pineda, 1987) and Brazil (Kincaid et al., 1996), and oral rehydration in The Gambia (McDowell & McDivitt, 1990). Knowledge and behavior maintenance may be more difficult for poor, uneducated people (Snyder, 1990).

Donor organizations have attempted to use institutionalization and capacity building as the way to increase the sustainability of behavior changes achieved by campaigns. Although local capacity is important, as stated above, it is inadequate as an approach to sustainability, implying that the local institutions must forever communicate on the behavior.

Rather, it is critical to understand how to sustain the behavior without constant communication from campaigns. Research is needed into how cultures take over the socialization of new behaviors, and then build appropriate activities into campaigns. If successive generations are taught a behavior (such as breastfeeding, teeth brushing, or taking children for immunizations) through informal channels at an appropriate time of their lives, then governments and other groups can move into a role of providing sustained support for the appropriate behavior but leave the majority of the communication on the behavior up to other socializing agents.

Campaigns starting from a position of respect for local cultures and recognition of community values may have more lasting impacts. The president of the World Bank, James Wolfensohn, said, "We are starting to understand that development effectiveness depends, in part, on 'solutions' that resonate with a community's sense of who it is" (World Bank, 1999). Currently, many campaigns seek to supplant traditional and informal channels of communication with government agents and media. When campaigns hurt local cultures by devaluing traditional sources or cultural forms, they are ethically irresponsible.

Coordinate Common Behavior Change

Because health campaigns are often organized by people focused on one disease, they miss opportunities to work across problems for common behavior change. For example, exercise promotion is common to cancer, diabetes, and heart disease campaigns. Coalitions formed around behaviors and across problems could address common behaviors. The extent to which particular problems are emphasized should depend on which issues are of concern to the target groups.

Improved Theory of Campaigns Effects for Different Types of Behaviors

Although theories of persuasion have improved message design, more theoretical work is needed to understand information-seeking behavior and channel choice, social change processes for different types of behaviors in different contexts, and the process whereby an idea becomes self-sustaining within a culture over time.

Coordination of Different Activities

Campaign theorists (Hornik, 1988; Piotrow et al., 1997; Rogers, 1995) advise the use of multiple channels, but more needs to be done to understand how best to coordinate channels and activities, particularly to achieve sustainable changes. For example, family planning and breastfeeding campaigns are more effective when there are appropriate national, workplace, and hospital policies in place (Brown et al., 1994; Rogers, 1973). To compare combinations of activities, more programs need to make available data on both the effectiveness and cost-effectiveness of individual activities and for various combinations of activities; when there are enough campaigns with good evaluation data, it will be possible to do a meta-analysis to answer coordination questions.

Optimal Timing for Campaigns

People need information at different times in their lives due to changes in life status, emergencies, health changes, new breakthroughs, and need for new services, among other reasons. If we understood better how information flows take place over time for different topics, then it would be possible to design more efficient campaigns. Patterns of information seeking are also changing over time, particularly as interactive media become more available.

One issue is the optimal periodicity for successive campaigns over time for different types of behaviors. Periodicity will depend on the presence of new cohorts of people who are not performing the behavior, the need to maintain the behavior among those already performing it, periodicity of the problem, and prior success rates. Similarly, we need a better understanding of how to time bursts of campaign activities (called *pulsing* in the advertising literature) while a campaign is ongoing.

Another issue is the appropriate length for a campaign on a given topic. Short-term campaign effects in the United States are maximized when campaigns are one year or less and perhaps therefore more intense (Snyder & Hamilton, in press). Immunization campaigns lasting 18 months or more seemed to have a greater impact (Hornik et al., 1992), but very short immunization campaigns can also be successful (e.g., Balraj & John, 1986). Optimal length may relate to available channels and the reach and frequency of campaign messages, and the periodicity of the problem itself. A rheumatic fever campaign in Guadeloupe and Martinique took four years to bring rates down and continued through two more minor resurgences for a total of 10 years (Bach et al., 1996).

CONCLUSION

Communication campaigns can be useful tools in development. Much progress has been made in the past 20 years in how to plan, organize, and coordinate campaigns that have a greater likelihood of success. However, much more research is needed to know the comparative impact of campaigns and other types of activities, improve models of campaigns for different types of problems, increase the sustainability of campaigns, coordinate across problems that share common behavioral goals, and improve campaign timing and coordination of multiple activities. It appears that development communication campaigns have an average effect on behavior of between 3% and 14%. These figures can be useful for campaign planners establishing goals, evaluators setting sample size, and researchers comparing effectiveness across interventions.

NOTE

1. See the Children's Television Workshop online at http://www.ctw.org.

REFERENCES

AIDS analysis Africa. (1997, December). Vol. 7, No. 6, p. 3.

Ajzen, I., & Fishbein, M. (1980). *Understanding attitudes and predicting social behavior.* Englewood Cliffs, NJ: Prentice Hall.

Andreasen, A. R. (1995). *Marketing for social change: Changing behavior to promote health, social development, and the environment.* San Francisco: Jossey-Bass.

Austin, E. W. (1995). Reaching young audiences: Developmental considerations in designing health messages. In E. Maibach & R. L. Parrott (Eds.), *Designing health messages: Approaches from communication theory and public health practice* (pp. 114-144). Thousand Oaks, CA: Sage.

Bach, J. F., Chalons, S., Forier, E., Elana, G., Jouanelle, J., Kayemba, S., Delbois, D., Mosser, A., Saint-Aime, C., & Berchel, C. (1996). 10-year educational programme aimed at rheumatic fever in two French Caribbean islands. *Lancet, 347,* 644-648.

Balraj, V., & John, T. J. (1986). Evaluation of a poliomyelitis immunization campaign in a Madras City. *Bulletin of the World Health Organization, 64,* 861-865.

Bandura, A. (1986). *Social foundations of thought and action.* Englewood Cliffs, NJ: Prentice Hall.

Bauman, K. E. (1997). The effectiveness of family planning programs evaluated with true experimental designs. *Public Health Briefs, 87,* 666-669.

Benor, D., & Baxtor, M. (1984). *Agricultural extension: The training and visit system.* Washington, DC: World Bank.

Bertrand, J. T., Santiso, R., Linder, S. H., & Pineda, M. A. (1987). Evaluation of a communications program to increase the adoption of vasectomy in Guatemala. *Studies in Family Planning, 18,* 361-370.

A better world for all [Online]. (2000). Available: http://www.paris21.org/betterworld (Organization for Economic Cooperation and Development)

Broadhead, R. S., Heckathorn, D. D., Weaklrem, D. L., Anthony, D. L., Madray, H., Mills, R. J., & Hughes, J. (1998). Harnessing peer networks as an instrument for AIDS prevention: Results from a peer-driven intervention. *Public Health Reports, 113,* suppl., 142-157.

Brown, V., Neumann, C., Sanders-Smith, M., & Snyder, L. (1994). *Mid-term evaluation: Wellstart International's expanded promotion of breastfeeding program.* Washington, DC: U.S. Agency for International Development, Division of Nutrition & Maternal Health, Office of Health & Nutrition.

Budget justification FY 2001 [Online]. (2000). Available: http://www.usaid.gov/pubs/bj2001/cent_prog/global/phn/936003.html (U.S. Agency for International Development)

Cartwright, D. (1949). Some principles of mass persuasion: Selected findings of research on the sale of United States war bonds. *Human Relations, 2,* 253-267.

Chaffee, S. H., & Roser, C. (1986). Involvement and the consistency of knowledge, attitudes, and behaviors. *Communication Research, 13,* 373-399.

Contado, T. E. (1997, October 1). The Strategic Extension Campaign: An FAO agricultural extension approach. In *Sustainable development dimensions* [Online]. Available: http://www.fao.org/sd/index_en.htm (U.N. Food and Agriculture Organization)

Dearing, J. W., Rogers, E. M., Meyer, G., Casey, M. K., Rao, N., Campo, S., & Henderson, G. M. (1996). Social marketing and diffusion-based strategies for communication with unique populations: HIV prevention in San Francisco. *Journal of Health Communication, 1*, 343-363.

D'Huys, P. (1998, December 11). Communication for development: The case of the Pan African Rinderpest Campaign (PARC). In *Sustainable development dimensions* [Online]. Available: http://www.fao.org/sd/CDdirect/CDan0021.htm (U.N. Food and Agriculture Organization)

Díaz Bordenave, J. (1976). Communication of agricultural innovations in Latin America: The need for new models. In E. M. Rogers (Ed.), *Communication and development: Critical perspectives* (pp. 43-62). Beverly Hills, CA: Sage.

Dissanayake, W. (1977). New wine in old bottles: Can folk media convey modern messages. *Journal of Communication, 27*, 122-124.

Fagen, R. (1969). *The transformation of political culture in Cuba.* Stanford, CA: Stanford University Press.

Fishbein, M., Guenther-Grey, C., Johnson, W. D., Wolitski, R. J., McAlister, A., Rietmeijer, C. A., & O'Reilly, K. (1996). Using a theory-based community intervention to reduce AIDS risk behaviors: The CDC's AIDS community demonstration projects. In S. Oskamp & S. C. Thompson (Eds.), *Understanding and preventing HIV risk behavior, safer sex and drug use* (pp. 177-206). Thousand Oaks, CA: Sage.

Freire, P. (1973). *Education for critical consciousness.* New York: Seabury.

Friend, J., Searle, B., & Suppes P. (Eds.). (1980). *Radio mathematics in Nicaragua.* Stanford, CA: Stanford University Institute for Mathematical Studies in the Social Sciences.

Grieser, M. (2000). Participation. In B. A. Day & M. C. Monroe (Eds.), *Environmental education and communication for a sustainable world: Handbook for international practitioners* (pp. 17-21). Washington, DC: Academy for Educational Development.

Grilli, R., Freemantle, N., Minozzi, S., Domenighetti, G., & Finer, D. (1999). Mass media interventions: Effects on health services utilization (Cochrane review). *The Cochrane Library, 4.* Oxford, UK: Update Software.

Groth-Marnat, G., Leslie, S., & Renneker, M. (1996). Tobacco control in a traditional Fijian village: Indigenous methods of smoking cessation and relapse prevention. *Social Science and Medicine, 43*, 473-477.

Hall, B. (1978). *Muntu ni Afya: Tanzania's health campaign.* Washington, DC: Academy for Educational Development.

Hornik, R., Contreras-Budge, E., McDivitt, J., McDowell, J., Yoder, P. S., Zimicki, S., & Rasmuson, M. (1992). Communication for child survival: Evaluation of "Healthcom" projects in ten countries. Unpublished manuscript.

Hornik, R., & McAnany, E. (1999). *Mass media and fertility change.* Manuscript.

Hornik, R. C. (1988). *Development communication: Information, agriculture, and nutrition in the Third World.* New York: Longman.

Hough, R. R., & Day, B. A. (2000). Addressing the social dimension: An application of systems thinking. In B. A. Day & M. C. Monroe (Eds.), *Environmental education and communication for a sustainable world: Handbook for international practitioners* (pp. 33-37). Washington, DC: Academy for Educational Development.

Ignacio Mata, J. (2000). El Salvador's national environmental education strategy. In B. A. Day & M. C. Monroe (Eds.), *Environmental education and communication for a sustainable world: Handbook for international practitioners* (pp. 91-103). Washington, DC: Academy for Educational Development.

Isbister, J. (1991). *Promises not kept: The betrayal of social change in the Third World.* Bloomfield, CT: Kumarian.

Janz, N., & Becker, M. (1984). The health belief model: A decade later. *Health Education Quarterly, 11*, 1-47.

Joint United Nations Programme on HIV/AIDS. (2000). *Social marketing: Expanding access to essential products and services.* Geneva: UNAIDS and Population Services International.

Kincaid, D. L., Payne Merritt, A., Nickerson, L., de Castro Buffington, S., de Castro, M. P. P., & de Castro, B. M. (1996). Impact of a mass media vasectomy promotion campaigns in Brazil. *International Family Planning Perspectives, 22*, 169-175.

Kiwanuka-Tondo, J., & Snyder, L. B. (in press). An organizational theory of health communication campaigns: Evidence from the Uganda AIDS campaign. *Journal of Health Communication.*

Korten, C. D. (1980, September). Community organization and rural development: A learning process approach. *Public Administrative Review,* pp. 480-511.

Kotler, P., & Zaltman, G. (1971). Social marketing: An approach to planned social change. *Journal of Marketing, 33,* 10-15.

Kumuk, T., & Van Crowder, L. (1996, July 18). Harmonizing T&V extension: Some experiences from Turkey. In *Sustainable development dimensions* [Online]. Rome: U.N. Food and Agriculture Organization. Available: http://www.fao.org/sd/EXdirect/EXan0011.htm

Lerner, D. (1958). *The passing of traditional society: Modernizing the Middle East.* Glencoe, IL: Free Press.

Liu, A. P. (1981). Mass campaigns in the People's Republic of China. In R. E. Rice & W. J. Paisley (Eds.), *Public communication campaigns* (pp. 199-223). Beverly Hills, CA: Sage.

Manheim, J. B. (1994). *Strategic public diplomacy and American foreign policy.* Oxford, UK: Oxford University Press.

Mankekar, P. (1993). National texts and gendered lives: An ethnography of television viewers in a North Indian city. *American Ethnologist, 20,* 543-563.

Marín, B. V., Peres-Stable, E. J., Marín, G., & Hauck, W. W. (1994). Effects of a community intervention to change smoking behavior among Hispanics. *American Journal of Preventive Medicine, 10*(6), 340-347.

Marthur, H. M. (1989). Government administered programs for people-centered development. *Planning and Administration, 1,* 40-49.

McAlister, A. (1995). Behavioral journalism: Beyond the marketing model for health communication. *American Journal of Health Promotion, 9,* 417-420.

McAlister, A. L., Fernandez-Esquer, M. E., Ramirez, A. G., Trevino, F., Gallion, K. J., Villarreal, R., Pulley, L., Hu, S., Torres, I., & Qing, Z. (1995). Community level cancer control in a Texas barrio: Part II. Baseline and preliminary outcome. *Journal of the National Cancer Institute Monographs, 18,* 123-126.

McAlister, A. L., Ramirez, A. G., Amezcua, C., Pulley, L., Stern, M. P., & Mercado, S. (1992). Smoking cessation in Texas-Mexico border

communities: A quasi-experimental panel study. *American Journal of Health Promotion, 6,* 274-279.

McAnany, E., & Lapastina, A. (1994). Telenovela audiences: A review and methodological critique of Latin American research. *Communication Research, 21,* 828-849.

McDivitt, J. A. (1991). *The Healthcom Project in Jordan: Final case study evaluation report* (Working Paper No. 1004). Philadelphia: Annenberg School for Communication.

McDowell, J., & McDivitt, J. (1990). *The Healthcom resurvey of oral rehydration therapy practices in The Gambia.* Menlo Park, CA: Applied Communication Technology.

Melkote, S. R. (1991). *Communication for development in the Third World: Theory and practice.* Newbury Park, CA: Sage.

McGuire, W. (1981). Theoretical foundations of campaigns. In R. E. Rice & W. J. Paisley (Eds.), *Public communication campaigns.* Beverly Hills, CA: Sage.

Mendelsohn, H. (1973). Some reasons why information campaigns can succeed. *Public Opinion Quarterly, 39,* 50-61.

Miller, P. (1965). *The life of the mind in America, from the Revolution to the Civil War.* New York: Harcourt, Brace & World.

Mody, B. (1978, September). Lessons from the Indian Satellite Experiment. *Educational Broadcasting International,* pp. 117-120.

Mody, B. (1991). *Designing messages for development communication.* Newbury Park, CA: Sage.

Monroe, M. C., & Chambers, N. (2000). Building capacity through training. In B. A. Day & M. C. Monroe (Eds.), *Environmental education and communication for a sustainable world: Handbook for international practitioners* (pp. 69-77). Washington, DC: Academy for Educational Development.

Montgomery, K. C. (1989). *Target: Prime time.* New York: Oxford University Press.

Myrick, R. (1998). In search of cultural sensitivity and inclusiveness: Communication strategies used in rural HIV prevention campaigns designed for African Americans. *Health Communication, 10,* 65-85.

Nyerere, J. K. (1973). Freedom and development. Uhuru na Mandeleo. A selection from writings and speeches 1968-1973 by Julius K. Nyerere. Dar es Salaam: Oxford University Press.

Ojha, K. N., Gupta, S., Dhingra, N., & Menon, D. K. (1993, January-June). Public awareness towards mental handicap: Within a CBR framework. *Indian Journal of Disability and Rehabilitation*, pp. 37-51.

Organization for Economic Cooperation and Development. (2000). *Aid at a glance* [Online]. Available: http://www.oecd.org/dac/htm/agdac. htm

Paisley, W. J. (1981). Public communication campaigns: The American experience. In R. E. Rice & W. J. Paisley (Eds.), *Public communication campaigns* (pp. 15-40). Beverly Hills, CA: Sage.

Palmer, E. (1981). Shaping persuasive messages with formative research. In R. E. Rice & W. J. Paisley (Eds.), *Public communication campaigns*. Beverly Hills, CA: Sage.

Pick, M. (1993). *How to save your neighborhood, city, or town: The Sierra Club guide to community organizing*. San Francisco: Sierra Club.

Piotrow, P. T., Kincaid, D. L., Rimon, J. G., III, & Rinehart, W. (1997). *Health communication: Lessons from family planning and reproductive health*. Westport, CT: Praeger.

Pratt, C. B., Silva-Barbeau, I., & Pratt, C. A. (1997). Toward a symmetrical and an integrated framework of norms for nutrition communication in sub-Saharan Africa. *Journal of Health Communication, 2*, 43-58.

Prochaska, J. O., & DiClemente, C. C. (1983). Stages and process of self-change of smoking: Toward an integrative model of change. *Journal of Consulting and Clinical Psychology, 51*, 390-395.

Ray, M. L. (1975). Marketing communication and the hierarchy-of-effects. In P. Clark (Ed.), *New models for mass communication research* (pp. 147-176). Beverly Hills, CA: Sage.

Roberts, R. S., Samb, M. C., Mitchell, M., Diop, D., Snyder, L., & Leye, I. (1988). Combatting diarrheal diseases—ORT: Mid-course evaluation of the CDD Program. Dakar, Senegal: Ministry of Public Health.

Rogers, E. M. (1962). *Diffusion of innovations*. New York: Free Press.

Rogers, E. M. (1973). *Communication strategies for family planning*. New York: Free Press.

Rogers, E. M. (1995). *Diffusion of innovations* (4th ed.). New York: Free Press.

Ross, J. A., & Mauldin, W. P. (1996). Family planning programs: Efforts and results, 1972-1994. *Studies in Family Planning, 27*(3), 137-147.

Rostow, W. W. (1960). *The stages of economic growth: A non-Communist Manifesto*. Cambridge, UK: Cambridge University Press.

Royal Danish Ministry of Foreign Affairs. (2000). *The power of culture: The cultural dimension in development* [Online]. Available: http://www. um.dk/danida/tpoc

Schramm, W. (1962). *Mass media and national development*. Palo Alto, CA: Stanford University Press.

Sida supports a project against sexual abuse and sexual exploitation in the Greater Mekong. (2000, March). *Health for Change Newsletter, 1, 2.*

Singhal, A., & Rogers, E. M. (1999). *Entertainment-education: A communication strategy for social change*. Mahwah, NJ: Lawrence Erlbaum.

Snyder, L. B. (1990). Channel effectiveness over time and knowledge and behavior gaps. *Journalism Quarterly, 67*, 875-886.

Snyder, L. B., & Hamilton, M. A. (in press). Meta-analysis of U.S. health campaign effects on behavior: Emphasize enforcement, exposure, and new information, and beware the secular trend. In R. Hornik (Ed.), *Public health communication: Evidence for behavior change*. Hillsdale, NJ: Lawrence Erlbaum.

Snyder, L. B., Hamilton, M. A., Mitchell, E. W., Kiwanuka-Tondo, J., Fleming-Milici, F., & Proctor, D. (in press). The effectiveness of mediated health communication campaigns: Meta-analysis of commencement, prevention, and cessation behavior campaigns. In R. Carveth & J. Bryant (Eds.), *Meta-analysis of media effects*. Mahwah, NJ: Lawrence Erlbaum.

Stern, M. P., Farquhar, J. W., Maccoby, N., & Russell, S. H. (1976). Results of a two-year health education campaign on dietary behavior: The Stanford Three Community Study. *Circulation, 54*, 826-833.

Uganda communication campaigns spur integrated health programs. (1999, October). In *Commu-*

nication impact! (No. 6, pp. 1-2). Baltimore: Johns Hopkins University Center for Communication Programs.

United Nations Children's Fund. (2000). *State of the world's children, 2000* [Online]. New York: Author. Available: http://www.unicef.org/sowc00

U.S. Agency for International Development Combating Polio in Madagascar [Online]. (2000). Available: http://www.usaid.gov/regions/afr/new_day/a59.txt

Valente, T. W., Kim, Y. M., Lettenmaier, C., Glass, W., & Dibba, Y. (1994). Radio promotion of family planning in The Gambia. *International Family Planning Perspectives, 20,* 96-100.

Valente, T. W., Poppe, P. R., & Payne Merritt, A. (1996). Mass-media-generated interpersonal communication as sources of information about family planning. *Journal of Health Communication, 1,* 247-265.

Wallack, L., Dorfman, L., Jernigan, D., & Themba, M. (1993). *Media advocacy and public health: Power for prevention.* Newbury Park, CA: Sage.

Weinreich, N. K. (1999). *Hands-on social marketing.* Thousand Oaks, CA: Sage.

Williamson, H. A. (1991). The Fogo Process: Development support communication in Canada and the developing world. In F. Casmir (Ed.), *Communication in development.* New York: Ablex.

World Bank. (1999). *Culture and sustainable development: A framework for action.* Washington, DC: Author.

World Bank. (2000/2001). *World development report: Attacking poverty* [online]. Washington, DC: Author. Available: http://www.worldbank.org/poverty/report/index.htm

World Health Organization. (1996). *World health report, 1996* [Online]. Geneva: Author. Available: http://www. who.int/whr

Yun, H., Govinder, K., & Mody, B. (2001). Factoring poverty and culture in to HIV-AIDS campaigns: Empirical support for audience segmentation. *Gazette, 64,* 73-95.

11

Communication Technology and Development

Instrumental, Institutional, Participatory, and Strategic Approaches

J. P. SINGH
Georgetown University

The current hype and importance given to sophisticated communication technologies for the developing world are in contrast to the lack of importance the "communication sector" received in the immediate postcolonial era from policymakers.[1] By the late 1950s, burgeoning literatures on communication and development, mostly in the United States, began to make a lot of the "promise" of communication technologies.[2] However, communication issues did not come of age until the 1960s. After less than 50 years, communication programs and development issues are now prominent in academic offerings worldwide. Policymakers, international governmental and nongovernmental organizations (IGOs and INGOs), nongovernmental organizations (NGOs), advocacy groups, and individuals alike chant the mantra of communication technologies.

This chapter culls a few themes in the literature on communication and development over the past 50 years. For pedagogical purposes, three time periods are distinguished. Dominant and alternative positions mostly in scholarship, but also in policy, are identified for each period. The chapter begins with a discussion of the changing conceptions of development to frame the debates on communication technologies followed by three subsections on the time periods. The first period (1950s to 1970s) deals with mass media theories and the overhaul of people's lives that was posited. The second period (1970s to 1990s) emphasized satellite and telecommunication technologies and made

AUTHOR'S NOTE: I thank Bella Mody and two anonymous referees for comments on earlier drafts and Simona Folescu for valuable research assistance.

much of their two-way interactive potential. The last period discussed (1990s onward) looks at the effects of micro-electronic information networks.

The main arguments are the following. The modernization model of state-led, top-down, mass media-oriented, national communication technology deployment gave way in the late 1960s to a considerable emphasis on sociopolitical institutional contexts. The modernization literature advocated putting mass media in the same pride of place as other grand development projects (e.g., hydroelectricity, railways, mineral extraction) in the immediate postcolonial era. Much faith was placed in central planning. The 1970s brought a few sobering and specific insights. Instrumental thinking, positing technology as the panacea for all socioeconomic problems, still ruled but the context of governmental, societal, and capitalist structures and institutions for technological diffusion became obvious, too. The conceptualizations of new technologies (telecommunications, satellites) were limited to economic and sociological features as opposed to the psychological reconditioning of people's daily lives planned in the mass media era. Emphasis was also placed on two-way communications. Throughout both these eras, radical and structuralist scholarship focused on the constraints posited by historically powerful socioeconomic institutions (class, private capital, bourgeois state) and argued that communication technologies legitimized the interests of Western capitalism.

Finally, the current "Internet era" is marked both by an optimism about group-specific participatory and strategic approaches and the radical/structuralist pessimism regarding the potential of communication technology for development. For the optimists, the cost structure of technologies has now changed to facilitate diffusion without massive state support, which led to many forms of state abuse in the past. The instrumentalist, structural-

ist, and radical perspectives now also coexist and draw inspiration and critical thunder from newer perspectives such as constructivist ones, discourse analysis, and ethnographic approaches.[3] Table 11.1 summarizes the main arguments.

THE MACRO DEVELOPMENT CONTEXT

"Now India," said India's prime minister Jawaharlal Nehru in 1956, "we are bound to be industrialized, we are trying to be industrialized, we must be industrialized." Grand projects accompanied by central planning were conceived. The promise of information technology presented today in significant ways mimics the expectations from industrial technology.

Three economic ideas helped to shape the development debates of the 1950s, and subsequently the way communication technologies were conceived and deployed. These three were Keynesian industrialization strategies, import substitution industrialization, and central planning. Keynes's (1936) ideas helped convince the industrialized world that without adequate public policy, capitalism could not sustain itself. The impetus to public policy suited the mood of the Third World that equated capitalism with colonialism.[4] Keynesian theory also argued that the ripple effects of initial capital investment or demand would be limited due to structural bottlenecks in the economy that could not respond to market signals adequately. State intervention for ensuring industrial growth was thus necessary. From the 1940s to the 1960s, a time dubbed by Hirschman (1981) as an eminently exciting era in development economics, several state-led strategies were suggested to beget rapid industrialization. Central planning, modeled mostly on Gosplan (Soviet state planning agency) models, was also introduced, and the

Table 11.1 Communication Technology and Development: The Past 50 Years

Period[a]	Late 1950s to Early 1970s	Early 1970s to Early 1990s	1990s to Present
Communication technologies emphasized	Mass media (print, radio, TV broadcasting)	Satellites (television), telecommunications	Computers, Internet
Dominant characteristics	Instrumental beliefs about technology	Appreciation of institutional and structural constraints	Pluralistic, strategic, and participatory approaches
Dominant goal	Shift in mind-sets toward "modern" and achievement-oriented thinking	Economic growth	NGO empowerment and networking; economic growth and private profit
Emphases in alternative perspectives	Institutionalist: Context of diffusion Critique of international capitalism	Advocacy for NWICO Pluralistic/participatory perspectives	Radical traditions emphasizing structuralist forces Neoliberal perspectives
Cost structure of technology	High fixed and variable costs	High fixed and low or high variable costs	Low fixed and variable costs
Chief proponents[b] (1) dominant (2) alternative	(1) McClelland, Lerner, Schramm, Pool (2) Smythe, Schiller	(1) Hudson, Parker, Saunders et al., Rogers (2) Mody, Sussman, NWICO school	(1) Social movements literature (Wilkins, Castells), international organizations (Mansell and Wehn)
Promotional agencies	National governments, prominent individuals	LOs, national governments, research institutes, MNCs	Private sector, LOs (IGOs and INGOs), MNCs, national governments
Policy instruments	Central planning, trust in the state	Cautious moves away from the state to involve communities and private capital	Privatization and MNCs, donor agency funds, state and NGO strategies
Development context	Grand macro projects, Keynesian beliefs, central planning	Sociopolitical constraints emphasized; private sector ascendancy; micro approaches develop	Appreciation both of structural constraints and micro contexts of empowerment
Unit of analysis	Nation-state	Nation-state, subnational units	Subnational and transnational units
Methods in scholarship	Empiricist and behavioral	Empirical, historical-institutionalist	Empirical, institutionalist, ethnographic, discourse analysis

NOTE: IGO = international governmental organization, INGO = international nongovernmental organization, IO = international organization, MNC = multinational corporation, NGO = nongovernmental organization, NWICO = New World Information and Communication Order.

a. Each period might also include features of earlier periods.

b. See references for citations.

191

government elite in various developing countries set out to effect carefully orchestrated industrialization in a short period of time. The third guiding pillar, and a direct fallout of colonialism, was that developing countries could not hope to gain from a Western-type industrialization. Imports were expensive and unnecessary and would result in unwanted dependencies. Thus, areas of import-intensive industrialization were identified and policymakers sought to jump-start indigenous programs. Thus was born the strategy of import substitution industrialization (ISI).

By the late 1960s, the high growth rates expected from ISI had not materialized. Although many factors were to be blamed, economists focused increasingly on the institutional contexts. Neoclassical liberalism found a scapegoat in the rent-seeking state, which had become corrupt and inefficient and thus incapable of accelerating economic growth (for an overview, see Belassa, 1989). A subtler critique came from economic historians who reexamined Europe's industrial past to find cues to growth. What they discovered was that Europe's industrialization was itself an outcome of Europe's rationalized system of property rights enforced by increasingly democratizing states in history (see North, 1981; North & Thomas, 1973). In fact, they argued, it was this mix of favorable institutional factors that ensured that England outpaced continental Europe in the nineteenth century.

An important challenge to economic orthodoxy came from Latin American economists who questioned the value of free trade ties with the North when the terms of trade were not in their favor. An early exponent was Raul Prebisch, whose ideas helped in the formation of the United Nations Conference on Trade and Development (UNCTAD) as an alternative to the General Agreement on Tariffs and Trade (GATT). Later such ideas became the province of the dependency school, which in its sophisticated versions employed class analysis to show that the core elite of the developed and the developing worlds kept the periphery of the developing world in a state of dependency and impoverished development (Cardoso & Faletto, 1971/1979; Evans, 1979). Although empirically questionable, ideas of the dependency, structuralist (à la Prebisch), and radical schools provided the intellectual backing to the North-South political-economic confrontations beginning in the late 1960s.

Two political developments in the 1980s changed the course of Third World economic strategies. One was the debt crisis. ISI was import intensive for its capital needs, and international finance had been used to support these imports since the late 1960s. The debt crisis began with Mexico's acknowledgment that it could not pay on its more than $85 billion foreign debt in 1982. The total developing country debt owed to the North in 1989 was $1.3 trillion. The second was the ascendancy of liberal ideas favoring private capital and market-based solutions under Reagan in the United States and Thatcher in the United Kingdom. If the foreign debt crisis, widely blamed on government-led ISI expenditures, broke the back of state-led strategies, the rise of liberal ideas sought to fill that void. The property rights school, however, warned that without institutional mechanisms in place, liberal economic policies would also founder (Olson & Kähkönen, 2000; Williamson, 1985).

The old belief in conceiving grand development projects is now gone, partly because of the failure of the top-down grand strategies favored by states and international organizations in the past and partly because of bottom-up participatory development pressures from local groups (see the chapter by Huesca in this volume). By 1990s, micro-projects and micro-financing were the buzzwords of development agencies worldwide. As the faith in government-led development policies decreased,

NGOs tried to step in to pick up the challenge of grassroots development. NGOs, many of them linked globally through donor agencies and INGO networks, also emphasized micro-level policies. The current period is interesting because although agencies of international capital (private sector, powerful governments, and international organizations such as the World Bank and International Monetary Fund) have defined the "Washington consensus" around neoliberal policies favoring private markets, the latter is being heavily contested not just in scholarship but also by grassroots and transnational social movements. It remains to be seen if the Washington consensus will wipe out the small opening for alternative development designs. What is also beginning to emerge is a synthesis of the two. The creation of market institutions demands oversight by governments and other groups to ensure transparency and a level playing field and might even mean new types of partnerships among governments and private sector and societal groups to ensure that social empowerment does indeed take place (Mansell & Wehn, 1998; I will pick up on this theme later).

The dirigiste projects of the 1950s, the appreciation of the institutional constraints beginning with the late 1960s, and the current dual foci on privatization and market-based institutions, on one hand, coupled with micro-strategic approaches, on the other, all find their counterparts in the way communication technology has been conceptualized in the past 50 years.

THE ERA OF GRAND PROJECTS: MASS MEDIA

One of the legacies of the Western world's industrialization experience, along with the spread of liberal ideas, was what it meant to be a "modern" human being. Associated ideas of "modernization," the desirability of democracy, and U.S. Cold War aims influenced the study of communication as it began to emerge in universities in the United States. Interestingly, though, in spite of the links with democracy and capitalism, communication technologies were first introduced to the developing world as centrally planned state-led grand projects.

David Lerner (1958) stated the link between modernity and communication categorically in the preface of his influential book: "Modernity is primarily a state of mind—expectation of progress, propensity of growth, readiness to change" (p. viii). It was merely serendipitous that Western Europe had first developed this state of mind. It could be produced anywhere and herein lay its development potential. "The Western model must, in this sense, be *freed* from the constraints of ethnocentrism in order to function effectively" (p. ix). Scholars such as Lerner, followed by McClelland (1961), Schramm (1964), and Rogers (1962), effectively established a groundwork for this desired outcome from mass media dissemination. (Many chapters in this handbook—McDowell, Melkote, and Mody and Lee—cover these ideas; therefore, only a summary is presented here.)

Lerner (1958) argued that modernity and democracy needed checks on tribalism and isolation, to check "traditional" ways of thinking. Modernity demands active participation, empathy, and people's ability to imagine alternative futures. The march toward modernity could be effected by accelerating the following sequence:

increasing urbanization → high rates of literacy → mass media dissemination → political participation and economic growth.

The broadcast-oriented channels of mass media communication, as opposed to the traditional interpersonal ones, can help in replacing the traditional ways with much needed secular mind-sets. In fact, high levels of literacy are not necessary for understanding television and radio and thus would be particularly effective for bringing awareness. Lerner's thesis was supported by McClelland's (1961) psychological and empirical insight into the "achievement motivation," which can be measured by a modern society's members' ability to fantasize and indulge in free associations liberating them from traditional mind-sets.

The ideas about modernization and mass media found full expression in Wilbur Schramm's writings. His seminal contribution, *Mass Media and National Development* (1964), held information flows as essential to the development process. The book was quite influential in recommending and planning the mass media programs in the developing world during the 1960s. It cited several studies correlating communication infrastructures with economic growth, affirming Lerner's belief that the former were a "great multiplier" (p. 47). Thus, communication development projects all over the world were used to provide distance education and information on health, nutrition, weather, farming, and so on. The broader conclusions regarding effects of mass media on political participation were also supported by other prominent theorists such as Pool (1963) and Pye (1963).

A closely related thesis to Schramm's, in that it, too, noted how stimuli/innovations (including communication) can change the way a social system operates, was Everett M. Rogers's *Diffusion of Innovations* (1962). Rogers (1983) posited diffusion as "the process by which (1) an *innovation* is (2) *communicated* through certain *channels* (3) *over time* (4) among the members of a *social system*" (p. 10). Central to diffusions is the communication of ideas. Rogers refined the thesis on the role of mass media by borrowing from

Lazarsfeld, Berelson, and Gaudet (1944) and Katz's (1957) two-step model of communication. "Mass-media channels are primarily knowledge creators, whereas interpersonal networks are more important at persuading individuals to adopt or reject" (Rogers, 1983, p. 273). Thus, Rogers attributed to opinion leaders the kinds of modern characteristics that Lerner and others privileged but also emphasized the role of interpersonal communication that they had marginalized.

The models of mass media communication noted so far are often critiqued for being conservative, Eurocentric, and ignorant of local context. The critiques may be exaggerated. The fact that these media were introduced to many in the developing world under the auspices of central planning has been almost missed by these critiques and deserves attention historically. So convinced were scholars of the usefulness of mass media models that they seldom questioned the efficacy of central planning instruments, hardly a feature of any kind of reactionary scholarship, deployed to disseminate radio and television. Planners in developing countries were enamored with the socialist experiment of countries such as the Soviet Union and in Eastern Europe where mass media had been deployed to influence and change mind-sets, too. Many of the central plans, which included mass media programs, were modeled after the Soviet Gosplan's exercises, and "central planning" economists such as Wassily Leontif, Oskar Lange, and Jan Tinbergen either were from Eastern Europe or were heavily influenced by central planning ideas that came from there. In Oskar Lange's (1975) words: "In the socialist countries and in the countries following a national revolutionary pattern we plan economic development, because economic development would not, under historic conditions existent, take place by itself automatically. Consequently it must be planned" (p. 695).

Furthermore, by the late 1960s, many scholars themselves questioned the need for Western-style urbanization that Lerner had earlier seen as a prerequisite for development (Lerner & Schramm, 1967). People such as Schramm also emphasized that mass media would be counterproductive if deployed without concern for local conditions. Schramm et al. (International Institute for Educational Planning, 1967a, 1967b) assessed the effectiveness of mass media for education by outlining the set of technical, organizational, political, and planning elements that are necessary along with emphasizing how the media system needs to fit the educational problem at hand and not the other way around. They noted that the mass media were not "miracle drugs." Similarly, Rogers's emphasis on interpersonal communication took stock of the necessity of local communication channels in diffusion of innovations.

It is, nevertheless, undeniable that the challenges and failures of the modernization model not only helped to shape the dominant communication development models but also the critiques from the left. Attention focused on these models' grand design, their top-down instrumentality, and their expectations (and unquestioned acceptance) about the suitability of representational democracy. Just as economists sought to boil the task of development down to a singular activity such as demand or investment, communication scholars similarly conjectured about the desired effects of mass media in producing modern mind-sets, secular thinking, and cosmopolitanism. The thinking is linear and causal, in accordance with the methodological trends then. Rogers (1976) noted that models like those of Lerner "led communication scholars to expect the mass media to be kind of a magic multiplier for development in other developing nations . . . consistent with the general upbeat opinion about the possibilities for

rapid development" (p. 134). The top-down instrumentality is obvious even in the models advocating concern for local conditions: The task is that of communicating preconceived models (means and ends) effectively through localized communication channels.

The expectation that mass media cause democracy was empirically unfounded and was perhaps the most blatantly ideological element of early mass media thinking. Leading political scientists such as Lipset (1959), Pool (1963), and Pye (1963) questioned the effectiveness of mass media alone in producing attitudes favoring political participation. Nonetheless, these scholars elsewhere held great hopes for these technologies in producing political freedoms (Pool, 1963).[5]

The biggest critique of modernization came from radical approaches critical of the spread of capitalism. The latter was implicitly built into modernization models and partly ignored, as these models often overlooked the global context in which they were to be implemented. The fiercest early critiques came from Schiller and Smythe (the latter a colleague of Schramm's at Illinois). Schiller (1969) warned that a global communication network had emerged dominated by the United States and reflected the political ambitions of its government and the military-industrial complex surrounding it. Instead of being enlightening, mass media such as radio and television danced only to the tune of markets and profitability. Schiller warned developing countries not to model their communication systems after those of the United States. Later, Schiller (1973) warned that the knowledge itself was big business supported by big government. Smythe's (1994) writings are concerned with the way mass media are used to perpetuate capitalism, binding people (consumers) in a nonenlightening ideology. His work seeks to lay bare the myths and ideologies surrounding mass media, forever calling attention to how institutions of market capitalism impose pre-determined solutions on their audiences rather than shaping technologies with audience participation. Smythe and Schiller's insights served to check the instrumental optimism of mass communication models and they pioneered alternative traditions in communication scholarship (including providing intellectual impetus to radical ideas to correct information imbalances between the North and South, analyzed in the next subsection). Both theorists were, however, also critiqued for making sweeping statements that are hard to substantiate empirically.

By the 1970s, the communication technology and development literature had come a long way, its practitioners both aware of the internal contradictions and challenges of their models and many of them critical of the values of capitalism that were being passed to the developing world without questioning.

THE INSTITUTIONAL CONTEXTS: SATELLITES AND TELECOMMUNICATIONS

The period from early 1970s to early 1990s was guided by lessons learned from implementation of the first few communication development programs and the increasing importance, in scholarship and later in policy, of technologies such as satellites and telecommunications. It was hard to reduce the problem of development to that of changing mindsets via mass media information dissemination. Furthermore, communication development programs faced significant societal and governmental barriers in their implementation. These and other findings narrowed the goals for the introduction of newer technologies that were conceived only in terms of the need to reach remote areas and in terms of boosting the rates of economic growth, a

far cry from the earlier mass media era when an entire overhaul of a society's ways was planned.

Satellites come with many attractive features. First, geographic isolation can be bridged and the remotest areas accessed, not possible even with microwave-based radio. Second, broadcasting can be more effective by allowing for voice and image streams allowing television to reach places where only radio might have done so earlier. Third, satellites allow for interactive two-way communications. This tallies well with the early results from communication development, including diffusions research, which underscored the importance of and need for interpersonal communication.

The case for satellite communication came to be made in policy circles more effectively than in scholarship initially, reversing the ideational-policy chain of the mass media. Whereas the share of developing countries in Intelsat, the global satellite consortium owned by most of the world's governments, was only about 30% (Hudson, 1990, p. 149), it still allowed many developing countries to think and to plan for provision of satellite-based services in the 1960s. Hudson (1990), who makes a forceful case for satellites, noted: "Satellite technology has an almost seductive appeal. The capability of satellites to reach virtually any location from a single point is a powerful attraction for television broadcasters and for governments concerned with building or preserving national unity" (p. 175). Although the cost barriers for owning satellite systems are formidable, a few large countries such as Brazil, India, Indonesia, Mexico, and China were early converts. Many others either leased capacity from Intelsat or joined regional satellite systems such as Arabsat or Indonesia's Palapa B system, which provided services to Southeast Asia (Hudson, 1990). Nevertheless, by the time scholars began to analyze the case of satellites in the 1980s, policymakers in the developing world, often with help from international donor agencies, had already planned ambitious initiatives for satellites.

Scholars such as Hudson (1985) led the way in documenting the benefits of satellites effectively raising their stature for providers, international development agencies, and national governments. She also documented their economic benefits, especially in provision of telephony. But as with mass communication, the promise was tampered by politics. Hudson (1990) called attention to the institutional barriers to satellite diffusion noting that Intelsat, in spite of its commitment to development, was too organizationally unmanageable and monopolistic to intervene effectively. National governments, on the other hand, faced a number of organizational, resource, and capability barriers preventing them from realizing the full benefits of this technology. These institutional barriers were, however, noted in broad strokes only.

The big break with the mass media-oriented era came from the two-way communication potential of satellites.

> Despite the popularity of television or video, it should be noted that this is generally not the greatest communication need in rural and remote areas. Around the world, isolated people agree that reliable two-way communication is their top priority, so that they can get help in emergencies, stay in touch with families and friends, and get the information they need for economic survival. (Hudson, 1990, p. 180)

The case for rural telephony, and the socioeconomic benefits thereof, is made by Hudson with her coauthor Edwin Parker in a number of works including Hudson et al. (1983) and Parker, Hudson, Dillman, and Roscoe (1989).

The socioeconomic benefits of two-way telephony began to be documented as early as the 1960s, but in the 1970s these efforts received a big push from the International Telecommunication Union (ITU) that not only sponsored many influential studies (including many by Parker and Hudson) but also led the organization to declare 1984 as the International Communication Year. The ITU's (1984) Maitland Commission report urged developing countries to put a telephone within a short distance of every member of their population. Other studies emphasized the benefits of telecommunications such as diversifying the rural and urban economic bases, reducing business and administrative costs, and for delivering social services such as health, education, and emergency services (ITU, 1984; National Telecommunications and Information Administration, 1992; Parker et al., 1989; Saunders, Warford, & Wellenius, 1994). Countries such as early Singapore and Brazil and Korea made telecommunications a priority in the 1970s, and a number of developing countries did so in the 1980s.

Just as telecommunications became a development priority, the grand projects of the immediate postcolonial era, in communication and elsewhere, were coming undone. Faith in central planning and the state had resulted in few positive results. Cash-strapped and debt-laden developing country governments, often under a host of domestic and international pressures including ideational pressures, began to move away from ISI. In telecommunications, this meant ushering in privatization and market-oriented liberalization to boost telecommunication infrastructures. Liberalization was then the institutional-fix that was introduced, and it was legitimized by the Washington consensus, to expand telecommunication infrastructures in the developing world.

It is now increasingly clear that most satellite and telecommunication expansion programs were (and are) too supply driven or technologically determinist. A critique of the Hudson-Parker thinking, such as one offered by Shields (1989), is illustrative. First, although these authors are aware of the institutional constraints, they do not effectively document them. Their main concern is with how technologies, if introduced somehow, would produce desired conditions. Second, Shields is particularly critical of one such desired condition, namely, that rural areas should all have a public call office that allows them to call urban areas. This urban bias makes assumptions about how rural populations interact and might be centered too much on Parker and Hudson's earlier research in Alaska. Even within the neoliberal paradigm, through which Parker and Hudson operate, recent research (Pernyeszi, Rao, Yadagiri, & Kumar, 2000) shows that rural areas benefit most when they have large internal networks. Third, the predominant focus on technology sidesteps distributive questions. Shields implies that Hudson and Parker were so beholden to the international agencies sponsoring their research that they found it expedient to ignore these distributive questions.

For detailed analyses of institutional barriers to technological diffusion and its distributional effects, structural and radical scholarships are useful. Mody (1987), for example, documents the political obstacles underlying India's experience with the Satellite Instructional Television Experiment (SITE) that began to be proposed by the Indian Space Research Organization in the mid-1960s in collaboration with the National Aeronautics and Space Administration (NASA) [6] and began service in a pilot project in 1975. An Indian satellite system, INSAT, which was to boost SITE efforts, was approved in 1975 and became operational in 1983. By the time of INSAT's launch, the educational goals of SITE were sidetracked by political prerogatives such as controlling news flows to the public or economic ones such as the need for the national television carrier, Doordarshan, to earn revenues. Mody (1987) notes that India took 20 years to launch the technology because of its desire to develop indigenous technology, and she concluded that "the nature of the civil service bureaucracy and multi-part organization of the political system in India required more time-consuming establishment of consensus at several levels" (p. 158).

While the developing world headed toward liberalization in the 1980s, the structuralist and radical critiques continued to gain momentum. Both Hudson and Mody, as noted above, had drawn attention to the power structures that constrained the adoption and diffusion of technology. However, Mody meets the challenge of distributive questions head-on. An early evaluation (Shingi & Mody, 1976) of television in disseminating agricultural information concluded that better educated farmers had the most access to television, whereas those who needed it the most, farmers with low levels of knowledge, had less access. Mody (1987) noted that SITE and INSAT were being used by politicians to effect political gains and by Doordarshan (India's TV channel) for economic gains. She also noted the urban bias of satellite-based television, areas that were relatively information rich already.

At the international level, the radical critique led directly to examining the information imbalances within and beyond less developed countries (LDCs), especially between industrialized and developing countries. Scholars noted that global information flows were from the North to the South, with the latter controlling information production, distribution and consumption. (See Mowlana,

1997, for an overview of "flows" research.) This later came to be known as the "communication gap" (ITU, 1984; O'Brien, 1983). These events also coincided with and provided impetus internationally to the demand for a New World Information and Communication Order (NWICO), a call emboldened by moves from the United Nations Educational, Scientific and Cultural Organization (UNESCO) where much of the early flows research took place.[7] Cees Hamelink (1983) at UNESCO and Galtung (1982) likened the processes sustaining the communication gap to cultural imperialism.

Initially, NWICO laid importance on correcting the one-way flow of negative news and information via mass media from LDCs to developed countries. But by the time of the MacBride Commission report (1979) and the influential work *Many Voices, One World* (International Commission for the Study of Communication Problems, 1980), developing self-reliant communication infrastructures within LDCs became important. The MacBride Commission thus wrote that,

> Communication be no longer regarded merely as an incidental service and its development left to chance. Recognition of its potential warrants the formulation by all nations, and particularly developing countries, of comprehensive communication policies linked to overall social, cultural, economic and political goals . . . with broad public participation . . . within the wider frame of national development in an interdependent world. (quoted in Pavlic & Hamelink, 1985, p. 22)

What emerged from NWICO were ideas emphasizing self-reliance in individual LDCs and collective reliance across them. Many authors and organizations during the 1970s, although not expressly endorsing NWICO, recognized the importance of self-reliance in telecommunications and also emphasized making transfers of technology from developed countries more suitable to LDCs (see Galtung, 1982; Pitroda, 1976). To sum up, the NWICO line of thinking shows that telecommunications was becoming increasingly recognized as a priority even before LDCs began moving away from an ISI strategy in the 1980s. Thus, it could be argued counterfactually that LDCs would have continued to make telecommunications a priority even without abandoning ISI.[8] The current fashion, especially in the trade press, of noting that telecommunication prioritization owes its origins to the ascendancy of neoliberal policies in the developing world is incorrect.

While the radical critiques challenged the efficacy of spreading broadcast or two-way communication technology via the market system, especially in the calls for NWICO, an alternative line of reasoning looking at detailed technical and organizational aspects developed mostly from observation of grassroots communication development models. The language of small-scale "participatory development" programs thus begins to find expression in scholarship (see the Huesca chapter in this volume) in which those affected take part in the planning as well as the implementation of development programs. Hornik (1988) summarizes this literature to argue that effective communication development programs require multiple channels of communication, carefully developed messages, appropriate feedback effects, administrative coordination among various agencies, political attractiveness, institutional support, and lots of patience. The jury is still out on whether the adoption of the language of participatory development by international development agencies, beginning in the late 1980s, is a rhetorical appropriation or a significant change in focus. Thus, for example, whereas providing phones through micro grassroots initiatives is heralded as a success story of rural empowerment by international organizations (Bhatnagar & Schware, 2000), it is critiqued as perpetuating the status quo by others (see Quadir, in press).

To summarize, it was clear by the late 1980s that the grand state-supported projects of the past era had failed. The radical critiques had lost much of their political constituency as the developing world adopted liberalization strategies. In the meantime, mainstream conceptualizations of communication had benefited from these critiques and their own to think of communication technology in its institutional, micro, and interactive (two-way) contexts.

NETWORK STRATEGY, PARTICIPATION, AND PLURALISM: COMPUTERS AND THE INTERNET

By the 1990s, attention focused on technologies that made communication less hierarchical, more two-way and interactive. The thinking both reflected and was shaped by still newer communication technologies: computers and the Internet. Although the radical critiques continued (Sussman, 1997), many approaches toward communication emphasized networking strategy, participation, and pluralism (Mansell & Wehn, 1998; Wilkins, 2000).

What broadcasting was to mass media, two-way communication to satellites and telecommunications, *networks* are to computers and the Internet. Instead of the mere interaction of two-way information flows, networks allow for multiple channels of communication running through multiple parties, allowing for multiple types of messages. In Castells's (1996) words: "Networks constitute the new social morphology of our societies, and the diffusion of networking logic substantially modifies the operation and outcomes in pro-

cesses of production, experience, power and culture" (p. 469).

Where the language of networking parts company with prior analyses is in the positing of the many new and old actors involved and the various methods by which they interact over these communication networks. No longer are analyses limited to speaking of government or international aid agency-led communication development programs. In fact, the very language of "development communication," now significantly in disuse, smacks of a top-down goal-ordered instrumentality. What analysts are positing/discovering are actors such as NGOs, social movements, and other human (institutional and cultural) groupings that now employ communication media such as the Internet in ways whose outcomes cannot always be prespecified. In a volume on the changing urban geography, but equally applicable for communication media in the developing world, Graham and Marvin (1996) critique both the linear instrumental thinking and also the grand claims of radical political economy regarding capitalism: "Both, we argue, are unhelpful. . . . Social action shapes telecommunications applications in cities in diverse and contingent ways, even if this goes on against the backcloth of broader political economic trends" (p. 381).

The diverse and contingent ways in which networks function are perhaps best appreciated by approaches that embed and contextualize networks in sociopolitical institutions, in new conceptions of power, and possible uses of network strategy. At their core, however, they are concerned with how marginalized and excluded groups in the developing world may or may not benefit from information networks linking computers and the Internet. Whereas these approaches are themselves multifaceted, they stand in contrast to the grand approaches, both neoliberal and radical, alluded to by Graham and Marvin. Their understanding of institutions and power is also more nuanced and subtle than previously understood.

Earlier critiques of technological instrumentality almost unknowingly sanctioned another type of instrumentality, in understanding power and institutions. Instrumental power focuses on the capacity of power holders to effect particular outcomes, and most analyses above have this definition at their core, be it in the instrumental understanding of technology or in the exclusion of the disadvantaged from it. This almost reduces the problem of development to that of access. Both radical and liberal scholarships advocate particular solutions to access ranging from trickle-down diffusion theories to the radical strategies advocating a structural overhaul (see NWICO debates).

But power is both instrumental and constitutive (Singh, 2001). The latter refers to the collective understanding of power holders (as well as those without) in promoting particular development ideas, often referred to as ideologies or discourses. For Wilkins (2000), "Development communication may be seen as a special case in which institutions engage in ideological production through strategic intervention using communication processes and technologies" (pp. 198-199). The intellectual antecedents to these approaches may be traced in the participatory approaches to development from Latin America starting with Freire (1970/2000) and discourse analyses of power by philosophers such as Foucault (2000). There is a double bind here. The dominant development discourse fashions the actions of power holders and it conditions the subservience of the disenfranchised by conditioning their actions within that discourse.

In their conceptualizations of the new media (computers and the Internet), scholars are, therefore, exploring the contexts in which such discourse may be transformed or overcome. Freire (1970/2000) offers a guide here: "For the oppressed to be able to wage the struggle for their liberation, they must perceive the reality of oppression not as a closed world from which there is no exit, but as a limiting situation they can transform." Such a task is not easy but begins with fashioning a new collective understanding by the oppressed about their identity rather than affixing it to the one offered by the oppressing ideology. Information networks, which are inherently interactive, may be allowing a limited voice to the underprivileged in helping them voice their concerns to like-minded individuals locally, regionally, and globally (Wilkins, 2000), allowing for new forms of identity to emerge. It is no surprise here that the constitutive power of information networks is often noted in the context of the social movements and international and domestic NGOs that can often work outside the purview of traditionally powerful state and capitalist interests (Keck & Sikkink, 1998; Mathews, 1997). Of particular note is the growing body of scholarship that examines questions of identity, collective-conscience formation, and collective action for women's networks worldwide, including the developing world (see essays in Harcourt, 1999; Keck & Sikkink, 1997; Wilkins, 2000). It is important to note that although strategic and constitutive network interactions are being noted, scholars, including those mentioned above, have not overlooked the way that the underprivileged are often excluded from the very networks that may be a source of liberation for them.

The radical scholars are particularly careful to point out the business-as-usual aspect of the new information networks. For Castells (1996, 1997, 1998), the primary function performed by networks is that of sustaining and coordinating global financial, production, and distribution flows. Labor, on the other hand, is fragmented (Castells, 1996, p. 475). Social movements, including feminist ones, can challenge dominant structures using subordinate networks through "conscious, purposive social action" (Castells, 1998, p. 380), but this is not a fait accompli. Castells posits feminist movements challenging patriarchal structures in favorable light. Women's NGOs, for example, approximate what Castells (1997, p. 200) calls "practical feminists" who, apart from their presence in the developed world, represent "the widest and deepest stream of women's struggles in today's world, particularly in the developing world." But he also sees them as being quite elitist. In the end, networked capitalism, in replacing industrial capitalism, creates fragmented and multiple social identities, including feminist ones.

Castells's themes are reflected well in the radical communication scholarship that began with Schiller and Smythe and sustained through NWICO debates. Recently, many authors (including Schiller) in a volume edited by Thussu (1998) note that global capitalism, supported by national governments and international organizations, in the information age is best seen through the emergence of "electronic empires" headed by media barons such as Ted Turner, Rupert Murdoch, and Bill Gates. These authors challenge the popular view that declining costs of technology and globalization will lead to a global village in which ordinary lives may be improved. Golding (1998) notes that contrary to the revolutionary hype about the Internet, "its commercialization in the mid-1990s looks all too familiar to observers of past technological promise." In radical scholarship, the pursuit of private profit through activities as diverse as infotainment and the control of digital networks is incompatible with the universalistic and emancipatory promises that have accompanied these technologies.

A middle-of-the-road position ideologically (called "practical liberal" here) is offered by Mansell and Wehn (1998) in a report prepared for the United Nations Commission on Science and Technology. The report is concerned with the exclusion of the underprivileged from sophisticated information and communication technologies (ICTs) and the limited strategic ways in which the latter might better their conditions. The commission authors are wary of instrumental notions: ICTs, to be effective, need to be examined in their organizational contexts. In particular, for technologies such as the Internet to be adopted, educational capabilities (including technical skills) first need be improved. "Overemphasis on 'access' to links in the information 'highways' means that insufficient attention may be given to other crucial matters. Development needs, preparedness, affordability, and skills development all need to be considered systematically" (Mansell & Wehn, 1998, p. 115). However, only a few developing countries are ready for the sophisticated ICTs through comprehensive national policies. In contrast to radical scholars, the report notes the possibility of a "new" development model in which governments and businesses are working together not only to expand markets but also to enhance the kinds of capabilities that are necessary to take advantage of ICTs.

The Mansell and Wehn (1998) conclusions are complemented by Singh (1999). Only a few "catalytic" states are capable of formulating the kind of comprehensive national information policies and articulating the kind of property rights that would have widespread and beneficial distributional effects. Singh provides a user-group demands and government-led supply model to show that most developing countries are unable to resolve the myriad pressures they face in providing information infrastructures effectively. Nevertheless, it is still possible for states, businesses, and civil society to come together to forge a consensus toward mutually beneficial information policies.

The practical liberal position needs to be distinguished from other neoliberal models. The neoliberal solutions Levy and Spiller (1996) and the World Bank (1998) have focused on are the kinds of property rights that governments must provide to optimize network expansion. The neoliberal property rights school includes political institutions but only inasmuch as they create or hinder network "efficiencies" (Levy & Spiller, 1996) or privilege powerful political actors to the detriment of others (Singh, 2000). Although this view is obviously endorsed by powerful agencies such as the World Bank and many multinational corporations in arguing for market-based solutions, its normative position favoring markets is also under heavy fire for producing a "digital divide." For many scholars, this view may also represent the dominant position today with its hold over defining national and international policy outcomes favoring private capital.

The various liberal positions are often critiqued by radical scholarship as being too naïve or optimistic when it comes to the effects of global capitalism. However, they share the concern for institutional strategy and collective action that discourse-based scholars such as Wilkins (2000) underscore. This chapter takes both the liberal and the discourse-based positions to be defining the mainstream of scholarly enquiry and the critical and constructivist schools to be providing useful counterpoints and relevant critiques.

CONCLUSION

Fifty years of communication and development scholarship offer many results, but it is informed by the dialectic of technology as a panacea versus its effects being circumscribed by the social, political, and economic contexts in which it is introduced. The former position, often characterized as a "field of dreams" build-it-and-they-will-come approach, is supply driven and posits bold conclusions such as overhauling people's lives through mass media, making the world interactive and empowered through introduction of information highways. This technologically instrumentalist view continues to be supported not just by many hues of scholarship, but more important, it finds powerful constituencies of support among international organizations, businesses, and many national governments.

The alternatives to thinking of technological instrumentality are many, but three important themes stand out. First, distributional questions are often skirted or not fully answered by traditional accounts. If instrumental scholarships note that technologies enhance capabilities, structural views call attention to the social, political, and economic environments that govern, shape, and often preempt capability enhancements. For example, what good is it to talk about the double-digit growth rates of telephones, cellular, and the Internet in China when most of these services accrue to the politically powerful export-oriented coastal provinces and to governmental elite, and content censorship can result in draconian punishments for those participating in the use of the Internet? Second, top-down models of technology do not work but the bottom-up ones are equally limited (or politically powerless) in their application. Numerous obstacles stand in the way of individuals from all kinds of gender, class (and caste in South Asia), racial (including North-South divisions), skill and education levels, and geographic and regional hierarchies from participating in the use of communication technologies. What promise does the Internet offer women in the global South struggling with all kinds of oppression and caught in low skill and education levels? Third, and on a slightly more optimistic note, if technologies embody politics, then critical thinking (both everyday and intellectual) can help to disembody these politics. Technologies are not merely instruments and structures but apparatuses that help to constitute identities. This raises questions about structure and agency as, for example, when a Chinese student downloads prohibited materials in Beijing or when a housewife in India or Mexico watches a television soap opera in which women do not play out traditional roles.

Barring those who attribute insidious motives to scholars or those who eschew the idea that scholarship serves a social purpose, most communication development scholars seek to find ways in which technologies might help the disadvantaged and the disenfranchised. The controversies on how to effect or define these development goals are neither resolvable, nor should be so. In fact, as this chapter shows, the dialectic of critique and counter-critique has informed and (it is hoped) strengthened successive waves of scholarship. The practical liberal position suggested above and still emerging is thus appreciative of the positive role of communication media as well as the organizational, skill-level and educational, and political difficulties that almost make it difficult to employ these communication media for socially useful tasks. This perspective offers limited hopes about forging partnership among governance institutions, businesses, and civil society, but it also challenges one to think of strategic, participatory, and micro ways in which communication technologies might be employed. It also offers a respite from naïve views and hype about communication media rampant in the stories about our always newly empowered global village from yet another new technology.

NOTES

1. Colonial rulers had placed great importance on the control of communication infrastructure and flows for enforcing imperialism. See Innis (1950).

2. The McDowell and Melkote chapters in this volume note that the agenda of the early communication researchers was influenced by Cold War calculations and thus communication development projects were often tied to the need for peddling American influence abroad.

3. Constructivist schools look at the interactive social processes that bring about common understandings in groups (Berger & Luckmann, 1966); discourse analyses examine how powerful human agencies legitimate and enforce particular systems of ideas (Foucault, 2000); and ethnographic approaches, arising from anthropology (Geertz, 1973), describe the cultural understandings of groups through detailed observations.

4. For members of the nationalist elite, there was no dearth of theories that saw imperialism as a stage of capitalism. See Brewer (1980).

5. Schramm, Pool, and Pye were patriotic American men who supported freedoms of speech and press. But there were rumors that Schramm was an FBI informant (Smythe, 1994). Both Pool and Pye supported American aims in Vietnam to check the spread of communism.

6. Mody (1987, p. 154) notes that NASA's choice of India over Brazil was influenced by Wilbur Schramm and fellow Stanford University colleague Lyle Nelson's study of the two countries' appropriateness.

7. Just as American aims in the Cold War had influenced early communication development programs, Soviet designs influenced the NWICO debate, leading ultimately to U.S. withdrawal from UNESCO in 1983. Many NWICO scholars and policymakers were known to have close ties to the USSR and their advocacy was often characterized by the Western media (including the *New York Times*) as fighting a proxy Cold War.

8. This case is also supported by Braman (1993): NWICO "demonstrated that a generalized consciousness of the centrality of information to society was already felt beyond the Western industrialized world" (p. 136).

REFERENCES

Belassa, B. (1989). *New directions in the world economy.* Washington Square: New York University Press.

Berger, P. L., & Luckmann, T. (1966). *Social construction of reality: A treatise in the sociology of knowledge.* New York: Anchor.

Bhatnagar, S., & Schware, R. (Eds.). (2000). *Information communication technology in rural development: Case studies from India.* WBU Working Papers. Washington, DC: World Bank Institute.

Braman, S. (1993, Summer). A harmonization of systems: The third stage of the information society. *Journal of Communication, 43.*

Brewer, A. (1980). *Marxist theories of imperialism: A critical survey.* London: Routledge & Kegan Paul.

Cardoso, F., & Faletto, E. (1979). *Dependency and development in Latin America.* Berkeley: University of California Press. (Original work published 1971)

Castells, M. (1996). *The information age: Economy, society and culture: Vol. 1. The rise of the network society.* Oxford, UK: Basil Blackwell.

Castells, M. (1997). *The information age: Economy, society and culture: Vol. 2. The power of identity.* Oxford, UK: Basil Blackwell.

Castells, M. (1998). *The information age: Economy, society and culture: Vol. 3. End of millennium.* Oxford, UK: Basil Blackwell.

Evans, P. (1979). *Dependent development: The alliance of multinational, state and local capital in Brazil.* Princeton, NJ: Princeton University Press.

Foucault, M. (2000). *Power: Essential works of Foucault, 1954-1984* (Vol. 3, J. D. Faubion, Ed.). New York: New Press.

Freire, P. (2000). *Pedagogy of the oppressed* (30th anniversary ed.). New York: Herder and Herder. (Original work published 1970)

Galtung, J. (1982). The new international order: Economics and communications. In M. Jussawalla & D. M. Lamberton (Eds.), *Communication economics and development.* Honolulu, HI: East-West Center.

Geertz, C. (1973). *The interpretation of cultures.* New York: Basic Books.

Graham, S., & Marvin, S. (1996). *Telecommunications and the city: Electronic spaces, urban places.* London: Routledge.

Golding, P. (1998). Worldwide wedge: Division and contradiction in the global information infrastructure. In D. K. Thussu (Ed.), *Electronic empires: Global media and local resistance.* London: Edward Arnold.

Hamelink, C. (1983). *Cultural autonomy in global communications.* New York: Longman.

Harcourt, W. (Ed.). (1999). *Women @ Internet: Creating new cultures in cyberspace.* London: Zed.

Hirschman, A. (1981). The rise and decline of development economics. In A. Hirschman, *Essays in trespassing: Economics to politics and beyond.* Cambridge, UK: Cambridge University Press.

Hornik, R. C. (1988). *Development communication: Information, agriculture, and nutrition in the Third World.* New York: Longman.

Hudson, H. E. (1985). *New directions in satellite communications: Challenges for North and South.* Dedham, MA: Artech House.

Hudson, H. E. (1990). *Communication satellites: Their development and impact.* New York: Free Press.

Hudson, H. E., et al. (1983). *Projections of the impact of installation of telephones and their route satellite Earth stations on rural development: A report to the International Telecommunication Union.* Geneva.

Innis, H. (1950). *Empire and communications.* Oxford, UK: Clarendon.

International Commission for the Study of Communication Problems. (1980). *Many voices, one world: Towards a new, more just and more efficient world information and communication order.* Paris: UNESCO.

International Institute for Educational Planning. (1967a). *New educational media in action: Case studies for planners.* Paris: UNESCO.

International Institute for Educational Planning. (1967b). *The new media: Memo to educational planners.* Paris: UNESCO.

International Telecommunication Union. 1984. *The missing link: Report of the Independent Commission for World Wide Telecommunications Development.* Geneva: Author.

Katz, E. (1957). The two-step flow of communication. *Public Opinion Quarterly, 21.*

Keck, M. E., Sikkink, K. (1998). *Activists beyond borders: Advocacy networks in international politics.* Ithaca, NY: Cornell University Press.

Keynes, J. M. (1936). *The general theory of employment, interest, and money.* London: Macmillan.

Lange, O. (1975). Planning economic development. In G. Meier (Ed.), *Leading issues in economic development* (pp. 695-700). Hong Kong: Oxford University Press.

Lazarsfeld, P. F., Berelson, B., & Gaudet, H. (1944). *The people's choice.* New York: Duell, Sloan and Pierce.

Lerner, D. (1958). *The passing of traditional society: Modernizing the Middle East.* Glencoe, IL: Free Press.

Lerner, D., & Schramm, W. (Eds.). (1967). *Communication and change in the developing countries.* Honolulu, HI: East-West Center.

Levy, B., & Spiller, P. T. (Eds.). 1996. *Regulations, institutions and commitment: Comparative studies of telecommunications.* Cambridge, UK: Cambridge University Press.

Lipset, S. M. (1959). Some social requisites of democracy: Economic development and political legitimacy. *American Political Science Review, 53.*

MacBride Commission. (1979). *Many voices, one world: Communication and society, today and tomorrow: Toward a new, more just and more efficient world information and communication order.* London: Kogan Page.

Mansell, R., & Wehn, U. (Eds.). (1998). *Knowledge societies: Information technology for sustainable development.* New York: Oxford University Press.

Mathews, J. T. (1997, January/February). Power shift. *Foreign Affairs, 76*(1).

McClelland, D. C. 1961. *The achieving society.* Princeton, NJ: Van Nostrand.

Mody, B. (1987). Contextual analysis of the adoption of a communication technology: The case of satellites in India. *Telematics and Informatics, 4*(2), 151-158.

Mowlana, H. (1997). *Global information and world communication: New frontiers in international relations* (2nd ed.). London: Sage.

North, D. C. (1981). *Structure and change in economic history.* New York: Norton.

North, D. C., & Thomas, R. T. (1973). *The rise of the Western world: A new economic history.* Cambridge, UK: Cambridge University Press.

National Telecommunications and Information Administration. (1992). *The NTIA infrastructure report: Telecommunications in the age of information.* Washington, DC: U.S. Department of Commerce.

O'Brien, R. C. (Ed.). (1983). *Information, economics and power: The North-South dimension.* Boulder, CO: Westview.

Olson, M., & Kähkönen, S. (Eds.). (2000). *A not-so-dismal science: A broader view of economies and societies.* Oxford, UK: Oxford University Press.

Parker, E. B., Hudson, H. E., Dillman, D. A., & Roscoe, A. D. (1989). *Rural America in the information age: Telecommunications policy for rural development.* Lanham, MD: Aspen Institute and University Press of America.

Pavlic, B., & Hamelink, C. J. (1985). *The new international economic order: Links between economics and communications.* Paris: UNESCO.

Pernyeszi, J., Rao, M., Yadagiri, P., & Kumar, U. (2000, November). *Micro-surveys of rural Telecom in India and USA, and their implications for India's public policy.* Paper presented at the Telecom in India conference, Asia/Pacific Research Center, Stanford University, Stanford, CA.

Pitroda, S. G. (1976, July). Telecommunications development—The third way. *IEEE Transactions on Communications, 24*(7).

Pool, I. de S. (1963). The mass media and politics in the modernization process. In L. Pye (Ed.), *Communication and political development.* Princeton, NJ: Princeton University Press.

Pye, L. (Ed.). (1963). *Communication and political development.* Princeton, NJ: Princeton University Press.

Quadir, F. (in press). Promoting democratic governance at the grassroots in the twenty-first century? Myths and realities of NGO programs in Bangladesh. In F. Quadir, S. J. Maclean, & T. M. Shaw (Eds.), *Prospects for governance in Asia and Africa*. Brookfield, VT: Ashgate.

Rogers, E. M. (1962). *Diffusion of innovations*. New York: Free Press.

Rogers, E. M. (Ed.). (1976). *Communication and development: Critical perspectives*. Beverly Hills, CA: Sage.

Rogers, E. M. (1983). *Diffusion of innovations* (3rd ed.). New York: Free Press.

Saunders, R. J., Warford, J. J., & Wellenius, B. (1994). *Telecommunications and economic development* (2nd ed.). Washington, DC: World Bank.

Shieds, P. (1989). *Telecommunication and development: Continuities and discontinuities with the mass communication research tradition*. Master's thesis, Ohio State University, Columbus, OH.

Schiller, H. I. (1969). *Mass communications and American empire*. New York: A. M. Kelley.

Schiller, H. I. (1973). *The mind managers*. Boston: Beacon.

Schramm, W. L. (1964). *Mass media and national development: The role of information in the developing countries*. Stanford, CA: Stanford University Press.

Shingi, P. M., & Mody, B. (1976). The communication effects gap: A field experiment on television and agricultural ignorance in India. In E. M. Rogers (Ed.), *Communication and development: Critical perspectives* (pp. 79-98). Beverly Hills, CA: Sage.

Singh, J. P. (1999). *Leapfrogging development: The political economy of telecommunications restructuring*. Albany: State University of New York Press.

Singh, J. P. (2000, November). The institutional environment and effects of telecommunication privatization and market liberalization in Asia. *Telecommunications Policy, 24*.

Singh, J. P. (2001). Introduction: Information technologies and the changing scope of global power and governance. In J. N. Rosenau & J. P. Singh (Eds.), *Information technologies and global politics: The changing scope of power and governance*. Albany: State University of New York Press.

Smythe, D. W. (1994). *Counterclockwise: Perspectives on communication* (T. Guback, Ed.). Boulder, CO: Westview.

Sussman, G. (Ed.). (1997). *Communication, technology, and politics in the information age*. Thousand Oaks, CA: Sage.

Thussu, D. K. (Ed.). (1998). *Electronic empires: Global media and local resistance*. London: Edward Arnold.

Wilkins, K. G. (2000). *Redeveloping communication for social change: Theory, practice, and power*. Lanham, MD: Rowman & Littlefield.

Williamson, O. E. (1985). *The economic institutions of capitalism*. New York: Free Press.

World Bank. 1998. *World development report 1998/99: Knowledge for development*. Washington, DC: Author.

12

Participatory Approaches to Communication for Development

ROBERT HUESCA
Trinity University

The dominant paradigm of development underwent far-reaching interrogation and criticism in the 1970s by scholars and practitioners across disciplines and from around the globe. Perhaps the most significant challenge to the dominant paradigm of development communication came from Latin American scholars who deconstructed and rejected the premises, objectives, and methods of modernization and its attendant communication approaches. This early criticism stimulated a range of research projects that has resulted in a robust literature exploring participatory communication approaches to development. Participatory approaches gained momentum in the 1980s and 1990s and have evolved into a rich field standing in stark contrast to models and theories of the first development decades. In fact, scholars have noted that few contemporary development projects—regardless of theoretical orientation—are conducted with-

out some sort of participatory component, even if this notion is honored more on paper than in practice (Ascroft & Masilela, 1994, Fraser & Restrepo-Estrada, 1998; Mato, 1999; S. A. White, 1994). Despite its widespread use, however, the concept of participatory communication is subject to loose interpretation that appears at best to be variable and contested and at worst misused and distorted (Arnst, 1996; Jacobson & Servaes, 1999).

Indeed, the Latin American challenge for scholars to embrace more appropriate, ethical, and responsive theories of development communication remains unrealized to some extent, creating a sense of conceptual and practical stagnation. One way of reinvigorating this field of study is to review the key elements of the challenge from Latin America and of the subsequent research that has refined our sense of participatory approaches

of development communication. Such a review is intended to illuminate the conceptual
directions that have been emphasized, elaborated, neglected, and ignored over time. By
reviewing the variety of directions that have
been explored over time, future paths of
research and practice will be suggested for the
continued theoretical advance of this field.

This chapter will begin with an abbreviated
history of the challenge to the dominant paradigm of development communication that
emerged from Latin America in the 1970s.[1] It
will then provide a thematic review of the
participatory communication research that
has emerged since then, identifying the
various directions taken by scholars in this
field. Placing this thematic review into relief
with the Latin American critique will provide a historical map of ideas and interests
that will point to future directions. The final
section of the chapter will conclude by recovering specific themes that hold the promise of advancing participatory development
communication.

CHALLENGING THE DOMINANT PARADIGM

In the 1970s, scholars from Latin America began deconstructing the dominant paradigm of
communication for development and pointing to new directions for research. This section briefly summarizes this deconstruction
and reconstruction, beginning with an examination of the assertions that development efforts were ideologically and materially related to neocolonialism and the extension of
capitalist relations. It continues by introducing key, alternative directions for development efforts, including notions of praxis, dialogue, and communication process.

Communication Domination

Prior to the 1970s, almost all of Latin American communication development theory and
practice were based on concepts and models
imported from the United States and Europe
and used in ways that were both incommensurable with and detrimental to the region's
social context (Beltrán, 1975). These concepts
and models were guided philosophically by a
combination of behaviorism and functional-
ism prevalent in the social sciences and by persuasion definitions of communication dating
back to Aristotle in the humanities (Beltrán,
1980). The development programs and research projects falling out of this philosophical frame tended to focus on individual attitudes and effects while ignoring social,
political, and economic structures that frequently stood in contradiction to development goals. Development was often defined in
terms of the adoption of new behaviors or
technologies, which were rarely, if ever, examined in terms of their social, political, and economic dimensions. Beltrán (1975) concluded,
"The classic diffusion model was based on an
ideological framework that contradicts the
reality of this region" (p. 190). This persuasion, attitude focus of research not only
reflected the culture and philosophy of the
Western tradition, it resulted in theories that
blamed individuals, not systems, for continued underdevelopment.

But more than merely reflecting the intellectual and cultural history of Western
research, early development projects were
criticized as a form of domination and manipulation. Freire (1973b) analyzed the term
extension used in agricultural projects, in
terms of its "associative fields" and concluded
that they invited "mechanistic," "transmission," and "invasion" models of communication development. The vertical structure of
many extension projects paralleled the hierarchical organization of landlord-peasant

relations preceding it in Latin American *latifundios,* resulting in an unintended continuity of inegalitarian relations. The sense that development projects frequently perpetuated the interests of dominant elites was echoed by numerous scholars at the First Latin American Seminar on Participatory Communication sponsored in 1978 by the Center for Advanced Studies and Research for Latin America (CIESPAL). Influenced by dependency theory that was prevalent at the time, scholars there concluded that uses of mass media in development imposed the interests of dominant classes on the majority of marginalized people, resulting in the reinforcement, reproduction, and legitimation of social and material relations of production (O'Sullivan-Ryan & Kaplún, 1978).[2]

The Latin American critique of the dominant paradigm, then, moved from the level of specific and misguided models of communication to the level of historical and global theories of domination and inequity. Early on, Latin American scholars suggested that development communication be interpreted from within a global framework guided by dependency theory (O'Sullivan-Ryan & Kaplún, 1978). That is, development projects should be analyzed as integral elements in a global system that essentially acts to maintain asymmetrical relations. Freire (1973a) went as far as to label the various top-down, modernization projects as "assistentialism," or social and financial activities that attack symptoms, not causes, of social ills that function as disguised forms of colonial domination. These early suspicions have been confirmed by a more recent analysis of health and nutrition programs in Latin America, which concluded that development projects functioned as an extension of the geopolitical struggle between the capitalist West and the communist East (Escobar, 1995). Moreover, the categories of assistance constructed by donor nations allowed "institutions to distribute socially individuals and

populations in ways consistent with the creation and reproduction of modern capitalist relations" (Escobar, 1995, p. 107). The deconstruction of the dominant paradigm of development, then, was a protest against the perpetuation of historical inequities and a call for the invention of humane, egalitarian, and responsive communication theories and practices.

Toward Dialogic Praxis

Embracing the notion of praxis—self-reflexive, theoretically guided practice—was an immediate and obvious outcome of the Latin American critique of the dominant paradigm. The modernization project and its concomitant theories of development themselves had been shown to illustrate the inextricable connection between theory and practice (Beltrán, 1975, 1980; Escobar, 1995). Through its assumptions regarding the locus of social problems, models of communication as information transfer, methods that placed human objects under the antiseptic gaze of scientists, and findings that confirmed micro explanations of persistent underdevelopment, the modernization approach unconsciously demonstrated the reciprocal and self-confirming relationship between theory and practice. One of the earliest recommendations of the Latin American critics was to acknowledge consciously this relationship, to turn away from scientific positions of objectivity, and to embrace an orientation toward research as praxis.

Much of the inspiration for this shift came from the work of Freire (1970), whose experience in traditional pedagogy was seen as analogous to modernization approaches to development. In traditional pedagogy, teachers typically viewed students as objects characterized by some sort of deficiency and in need of knowledge that could be transferred to them in a linear fashion. Freire denounced this objectivist orientation as sadistic and oppressive and claimed that humane practitioners could not view themselves as proprietors of knowledge and wisdom. In contrast to this oppressive pedagogy, Freire proposed a liberating approach that centered on praxis. Under this orientation, practitioners attempt to close the distance between teacher and student, development agent and client, researcher and researched to enter into a co-learning relationship guided by action and reflection. In a praxis approach to teaching, development, or research, people serve as their own examples in the struggle for and conquest of improved life chances.

The turn toward research praxis was a radical epistemological move that has been adopted and refined by scholars since then (e.g., Fals-Borda, 1988; Rahman, 1993). It posits that the combination of critical theory, situation analysis, and action creates a fruitful dialectic for the construction of knowledge, which is systematically examined, altered, and expanded in practice. The elimination of the dichotomy between subject and object, combined with an action-reflection orientation toward inquiry, resulted in a heightened moral awareness or *conscientização*. This liberating praxis generated "thinking which perceives reality as process, as transformation, rather than as a static entity—thinking which does not separate itself from action, but constantly immerses itself in temporality without fear of the risks involved" (Freire, 1970, p. 81). The turn toward praxis not only rejected dominant approaches to development as oppressive, it argued for integrating scholarship more directly with development practice.

Although this turn provided both a philosophical and epistemological framework for scholarship, it also provided a practical, commensurate method in the form of dialogue. Dialogic communication was held in stark contrast to information transmission models

emerging from Lasswell's (1948/1964) five-point question of who says what in what channel to whom with what effect. This required development researchers and practitioners to seek out the experiences, understandings, and aspirations of others to jointly construct reality and formulate actions (Beltrán, 1980). Freire (1970, 1973a) provided concrete exercises for initiating critical dialogues to, in effect, deconstruct social contexts, separate out their constituent parts, and reconstruct a thematic universe for pursuing social transformation. Such a process resulted in a "cultural synthesis" between development collaborators to arrive at mutually identified problems, needs, and guidelines for action.

Aside from its practical contribution, dialogue was promoted as an ethical communication choice within the development context. Freire (1970) argued that true humanization emerged from one's ability "to name the world" in dialogic encounters. This humanization not only was denied to marginalized or oppressed peoples but was something that leaders and elites were prevented from attaining, as well, in prevailing communication environments. Grounded in Buber's notion of "I-Thou" communication, Freire argued that subject-object distinctions were impossible to maintain in true dialogue because one's sense of self and the world is elicited in interaction with others. The resulting fusion of identities and communal naming of the world did not emerge merely from an exchange of information, however; it required a moral commitment among dialogue partners. "Being dialogic is not invading, not manipulating, not imposing orders. Being dialogic is pledging oneself to the constant transformation of reality" (Freire, 1973b, p. 46). This highly developed sense of dialogue— simultaneously practical and rarefied—pushed scholars to conceptualize the phenomena of their study away from states (attitudes) and entities (media) toward process.

Communication as Process

More than any other aspect of the Latin American critique, the observation that communication was frequently conceptualized in static, rather than process, terms constituted the greatest challenge for development practitioners. Scholars from the North had been struggling with process models of communication since Berlo's (1960) work so convincingly argued in their favor. Yet Berlo's construction of the sender-message-channel-receiver model of communication demonstrated the tenacity of static, linear models that identified components amenable to survey research and development program design. It also demonstrated the elusiveness of the dynamic, process nature of communication.

Latin American scholars introduced a phenomenological orientation, which radically altered the conceptualization, study, and practice of development communication.[3] Rather than focusing on the constituent parts of communication, Latin American scholars introduced more fluid and elastic concepts that centered on how-meaning-comes-to-be in its definition. These more fluid and meaning-centered conceptualizations of communication emphasized co-presence, inter-subjectivity, phenomenological "being in the world," and openness of interlocutors (Pasquali, 1963). This view introduced a sophisticated epistemology arguing that the understanding of social reality is produced between people, in material contexts, and in communication. Freire (1973b) captured the sense of the phenomenological orientation toward communication writing:

> One's consciousness, "intentionality" toward the world, is always consciousness of, and in permanent movement toward reality. . . . This relationship constitutes, with this, a dialectical unity in which knowing-in-solidarity is generated in

being and vice versa. For this reason, both objectivist and subjectivist explanations that break this dialectic, dichotomizing that which is not dichotomizable (subject-object), are not capable of understanding reality. (p. 85)

In other words, traditional development approaches of "understanding reality" through the unilateral definition of problems, objectives, and solutions were criticized as violating the very essence of communication.

Pasquali (1963) went as far as stating that the notion of "mass communication" was an oxymoron and that Latin American media constituted an "information oligarchy" that cultivated a social context characterized by "communicational atrophy." Though his analysis was aimed at issues of media and culture broadly, the kinds of development communication projects typical of the period were consistent with his analysis. This fundamental criticism of static models of communication led to calls in development to abandon the "vertical" approaches of information transmission and to adopt "horizontal" projects emphasizing access, dialogue, and participation (Beltrán, 1980). The Latin American critique of the dominant paradigm as an extension of domination and the call for more egalitarian and responsive approaches to development were followed by a robust body of research into participatory development communication, which is thematically summarized in the next section.

THE RISE OF PARTICIPATORY COMMUNICATION

In the decades following the Latin American call for participatory approaches to development communication, a wide range of theoretical responses emerged. At one end of the participatory spectrum, scholars coming out of the behaviorist, mass media effects tradition acknowledged the critique and have in-corporated participatory dimensions—albeit to a limited extent—into their research. On the other end of the spectrum, scholars criti-cal of traditional development communica-tion research embraced participation virtu-ally as an utopian panacea for development. These distinct theoretical positions essen-tially mark ends on a continuum, where par-ticipation is conceptualized as either a means to an end or an end in and of itself. In this sec-tion, I will present these two positions more fully before moving on to review a variety of other themes that reside somewhere between these two extremes.

Participation: Technical Means or Utopian End?

Almost as quickly as Latin American schol-ars articulated their objections to mainstream approaches to development communication, some of the leading figures of the dominant paradigm acknowledged the criticisms and re-formed their projects (Lerner, 1976; Rogers, 1976; Schramm, 1976). They acknowledged that their conceptualization of development had been oversimplified by focusing narrowly on individuals as the locus for change, theoriz-ing in a universal, evolutionary manner, ignor-ing cultural specificity, and emphasizing mass media. But this recognition did not lead to the wholesale rejection of their empiricist ap-proach. In fact, Lerner (1976) defended social science's inviolable methodological assump-tions of ontological continuity and social regularity, which were threatened by the Latin American rejection of objectivism and pro-motion of communication-as-process. Rather, dominant paradigm scholars acknowledged the general value of popular participation in development, recognized new uses of me-dia to "unlock local energies" (Lerner & Schramm, 1976, p. 343), and expanded re-

search to include interpersonal networks in addition to opinion leaders. To an extent, the concept of participation served to reform the dominant paradigm, making it—in the words of its proponents—more expansive, flexible, and humane (Rogers, 1993).

Such reformist approaches to participation are used by major institutions such as the World Bank and Mexico's dominant Institu-tional Revolutionary Party (PRI) (Mato, 1999; K. White, 1999). Their top-down ef-forts are supported by theoretical arguments that participation be conceptualized in ways that disassociate it from any particular ideol-ogy (Chu, 1987, 1994). By ideologically neu-tralizing it, participation is seen as compatible with social marketing, capitalist expansion, and global trade (Moemeka, 1994). In fact, King and Cushman (1994) have argued that participation be conceptualized on a highly abstract level where a "nation's people and its government" fashion themselves as global competitors participating in the arena of world trade. They discard the value of grass-roots participation, local knowledge, and cultural beliefs as "old myths" that are in-compatible with the contemporary reality of globalization.

Less dismissive of grassroots participa-tion but still consistent with empiricist, top-down approaches to development is recent research in entertainment-education (Singhal & Rogers, 1988; Storey, 1999). Rather than neutralizing the ideological element of partici-pation, entertainment-education draws on findings emerging from cultural studies to advance predetermined objectives in areas such as "reproductive health." A sophisticated theoretical framework drawing from studies in reception and popular culture has been con-structed to conceptualize texts as open sys-tems activated by audience participants that render media products incapable of manipula-tion (Storey, 1999, 2000). Rather than using this assertion as the basis for promoting grassroots communication broadly, the notion of "open texts" has functioned primarily as a justification for expert-produced, entertainment-education products. Coupled with the theoretical contributions of Mikhail Bakhtin, this approach uses the concept of participation both to guide the development of "pro-social content" through audience surveys and focus groups and, more important, to impute wide-ranging and long-term consequences via the "social dialogue" of individuals, institutions, and culture. More than any other research genre, entertainment-education has used the concept of participation to bolster the administrative position of the dominant paradigm.

The apparent contradiction of using participatory elements to enhance the status of traditional development practices has received intense attention by communication scholars. A recent, historical analysis focusing on the discourse of development suggests that the Latin American call for participation constituted a counter discourse to the dominant paradigm that was "easily co-opted by the established system and rendered ineffective or counter productive" (Escobar, 1999, p. 326). Indeed, the most pernicious instances of instrumental uses of participation appear to be attached to large agencies connected to the state or to transnational regimes such as the U.S. Agency for International Development or the World Bank (K. White, 1999; Mato, 1999). The role of scholars who have integrated participation into essentially top-down development theories has been interpreted as akin to engaging in a "conspiracy theory" to redeem the dominant paradigm from the interrogation it experienced in the 1970s (Ascroft & Masilela, 1994; Lent, 1987). When put into practice, such uses of participatory communication exemplify, at best, passive collaboration, and at worst, manipulative consultation done only to help advance a predetermined objective (Díaz Bordenave, 1994;

Dudley, 1993). In fact, one development practitioner argues that any uses of participation will evolve into an "insidious domination tactic" if incorporated into the development discourse due to its historical association with Western political hegemony (K. White, 1999).

Few scholars would agree with this extreme position, especially those reviewed above who advocate administrative uses of participation. Moreover, a group of scholars conceptualizing participation as an end in and of itself has articulated utopian visions of the role of people in their own development. These visions are premised on a somewhat romantic belief that peasants, Indians, and other marginalized persons possess local wisdom and a virtuous cultural ethos and that participatory processes are inherently humanizing, liberating, and catalyzing (Dissanayake, 1985; Vargas, 1995; S. A. White, 1994). Beginning from such premises, scholars have prescribed totalizing processes of participatory communication where all interlocutors experience freedom and equal access to express feelings and experiences and to arrive at collective agendas for action (Díaz Bordenave, 1994; Kaplún, 1985; Nair & White, 1994a). Under these circumstances, all people are said to take ownership of communication and to experience empowering outcomes. These utopian visions of development communication have been called "genuine" and "authentic" participation, as opposed to the manipulative, pseudo participation reviewed above.

The generalized premises and prescriptions of utopian scholars have been accompanied by equally optimistic renditions of participation by researchers who offer more concrete directions for development practice. For example, various phases in development—identifying problems, setting goals and objectives, planning procedures, assessing actions—have been identified, each one necessitating the full participation of intended beneficiaries (Kennedy, 1984; Midgley, 1986; Nair &

White, 1994b). This has been accompanied by policy recommendations for the reorganization of major social institutions, such as the media system, to bring communication structures in line with participatory communication development approaches (Servaes, 1985). Placed on a continuum, these utopian, normative theories stand as polar opposites to the functional, administrative notions of participation advanced by scholars approaching development from a more conventional perspective.

The evolution of polarized conceptualizations of participatory development communication has been noted in a number of scholarly reviews that have distinguished the two poles in slightly different ways. In fact, early research in this area suggested that participatory communication functions as both a means and an end in development, thus foreshadowing the distinct conceptual paths that would be followed in the decades to come (O'Sullivan-Ryan & Kaplún, 1978). A number of scholars have interpreted this means-end division as a convenient and fruitful way of guiding communication decisions in development projects (Chu, 1994; Decker, 1988; Kaplún, 1989; Rodriguez, 1994). That is, a limited role for communication-participation-as-means may be appropriate in projects focused on teaching skills, carrying out prescribed objectives, or producing highly polished media products. Under such circumstances, social impacts are viewed as ephemeral, goals are immediate, and interaction is formal. In contrast, an expansive role for communication-participation-as-end is appropriate in projects aimed at organizing movements, transforming social relations, and empowering individuals. Under such circumstances, social impacts are perpetual, goals are long range, and interaction is fluid. Other scholars noting the means-end continuum in the research have been more critical of the distinction, arguing that participation-as-

means is nothing more than a thinly veiled reincarnation of the dominant paradigm (Melkote, 1991; Vargas, 1995; S. A. White, 1994). They argue that this approach invokes participatory communication in an instrumental, manipulative, dominating manner that undercuts its theoretical legitimacy. Although they recognize the existence of the gradations in the evolution of the concept of participation, they reject the means-to-an-end perspective as an illegitimate appropriation. Regardless of the subtle distinctions characterizing the ends of this continuum, these scholars have noted that most theory development of participation has not been predominantly means or end, teaching or organizing, pseudo or genuine, but some version that resides between the poles. The remainder of this section reviews major concepts and issues that have emerged over the years but that defy convenient location at either end of the conceptual continuum.

From General Theories to Concrete Practices

The bulk of theoretical research into participatory communication does not claim an exclusive means or ends focus, but does vary in terms of level of abstraction, issue of attention, or topic of interest. This section of the chapter briefly summarizes these various theoretical contributions moving from general and abstract scholarship to more applied and concrete research. This review will touch on the general notions of multiplicity, power, and popular mobilization as well as specific attention to levels of participation, media applications, and concrete methods of inquiry. The purpose of doing this is to display the various degrees of participation that have emerged over the years and to stake out some of the dominant patterns of interest that this field has generated. Holding these general patterns in relief to the origins of interest in participatory communication will form the basis for making recommendations for future research.

One of the more general and fully articulated concepts to emerge from the participatory communication tradition is the notion of multiplicity in one world (Servaes, 1985, 1986, 1989). This approach recommends strong, grassroots participation in development efforts but explicitly rejects universal approaches to its application (Servaes, 1986, 1996a). Instead, it emphasizes the terms *diversity* and *pluralism,* suggesting that nations and regions cultivate their own, responsive approaches to self-determined development goals that emerge out of participatory processes. The reluctance to advocate universal theorizing stems from the observation that even within fairly homogeneous cultures, competing political, social, and cultural interests and groups will be found (Servaes, 1985). The conflicts inherent in all social systems suggest that "rigid and general strategies for participation are neither possible nor desirable. It is a process that unfolds in each unique situation" (Servaes, 1996a, p. 23). Eschewing even "general strategies for participation" constitutes a naïve faith in the power of communication to negotiate stark political differences and casts multiplicity into a relativistic arena that has difficulty sustaining coherence within the larger discourse of development.

The strain on theoretical coherence is evident in the introduction of universal principles and totalizing concepts that accompany this relativized communication approach. The early multiplicity research, for example, claimed that a universal "right to communicate" formed the basis for all multiplicity approaches to development communication (Servaes, 1986). Later scholars adopting the multiplicity framework reiterated this position and added that "cultural processes" should be granted primacy in both the study and practice of development communication

(R. White, 1994; Wildemeersch, 1999). Most recently, Servaes (1998) has suggested that a "global ethics" grounded in principles of democracy and respect for human rights be adopted unilaterally by development agencies. This tension between a rejection of universal approaches and the advocacy of global principles is a contradiction that permeates the development communication field generally in its attempts to reconcile subjectivity/agency and structure/political economy (Dervin & Huesca, 1997, 1999). Moreover, it is emblematic of a widespread reluctance among scholars to establish normative standards of participatory communication on philosophical grounds (Deetz, 1992). Although this contradiction does represent theoretical incoherence, it more significantly demonstrates the desire to honor differential forms of human agency that generate diverse cultural practices while reckoning with the material constraints of an undemocratic, profit-driven communication environment.

Another area of general, theoretical attention in participatory communication has centered more closely on those material constraints by focusing on the role of power in development. Early advocates of participatory approaches either ignored the issue of power or naïvely called for its general redistribution within and between nations. More recent research has focused explicitly on power and conceptualized it in a nuanced and problematic way. For the most part, power has been theorized as both multicentered—not one dimensional—and asymmetrical (Servaes, 1996c; Tehranian, 1999). This role acknowledges the force of institutions and structures, but emphasizes the role of human agency in reproducing and transforming them (Tehranian, 1999). Within this generalized framework of power, participatory communication is seen by some as being a potential source of social transformation (Nair & White, 1994a; Riaño, 1994). By virtue of the differences—ethnic, gender, sexual, and the like—that multiple social actors bring to development projects, participatory communication reveals how power functions to subordinate certain groups of people (Riaño, 1994). Furthermore, participation functions to cultivate "generative power" where individuals and groups develop the capacity for action, which can be harnessed to reshape and transform conditions of subordination (Nair & White, 1994a). While mindful of the asymmetrical characteristics of power in society, these positions are generally optimistic regarding the prospects of transformation via participatory communication.

Less optimistic are scholars who see participation as either insufficient or problematic in and of itself in terms of altering power relationships in society. For these scholars, participatory communication may be helpful in attaining structural transformations in the land tenure, political, or economic arrangements of society, which are viewed as the root sources of subordination (Hedebro, 1982; Lozare, 1994; Nerfin, 1977). As such, participatory communication is necessary but not sufficient for engaging and altering power relationships. In fact, participatory communication that is not guided toward an a priori structural goal, such as building progressive institutions or deconstructing dominating discourses, runs the risk of dissolving into a self-indulgent exercise or being co-opted by an established and elitist organization (Escobar, 1999; O'Connor, 1990). Worse yet, participatory communication by itself is capable of reproducing inegalitarian power structures, especially in regard to gender relations (Wilkins, 1999, 2000). For these authors, the relationship between participatory communication and dominant power structures is neither transparent nor unproblematic.

An approach to the issue of participatory communication and power that most explicitly bridges the agency-structure divide is the scholarship that focuses on the role of participation in relation to popular movements. One position in this research argues that popular movements are inherently linked to participatory communication projects because "liberation" is an axiomatic quality of participation (Riaño, 1994). That is, the openness required of participatory communication leads to awareness of differences that reveals inequalities and results in movements to address and transform them. A distinct but related perspective notes that participation emerges from popular movements that engage in structural reforms but rely on continual regeneration through broad social involvement (Servaes, 1996b; R. White, 1994). Large-scale popular movements, therefore, serve as valuable laboratories for breaking through artificial boundaries that obscure the role of participatory communication in the transformation and reproduction of dominant relations. Some scholars have gone farther and suggested that development research actively align itself with popular movements to yield insights that contribute directly to participatory, social change projects (Rahman, 1993; Servaes & Arnst, 1999). This nexus between participation and popular liberation movements constitutes an entry point for negotiating problematic issues of power.

Concrete Applications and Operationalizations

Research attending to abstract theoretical concerns of multiplicity, power, and mobilization demonstrates the negotiation of the means-end polarity in the participatory communication literature. But a range of scholarship focused on more specific issues and concerns defies simple means-end classification as well. This section of the chapter briefly reviews scholarship focusing on more concrete issues such as levels of participation, media applications, and research methods.

A number of researchers have worked to identify differential levels and intensities of participation in development projects. These scholars have identified stages of participation, ranging from initial access to communication resources to active identification of development issues and goals to full authority in project governance (Fraser & Restrepo-Estrada, 1998; Krohling Peruzzo, 1996; Servaes, 1996a). These stages are usually conceptualized as being guided either by contextual qualities of the participants themselves or by organizational constraints of the supporting development institutions. For example, Thapalia (1996) suggested that development practitioners cultivate a stronger, more directive role for themselves—something she labeled "transformational leadership"—aimed at constructing a shared vision and commitment to action in a community. She argues for resurrecting the discredited notion of "leadership" because egalitarian participation is frequently incommensurable with the desires and interests of local people. Like the constraints created by local cultural contexts, organizational characteristics impose limitations on participation as well. Large development agencies most frequently implement participation on limited level, such as using focus groups in the initial phase of an information campaign, because of organizational goals and limitations on time and resources (McKee, 1994; Wilkins, 1999). The various levels identified by these researchers are conceptualized in a complex interaction with contextual and structural constraints that move beyond the binary means-end continuum suggested by other scholars. Furthermore, they are acutely concerned with concrete applications of participatory communication in development.

Another area of scholarship that has focused on communication applications concerns participatory uses of media in development. Soon after the Latin American challenge to the dominant paradigm of development, scholars began focusing on participatory applications in media. Fueled by a series of United Nations Educational, Scientific and Cultural Organization (UNESCO) meetings that led to the declaration for a New World Information and Communication Order, these scholars identified the concepts of access (to communication resources), participation (in planning, decision making, and production), and self-management (collective ownership and policy making) in media development (Berrigan, 1981; O'Sullivan-Ryan & Kaplún, 1978). Since then, systematic attention has been given to various aspects of participatory media, including audience involvement in message creation (Mody, 1991; Nair & White, 1993a, 1993b, 1994b; Thomas, 1994), identity construction (Rodriguez, 1994), and institution building (Díaz Bordenave, 1985; Fadul, Lins da Silva, & Santoro, 1982). In fact, an entire communication subfield of "alternative media" has spun off of the initial criticisms of the dominant paradigm and call for participatory approaches to social change (see Atwood & McAnany, 1986; Huesca & Dervin, 1994; Reyes Matta, 1983; Simpson Grinberg, 1986).

Whereas scholarly attention has been given to many abstract and concrete issues relevant to participatory communication, the area of research methods has been neglected to some extent (Ascroft & Masilela, 1994; Melkote, 1991). Recently, this situation has begun to change, however, with scholars emphasizing the importance of advancing research methods that are commensurate with the philosophy and theory that underpin participatory communication for development (Dervin & Huesca, 1997, 1999; Jacobson, 1996; Servaes & Arnst, 1999; R. White, 1999). At the level of methodology, this requires thinking through the ontological and epistemological assumptions that mandate the dissolution of subject-object relations and lay the groundwork for participatory communication for development (Dervin & Huesca, 1999; Jacobson, 1993, 1996). It also requires the establishment of criteria of validity in order to fulfill the self-reflexive, evaluative dimension of research, as well as to advance comparative studies in the field. Such criteria might be imported from parallel communication theories, such as Habermas's ideal speech situation (Jacobson & Kolluri, 1999), or they might emerge from the practical outcomes of the research process itself (Escobar, 1999; Servaes & Arnst, 1999). At the level of method, an orientation toward participatory action research has been suggested as perhaps the most compatible approach to the study of participatory communication (Einsiedel, 1999; Escobar, 1999; Jacobson, 1993; R. White, 1999). Such methods are explicitly political, calling on researchers to align themselves with specific social actors and to embrace their goals and purposes. The recent attention to methodology and method may foreshadow renewed interest in conducting empirical research into participatory communication for development.

This brief sketch of the multiple issues receiving scholarly attention was intended to identify the major patterns shaping our understanding of participatory communication for development. By examining these patterns against the issues raised in the Latin American challenge to the dominant paradigm, I intend to identify some fruitful directions for future research in the concluding section of this chapter.

REVISITING KEY CONCEPTS

The future of participatory communication for development is uncertain because of serious practical and conceptual impediments facing it. Practical impediments include a lack of institutional support as the approach's long-range, time-consuming, and symbolic (*conscientização*, empowerment) dimensions do not conform to the evaluative criteria of many development bureaucracies (Arnst, 1996; Fraser & Restrepo-Estrada, 1998; Servaes, 1998; Servaes & Arnst, 1999; Wilkins, 1999). These same scholars note that strong participatory projects transfer control from officials to beneficiaries and are often met with resistance from experts whose power is jeopardized. Conceptual impediments include definitional fuzziness, exemplified by the wide-ranging scholarship outlined above (Ascroft & Masilela, 1994; Jacobson, 1994; Vargas, 1995; S. A. White, 1994). Several scholars have noted that because of this definitional fuzziness, dominant communication patterns and oppressive social relationships can be and are reproduced under the guise of participation (Kaplún, 1985, 1989; Wilkins, 1999).

Although the challenges to participatory communication for development appear formidable, reasons for optimism are provided by scholars who have documented renewed interest in this approach (Ascroft & Masilela, 1994; Fraser & Restrepo-Estrada, 1998; Melkote, 1993; Nair & White, 1993c; Vargas, 1995). Attention to participation as a component in development is being embraced by both small, nongovernmental organizations and large institutions, albeit in problematic forms as documented above. The challenge before contemporary scholars is to continue advancing this area of theory and practice in light of the practical and conceptual impediments currently facing it. Such advancement can occur by revisiting key notions that have been pursued and neglected in the 30-year-old call to participatory communication.

On the conceptual level, scholars should redouble their efforts to base development practices and analyses on definitions of communication that emphasize its dynamic process nature. Much of the conceptual fuzziness in this field is due to instrumental adoptions and adaptations of participation in projects that are essentially attempts to improve information transfers and cloak them as communication. Furthermore, this fuzziness is compounded when participation is incorporated into applications clearly based on linear models of communication, such as "message development." Freezing communication action into static components effectively ignores the dynamic process roots of the Latin American challenge and slides back into the linear models that guided modernization and its top-down projects. Concerns about moving from state-entity concepts to process-dynamic models are evident not only in communication but in other social science disciplines as well (Bruner, 1986; Dervin, 1993; Fals-Borda, 1991). Adopting process models as the foundation of theory and practice will provide conceptual guidance for negotiating the means-end polarity and for distinguishing participatory communication from information transfer.

Other conceptual components worthy of recovering and reinforcing are the ethical and political mandates that underpinned the Latin American call for participatory communication. These mandates have become obscured, if not lost altogether, as scholars have emphasized multiplicity, the primacy of culture, and other notions that have effectively relativized the meaning of participation. Although the early denunciations of the dominant paradigm called for dialogue, democracy, and participation, they did so with a clear sense of moral commitment to strive for social justice. The claim to moral authority was grounded in the liberation theology movement popular at the time but never claiming a prominent place in the theoretical challenges to the dominant paradigm. Consequently, the liberation theology connection to the call for participatory communication has been lost in all but a few research projects conducted in subsequent years (Díaz Bordenave, 1994; Fals-Borda, 1988; Tehranian, 1999; Vargas, 1995). Nevertheless, the work of Freire—whose adult education project in Recife was modeled on Catholic base community meetings—has been infused consistently with references to theologians and declarations of faith and commitment to oppressed groups in society (Freire, 1970, 1973a, 1973b, 1997; Horton & Freire, 1990). The intensity of these dimensions was maintained in his most recent analyses of neoliberal Brazil in the 1990s, when he suggested, "It is urgent that the disowned unite and that we all fight in favor of liberation, transforming this offensive world into a more people-oriented one, from both a political and an ethical standpoint" (Freire, 1997, p. 46). Strengthening the ethical and political grounds of participatory communication for development will function to enhance conceptual clarity and to reduce the likelihood that participatory projects will reproduce inegalitarian relationships.

One practical step that researchers can take to advance the agenda of participatory communication for development is to begin aligning themselves with new social movements that have emerged recently worldwide. New social movements constitute a nexus where concerns for communication process, social justice, and broad participation converge as natural laboratories for exploring participatory communication for development. A number of researchers noted above have already identified popular movements as an arena worthy of scholarly attention. Their suggestion is further strengthened by the recent attention given to method and methodology, particularly those that advocate an action orientation to scholarship of and for social change. The intensive study of new social movements not only will give scholars direction in their research, it might address some of the issues of efficacy raised by development bureaucracies that demand demonstrable evidence of broad, material consequences of specific projects.

The concept of participatory communication for development is the most resilient and useful notion that has emerged from the challenges to the dominant paradigm of modernization. It has generated a diverse body of scholarship that has issued new challenges, identified problems, documented achievements, and advanced theoretical understanding. The past 30 years of research demonstrate substantial progress, but more than that, this past research contains important traces for the continued advancement of scholarship in this area.

NOTES

1. Although this history draws primarily from Latin American authors, readers should note that the dominant paradigm of development received criticisms across geographic boundaries. Flaws in the conceptualization and administration of diffusion of innovations projects, for example, were identified in both Africa and Asia (Röling, Ascroft, & Chege, 1976; Shingi & Mody, 1976).

2. Dependency was a school of thought emerging in Latin America in the 1960s that explained underdevelopment as the result or by-product of capitalist expansion. Furthermore, the development of underdevelopment was interpreted as part of a process of continuous political-economic relations occurring globally between the developed North and the impoverished South, or what has been termed "core-periphery" relations. Key authors include Cardoso and Faletto (1979) and Frank (1967).

3. Antonio Pasquali was fundamental in introducing continental proponents of phenomenology to Latin American critics of the dominant paradigm of development communication. Relying most heavily on the work of Heidegger and Merleau-Ponty, Pasquali argued that knowledge of development needed to be generated phenomenologically, that is, through presuppositionless, intentional action in the world. This position

undermined—on the most fundamental level—modernization approaches that assumed a separation between subject and object, researcher and development recipient.

REFERENCES

Arnst, R. (1996). Participation approaches to the research process. In J. Servaes, T. L. Jacobson, & S. A. White (Eds.), *Participatory communication for social change* (pp. 109-126). New Delhi: Sage.

Ascroft, J., & Masilela, S. (1994). Participatory decision making in Third World development. In S. A. White, K. S. Nair, & J. Ascroft (Eds.), *Participatory communication: Working for change and development* (pp. 259-294). New Delhi: Sage.

Atwood, R., & McAnany, E. G. (Eds.). (1986). *Communication and Latin American society.* Madison: University of Wisconsin Press.

Beltrán, L. R. (1975). Research ideologies in conflict. *Journal of Communication, 25,* 187-193.

Beltrán, L. R. (1980). A farewell to Aristotle: "Horizontal" communication. *Communication, 5,* 5-41.

Berlo, D. (1960). *The process of communication: An introduction to theory and practice.* San Francisco: Holt, Rinehart & Winston.

Berrigan, F. J. (1981). *Community communications: The role of community media in development.* Paris: UNESCO.

Bruner, E. M. (1986). Experience and its expressions. In V. W. Turner & E. M. Bruner (Eds.), *The anthropology of experience* (pp. 3-30). Urbana: University of Illinois Press.

Cardoso, F. H., & Faletto, E. (1979). *Dependency and development in Latin America* (M. Mattingly Urquidi, Trans.). Berkeley: University of California Press.

Chu, G. C. (1987). Development communication in the year 2000: Future trends and directions. In N. Jayaweera & S. Amunugama (Eds.), *Rethinking development communication* (pp. 95-107). Singapore: Asian Mass Communication Research and Information Centre.

Chu, G. C. (1994). Communication and development: Some emerging theoretical perspectives. In A. Moemeka (Ed.), *Communicating for development: A new pan-disciplinary perspective* (pp. 34-53). Albany: State University of New York Press.

Decker, P. (1988). *Portable video in grass-roots development.* Paper from the Institute for Communication Research, Stanford University, Stanford, CA.

Deetz, S. A. (1992). *Democracy in an age of corporate colonization: Developments in communication and the politics of everyday life.* Albany: State University of New York Press.

Dervin, B. (1993). Verbing communication: A mandate for disciplinary invention. *Journal of Communication, 43,* 45-54.

Dervin, B., & Huesca, R. (1997). Reaching for the communicating in participatory communication. *Journal of International Communication,* 4(2), 46-74.

Dervin, B., & Huesca, R. (1999). The participatory communication for development narrative: An examination of meta-theoretic assumptions and their impacts. In T. L. Jacobson & J. Servaes (Eds.), *Theoretical approaches to participatory communication* (pp. 169-210). Cresskill, NJ: Hampton.

Díaz Bordenave, J. E. (1985). *Comunicación y sociedad* [Communication and society]. La Paz, Bolivia: CIMCA.

Díaz Bordenave, J. (1994). Participative communication as a part of building the participative society. In S. A. White, K. S. Nair, & J. Ascroft (Eds.), *Participatory communication: Working for change and development* (pp. 35-48). New Delhi: Sage.

Dissanayake, W. (1985). From a piecemeal approach to an integrated strategy for development. *Media Development, 4,* 20-22.

Dudley, E. (1993). *The critical villager: Beyond community participation.* London: Routledge.

Einsiedel, E. F. (1999). Action research: Theoretical and methodological considerations for development. In T. L. Jacobson & J. Servaes (Eds.), *Theoretical approaches to participatory communication* (pp. 359-379). Cresskill, NJ: Hampton.

Escobar, A. (1995). *Encountering development: The making and unmaking of the Third World.* Princeton, NJ: Princeton University Press.

Escobar, A. (1999). Discourse and power in development: Michel Foucault and the relevance of his work to the Third World. In T. L. Jacobson & J. Servaes (Eds.), *Theoretical approaches to participatory communication* (pp. 309-335). Cresskill, NJ: Hampton.

Fadul, A., Lins da Silva, C. E., & Santoro, L. F. (1982). Documento básico do IV ciclo de estudos interdisiplinares da comunicação [Basic document of the IV cycle of interdisciplinary studies of communication]. In C. E. Lins da Silva (Ed.), *Comunicação, hegemonia, e contra-informação* [Communication, hegemony, and counter-information] (pp. 9-16). São Paulo: Cortel Editora/Intercom.

Fals-Borda, O. (1988). *Knowledge and people's power: Lessons with peasants in Nicaragua, Mexico and Colombia.* New Delhi: Indian Social Institute.

Fals-Borda, O. (1991). *Knowledge and social movements.* Santa Cruz, CA: Merrill.

Frank, A. G. (1967). *Capitalism and underdevelopment in Latin America.* New York: Monthly Review Press.

Fraser, C., & Restrepo-Estrada, S. (1998). *Communicating for development: Human change for survival.* London: I. B. Tauris.

Freire, P. (1970). *Pedagogy of the oppressed* (M. Bergman Ramos, Trans.). New York: Herder and Herder.

Freire, P. (1973a). *Education for critical consciousness.* New York: Seabury.

Freire, P. (1973b). *¿Extensión o comunicación?* [Extension or communication?] (L. Ronzoni, Trans.). Buenos Aires: Siglo XXI.

Freire, P. (1997). *Pedagogy of the heart* (D. Macedo & A. Oliveira, Trans.). New York: Continuum.

Hedebro, G. (1982). *Communication and social change in developing nations.* Ames: Iowa State University Press.

Horton, M., & Freire, P. (1990). *We make the road by walking: Conversations on education and social change.* Philadelphia: Temple University Press.

Huesca, R., & Dervin, B. (1994). Theory and practice in Latin American alternative communication research. *Journal of Communication,* 44(4), 53-73.

Jacobson, T. L. (1993). A pragmatist account of participatory communication research for national development. *Communication Theory, 3*(3), 214-230.

Jacobson, T. L. (1994). Modernization and post-modernization approaches to participatory communication for development. In S. A. White, K. S. Nair, & J. Ascroft (Eds.), *Participatory communication: Working for change and development* (pp. 60-75). New Delhi: Sage.

Jacobson, T. L. (1996). Conclusion: Prospects for theoretical development. In J. Servaes, T. L. Jacobson, & S. A. White (Eds.), *Participatory communication for social change* (pp. 266-277). New Delhi: Sage.

Jacobson, T. L., & Kolluri, S. (1999). Participatory communication as communicative action. In T. L. Jacobson & J. Servaes (Eds.), *Theoretical approaches to participatory communication* (pp. 265-280). Cresskill, NJ: Hampton.

Jacobson, T. L., & Servaes, J. (1999). Introduction. In T. L. Jacobson & J. Servaes (Eds.), *Theoretical approaches to participatory communication* (pp. 1-13). Cresskill, NJ: Hampton.

Kaplún, M. (1985). *El comunicador popular* [The popular communicator]. Quito: CIESPAL.

Kaplún, M. (1989). Video, comunicación y educación popular: Derroteros para una búsqueda [Video, communication and popular education: Action plan for a quest]. In P. Valdeavellano (Ed.), *El video en la educación popular* [Video in popular education] (pp. 37-58). Lima: Instituto Para América Latina.

Kennedy, T. W. (1984). Beyond advocacy: An animative approach to public participation (Doctoral dissertation, Cornell University). *Dissertation Abstracts International, 45,* 09A.

King, S. S., & Cushman, D. (1994). Communication in development and social change: Old myths and new realities. In A. Moemeka (Ed.), *Communicating for development: A new pandisciplinary perspective* (pp. 23-33). Albany: State University of New York Press.

Krohling-Peruzzo, C. M. (1996). Participation in community communication. In J. Servaes, T. L. Jacobson, & S. A. White (Eds.), *Participatory communication for social change* (pp. 162-179). New Delhi: Sage.

Lasswell, H. D. (1964). The structure and function of communication in society. In L. Bryson (Ed.), *The communication of ideas* (pp. 37-51). New York: Cooper Square. (Original work published c. 1948)

Lent, J. (1987). Devcom: A view from the United States. In N. Jayaweera & S. Amunugama (Eds.), *Rethinking development communication* (pp. 20-41). Singapore: Asian Mass Communication Research and Information Centre.

Lerner, D. (1976). Toward a new paradigm. In W. Schramm & D. Lerner (Eds.), *Communication and change: The last ten years—And the next* (pp. 60-63). Honolulu: University Press of Hawaii.

Lerner, D., & Schramm, W. (1976). Looking forward. In W. Schramm & D. Lerner (Eds.), *Communication and change: The last ten years—And the next* (pp. 340-344). Honolulu: University Press of Hawaii.

Lozare, B. V. (1994). Power and conflict: Hidden dimensions of communication, participative planning, and action. In S. A. White, K. S. Nair, & J. Ascroft (Eds.), *Participatory communication: Working for change and development* (pp. 229-244). New Delhi: Sage.

Mato, D. (1999). Problems of social participation in "Latin" America in the age of globalization: Theoretical and case-based considerations for practitioners and researchers. In T. L. Jacobson & J. Servaes (Eds.), *Theoretical approaches to participatory communication* (pp. 51-75). Cresskill, NJ: Hampton.

McKee, N. (1994). A community-based learning approach: Beyond social marketing. In S. A. White, K. S. Nair, & J. Ascroft (Eds.), *Participatory communication: Working for change and development* (pp. 194-228). New Delhi: Sage.

Melkote, S. R. (1991). *Communication for development in the Third World.* New Delhi: Sage.

Melkote, S. R. (1993). From Third World to First World: New roles and challenges for development communication. *Gazette, 52,* 145-158.

Midgley, J. (1986). Community participation: History, concepts and controversies. In J. Midgley (Ed.), *Community participation, social development and the state* (pp. 13-44). London: Methuen.

Mody, B. (1991). *Designing messages for development communication: An audience participation-based approach.* New Delhi: Sage.

Moemeka, A. A. (1994). Development communication: A historical and conceptual overview. In A. Moemeka (Ed.), *Communicating for development: A new pan-disciplinary perspective* (pp. 3-22). Albany: State University of New York Press.

Nair, K. S., & White, S. A. (1993a). The development communication process. In K. S. Nair & S. A. White (Eds.), *Perspectives on development communication* (pp. 47-70). New Delhi: Sage.

Nair, K. S., & White, S. A. (1993b). Introduction. In K. S. Nair & S. A. White (Eds.), *Perspectives on development communication* (pp. 12-31). New Delhi: Sage.

Nair, K. S., & White, S. A. (1993c). Preface. In K. S. Nair & S. A. White (Eds.), *Perspectives on development communication* (pp. 9-11). New Delhi: Sage.

Nair, K. S., & White, S. A. (1994a). Participatory development communication as cultural renewal. In S. A. White, K. S. Nair, & J. Ascroft (Eds.), *Participatory communication: Working for change and development* (pp. 138-193). New Delhi: Sage.

Nair, K. S., & White, S. A. (1994b). Participatory message development: A conceptual framework. In S. A. White, K. S. Nair, & J. Ascroft (Eds.), *Participatory communication: Working for change and development* (pp. 345-358). New Delhi: Sage.

Nerfin, M. (1977). Introduction. In M. Nerfin (Ed.), *Another development: Approaches and strategies* (pp. 9-18). Uppsala, Sweden: Dag Hammarskjöld Foundation.

O'Connor, A. (1990). Radio is fundamental to democracy. *Media Development, 4,* 3-4.

O'Sullivan-Ryan, J., & Kaplún, M. (1978). *Communication methods to promote grass-roots participation: A summary of research findings from Latin America, and an annotated bibliography.* Paris: UNESCO.

Pasquali, A. (1963). *Comunicación y cultura de masas* [Communication and mass culture]. Caracas: Universidad Central de Venezuela.

Rahman, M. A. (1993). *People's self development: Perspectives on participatory action research.* London: Zed.

Reyes Matta, F. (Ed.). (1983). *Comunicación alternativa y búsquedas democráticas* [Alternative communication and democratic quests]. Mexico City: Instituto Latinoamericano de Estudios Transnacionales y Fundación Friedrich Ebert.

Riaño, P. (1994). Women's participation in communication: Elements of a framework. In P. Riaño (Ed.), *Women in grassroots communication* (pp. 3-29). Thousand Oaks, CA: Sage.

Rodriguez, C. (1994). A process of identity deconstruction: Latin American women producing video stories. In P. Riaño (Ed.), *Women in grassroots communication* (pp. 149-160). Thousand Oaks, CA: Sage.

Rogers, E. M. (1976). Communication and development: The passing of the dominant paradigm. *Communication Research, 3*(2), 213-240.

Rogers, E. M. (1993). Perspectives on development communication. In K. S. Nair & S. A. White (Eds.), *Perspectives on development communication* (pp. 35-46). New Deli: Sage.

Röling, N. G., Ascroft, J., & Chege, F. W. (1976). The diffusion of innovations and the issue of equity in rural development. In. E. M. Rogers (Ed.), *Communication and development: Critical perspectives* (pp. 63-79). Beverly Hills, CA: Sage.

Schramm, W. (1976). End of an old paradigm? In W. Schramm & D. Lerner (Eds.), *Communication and change: The last ten years—And the next* (pp. 45-48). Honolulu: University Press of Hawaii.

Servaes, J. (1985). Towards an alternative concept of communication and development. *Media Development, 4,* 2-5.

Servaes, J. (1986). Development theory and communication policy: Power to the people! *European Journal of Communication, 1,* 203-229.

Servaes, J. (1989). *One world, multiple cultures: A new paradigm on communication for development.* Louvain, Belgium: Acco.

Servaes, J. (1996a). Introduction: Participatory communication and research in development settings. In J. Servaes, T. L. Jacobson, & S. A. White (Eds.), *Participatory communication for social change* (pp. 13-25). New Delhi: Sage.

Servaes, J. (1996b). Linking theoretical perspectives to policy. In J. Servaes, T. L. Jacobson, &

S. A. White (Eds.), *Participatory communication for social change* (pp. 2943). New Delhi: Sage.

Servaes, J. (1996c). Participatory communication research with new social movements: A realistic utopia. In J. Servaes, T. L. Jacobson, & S. A. White (Eds.), *Participatory communication for social change* (pp. 82-108). New Delhi: Sage.

Servaes, J. (1998). Human rights, participatory communication and cultural freedom in a global perspective. *Journal of International Communication, 5*(1-2), 122-133.

Servaes, J., & Arnst, R. (1999). Principles of participatory communication research: Its strengths (!) and weaknesses (?). In T. L. Jacobson & J. Servaes (Eds.), *Theoretical approaches to participatory communication* (pp. 107-130). Cresskill, NJ: Hampton.

Shingi, P. M., & Mody, B. (1976). The communication effects gap: A field experiment on television and agricultural ignorance in India. In E. M. Rogers (Ed.), *Communication and development: Critical perspectives* (pp. 79-98). Beverly Hills, CA: Sage.

Simpson Grinberg, M. (Ed.). (1986). *Comunicación alternativa y cambio social* [Alternative communication and social change]. Tlahuapan, Puebla, Mexico: Premiá Editora de Libros.

Singhal, A., & Rogers, E. M. (1988). Television soap operas for development in India. *Gazette, 41*(2), 109-126.

Storey, D. (1999). Popular culture, discourse, and development. In T. L. Jacobson & J. Servaes (Eds.), *Theoretical approaches to participatory communication* (pp. 337-358). Cresskill, NJ: Hampton.

Storey, D. (2000). A discursive perspective on development theory and practice: Reconceptualizing the role of donor agencies. In K. G. Wilkins (Ed.), *Redeveloping communication for social change: Theory, practice, and power* (pp. 103-117). Lanham, MD: Rowman & Littlefield.

Tehranian, M. (1999). *Global communication and world politics: Domination, development and discourse.* Boulder, CO: Lynne Rienner.

Thapalia, C. F. (1996). Animation and leadership. In J. Servaes, T. L. Jacobson, & S. A. White

(Eds.), *Participatory communication for social change* (pp. 150-161). New Delhi: Sage.

Thomas, P. (1994). Participatory message development communication: Philosophical premises. In S. A. White, K. S. Nair, & J. Ascroft (Eds.), *Participatory communication: Working for change and development* (pp. 49-59). New Delhi: Sage.

Vargas, L. (1995). *Social uses & radio practices: The use of participatory radio by ethnic minorities in Mexico.* Boulder, CO: Westview.

White, K. (1999). The importance of sensitivity to culture in development work. In T. L. Jacobson & J. Servaes (Eds.), *Theoretical approaches to participatory communication* (pp. 17-49). Cresskill, NJ: Hampton.

White, R. (1994). Participatory development communication as a social-cultural process. In S. A. White, K. S. Nair, & J. Ascroft (Eds.), *Participatory communication: Working for change and development* (pp. 95-116). New Delhi: Sage.

White, R. (1999). The need for new strategies of research on the democratization of communication. In T. L. Jacobson & J. Servaes (Eds.), *Theoretical approaches to participatory communication* (pp. 229-262). Cresskill, NJ: Hampton.

White, S. A. (1994). The concept of participation: Transforming rhetoric to reality. In S. A. White, K. S. Nair, & J. Ascroft (Eds.), *Participatory communication: Working for change and development* (pp. 15-32). New Delhi: Sage.

Wildemeersch, D. (1999). Transcending the limits of traditional research: Toward an interpretive approach to development communication and education. In T. L. Jacobson & J. Servaes (Eds.), *Theoretical approaches to participatory communication* (pp. 211-227). Cresskill, NJ: Hampton.

Wilkins, K. G. (1999). Development discourse on gender and communication in strategies for social change. *Journal of Communication, 49,* 46-68.

Wilkins, K. G. (2000). Accounting for power in development communication. In K. G. Wilkins (Ed.), *Redeveloping communication for social change: Theory, practice, and power* (pp. 197-210). Lanham, MD: Rowman & Littlefield.

13

Development Communication as Marketing, Collective Resistance, and Spiritual Awakening

A Feminist Critique

H. LESLIE STEEVES
University of Oregon

As in all subfields of communication studies, development communication scholars and practitioners have constructed frameworks for talking about and practicing communication. Most discourse on development communication assumes an overall *economic* framework, concerned primarily with the creation and distribution of material resources in society and the role of communication in these processes. Whereas some who make critical, political-economic arguments do at times acknowledge ideological influence (e.g., issues of cultural imperialism), these arguments usually are secondary to questions of power over capital resources. The globalization of the economy has reinforced the dominance of economic perspectives.

Nonmaterial considerations of religion and spirituality are seldom examined in the scholarship or practice of Western development aid—except as obstacles to change under the dominant paradigm of modernization. Likewise, the purpose of communication usually is defined as personal influence and marketing (modernization perspectives) or political solidarity and resistance to modernization (critical perspectives), with little attention to religion or spirituality. In the larger, umbrella field of communication theory, the notion of religious or spiritual practice as a form of communication has been seriously considered by only a handful of communication scholars, with most focusing on other practical communication functions (Craig, 1999).[1]

The neglect of the nonmaterial in development communication has been accompanied by a neglect of gender considerations. Yet the field of development studies—as well as of media studies—reveals three decades of scholarship on gender inequities. This research is often traced to Ester Boserup (1970), who used data from sub-Saharan Africa to show that women's historically productive roles in agriculture were harmed by colonial and postcolonial aid policies favoring men in the new cash economies. From this research, Boserup argued for integrating women in development, an argument that helped catalyze the 1975-1985 U.N. Decade for Women, and also the implementation of women-specific programs in most aid agencies. Many studies show, however, that these changes have been superficial, the changes have affected only limited categories of projects, and women continue to be neglected (e.g., Hoy, 1998; Rogers, 1980/1989; Staudt, 1985b; Wilkins, 1999).

Boserup's and others' liberal feminist emphasis on integrating women in development has been critiqued not only for its failures but also for ignoring women's reproductive work in measures of production and for exploiting their labor (Mohanty, 1991b; Rogers, 1980/1989; Sen & Grown, 1987). Hence, although adding women to development structures does address an affirmative action issue, it will not necessarily produce either project success or improvements in poor women's lives.

This insight led to a revision in women-in-development (WID) thinking. The gender-and-development (GAD) framework recognizes the importance of considering the *gendered* context of every situation, including women's and men's historic roles, and other relevant social divisions.[2] Aid agencies such as the U.S. Agency for International Development (USAID) have embraced the rhetoric of GAD (*Gender Action,* 1997, p. 4). However, as with WID stipulations, GAD applies only to certain categories of USAID projects, and it is unclear how much impact GAD policy will have.

Alongside the literature of women in development is a large body of literature on women and media (e.g., Steeves, 1987; van Zoonen,

1993). Most of this research has been carried out in North America and Europe over the past three decades. Much of the early scholarship counted women represented in media content or employed in media organizations, assuming that adding women to media would reduce inequities. As this remedy proved ineffective—and the research did little more than confirm the obvious—scholars began developing more complex approaches. Some drew on Marxian theory (to be discussed) to critique the role of the dominant ideology, including oppressive gender and class representations, in sustaining patriarchy. Others followed more radical feminist perspectives in arguing for the necessity of alternative feminist media.

There have been comparatively few studies of gender inequities in relation to communication in developing countries (for exceptions see, e.g., Gallagher, 1995; Gallagher & Quindoza-Santiago, 1994). Most such studies have analyzed media content from liberal feminist frameworks. Although these studies are important, they need to be linked more clearly to larger issues of development policy and practice. Also, many areas of study remain underexamined, including women's uses of media content; women's employment in communication organizations (including development organizations that carry out strategic communication), women's participation in policy making, and women's access to information and communication technologies. Furthermore, there is a need to reveal the societal consequences of inequities and how they vary contextually.

This chapter draws on feminist theory and feminist scholarship in development studies and communication studies to examine how feminism challenges development communication in three, overlapping traditions, conceptualizing communication as (1) information delivery for persuasive marketing, (2) collective resistance, and (3) spiritual practice for liberation or empowerment. These three frameworks are evident at all levels of society, from the global level to the grassroots (Melkote & Steeves, 2001). Building a feminist framework to address this complexity is a daunting challenge, discussed in the next section.

FEMINIST FRAMEWORK

Contextual considerations are crucial at all levels of development communication. At the global level, attention to regional differences is necessary for meaningful analysis. At more local levels, scholars often analyze project failures by seeking blind spots in the planning process, that is, significant omissions in analyzing the context of a problem.

In the WID/GAD literature, context has been a major theme. This is partly because much of the research and practice have been generated by Western scholars and consultants, often with contextually inaccurate assumptions. Chandra Mohanty (1991a) argues that Western feminists "discursively colonize" the lives of women in developing countries and assume a "composite, singular 'third world woman'" (p. 53). This monolithic woman is victimized by a "monolithic notion of patriarchy" as well (pp. 53-54). Mohanty discusses six overlapping areas of victim status commonly assumed by feminist scholars, that is, women as victims of male violence, universal dependency, colonial process, religion, familial systems, and development. Minority and Third World feminists have increasingly critiqued the assumptions and agendas of earlier frameworks as ethnocentric and irrelevant to their lives (e.g., hooks, 1984; Minh-ha, 1986-1987; Mohanty, 1991a, 1991b; Spivak, 1988).

The feminist perspective assumed here draws partly on socialist feminism, which assumes (from Marx) that individuals cannot develop their potential in class-based societies. Hence, socialist feminism rejects the individualistic premise of liberal feminism. It also rejects feminisms that assume an essential biological human nature, including some forms of radical feminism. From Marx, it assumes that human nature is a dialectical product of many factors and constraints—biological, social, economic, and political. Socialist feminism further assumes that the capitalist mode of production and capitalist classes contribute to women's oppression by encouraging men's control over women's labor. It does not focus exclusively on capitalism as the source of women's oppression, however, recognizing that women were oppressed before capitalism. Hence, there is a need for a theory of "capitalist patriarchy" (e.g., Barrett, 1985; Eisenstein, 1979).

Yet theories of capitalist patriarchy remain problematic. Most significant are problems of conceptualizing patriarchy in terms other than capitalism, especially in nonmaterial terms, such as ideology, representation, culture, spirituality, and individual identity and subjectivity. Finding a material basis for nonmaterial aspects of society remains an obstacle to theorizing links between capitalism and patriarchy (Barrett, 1999; Steeves & Wasko, in press).

In addition, in the past two decades feminism in general has turned away from an emphasis on material experiences (e.g., of illiteracy and low pay) to an emphasis on symbols and representations (Barrett, 1999). Poststructuralist theorists such as Foucault have argued that material objects alone are meaningless, but are given meaning by signs and discourses. Also, they have challenged the validity of causal explanations of inequality, arguing that it is more useful to analyze representational meaning. Poststructuralism has been supported by postmodernism, which also rejects causal theories in favor of a plurality of meanings. In addition to these influences, minority and Third World feminists, noted above, have critiqued the white, middle-class biases of Western feminisms as irrelevant to their lives. They tend to agree with poststructuralists' and postmodernists' rejection of unified theory, yet their material political agenda departs from a primary focus on words and symbols.

As development communication scholarship and practice have centralized the economic concerns of women in developing countries, it is likewise necessary to critique the political-economic structures and processes that contribute to their concerns. At the same time, the role of nonmaterial factors in women's oppression—including ideology, religion, and spirituality—cannot be discounted. In addition, none of these considerations are fixed, but vary by context.

I have argued elsewhere that the solution is not to confine scholars, practitioners, and activists to their contextual boundaries, but rather to work harder to understand our differences and commonalities, to collaborate and to build coalitions (Steeves, 1993a). Gender is a crucial contextual consideration at all levels of development communication scholarship and practice. The remaining sections of this chapter will critique three broad perspectives on communication and development, concluding with the most neglected area: communication as spiritual awakening.

COMMUNICATION AS MARKETING: THE LIBERAL-CAPITALIST BASIS OF DEVELOPMENT COMMUNICATION

Most development communication practice and scholarship are consistent with "modernization" theory, which is based on liberal political theory and rests on the same philosophical principles as Western science. Modernization (and related neoclassical economic)

approaches extol scientific rationality and individualism. Economic growth via building up infrastructure and acquiring technologies is prioritized, and communication is viewed as a product and reinforcer of economic growth (Lerner, 1958; Schramm, 1964). Participation in world trade is assumed necessary as well. At the macro level, communication scholars have supported global and national policies that facilitate "free flows" of communication content and technologies, as they view these products as crucial for participation in the global economy. At the micro level, they support persuasive marketing campaigns as an efficient means to transform traditional societies.

Although profit motives and liberal-capitalist ideologies constitute powerful national forces, and hence cannot be easily dismissed, it is clear that women have been neglected and harmed by their uncritical application, an omission that also has resulted in many project failures. Another modernization theme is an increased reliance on the new telecommunication technologies and the Internet to disseminate information and to network like-minded groups, yet the implications for women and other marginalized groups need to be considered.

The impact of modernization is perhaps most evident in the global power of transnational corporations (TNCs). These corporations usually receive much support from the governments of their home countries, from global financial institutions, and also from aid agencies, which sell or otherwise promote their products in developing countries, resulting in a financial drain on recipient countries. In the communication/information sector, there have been a number of "mega-mergers." Corporate mergers and the resulting expansion and diversification of TNCs allow them to increase their profits while reducing their risk (e.g., Melody, 1991, pp. 35-37).

Castells's (1996, 1997, 1998) three-volume series on the network logic of the information age describes a new global paradigm in which power and wealth increasingly are "diffused in global networks." The state, TNCs, and ideological institutions (schools, churches, media) no longer constitute the exclusive sites for the concentration of power (Castell, 1996, p. 359).

Certainly, Castells is right in observing power shifts accompanying the increased transcendence of time and space by information networks. However, to the extent that networks generate profits, these shifts will not produce much change in the basic reward structure of the market, which assumes interrelated divisions of labor, knowledge, and wealth. In this global network/market system, the benefits will continue to go to those at the top, most of whom live in industrialized nations. In addition, Castells concludes that the network society will continue to widen the gap between haves and have-nots, increasingly divided into those with access to cyberspace and other forms of mobility and those without access. Although increased globalization is rendering national boundaries less relevant, Castells (1998) concedes that a "fourth world" that consists of large parts of Africa, South America, and Asia will be almost completely excluded as irrelevant to the global network economy.

These predictions do not bode well for women, who historically have been marginalized in public life. All over the world and especially in developing countries, unemployment is higher among women than men, female wages are lower than male wages, and numbers of women decrease at higher organizational levels. Women also constitute the vast majority of the unpaid family workers. The International Conference on Population and Development held in Cairo in 1994 concluded that equality for the girl-child will be necessary for women to achieve equality with men in public life. Yet there remains much evidence globally of discriminatory health practices, including prenatal sex selection and female infanticide, and gender discrimination in school enrollment, literacy, and child labor.[3] The child labor situation has been exacerbated by electronics, clothing, and other plants in developing countries, which often prefer young women and girls as employees, and by sex trafficking.[4]

Given the exclusion and oppression of women in most aspects of public life, to what extent do women participate in global communication? Empirical studies show that women usually are devalued in representations, employment, and media education (e.g., Steeves, 1993b; United Nations Educational, Scientific and Cultural Organization [UNESCO], 1999). In content, women are represented less often than men, and where present, they are usually parents, homemakers, sex objects, or victims. Even the press coverage of serious women's events and issues, such as the 1995 Fourth World Conference on Women in Beijing, reveals negative stereotypes, with little attention to the issues the conference addressed (e.g., Akhavan-Majid & Ramaprasad, 2000; Danner & Walsh, 1999). In addition, advertising images in developing countries reveal the increased adoption of Western consumer values and associated conventions of gender representation (e.g., Griffin, Viswanath, & Schwartz, 1994).

Liberal feminism suggests that adding more women to media organizations would transform representations of women. From a civil rights standpoint alone, more women are needed (Gallagher, 1995). However, evidence thus far indicates that adding women to media structures, like development structures, will not readily transform them. Rather, it is more likely that women will conform to organizational norms (e.g., van Zoonen, 1994).

Clearly, the modernization paradigm has not brought gender equality, but rather has led to new forms of gender and class oppression. It has also helped create an impoverished fourth world, a world unlikely to benefit from the information revolution. All over the world, but especially in developing countries, women are disproportionately excluded from new information technologies, as they have been from mass media.

The fact that women's organizations are using the Internet to access information and network globally does not change the dominant uses of the Internet in development or overall gender disadvantage. In a study of 40 development projects that use computer technologies, Wilkins and Waters (2000) conclude that these technologies have not altered traditional approaches to—or participants in—communication and social change: "Instead, current institutional discourse continues to promote traditional development paradigms, focusing on economic integration rather than collective resistance" (p. 59). Hamada (1999) argues that the Internet is widening information gaps and intensifying the expansion of Western consumer culture. Gersch (1998, p. 307) and others have pointed out that the Internet is a part of computer culture and requires at least some technical expertise, expertise that has been historically male. Siew and Kim (1996, p. 76) observe that in Malaysia the cost of developing new technologies has been borne by the government and business sectors. As women's status and roles have been marginalized in these sectors, women's access to the Internet and other new technologies has been likewise limited.

At the local level of projects to support specific development goals, the technological orientation of projects often has disadvantaged women, who have not played major roles in developing these technologies. For instance, population projects have promoted technological "cures" for fertility, with little consideration of negative side effects or alternative solutions (e.g., Jaquette & Staudt, 1985).

All development projects depend on communication in order to succeed. Yet studies show that women benefit less than men. This is partly because aid agencies have tended to overlook women except in relation to traditional Western roles as mothers and homemakers. Hence, women are "targeted" in health, nutrition, population, and immunization campaigns, but are overlooked in campaigns related to agriculture and economic infrastructure. Gallagher (1987, p. 26) notes that the joint U.S.-Indian Satellite Instructional Television Experiment (SITE) either ignored or inaccurately stereotyped women's needs both in scheduling and in program content. The neglect of women can similarly be observed in many development communication texts, which mention women only in passing and in relation to traditional female roles.

Several studies have examined gender and class biases in national extension systems, which receive grants from aid agencies to plan and implement project communication. Research beginning in the 1970s indicated that most extension programs neither employ many women nor function in a gender-sensitive manner (e.g., Hale, 1982; Spens, 1986). In a study in western Kenya, Staudt (1985a) found that "female-managed farms always received fewer services than jointly managed farms, and gaps increased as the services became more valuable" (p. xii). Her recommendations included making greater use of women's groups and networks; recruiting more female extension agents; emphasizing group extension; and improving management, so that gender sensitivity is incorporated throughout organizations. Projects, new programs, and studies since then have supported the validity of Staudt's conclusions. However, their implementation has been slow, especially at managerial levels, and women remain marginalized in development (e.g., Staudt, 1985b; Wilkins, 1999).

In addition, the market values of the global economy have affected all areas of development planning. For instance, structural adjustment policies are forcing a trend toward the privatization of formerly public services, including mass media, health care, and education. Aid funds are increasingly being directed to micro-credit and micro-enterprise initiatives that will enable individuals to achieve economic independence (Hoy, 1998, p. 36). Few of these projects have a collective orientation, even when such an orientation would be more consistent with the local culture (e.g., Rapley, 1996, pp. 170-172). Also, these projects often fail to consider the gendered context of local situations, and merely add new responsibilities to women's domestic work, with no change in men's roles (e.g., Kellow, 1998; Rozario, 1997).

In local-level development communication, diffusion campaigns have increasingly been replaced by social marketing campaigns (Clift, 1989; Luthra, 1991; Wilkins, 1999; Worthington, 1992). These campaigns apply marketing concepts to socially desirable goals —such as improved nutrition, immunization, or family planning. Following research to assess user needs and constraints, marketing strategies are formulated around the "four Ps": product, price, place, and promotion (Kotler, 1984; Manoff, 1985). Although socially desirable outcomes are emphasized, in reality actual products—whether contraceptives or food items—are promoted in most projects. This means that commercial interests have the potential to dominate planning and may negatively affect both the projects' social mission and women's needs, as demonstrated empirically by Luthra (1991) and Worthington (1992).

As the modernization paradigm has not produced substantial gender equality in development communication—that is, beyond affirmative action gains for some women—I next explore critical perspectives, emphasizing communication in support of equitable economic arrangements.

COMMUNICATION AS COLLECTIVE RESISTANCE: THE CRITICAL BASIS OF DEVELOPMENT COMMUNICATION

Critical (including Marxist, dependency, and world systems) theorists have offered alternatives to modernization approaches, which they believe have resulted in project and foreign policy failures by creating intractable class systems where the few increase their wealth at the expense of the majority. These systems operate both within and between (and increasingly beyond) nations. At the global level, TNCs based in wealthier countries increase their profits by exploiting the resources of developing countries.

Critical approaches stem from Lenin's (1939) prediction that imperialism is the highest or "monopoly" stage of capitalism. Indications of this stage would be great increases in the sizes of firms, in the export of capital, and in monopoly ownership. Interpretations of the consequences of these phenomena have varied. Lenin predicted that capitalist imperialism would play a progressive role in establishing the material preconditions for socialism. Later observations led to more pessimistic predictions. Frank (1967) and Wallerstein (1974), among others, observed a growing world system of exploitation, where "core" countries exploit the resources and labor of "periphery" countries, and where the elite in periphery countries also profit from this system.

These observations are consistent with dependency theory, which emerged in Latin America in the late 1960s and 1970s in response to the growing economic dependency of these countries, due to debt and reliance on single export crops. Scholars also began applying the framework to critique the role of communication in sustaining a global power pyramid of imperialism (e.g., Schiller, 1969). The early scholarship focused on the economic expansionist goals of the nation-state, but in the 1990s these goals were increasingly framed within the context of TNCs and the global network society (Castells, 1996, 1997, 1998; Nordenstreng & Schiller, 1993).

Like modernization perspectives, critical perspectives tend to be secular and emphasize economic growth, though obviously they favor economic growth in a just and equitable manner. They disagree on how equitable growth should be accomplished. Early theorists assumed the necessity of revolution (Frank, 1967). By the 1970s, however, critical scholars were increasingly seeking alternatives that would allow for progressive development despite dependency (e.g., Cardoso & Faletto, 1979). Political organization to create structures for redistributive equality and to empower individuals is viewed as a prerequisite for economic growth. In addition, scholars examined the role of communication in challenging modernization, as communication is necessary to generate the awareness and organization necessary for resistance. Some have encouraged rather extreme policies of cultural dissociation (e.g., Hamelink, 1983). Most encourage bottom-up participatory forms of communication, the creation of alternative media, and national policies consistent with the values of each country (e.g., Hudson, 1994; International Commission for the Study of Communication Problems, 1980; Mowlana & Wilson, 1988).

Although critiques of capitalism and the emphasis on redistributive equality may seem to speak to women's oppression (as argued by socialist feminists), women generally remained oppressed in socialist states. Furthermore, few critical, international communication scholars have considered gender in their analyses. This indicates the strength of ideologies of gender inequality and also the fact that inequality does not depend on capi-

talism, but may pervade noncapitalist structures and processes as well.

Of the critical feminist communication studies, most have examined representations of women in media. These studies assume that mainstream media contribute to systems of representation, which make up ideological structures and processes in society and usually support hegemonic values of capitalism and patriarchy. They also assume that exposure alone challenges hegemony. Hence, it is worthwhile to reveal patriarchal processes in media texts, including news, entertainment, and advertising. These studies usually go beyond critique, to identify openings for possible hegemonic change as well. There are many examples, including the previously cited studies of news coverage of the Beijing conference and of the transfer of Western conventions to the advertising of developing countries. Studies examining how issues of particular concern to women are covered in local media news include Steeves's (1997) analysis of how the Kenyan press reported a crime of gender violence, Worthington's (2001) analysis of a Kenyan newsmagazine's coverage of a Mothers of Political Prisoners hunger strike, and Luthra's (1999) study of the coverage of an Indian campaign against female feticide. The many historically situated studies analyzing representations of women in media entertainment include Glasser's (1997) study of stereotypes in Chinese magazine fiction and Yanru's (1998) examination of a recent Chinese TV drama series "*on* women, *by* women, and *for* women."[5]

In contrast to the many studies critiquing content, only a few have examined women's reception of media in developing countries, assessing women's resistance to, as well as acceptance of, hegemonic representations. Exceptions include Mankekar's (1999) ethnography of television and womanhood in postcolonial India and Parameswaran's (1999) ethnography of the consumption of

Western romance fiction by middle-class Indian women. Parameswaran concludes that the reception of popular culture is complex and must "take into account the form of the media (print or electronic), the language in which these media are consumed (colonial or vernacular), and the differences of class, gender, and cultural capital among heterogeneous audiences" (p. 100).

Given critical scholars' assumptions about roles of communication and information in reinforcing hegemonic ideologies, some feminist scholars have argued for the need to contribute to discussions about communication and information policy (Gallagher, 1995, p. 8). Certainly, women and media has been a key topic at the conferences associated with the 1975-1985 Decade for Women, and was one of twelve critical areas of concern discussed at the Fourth World Conference on Women in Beijing. Also, in 1979, the U.N. General Assembly adopted the Convention on the Elimination of All Forms of Discrimination Against Women (CEDAW), which is the most comprehensive international treaty addressing women's human rights.[6] So far, 161 nations (excluding the United States) have ratified CEDAW, though often with qualifications attached. Obviously, the Beijing report and treaties such as CEDAW can only be as effective as the local and national will to enforce them. The Women's Environment and Development Organization (WEDO) was established in 1990 by an international group of activists, in large part to monitor, analyze, and publicize each nation's progress in implementing U.N. conference agreements and policies at all levels.[7] Although there is a long way to go, WEDO represents a start in women's collective organizing for change.

At the national level of communication and information policy, women face a daunting challenge in revising policy in gender-sensitive directions. Here it will be useful to draw on the works of feminists studying other areas of politics, policy, and law (see, e.g., Nelson & Chowdhury, 1994; Staudt, 1997). Feminists have had some success in influencing policy in industrialized nations, notably broadcast policy in Canada.[8] Steeves (1996) analyzed attempts to develop communication and information policy in Kenya, identifying areas that need to be addressed in gender-sensitive policy, women's employment, women's access to technologies, representations of women, and gender-sensitive criteria in choices of technologies. Bruin (1999) makes consistent points in a discussion of policy in the Caribbean.

Issues of representation and participation cannot depend on macro-level change alone. Feminist scholars and activists must recognize that the democratization of communication is irrelevant to the majority of the world's women, who remain excluded from access to media or information technologies. Hence, projects focusing on basic access are crucial. These include efforts to increase women's and girls' literacy and to make greater use of indigenous communication (Morrison, 1993), traditional women's groups and networks (March & Taqqu, 1986), and democratic media such as community radio (Lucas, 1999). Riano (1994) and Allen, Rush, and Kaufman (1996) provide additional examples globally. None of these projects are easy to implement and sustain, as the trend toward globalization and privatization drains resources from marginalized groups, especially in rural areas (e.g., Heath, 1988; "Women Organize," 1994). However, the continued initiation and success of some such projects do indicate openings for progressive social change within mainstream structures.

In addition, issues of education and economic empowerment are interdependent, and both may be necessary before women have access to communication and information. To increase grassroots involvement in development, critical scholars have written much about alternative, participatory, empowerment-oriented approaches. These are varied, and they are not mutually exclusive.[9] Rowlands (1997) and Rozario (1997) trace the history of the empowerment concept, which both say is overused. Rozario divides empowerment into two primary models: One model "is based on empowering the individual, not on encouraging collective social action by the oppressed" (p. 46). The other model, consistent with critical arguments, has emerged from Paulo Freire's approach, which emphasized "conscientization and radical social action" (p. 47).

Freire's assumptions of what development communication should do are radically different from the assumptions of modernization, emphasizing message transfer supportive of economic gain. Rather, development communication is emancipatory dialogue that leads to expanded individual and communal consciousness and power, with no hierarchical distinction among participants in dialogue. Freire argued that once people named their sources of oppression, as well as their sources of power, they would then be able to find solutions. For development communication practice, the central focus should be face-to-face egalitarian dialogue to initiate and sustain a collective process of reflection and action (e.g., Freire, 1970, 1973).[10]

As women have been neglected in economic development projects, noted earlier, a number of projects have tried to implement Freirian approaches. Micro-credit organizations and projects to enable women or women's collectives to start income generation projects are among these. For instance, since 1979 the Grameen Bank in Bangladesh has given unsecured loans to thousands of women for income-generating activities (Mizan, 1994). Although this and similar organizations have helped many in some ways, evidence indicates that these organizations do not seek to alter existing gender and class hierarchies as

grounded in a combination of local tradition and the global economy. This appears true even for more radical micro-credit nongovernmental organizations (NGOs) that claim goals of consciousness-raising and collective mobilization alongside improvement in economic status (Rozario, 1997). Even here, it appears that women add new tasks to their domestic responsibilities, with no changes in gender roles. Hence, although micro-credit organizations allow for the self-improvement of some, the underlying system of inequality is left intact.

Alongside efforts to create new kinds of economic development projects for women's empowerment, feminists are creating alternative media and networking structures. These forms of communication support other nonmainstream approaches by providing mechanisms for unfettered discussion and information dissemination, therefore opening new spaces for resistance. At the global level, alternative resources include the Women's Feature Service, a women's news agency based in New Delhi; Women's International Newsgathering Service (WINGS), a radio service based in the United States; *Women's International Net* (*WIN*) magazine, also based in the United States and now available free online; and the AVIVA Web site and news service, also free online, which connect women globally to exchange information and provide other forms of support. Successful national-level organizations include the Manushi collective in India, which publishes *Manushi* magazine and provides many other services for women; Kali for Women in India, which publishes a wide range of books and other materials; the Feminist International Radio Endeavor in Costa Rica; and the Tanzania Media Women's Association.[11] In addition, women are increasingly finding creative ways to use the Internet to link individuals and groups globally while still recognizing access barriers. The Internet was especially beneficial in the planning and follow-up for the Beijing conference.

In general, feminists with critical leanings have struggled in varied ways and at all levels to understand and address the complexities associated with the role of communication and information in supporting or challenging modernization in a context of increased globalization. However, one problem with most of these approaches is their secular orientation and lack of attention to nonmaterial motivations.

COMMUNICATION AS AWAKENING: THE SPIRITUAL BASIS OF DEVELOPMENT COMMUNICATION[12]

The religious and spiritual basis of development communication is rarely explicit in the literature, with many authors using the language of "empowerment," "emancipation," "liberation," and "dialogue," but few delving further, and fewer yet considering their meaning for women. At the macro level, some of the most profound social changes are inspired by the actions of religious leaders. These include the civil rights movement in North America, the antiapartheid movement in South Africa, and the anticolonial resistance movement in India. At the same time, religion is often a greater force of oppression than empowerment, as in many mission interventions and in fundamentalist movements. For women, the benefits of religion have been mixed at every level, with profound rewards, but much neglect and harm as well. This section seeks to reveal the religious and spiritual motivations underlying development communication as spiritual awakening for liberation, the importance of these motives, and women's strengths and weaknesses in relation to religion and spirituality in development.

As noted earlier, both capitalist and Marxian approaches to development are largely secular and reject religious expressions as contrary to the material concerns of modernity. To complicate matters further, Western feminists have tended to assume religion is fundamentally sexist (e.g., Daly, 1973) and to view women in developing countries as victims of religion (Mohanty, 1991a).

Although critical and feminist scholars and practitioners often draw freely on Freire (1970) to promote empowerment, they usually forget that Freire's argument rested on Christian liberation theology, one of several forms of "socially engaged spirituality" (e.g., Rothberg, 1993a). More specifically, themes of socially engaged spirituality are evident in the activism and writings of Christian liberation theology (e.g., Gutiérrez, 1973), of engaged Buddhism,[13] of Gandhi's approaches to nonviolent social change (e.g., Gandhi, 1967), of feminist theology (e.g., Grey, 1999), of feminist interpretations of Islam (e.g., Mernissi, 1987), and elsewhere.

These approaches have certain commonalities in that they respond actively to social suffering, injustice, and inequality. They are highly context based and consider the role of economic and political structures in contributing to suffering. They make use of *hermeneutics*, which involves the interpretation of sacred texts within historically specific contexts to argue for liberation from injustice, discrimination, and prejudice wherever they occur, including within their own religious organizations. Hence, these approaches reject dogmatic religions that legitimize or deny social injustice. Faith and spiritual practice are important, but the goal is not just individual enlightenment, but collective activism leading to social change as well.

As suggested above, in applications of liberation theology to development communication and education, Freire (e.g., 1970) has been probably the most influential scholar.[14]

The impact of his arguments and methodologies has been broad, beginning in Latin America and spreading globally. For Freire, the success of the awakening process via dialogue requires spiritual practice, which is communication, though a form of communication seldom examined by Western communication specialists. The assumption is that spiritual practice by individuals and groups assists in tapping resources that provide the necessary consciousness, energy, and motivation for change. Other forms of religious communication also may be significant in the liberation or empowerment communication process. These forms are unique to each religious tradition and culture and may include song, dance, storytelling, and gatherings of demographic groups with shared needs.

There is a need to attend more to these perspectives in development communication. There is also a need to find out how women fit in, and to what extent awakening projects encourage feminist awakening. Certainly, at the macro level, although women have played active roles in major resistance movements, they have been marginalized from the leadership of these movements. At the micro level, much more research remains to be done, but limited evidence indicates that spiritually motivated empowerment projects do not always encourage *feminist* empowerment.

An example is the Sarvodaya Shramadana Movement in Sri Lanka. The movement began in 1958 when its leader, A. T. Ariyaratne, first organized a *shramadana* (labor assistance) camp in a poor village. Today, the movement is the largest NGO in Sri Lanka and is active in more than 9,000 villages, about a third in the country. The primary goals are individual and collective awakening, accomplished by the voluntary sharing of time, resources, and labor. Spiritual practice involving meditation in the Buddhist tradition is a key feature of the movement. Yet the movement also aims to be inclusive of all religious traditions.[15]

The Sarvodaya movement has taken place in a country where women are considered inferior to men and are encouraged to pursue traditional roles (Risseeuw, 1988, p. 273). Yet the movement includes a legally independent Women's Movement, which claims that "Sarvodaya has always fully involved women in its development process." Evidence shows that although women do constitute the majority of the unpaid volunteers, they remain the minority (12%) of the leaders. Also, Women's Movement goals highlight women's traditional roles as mothers: "to ensure the mental and physical well being of children . . . to bring about the total development of women as mothers, social workers, income generators and spiritual leaders."[16]

Pace (1993) did field research to find out to what extent the awakening concept encouraged women to question gender roles. She found that although the movement emphasizes the necessity of personal transformation for societal transformation, it also idealizes village life, including traditional gender roles. These values are evident in Sarvodaya's official literature, including the Web site for the Women's Movement and Ariyaratne's speeches.[17] Also, women's predominant involvement with the movement has been via the concerns and activities of the mother's group, the preschools, and the youth group. These gendered family values were evident in Pace's interviews, where she asked female participants what the movement means by awakening, whether anything should be changed about women's status in Sri Lanka, and whether the women perceived links between the two areas of questions. Most women did not question traditional roles or inequalities associated with these roles. Some women had asked these questions, but not because they were encouraged by the movement.

Pace (1993) concluded that the movement "remains radical in terms of its ideology around issues of spiritual and community development, yet it is conservative with re-gards to its perspectives on prescribed roles for men and women" (p. 73). In addition, although income-generating projects have helped some women, these new responsibili-ties are merely added to women's domestic responsibilities with no change in gender roles. This finding is consistent with Rozario's (1997) study of secular empowerment proj-ects for women in Bangladesh, and also of Kellow's (1998) study of an income-generating project in a refugee camp in Uganda. Yet Sarvodaya's goals of village self-reliance, human development, and ecological balance constitutes a challenge to some of the macro-level causes of women's oppression, even if women are not aware of this. Also, women's experiences in new roles are person-ally empowering, even if these experiences do not result in feminist political activism.

The Sarvodaya movement in Sri Lanka is just one example of many movements and projects that reveal the central role of religion and spirituality in much development commu-nication.[18] All of these projects need feminist analysis and intervention. However, feminist studies of the role of religion and spirituality in development are vulnerable to two cri-tiques: They may contribute to the Western tendency to *over*identify women in develop-ing countries with religion, and they may con-tribute to the Western tendency to *negatively* and *inaccurately* miscast women as victims of religion (Mohanty, 1991a). I argue that the reality is neither. Many women in developing countries are involved with religion, but they obviously have many other affiliations too. Furthermore, women globally are reinterpret-ing sacred texts in feminist directions and challenging patriarchal practices in religious organizations. Few development communica-tion scholars have considered the positive role and power of religious communication in transforming individuals and communities. Those few who have done so usually have

neglected women's struggle to participate in these empowerment-oriented settings char-acterized by socially engaged spirituality. Therefore, there is a need to tell some of these stories and see what lessons there may be for development communication theory and practice.

CONCLUSION

The structures and processes of development communication may be conceptualized as serving at least three, overlapping practical goals: marketing, collective resistance, and/or spiritual awakening. These frameworks are evident at all levels of society. The globaliza-tion of the economy has reinforced the domi-nance of the marketing framework. Critical and liberation frameworks remain viable ave-nues for scholarship and practice, yet these projects take place within the ongoing con-straints, contradictions, and turmoil of mo-dernity. This chapter seeks neither to con-demn nor promote the theoretical or applied frameworks discussed, including moderniza-tion, but rather concludes that all have blind spots—in relation to each other, to feminism, and also to additional issues not explored here that cross perspectives (such as environ-ment, basic needs, and human rights). Gen-der-sensitive scholarship and revisions are needed in each instance. In addition, the path to women's individual and collective empow-erment is complex, as each gendered context has its own obstacles of tradition and social conflict. The transformation of self and world is a daunting and elusive goal, requiring a highly nuanced understanding of feminism, great self-reflexivity, and immense endurance.

NOTES

1. Craig (1999) divides communication the-ory into seven traditions according to underlying

conceptions of communication practice: rhetorical, semiotic, phenomenological, cybernetic, sociopsychological, sociocultural, and critical. Craig suggests a spiritual tradition as a neglected area that might be further developed (p. 151).

2. Especially important in early critiques of WID was DAWN (Development Alternatives with Women for a New Era), a group of activists, researchers, and policymakers that formed during the Decade for Women (Sen & Grown, 1987).

3. For statistics substantiating these statements, see, for example, annual reports of the World Bank and the United Nations Development Programme (UNDP), *World Development Report* and *Human Development Report,* respectively. See also Web sites of international organizations concerned with women and girls, listed and linked at the following address: http://www.unescobkk.org/infores/pips/girl.htm.

4. For analyses of sex trafficking, see, for example, Bales (1999) and Bishop and Robinson (1998). For analyses of gender discrimination in the global economy see, for example, Waring (1988), Ward (1990), and Pena (1997).

5. See also Steeves (1993b) for earlier citations.

6. For documents from all of these conferences, see United Nations (1996).

7. See WEDO's Web site: http://www.wedo.org.

8. Canada's "Sex Role Portrayal Code for Television and Radio Programming" is available online at http://www .ccnr.ca/english/codes/sexrole.htm.

9. Overlapping lines of argument include communitarian theory (e.g., Tehranian, 1994) and eco-feminism.

10. Development communication texts that promote Freirian and related approaches include Mody (1991), Nair and White (1993), and White, Nair, and Ascroft (1994). Freirian arguments have been extended to critiques of power differentials in using traditional data-gathering methods in non-Western contexts, with alternative proposals favoring egalitarian ethnographic approaches that contribute to social change. See other chapters in this volume for discussions of participatory action research (PAR).

11. See Steeves (1993b) and "Women Organize" (1994) for more information on these and other feminist media organizations. See also the Web site for each organization.

12. See Melkote and Steeves (2001), chapters 7 and 8, for more extended discussions of liberation approaches to development communication and women's roles therein.

13. For instance, the social activist and exiled Vietnamese monk Thich Nhat Hanh (e.g., 1987) and Sulak Sivaraska of Thailand (e.g., Rothberg, 1993b).

14. Although his ideas emerged initially from the Christian liberation theology movement of 1960s Brazil, he drew upon the writings and actions of liberation leaders from other traditions as well, especially Gandhi (1967).

15. See Liyanage (1988); also Sarvodaya: The Sarvodaya Shramadana Movement of Sri Lanka, online at http://www. sarvodaya.org/index.html. Previous essays on the movement in the context of development communication include Ariyaratne (1987).

16. See "Project 2000," http://www.sarvodaya.org/Project2000/index.htm.

17. His speeches have changed over the years, to show a greater recognition of gender inequality (Pace, 1993, pp. 14, 64-65).

18. For further discussion of the Sarvodaya Shramadana Movement as well as of the Base Ecclesial Community movement in Latin America, see Melkote and Steeves (2001) and Steeves (in press). Melkote and Steeves (2001) additionally discuss an example of a gender sensitive Muslim Family Life Education Project in Ghana. Another movement that certainly merits analysis is the radical NGO movement in Thailand.

REFERENCES

Akhavan-Majid, R., & Ramaprasad, J. (2000). Framing Beijing: Dominant ideological influences on the American press coverage of the Fourth U.N. Conference on Women and the NGO forum. *Gazette, 62*(1), 45-59.

Allen, D., Rush, R. R., & Kaufman, S. J. (Eds.). (1996). *Women transforming communications: Global intersections.* Thousand Oaks, CA: Sage.

Ariyaratne, A. T. (1987). Beyond development communication: Case study on Sarvodaya, Sri Lanka. In N. Jayaweera & S. Amunugama (Eds.), *Rethinking development communication* (pp. 239-251). Singapore: Asian Mass Communication Research and Information Centre.

Bales, K. (1999). *Disposable people: New slavery in the global economy.* Berkeley: University of California Press.

Barrett, M. (1985). Introduction. In F. Engels, *The origin of the family, private property and the state* (pp. 7-30). Harmondsworth, UK: Penguin. (Original work published 1884)

Barrett, M. (1999). *Imagination in theory: Essays on writing and culture.* Cambridge, UK: Polity.

Bishop, R., & Robinson, L. S. (1998). *Night market: Sexual cultures and the Thai economic miracle.* New York: Routledge.

Boserup, E. (1970). *Women's role in economic development.* New York: St. Martin's.

Bruin, M. de. (1999). Gender, media production and output. *Media Development, 46*(2), 50-54.

Cardoso, F. H., & Faletto, E. (1979). *Dependency and development in Latin America* (M. Mattingly Urquidi, Trans.). Berkeley: University of California Press.

Castells, M. (1996). *The information age: Economy, society and culture: Vol. 1. The rise of the network society.* Oxford, UK: Basil Blackwell.

Castells, M. (1997). *The information age: Economy, society and culture: Vol. 2. The power of identity.* Oxford, UK: Basil Blackwell.

Castells, M. (1998). *The information age: Economy, society and culture: Vol. 3. End of millennium.* Oxford, UK: Basil Blackwell.

Clift, E. (1989, Spring). Social marketing and communication: Changing health behavior in the Third World. *American Journal of Health Promotion,* pp. 7-24.

Craig, R. T. (1999). Communication theory as a field. *Communication Theory, 9*(2), 119-161.

Daly, M. (1973). *Beyond God the Father: Toward a philosophy of women's liberation.* Boston: Beacon.

Danner, L., & Walsh, S. (1999). "Radical" feminists and "bickering" women: Backlash in U.S.

media coverage of the United Nations Fourth World Conference on Women. *Critical Studies in Mass Communication, 16*(1), 63-84.

Eisenstein, Z. R. (Ed.). (1979). *Capitalist patriarchy and the case for socialist feminism.* New York: Monthly Review Press.

Frank, A. G. (1967). *Capitalism and underdevelopment in Latin America: Historical studies in Chile and Brazil.* New York: Monthly Review Press.

Freire, P. (1970). *Pedagogy of the oppressed.* New York: Continuum.

Freire, P. (1973). *Education for critical consciousness.* New York: Seabury.

Gallagher, M. (1987). Redefining the communications revolution. In H. Baehr & G. Dyer (Eds.), *Boxed in: Women & television* (pp. 19-37). New York: Pandora.

Gallagher, M. (1995). *An unfinished story: Gender patterns in media employment.* Paris: UNESCO.

Gallagher, M., & Quindoza-Santiago, L. (Eds.). (1994). *Women empowering communication: A resource book on the globalization of media.* New York: International Women's Tribune Centre.

Gandhi, M. (1967). *The mind of Mahatma Gandhi* (R. K. Prabhu & U. R. Rao, Eds.). Ahmedabad, India: Navajivan.

Gender action, A newsletter of the USAID Office of Women in Development (1997). Vol. 1, No. 3.

Gersch, B. (1998). Gender at the crossroads: The Internet as cultural text. *Journal of Communication Inquiry, 22*(3), 306-321.

Glasser, C. K. (1997). Patriarchy, mediated desire, and Chinese magazine fiction. *Journal of Communication, 47*(1), 85-108.

Grey, M. (1999). Feminist theology: A critical theology of liberation. In C. Rowland (Ed.), *The Cambridge companion to liberation theology* (pp. 89-106). Cambridge, UK: Cambridge University Press.

Griffin, M., Viswanath, K., & Schwartz, D. (1994). Gender advertising in the U.S. & India: Exporting cultural stereotypes. *Media, Culture & Society, 16,* 487-507.

Gutiérrez, G. (1973). *A theology of liberation: History, politics and salvation.* (Sr. C. Inda & J. Eagleson, Eds. & Trans.). Maryknoll, NY: Orbis.

Hale, S. M. (1982). Women as change agents: A neglected research area. *Resources for Feminist Research, 2*(1), 42-46.

Hamada, B. I. (1999). The initial effects of the Internet on a Muslim society. *Journal of Development Communication, 6*(2), 50-57.

Hamelink, C. (1983). *Cultural autonomy in global communications.* New York: Longman.

Hanh, T. N. (1987). *Being peace.* Berkeley, CA: Parallax.

Heath, C. (1988). Private sector participation in public service broadcasting: The case of Kenya. *Journal of Communication, 38*(3), 96-107.

hooks, b. (1984). *Feminist theory from margin to center.* Boston: South End.

Hoy, P. (1998). *Players and issues in international aid.* West Hartford, CT: Kumarian.

Hudson, H. (1994). Universal service in the information age. *Telecommunications Policy, 18*(8), 658-667.

International Commission for the Study of Communication Problems. (1980). *Many voices, one world.* Paris: UNESCO.

Jaquette, J., & Staudt, K. (1985). Women as "at risk" reproducers: Biology, science, and population in U.S. foreign policy. In V. Sapiro (Ed.), *Women, biology, and public policy* (pp. 235-268). Beverly Hills, CA: Sage.

Kellow, C. L. (1998). *Refugee needs and donor agendas: Communication and coordination of services in refugee aid programs.* Unpublished master's thesis, University of Oregon, Eugene.

Kotler, P. (1984). Social marketing of health behavior. In L. W. Frederiksen, L. J. Solomon, & K. A. Brehony (Eds.), *Marketing health behavior: Principles, techniques and applications* (pp. 23-39). New York: Plenum.

Lenin, V. I. (1939). *Imperialism: The highest stage of capitalism.* New York: International.

Lerner, D. (1958). *The passing of traditional society: Modernizing the Middle East.* Glencoe, IL: Free Press.

Liyanage, G. (1988). *Revolution under the breadfruit tree: The story of Sarvodaya Shramadana Movement and its founder Dr. A. T. Ariyaratne.* Nugegoda, Sri Lanka: Sinha.

Lucas, F. B. (1999). *A radio broadcasting model for rural women and farm households.* Bangkok, Thailand: Food and Agriculture Organization.

Luthra, R. (1991). Contraceptive social marketing in the Third World: A case of multiple transfer. *Gazette, 47*(3), 159-176.

Luthra, R. (1999). The Women's Movement and the press in India: The construction of female foeticide as a social issue. *Women's Studies in Communication, 22*(1), 1-24.

Mankekar, P. (1999). *Screening culture, viewing politics: An ethnography of television, womanhood, and nation in postcolonial India.* Durham, NC: Duke University Press.

Manoff, R. K. (1985). *Social marketing: A new imperative for public health.* New York: Praeger.

March, K., & Taqqu, R. (1986). *Women's informal associations in developing countries: Catalysts for change?* Boulder, CO: Westview.

Melkote, S. R., & Steeves, H. L. (2001). *Communication for development in the Third World: Theory and practice for empowerment.* New Delhi: Sage.

Melody, W. H. (1991). The information society: The transnational economic context and its implications. In G. Sussman & J. A. Lent (Eds.), *Transnational communications: Wiring the Third World* (pp. 27-41). Newbury Park, CA: Sage.

Mernissi, F. (1987). *Women and Islam: An historical and theological enquiry.* Oxford, UK: Basil Blackwell.

Minh-ha, T. T. (1986-1987). Difference: A special Third World woman issue. *Discourse, 8,* 11-38.

Mizan, A. N. (1994). *In quest of empowerment: The Grameen Bank's impact on women's power and status.* Dhaka, Bangladesh: University Press.

Mody, B. (1991). *Designing messages for development communication: An audience participation-based approach.* New Delhi: Sage.

Mohanty, C. T. (1991a). Introduction: Cartographies of struggle: Third World women and the politics of feminism. In C. T. Mohanty, A. Russo, & L. Torres (Eds.), *Third World women and the politics of feminism* (pp. 1-47). Bloomington: Indiana University Press.

Mohanty, C. T. (1991b). Under Western eyes: Feminist scholarship and colonial discourses. In C. T. Mohanty, A. Russo, & L. Torres (Eds.), *Third World women and the politics of feminism* (pp. 51-80). Bloomington: Indiana University Press.

Morrison, J. F. (1993). Communicating healthcare through forum theater: Egalitarian information exchange in Burkina Faso. *Gazette, 52,* 109-121.

Mowlana, H., & Wilson, L. (1988). *Communication technology and development* (UNESCO Reports and Papers on Mass Communication No. 101). Paris: UNESCO.

Nair, K. S., & White, S. A. (Eds.). (1993). *Perspectives on development communication.* New Delhi: Sage.

Nelson, B. J., & Chowdhury, N. (Eds.). (1994). *Women and politics worldwide.* New Haven, CT: Yale University Press.

Nordenstreng, K., & Schiller, H. I. (Eds.). (1993). *Beyond national sovereignty: International communications in the 1990s.* Norwood, NJ: Ablex.

Pace, M. (1993). *Awakening of all? A feminist appraisal of the Sarvodaya Shramadana Movement in Sri Lanka.* Unpublished master's thesis, University of Oregon, Department of International Studies.

Parameswaran, R. (1999). Western romance fiction as English-language media in post-colonial India. *Journal of Communication, 49*(3), 84-105.

Pena, D. G. (1997). *The terror of the machine: Technology, work, gender, and ecology on the U.S.-Mexico border.* Austin: University of Texas, Center for Mexican American Studies.

Rapley, J. (1996). *Understanding development: Theory and practice in the Third World.* Boulder, CO: Lynne Reinner.

Riano, P. (Ed.). (1994). *Women in grassroots communication: Furthering social change.* Thousand Oaks, CA: Sage.

Risseeuw, C. (1988). *The fish don't talk about the water: Gender transformation, power, and resistance among women in Sri Lanka.* Leiden, the Netherlands, and New York: E. J. Brill.

Rogers, B. (1989). *The domestication of women: Discrimination in developing societies.* London: Routledge. (Reprinted from 1980, New York: St. Martin's)

Rothberg, D. (1993a). The crisis of modernity and the emergence of socially engaged spirituality. *ReVision, 15*(3), 105-114.

Rothberg, D. (1993b). A Thai perspective on socially engaged Buddhism: A conversation with Sulak Sivaraksa. *ReVision, 15*(3), 121-127.

Rowlands, J. (1997). *Questioning empowerment: Working with women in Honduras.* London: Oxfam.

Rozario, S. (1997). Development and rural women in South Asia: The limits of empowerment and conscientization. *Bulletin of Concerned Asian Scholars, 30*(1), 45-53.

Schiller, H. I. (1969). *Mass communications and American empire.* New York: A. M. Kelley.

Schramm, W. L. (1964). *Mass media and national development: The role of information in the developing countries.* Stanford, CA: Stanford University Press.

Sen, G., & Grown, C. (1987). *Development, crises, and alternative visions: Third World women's perspectives.* New York: Monthly Review Press.

Siew, S., & Kim, W. L. (1996). Do new communication technologies improve the status of women? *Media Asia, 23*(2), 74-78.

Spens, T. (1986). *Studies on agricultural extension involving women* (Occasional Paper No. 3). New York: UNIFEM.

Spivak, G. C. (1988). Can the subaltern speak? In L. Grossberg & C. Nelson (Eds.), *Marxism and the interpretation of culture* (pp. 271-316). Urbana: University of Illinois Press.

Staudt, K. (1985a). *Agricultural policy implementation: A case study from western Kenya.* West Hartford, CT: Kumarian.

Staudt, K. (1985b). *Women, foreign assistance and advocacy administration.* New York: Praeger.

Staudt, K. (Ed.). (1997). *Women, international development, and politics.* Philadelphia: Temple University Press.

Steeves, H. L. (1987). Feminist theories and media studies. *Critical Studies in Mass Communication, 4*(2), 95-135.

Steeves, H. L. (1993a). Creating imagined communities: Development communication and the challenge of feminism. *Communication Theory, 43*(3), 218-229.

Steeves, H. L. (1993b). Gender and mass communication in a global context. In P. Creedon (Ed.), *Women in mass communication.* Newbury Park, CA: Sage.

Steeves, H. L. (1996). Sharing information in Kenya: Communication and information policy considerations and consequences for rural women. *Gazette, 56,* 157-181.

Steeves, H. L. (1997). *Gender violence and the press: The St. Kizito story.* Monographs in International Studies. Athens: Ohio University Press.

Steeves, H. L. (in press). Feminism, liberation, and development communication. *Communication Theory.*

Steeves, H. L., & Wasko, J. (in press). Feminist theory and political economy: Toward a friendly alliance. In E. Meehan & E. Riordan (Eds.), *Sex and money: Intersections of feminism and political economy in media.* Minneapolis: University of Minnesota Press.

Tehranian, M. (1994). Communication and development. In D. Crowley & D. Mitchell (Eds.), *Communication theory today* (pp. 274-306). Stanford, CA: Stanford University Press.

United Nations. (1996). *The United Nations and the advancement of women, 1945-1996* (United Nations Blue Books Series, Vol. 6, rev. ed.). New York: Author.

United Nations Educational, Scientific and Cultural Organization. (1999). *World communication and information report 1999-2000.* Paris: Author.

Wallerstein, I. (1974). *The modern world system.* New York: Academic Press.

Ward, K. (Ed.). (1990). *Women workers and global restructuring.* Ithaca, NY: Cornell University Press.

Waring, M. (1988). *If women counted: A new feminist economics.* New York: HarperCollins.

White, S. A., Nair, K. S., & Ascroft, J. (Eds.). (1994). *Participatory communication: Working for change and development.* New Delhi: Sage.

Wilkins, K. (1999). Development discourse on gender and communication in strategies for social change. *Journal of Communication, 49*(1), 46-68.

Wilkins, K., & Waters, J. (2000). Current discourse on new technologies in development communication. *Media Development, 47*(1), 57-60.

Women organize for alternative media. (1994). *Media Development, 41*(2), 18-24.

Worthington, N. (1992). *Gender and class in AIDS education: An analysis of the AIDSCOM project in Africa.* Unpublished master's thesis, University of Oregon, Department of Journalism.

Worthington, N. (2001). A division of labor: Dividing maternal authority from political activism in the Kenyan press. *Journal of Communication Inquiry, 25*(2), 167-187.

Yanru, C. (1998). In search of the essential woman in national development: China's first TV drama series *on* women, *by* women, *for* women. *Journal of Development Communication, 9*(2), 1-17.

Zoonen, L. van. (1994). *Feminist media studies.* London: Sage.

14

International Development Communication
Proposing a Research Agenda for a New Era

KARIN GWINN WILKINS
University of Texas at Austin

In this chapter, I describe some of the emerging issues in the field of development communication. Building on the broader concerns of communication scholarship, development communication research should extend from traditional studies of media effects, to include analyses of the structures and processes producing strategic communication, as well as the messages and modes of communicative texts. As the study of strategic responses to social problems through communication processes and technologies, development communication research may focus on the evaluation of interventions. Although many of these assessments produce valuable data in understanding the consequences of these practices, this field of scholarship needs to move beyond its concentration on applied work to consider the broader parameters of development communication in society.

Two central themes guide these observations: first, attention to communication about

development, or its discourse, and second, attention to communication for development, or institutional intervention for social change. Understanding development as discourse means examining the underlying assumptions of institutional texts, speech, and practice, about the nature of people, problems, and social change addressed through strategic intervention. Through discourse analyses, we discern how certain groups and conditions become visible in the ideological production of communication programs. Through their implementation of communication interventions, development institutions have the capacity to select and frame social conditions as problematic, and legitimize particular approaches toward their resolution.

Following a brief discussion of globalization, I apply these concerns with development discourse and intervention to four emerging issues: the privatization of programs designed to promote the public good, the role of new technologies in strategic social change, the efforts of social movements in resisting dominant actors and agencies, and the emergence of sustainability as an organizing metaphor for development. There are several other important issues in the field, such as a careful consideration of gender issues (see the Steeves chapter in this volume), participatory strategies (Huesca, this volume), and global-local dynamics (Boyd-Barrett, this volume; Braman, this volume; Mody, this volume). Although certainly not an exhaustive list of current concerns, the four areas identified here represent important areas for future research worthy of our attention.

CONTEXT OF GLOBALIZATION

Emerging issues need to be considered within a global context of economic, political, and social conditions, as well as of communication technologies. Current shifts toward economic capitalism, a restructuring of the role of the nation-state, the emergence of new social movements, and the migration of people, along with the development of new information technologies, converge toward a global context, in which transnational concerns take precedence over national interests (Appadurai, 1996; Castells, 1998; McMichael, 1996). Although analytically distinct, shifts in each of these sectors are intertwined with shifts in other arenas: A transformation of information technologies, for example, has facilitated the "globalization of wealth and information, and the localization of identity and legitimacy" (Castells, 1998, p. 2). Through enhanced digitalization and accelerated distribution of cultural texts, mobile groups may stay connected with a diasporic identity across territorial boundaries (Appadurai, 1996). The increased movement of social groups takes place within a

political context in which "Second World" nation-states have begun to disappear while more international governmental organizations have begun to flourish (Schiller, 1991).

Among these interconnected conditions, the most salient feature within this global context becomes the growing global capitalist economic structure, with an increasing concentration of transnational corporations. Economic development remains the central focus of transnational agencies (Schiller, 1991), as well as of many developing countries, particularly those in the Asian Pacific region (Castells, 1998). As transnational banks and corporations grew in strength, global interests began to transcend nationally directed economic policies, particularly after the debt crises of the 1980s (McMichael, 1996). According to McMichael (1996), the globalization of development policies involved moving toward market-based rather than state-managed strategies; emphasizing global market rules determined by the G-7 states; implementing global economic rules decided by the World Bank, International Monetary Fund, and World Trade Organization (WTO); concentrating economic power in transnational banks and corporations; and subordinating state social concerns to these global institutional interests (p. 177). Thus, the ruling authority in this context becomes the voice of the global marketplace. The following issues, concerning privatization, new technologies, social movements, and sustainable development, should be considered within this context.

PRIVATIZATION OF PUBLIC PROGRAMS

Within the context of a growing capitalist influence in the global economic structure, a central issue to be considered in the fuure of development communication becomes the privatization of programs designed for the public good. Historically, development emerged from national governments' interests in organizing strategic social change initiatives, partly in response to external political and economic agencies (McMichael, 1996). The Northern, Western approach that has dominated development practice has been driven by economic concerns with market behavior and technological solutions (McMichael, 1996), envisioning communication technologies as serving both commercial and modernizing functions in national development (Schramm, 1963). Although there has been an undercurrent within dominant development discourse historically that accepts unquestioningly the merits of free-market capitalism, there has been a growing emphasis on working with the private rather than the public sector in development programs (Bugliarello, 1995; Wilkins, 1999). This current trend toward privatization corresponds with broader policy shifts toward deregulation and privatization within and across political boundaries (Mohammadi, 1997; Moore, 1995).

Many U.S. Agency for International Development (USAID) programs foster this trend, working with private institutions through project intervention. Education programs for girls and women, for example, have replaced working with Ministries of Education with private "partners," from business, media, nongovernmental organizations (NGOs), and religious groups (USAID Office of Women in Development [USAID OWID], 1999a). In addition, many of the population, health, and nutrition programs rely on social marketing as a preferred approach to social change (Academy for Educational Development, 1995). This approach, in practice, connects project activity with the commercial sector. Not only are projects specifically working with for-profit entities, but they are also encouraging national governments to collaborate with the commercial sector. Privatizing

then moves toward commercializing development programs.

Micro-enterprise programs, designed to offer credit to collective groups to facilitate small-scale entrepreneurial initiatives, become closely aligned with commercial interests. Some projects, for example, introduce computer technologies to disadvantaged groups to facilitate their entry into global markets. Similarly, agribusiness enterprises for women are justified in terms that privilege the interests of the industry: "Industry employers need to expand and increase efficiency . . . not just to increase [women's] opportunities but also to improve productivity of agribusiness itself" (USAID OWID, 1999b, p. 4).

Growing attention to entertainment-education models can be seen as fitting a similar pattern. Popular media, often television and music, are used to educate viewers and listeners with socially beneficial messages, related to topics such as gender equity, health behavior, and HIV/AIDS prevention (Singhal & Rogers, 1999). This approach can be seen as a good way to reach a large audience with compelling messages. Although the professed goal of these programs is to promote social change, the proposed mechanism is through "commercially viable" media strategies (Singhal & Rogers, 1999, p. 8). These projects are described as successful when they are able to attract corporate sponsorship, as did a population communication project in the Philippines (Fraser & Restrepo-Estrada, 1998, p. 179).

Connecting public programs with the commercial sector tends to be justified as a cost-effective strategy by proponents, particularly when public funds for programs are decreasing. However, this alignment with the private sector appears to be described as a necessary part of the social change process, rather than as an alternative to a preferred strategy of relying on public funding. Entertainment-education, social marketing, education, population, and other programs could be conceived in other ways, without relying on the commercial sector.

A number of concerns can be raised about the evolving commercialization of development interventions. First, this practice focuses on short-term economic goals at the expense of long-term interests, such as improving human rights or women's status. For example, the emphases on women's rights and family planning were toned down in the Indian television drama *Hum Log,* in response to the desires of the commercial sponsors and the interests of the audience (Singhal & Rogers, 1989). As people become valued in terms of their ability to consume products and services (Wilkins, 1999), programs for the public good begin to neglect resource-poor and marginalized communities. Programs designed to improve health, for example, then become justified in terms of their benefits to the global economy, rather than in terms of human rights and dignity. As a way of legitimizing this approach to social change, programs focus on local efforts and individual-level change so that political-economic structural concerns are not brought into question. This not only affects international development agencies but also the development programs of national governments, who lose decision-making power over policy decisions, spending less on social services while prioritizing the needs of the global market (McMichael, 1996). While growing economic interdependence strengthens local elites across national boundaries, the resource-poor become even more marginalized (Fraser & Restrepo-Estrada, 1998; Mody, 1999).

Future research might examine the role of privatization in development discourse and intervention. First, following Moore's (1995) lead, one could explore the extent to which development discourse legitimates global capitalism in bilateral, multilateral, national, and nongovernmental agencies. This work needs to be conducted in a variety of fields, not just those that rather obviously connect public welfare to commercial integration, such as micro-enterprise programs. Moreover, research needs to be conducted to evaluate the effect of privatizing development programs over the long term. For example, how do health communication programs integrating intervention with the private sector differ from those working primarily with the public sector? Whether this concern with privatization is warranted could be assessed through longitudinal, comparative research.

NEW TECHNOLOGIES

Another emerging practice in development communication involves the enthusiastic use of new communication technologies in strategies for social change. The history of development communication discourse establishes a trend of excitement about one new technology after another, as scholars and practitioners proclaimed the benefits that radio, satellite television, video, and other channels would bring to development projects. Current attention to new computer technologies needs to be understood within this larger historical discourse on the assumptions made about media effects (Mody, 2000). At an earlier stage, Jacobson and Zimpfer (1993) documented the emergence of noncommercial computer networks directed toward national development efforts. Since then, computer technologies have become even more popular in development work.

New computer technologies may be seen as distinct from many other mediated channels given their interactive potential (Tomber & Bromley, 1998). New forms of digital communication technologies create the possibility for more participatory dialogue on social issues, thus obscuring the traditional dichotomy between mass and interpersonal communication

(Cerulo, 1997). Kellner (1995) contends that new technologies, such as computers, may promote a more democratic, or participatory, debate on political issues. Some posit computers as an alternative to dominant media systems, enabling users to build social capital as they interact (Friedland, 1996; Kern, 1997).

However, this technological potential remains dormant when only a small proportion of our global community have access to these channels. Mody (1999) documents almost all (97%) Internet host computers as residing within the domains of 29 wealthy nations, representing less than one quarter of the world's population. More equitable access would require investments in electrical and telecommunication infrastructures, computer hardware, and domestic economies, along with supporting appropriate regulation; even more important, if these technologies are to benefit marginalized groups, strategies will need to address capacities to produce relevant local content, to attain computer literacy, and to ensure other social infrastructures, such as adequate health services and employment opportunities (Mansell & Wehn, 1998; Mody, 1999).

The issue here is not how the industry or individuals use computer technologies but how they are employed by development institutions or other collective social groups to engage in social change. Graham and Marvin (1996) offer a theoretical framework for considering telecommunications as shaped by social action, with the potential to assist as well as exploit disadvantaged groups. Similarly, using new computer technologies for strategic social change has the capacity to both help and hurt participants. Many development interventions appropriate computer technologies to attempt to integrate marginal communities into the global marketplace, thus privileging the global economic over local interests (Wilkins & Waters, 2000). The United Nations and WTO support the Inter-national Trade Centre (ITC), for instance, to market the local products and services of developing countries in international arenas.[1] Overall, these projects tend to rely on computer technologies to promote the transmission of information, rather than promote dialogue, as advocated in participatory models, or promote resistance, as suggested in social movement approaches (Wilkins & Waters, 2000). This transmission approach may enhance the economic status of a few participants, but it does not facilitate the use of the technology as a form of resistance or engagement. Access to information, like other services, need not be commodified, but could be conceived as a human right.

Future research needs to do more to document the relationship between the growing emphasis on computer technologies in development practices and the trend toward commercialization in development discourse. Moreover, interventions could be examined in terms of the degree to which they are used to facilitate the creation of mediated content, and not just distribute existing information. It will be important to characterize access, as with any valuable resource, across individuals and communities, to the hardware (such as machines and a steady supply of electricity), software (considering issues such as literacy and language), and expertise needed to maintain these systems.

To understand the possibilities as well as the constraints of new communication technologies, more research could assess the extent to which new computer technologies facilitate the activities of social movement organizations (Escobar, 1995; Owen, 1998), labor unions (Drew, 1998), and other marginal groups (International Development Research Centre, 1992). One might also study the nature of discussion and practice within development networks, such as the United Nations Development Programme (UNDP) network on sustainable development (Fraser

& Restrepo-Estrada, 1998). The ability of these new technologies to facilitate change, particularly among emerging social movements, is another important subject for study (see Downing, 1999, for a useful discussion of network communities).

SOCIAL MOVEMENTS

Given the historical trajectory of the field, recognizing the contributions of social movements is an important step for development communication scholars. Initial development communication scholarship promoted a Western version of modernization, focusing on the individual as the agent of social change within a democratic and capitalist society (Lerner, 1958; Schramm, 1963). This approach was critiqued for its ethnocentric and hierarchical approach to development, particularly by academics working in non-Western territories and from political-economic traditions (for more comprehensive reviews of these critiques, see Melkote, 1991; Rogers, 1976). Attention to participatory development emerged in part as a response to these concerns (Freire, 1983).

When participatory approaches were conceptualized as an alternative to dominant strategies for social change, it was hoped that communication might be used to foster more horizontal and bottom-up development approaches than had been previously initiated (Mody, 1991). Participation has been conceptualized in many ways, by a variety of scholars and institutions, to imply quite different underlying approaches. Numerous publications on participatory development (documented in Fair & Shah, 1997), along with development programs promoting "democracy" and participatory governance, attest to the continued attention to this topic (see Huesca, this volume, for a more detailed review of participation). Following more than two decades of literature on the need for alternative development models, we should recognize that social change is a more complex process than artificial divisions between "top-down" and "bottom-up" would suggest. Focusing on social movements allows us to build on earlier concerns that we acknowledge the import of local groups mobilizing on behalf of an issue, while situating this social action as a form of resistance within a complex process of powerful actors and competing messages.

Like more traditionally conceived development communication projects, social movements engage in strategic social change. Groups are likely to coalesce within a defined community rather than within an institution, but not necessarily confined through geographic boundaries. Social change then is enacted by a collective group, rather than individuals, as implied in many development campaigns in agriculture, health, population, and nutrition. Whereas this latter approach intends to influence individuals to change their behaviors, social movements are more likely to attempt to change policies or norms, through intermediary goals such as mobilizing support and attracting sympathetic media attention. In sum, social movements "attempt to achieve or prevent social change, predominantly by means of collective protest" (Rucht, 1999, p. 207).

Based on a critical understanding of recent development practice, some observers promote the idea of "postdevelopment," focusing on social movements as radical alternatives by promoting marginal interests against dominant development structures and ideologies (Escobar, 1995; Moore, 1995). In this regard, social movements are not seen as a way to transform or improve development, but as a manifestation of resistance. Connecting struggles over cultural issues with those over technological resources, Castells (1998) argues that social change can indeed be perpetuated through "conscious, purposive social action, provided with information, and supported by legitimacy" (p. 380). Many of these social movements tend to be interested in nonmaterial values, concentrating on issues related to the civil rather than the economic sphere (Cohen, 1985). In this volume and elsewhere (1993), for example, Steeves addresses in more detail the role of women's movements in relation to development practice.

Social movements are beginning to transcend national boundaries, in accordance with similar trends in communication technologies and development programs. Although nation-states are still important arenas for decision making, the issues that groups engage, such as global capitalism, nuclear energy, environmental degradation, and women's rights, cross national borders. The growth of transnational social movements has been documented by several authors (Breyman, 1994; Webber, 1994). For example, the number of human rights organizations has grown from 90 in 1970 to 772 in 1990, and the number of international NGOs, such as Amnesty International, has risen from 178 in 1909 to 4,620 in 1991 (Rucht, 1999, p. 210). Having increased in number and size, transnational social movements have been growing also in visibility and legitimacy, in part through their active role in international conferences, such as the U.N. Conference on Environment and Development in 1992 (discussed in the next section) and the U.N. Beijing Conference on Women in 1995. Other movements are also beginning to combine efforts to contest the previously unquestioned authority of the WTO and World Bank. Although quite varied in character, many movements share this transnational trait.

The term *transnational* may be used to refer to the nature of the problem, targeted solution, or organization of people and other resources employed to engage in social change. Groups may mobilize in response to

processes of globalization or global events, such as the Gulf War, particularly when national governments have limited capacity to resolve these issues on a unilateral basis (Della Porta & Kriesi, 1999). Transnational mobilization is facilitated through the emergence of new communication and information technologies, making interactive dialogue on shared concerns faster and cheaper. The "libertarian spirit" underlying many of these movements may be seen as integrated with the emergence of more decentralized technologies (Castells, 1998, p. 360). Also, growing expertise in mobilizing resources, including the media, have enhanced these efforts.

Social movements use media for a variety of purposes, both internal and external to the collective organization. Communication technologies may work to mobilize constituents, plan strategies, and share information within the group. Beyond these more utilitarian roles, movements also target media attention to bring visibility and legitimacy to their issues (Gamson & Wolfsfeld, 1993). Seeing media as a site for symbolic struggle, a critical achievement for a social movement may be a shift in discourse toward the movement's preferred frames of the social problem (Gamson, 1988). Although media industries may have comparatively more power in this dynamic than social movements (Gamson & Wolfsfeld, 1993), the latter have some control over their ability to determine how they choose to work with the media, some employing media professionals to foster positive connections with mainstream journalists (Barker-Plummer, 1996).

Building on the work of other disciplines (Melucci, 1988; Morris & Mueller, 1992), development communication scholars could focus more attention on communication about and for social change initiated by social movements. Social movements are quite varied in their composition and goals, just as are development agencies. It may be useful to explore the growth of transnational issues in discourse about social movement strategies, documenting the degree to which movements are responding to global concerns and to corporate dominance. Research on media coverage of social movements may also illuminate how groups' strategic efforts relate to public discourse.

Future research could also examine how social movements use media to promote social change. Specifically, one might examine different approaches to attracting mainstream versus alternative mediated attention, and using industry (such as news stories) versus movement-controlled technologies (such as the Internet or a newsletter). Relative achievements need to be examined, understanding different types of success, such as changing the size of one's organization, media attention or sympathy, targeted policies, or public opinion. Observing dynamic relationships across media, movements, and other public and private institutions might also draw attention to the potential consequences of the commercialization of some movements. For example, would using large rock concerts to advocate political issues result in the mainstreaming of more radical or marginal concerns?

SUSTAINABILITY

The last issue that I highlight in this chapter concerns *sustainable development,* typically referring to development practice that attempts to meet "the needs and aspirations of present generations without compromising those of future generations" (Harris, 1997, p. 232). Sustainability has emerged as a central metaphor in organizing development discourse. Not only have many multilateral agencies engaged in what they refer to as sustainable development, but many other bilateral and nongovernmental development agencies have addressed long-term interests in environmental preservation as well. The

particular tenets of the approach, however, appear to vary greatly, ranging from a focus on environmental protection to a more inclusive concern with social, political, economic, and human resources.

Sustainable development first achieved mainstream attention in 1987 through the Brundtland report, titled *Our Common Future,* prepared by the U.N. World Commission on Environment and Development. The issues raised by environmental groups in the 1970s and 1980s were integrated into this more dominant economic approach toward modernization (McMichael, 1996; Peterson, 1997). This report addressed a variety of issues, including the need to reduce population growth, to revise agricultural methods, to reduce the loss of habitat and species, to create new energy sources, to halt pollution from industrial development, and to understand the problem of urban growth (Peterson, 1997, p. 21).

Five years later, the United Nations convened the Earth Summit in Rio de Janeiro to review the progress of the Brundtland report. The 1992 Conference on Environment and Development resulted in another report, *Agenda 21,* proposing a global strategy for the next century. The report emphasized the need for wealthy countries to invest in poorer nations, in sustainable development measures such as health, sanitation, education, and conservation, but also privileged the role of the market economy, from which wealthier nations benefit. In addition, the document stressed the need for global rather than national management of the environment.

The idea of sustainable development still dominates discourse in the field. In response to these conferences and reports, many development agencies are advocating development policies based on sustainability, including economic policies that do not damage the environment. As evidence of this topic's currency, the United Nations Education, Scientific and Cultural Organization (UNESCO) is compiling the *Encyclopedia of Life Support Systems (EOLSS)*, specifically building on sustainable development issues. A description of the project states that "science, technology, and management policies for sustainable use of life support systems will be emphasized together with issues of global change and their ecological, economic, social, cultural, and political dimensions" (UNESCO, 2000). The UNDP also supports many programs and publishes reports devoted to sustainable development principles, including a network program that distributes information through Internet services.[2]

Although this approach can be seen as advancing a more holistic and long-term approach to social change, several critiques have been raised about sustainable development discourse. First, environmental concerns are integrated within an economic framework, placing these issues under the logic of the global marketplace. By emphasizing economic growth "to reduce the pressure of the poor on the environment" (McMichael, 1996, p. 219), this approach blames the "irrationality" of the poor instead of other conditions, such as industrial practice or population growth, which support problematic practices. While drawing attention to the behaviors of the poor rather than the practices of the transnational corporation, these discussions refer to the importance of local participation, in that sustaining development would require the "informed and active participation" of intended beneficiaries (Harris, 1997, p. 232). Concentrating on individuals, as in a pluralist model of social change (Good, 1989), all people in a global environment are seen as sharing in responsibility for its protection; however, little attention is given to the structural conditions, such as inequitable access to resources, which perpetuate human suffering.

Building on these concerns, Escobar (1995) accuses the sustainable development strategy

of making "possible the eradication of poverty and the protection of the environment in one single feat of Western rationality" (p. 192). In other words, discourse on the topic has moved away from an understanding of "nature" to a managerial approach to controlling the "environment." The World Bank and other institutions' trend toward the privatization of natural resources reinforces this approach (Escobar, 1995, p. 198). This liberalization strategy means that national governments may commercialize natural resources to service international debt: For example, the massive increase in Chilean timber exports has depleted local forests beyond their ability to regenerate (McMichael, 1996, p. 152).

Although current discourse has been appropriated to integrate environmental concerns with an interest in global economic growth, sustainable development was introduced as a way of questioning development practices. As a contested term, others, such as Lester Brown from the Worldwatch Institute, advocated a sustainable approach that did not prioritize economic growth (Peterson, 1997, p. 9). Although Peterson argues that sustainable development ought to be more "about coordinating, rather than controlling, the relationship between humans and other life forms" (p. 185), she determines that current discourse resonates more closely with the project of modernity, emphasizing "consensus, control, prediction, and management" (p. 28).

Future research would do well to build on these examinations of discourse on sustainable development (Peterson, 1997) to understand how this approach becomes constructed and legitimated through institutional practice. A central concern here is the degree to which current discourse continues to rationalize the economic framework of global capital. This could be examined as it becomes manifest in the discourse of development institutions, social movements, and mediated texts. In terms of intervention, future research might contrast different approaches, across development organizations and social movements, to promoting sustainable development. To assess the long-term implications of these programs, one might create and monitor intermediate indicators over time.

CONCLUSION

Scholars of development communication need to build on critical approaches to social change, grounded in multiple social science disciplines and varied methodological approaches. Development communication analyses could draw more broadly from communication research, and from other disciplines, such as sociology, political science, anthropology, history, demography, and cultural studies, not only in terms of theoretical frameworks but also in terms of methodological approaches. Directing scholarship toward a more multidisciplinary approach may seem problematic, when the development field itself seems so compartmentalized (Fraser & Restrepo-Estrada, 1998, p. 224). However, a multidisciplinary framework, using a variety of research tools, would enhance our understanding of communication about and for development.

Development communication should be applauded for bridging theory with practice, in an effort to engage in strategic social change. This connection requires that both scholars and practitioners attempt to be reflective (Schön, 1979). Exploring communication about development, or its discourse, should enhance this reflection. Examinations of development discourse in explanations and processes of strategic intervention allow us to offer informed critiques. Along this vein, future research might consider the consequences of the incorporation of proposed alternative concepts, such as "participation" and "sustainable development," into a main-

stream discourse that privileges economic interests. Discourse might also be studied as it is manifest beyond the institutional domain, in mediated texts or social movements.

Critiquing dominant development discourse, although a necessary step in our reflective process, is not sufficient. We need to build on this reflection to consider ways to improve development practice, specifically how communication technologies and processes could be better used to promote beneficial social change. As one form of communication, the media may help to mobilize support, create awareness, foster norms, encourage behavior change, influence policymakers, or even shift frames of social issues. Future research might address specifically how projects advocating social change, whether from formal development organizations or collective social movements, use new technologies.

To understand how to improve our use of communication for development, we need more consistent and rigorous evaluations, not just of individual projects (Fraser & Restrepo-Estrada, 1998, p. 234) but also of groups of similar projects, over the long term. Such meta-evaluations need to be conducted on the consequences of projects, as well as on the processes through which certain issues and groups are selected and framed. The process of social change is complex, so that research on the role of communication needs to understand the conditions of production as well as the possibilities for effects. These concerns might be examined over time, within a broader context of global political and economic structures, of migration patterns, and of access to material resources, information, and services.

Recognizing that strategic intervention itself is not value neutral, but a political activity, means foregrounding power dimensions more clearly in our analyses. By acknowledging the political nature of the helping relationship, I am not attempting to dismiss or trivialize these efforts. Instead, articulating structural conditions and informal dynamics may help to illuminate the process through which social change may be enacted. These relationships across individuals, groups, and institutions with different levels of power might be understood in a variety of ways (Wilkins, 2000). One might decide to examine the process of normative or behavioral change, across groups with different levels of access to material resources and social capital. On another level, one might explore the degree to which development institutions and social movements have the power to select and frame social issues for intervention. Such a comparison of groups engaged in social change should be understood within their political-economic contexts, considering issues such as regulation and funding.

Currently, these power dynamics require attention to global conditions, particularly that of the global market. Having moved away from formal political control through colonial empires, we are now faced with a global economic empire, demanding the application of marketing principles to national decision making over economic as well as social issues (McMichael, 1996). Escobar (1995) suggests that social movements pose the best defense against global dominant forces, as a way of protecting cultural differences and "economic needs and opportunities in terms that are not strictly those of profit and market" (p. 226). The ability of transnational movements to mobilize and act across territorial boundaries may be enhanced through their use of new communication technologies (Escobar, 2000). But before we move toward conceptualizing social movements as a panacea for the problems inherent in development industry practice, we should remember that social movements themselves are also quite complex and varied, particularly in regard to their access to powerful agencies and their resonance with dominant discourse.

Emerging issues in the field of development communication remind us of the complexity of social change. Strategic attempts to direct social processes involve actors and agencies as producers of knowledge and distributors of ideologies and resources. We need to explore how this knowledge is appropriated and who benefits from these distributions. If current trends toward conceptualizing sustainable development and new technologies within the logic of global capitalism seem unsatisfactory, then we need to attempt to promote our concern with human rights, dignity, and equity (see, e.g., Whelan, 1998) through collective action.

NOTES

1. See the International Trade Centre online at http://www.intracen.org.
2. See the United Nations Development Programme online at http://www.undp.org.

REFERENCES

Academy for Educational Development. (1995). *Changing behavior and educating girls: Foundations for reproductive health*. Washington, DC: Author.

Appadurai, A. (1996). *Modernity at large: Cultural dimensions of globalization*. Minneapolis: University of Minnesota Press.

Barker-Plummer, B. (1996). The dialogic of media and social movements. *Peace Review, 8*(1), 27-34.

Breyman, S. (1994). Movements rising in the West. *Peace Review, 6*(4), 403-410.

Bugliarello, G. (1995). The global generation, transmission, and the diffusion of knowledge: How can the developing countries benefit? In *Marshaling technology for development: Proceedings of a symposium* (pp. 61-82). Washington, DC: National Academy Press.

Castells, M. (1998). *The information age: Economy, society and culture: Vol. 3. End of millennium.* Oxford, UK: Basil Blackwell.

Cerulo, K. (1997). Reframing sociological concepts for a brave new (virtual?) world. *Sociological Inquiry, 67*(1), 48-58.

Cohen, J. L. (1985). Strategy or identity: New theoretical paradigms and contemporary social movements. *Social Research, 52*(4), 663-716.

Della Porta, D., & Kriesi, H. (1999). Social movements in a globalizing world: An introduction. In D. Della Porta, H. Kriesi, & Dieter Rucht (Eds.), *Social movements in a globalizing world* (pp. 3-22). New York: St. Martin's.

Downing, J. D. (1999). Global networks toward new communities. In *Institute for Information Studies: The promise of global networks* (pp. 137-160). Queenstown: Aspen Institute.

Drew, J. (1998). *Global communications in the post-industrial age.* Ph.D. dissertation, University of Texas at Austin.

Escobar, A. (1995). *Encountering development: The making and unmaking of the Third World.* Princeton, NJ: Princeton University Press.

Escobar, A. (2000). Place, power, and networks in globalization and postdevelopment. In K. G. Wilkins (Ed.), *Redeveloping communication for social change: Theory, practice, and power* (pp. 163-174). Lanham, MD: Rowman & Littlefield.

Fair, J. E., & Shah, H. (1997). Continuities and discontinuities in communication and development since 1958. *Journal of International Communication, 4*(2), 3-23.

Fraser, C., & Restrepo-Estrada, S. (1998). *Communicating for development: Human change for survival.* London: I. B. Tauris.

Freire, P. (1983). *Pedagogy of the oppressed* (M. B. Ramos, Trans.). New York: Continuum.

Friedland, L. (1996). Electronic democracy and the new citizenship. *Media, Culture & Society, 18,* 185-212.

Gamson, W. (1988). Political discourse and collective action. *International Social Movement Research, 1,* 219-244.

Gamson, W., & Wolfsfeld, G. (1993). Movements and media as interacting systems. *The Annals of the American Academy of Political and Social Science, 528,* 114-125.

Good, L. (1989). Power, hegemony, and communication theory. In I. Angus & S. Jhally (Eds.), *Cultural politics in contemporary America* (pp. 51-64). London: Routledge.

Graham, S., & Marvin, S. (1996). *Telecommunications and the city: Electronic spaces, urban places.* London: Routledge.

Harris, P. (1997). Glossary. In P. Golding & P. Harris (Eds.), *Beyond cultural imperialism: Globalization, communication and the new international order* (pp. 208-240). London: Sage.

International Development Research Centre. (1992). *101 technologies: From the South for the South.* Ottawa: Author.

Jacobson, T., & Zimpfer, S. (1993). Noncommercial computer networks and national development. *Telematics and Informatics, 10*(4), 345-358.

Kellner, D. (1995). Intellectuals and new technologies. *Media, Culture & Society, 17,* 427-448.

Kern, M. (1997). Social capital and citizen interpretation of political ads, news, and Web site information in the 1996 presidential elections. *American Behavioral Scientist, 40*(8), 1238-1250.

Lerner, D. (1958). *The passing of traditional society: Modernizing the Middle East.* Glencoe, IL: Free Press.

Mansell, R., & Wehn, U. (Eds.). (1998). *Knowledge societies: Information technology for sustainable development.* New York: Oxford University Press.

McMichael, P. (1996). *Development and social change: A global perspective.* Thousand Oaks, CA: Pine Forge.

Melkote, S. R. (1991). *Communication for development in the Third World.* New Delhi: Sage.

Melucci, A. (1988). Getting involved: Identity and mobilization in social movements. In B. Klandermans, H. Kriesi, & S. Tarrow (Eds.), *International social movement research* (pp. 329-347). Greenwich, CT: JAI.

Mody, B. (1991). *Designing messages for development communication: An audience participation-based approach.* New Delhi: Sage.

Mody, B. (1999). The Internet in the other three-quarters of the world. In *Institute for Information Studies: The promise of global networks* (pp. 69-94). Cobh, Ireland: Aspen Institute.

Mody, B. (2000). The contexts of power and the power of the media. In K. G. Wilkins (Ed.), *Redeveloping communication for social change: Theory, practice, and power* (pp. 185-196). Lanham, MD: Rowman & Littlefield.

Mohammadi, A. (1997). An overview of communication technology, deregulation policy and their impact on the developing countries. In A. Mohammadi (Ed.), *International communication and globalization: A critical introduction* (pp. 50-66). London: Sage.

Moore, D. B. (1995). Development discourse as hegemony: Towards an ideological history— 1945-1995. In D. B. Moore & G. J. Schmitz (Eds.), *Debating development discourse: Institutional and popular perspectives* (pp. 153). New York: St. Martin's.

Morris, A. D., & Mueller, C. M. (Eds.). (1992). *Frontiers in social movement theory.* New Haven, CT: Yale University Press.

Owen, C. (1998). *New technologies and women's movements in Mexico.* Master's thesis, University of Texas at Austin.

Peterson, T. R. (1997). *Sharing the Earth: The rhetoric of sustainable development.* Columbia: University of South Carolina Press.

Rogers, E. M. (1976). Communication and development: The passing of the dominant paradigm. *Communication Research, 3*(2), 121-133.

Rucht, D. (1999). The transnationalization of social movements: Trends, causes, problems. In D. Della Porta, H. Kriesi, & Dieter Rucht (Eds.), *Social movements in a globalizing world* (pp. 206-222). New York: St. Martin's.

Schiller, H. I. (1991). Not yet the post-imperialist era. *Critical Studies in Mass Communication, 8,* 13-28.

Schön, D. (1979). Generative metaphor: A perspective of problem-setting. In A. Orthony (Ed.), *Metaphor and thought* (pp. 254-283). Cambridge, UK: Cambridge University Press.

Schramm, W. (1963). Communication development and the development process. In L. Pye (Ed.), *Communications and political development* (pp. 30-57). Princeton, NJ: Princeton University Press.

Singhal, A., & Rogers, E. M. (1989). Prosocial television for development in India. In R. E. Rice & C. K. Atkin (Eds.), *Public communication campaigns* (2nd ed., pp. 331-350). Newbury Park, CA: Sage.

Singhal, A., & Rogers, E. M. (1999). *Entertainment-education: A communication strategy for social change.* Mahwah, NJ: Lawrence Erlbaum.

Steeves, H. L. (1993). Creating imagined communities: Development communication and the challenge of feminism. *Journal of Communication, 43*(3), 218-229.

Tomber, H., & Bromley, M. (1998). Virtual soundbites: Political communication in cyberspace. *Media, Culture & Society, 20,* 159-167.

United Nations Education, Scientific, and Cultural Organization. (2000). *EOLSS: Encyclopedia of life support systems* [Online]. Available: http://www.eolss.co.uk

U.S. Agency for International Development Office of Women in Development. (1999a, June). *Educational partnerships for girls: Development successes* (Information Bulletin No. 2). Washington, DC: USAID.

U.S. Agency for International Development Office of Women in Development. (1999b, December). *Sowing the seeds of opportunity: Women in agribusiness* (Information Bulletin No. 7). Washington, DC: USAID.

Webber, M. J. (1994). Challenges to transnational movements. *Peace Review, 6*(4), 395-402.

Whelan, D. (1998). *Recasting WID: A human rights approach.* Washington, DC: International Center for Research on Women.

Wilkins, K. (1999). Development discourse on gender and communication in strategies for social change. *Journal of Communication, 49*(1), 44-64.

Wilkins, K. (2000). Accounting for power in development communication. In K. G. Wilkins (Ed.), *Redeveloping communication for social change: Theory, practice, and power* (pp. 197-210). Lanham, MD: Rowman & Littlefield.

Wilkins, K., & Waters, J. (2000). Current discourse on new technologies in development communication. *Media Development, 1,* 57-60.

PART III

A Retrospective Prospectus

15

Looking Back, Looking Forward

E VERETT M. R OGERS
University of New Mexico

W ILLIAM B. H ART
Old Dominion University

An individual entering any scholarly discipline is naturally interested in why certain questions are studied whereas others are ignored. Where did the main concepts and theories come from, and how have they been modified over the years? Which individuals played a major role in founding, and in the intellectual evolution of, the scholarly field? The present chapter traces the histories of international communication (INC) and development communication (DC). The INC and the DC fields were established mainly by mass communication scholars. INC and DC deal with macro-level information exchanges between and within nations. Initially, the fields of development and international communication each displayed a certain made-in-the-U.S.A. quality,

because their forebears and founders were mainly U.S. Americans, but in recent years each field evolved to become more multicultural in nature as communication study has grown to strength worldwide, particularly (1) in Latin America (especially in Mexico and Brazil, which together enroll more students than the some 2,000 U.S. universities with departments of communication) and (2) in certain Asian nations (e.g., South Korea and Taiwan). Culture obviously intrudes in the conceptualizations, methods, and the choice of what is studied in communication research, and especially so in the case of studies of communication and culture.

We use Thomas Kuhn's (1970) staged model of scientific evolution to organize the

AUTHORS' NOTE: We acknowledge the helpful comments of Krishna Kandath, University of New Mexico, on an earlier draft of the chapter.

histories of INC and DC. Kuhn's conceptualization consists of five stages: (1) preparadigmatic research, where unconnected researchers conduct sporadic studies that may not advance theory in a coherent manner; (2) appearance of a paradigm, which typically is set forth in a book or article that becomes a classic in the field; (3) normal science, when an invisible college (a network of scholars in a field who share a scientific paradigm) forms around the new paradigm; (4) anomalies, when research finds failures in the paradigm; and (5) exhaustion of the paradigm, when scholarly interest in the scientific paradigm wanes, and it may be replaced by a new paradigm. We recognize that a paradigm may have disadvantages for a scholarly specialty, such as influencing all scholarly work into a single conceptualization and thus limiting alternative explanations, as well as the advantage of greater coherence and concerted direction.

INTERNATIONAL COMMUNICATION

International communication (INC) is the study of heterophilous mass-mediated communication between two or more countries with differing backgrounds.[1] The communicating countries may differ ideologically, culturally, in level of economic development, and in language. The primary unit of analysis in INC is the interaction of two or more societies/nations that are linked by mass media communication (Markham, 1970). So INC takes place at the societal level, as opposed to the interpersonal level, which distinguishes it from ICC. INC is a type of mass-mediated communication (i.e., few-to-many communication mediated by technologies such as radio, television, and computers networks). Such INC across borders may pose threats to national sovereignty and may represent *media imperialism*, the process through which

one nation's culture is imposed on another country through mass media channels. Studies of the mass media system of a single nation, and comparative studies of different mass media systems, were precursors to the study of INC; however, the focus of INC, especially in the early decades of study, was often on the flows of information between, and among, nations. INC textbooks include those by Cherry (1971), Frederick (1993), Fortner (1993), Stevenson (1994), and Mowlana (1996). Histories of INC are Armand Mattelart's (1994) *Mapping World Communication*, Philip M. Taylor's (1997) *Global Communications, International Affairs, and the Media Since 1945*, and Cees J. Hamelink's (1995) *World Communication*.

International Communication: Preparadigmatic Work

The roots of INC can be traced to key intellectuals of late-19th-century Europe, primarily Charles Darwin and Karl Marx.[2] Darwin's evolutionary theory played an important role in the development of capitalism, which is involved in INC flows. A century before Darwin's evolutionary theory was published, the founder of economics, Adam Smith, described a political and economic philosophy in which national governments would play a minimal role in guiding a nation's economy. Smith promoted a free-market economy, which favored competition between individuals and corporations free of government intervention. This laissez-faire approach to economics served as a basic tenet of capitalism, along with a belief in the invisible hand of market forces in optimizing prices and wages.

Sir Herbert Spencer, a contemporary of Darwin's, was influenced by both Adam Smith and Charles Darwin. Like Smith, Spencer supported free-market capitalism. He used the phrase "survival of the fittest" to describe economic competition in which the units best fitting their environment rise to prominence in a free market. Spencer applied Darwin's biological evolutionary theory to social life (social Darwinism). In the late 19th century, Karl Marx became disillusioned with the beginnings of modern capitalism due to the growing gap between the capitalist class (the exploiting) and the working class (the exploited). He predicted that the working class would overthrow the capitalist class to form a classless, socialist society in which the government would control the production and distribution of wealth. Influenced by Darwin, Marx proposed that societies would develop through stages from capitalism to socialism and then to communism (a utopia with no ruling class and with wealth shared by all).[3] Free-market capitalism versus state-controlled socialism were the two powerful ideologies that would shape future INC during the Cold War era from 1945 to 1989.

At about the same time that these two political ideologies were being formed in the late 19th century, the communication technologies that would be important in INC were invented and diffused. The telegraph and the radio signaled the birth of modern INC (Fortner, 1993).[4] The telegraph enabled Western news agencies such as Reuters, the French Press Agency, and the Associated Press to form cartels to control the international flow of news (Frederick, 1993). The dominance of these international news agencies, who tended to impose a Western perception of news on the world, later became a topic of study by INC scholars (Nafziger, 1940). This Western bias was shown, for example, in the relatively greater attention given to news events occurring in Europe and North America and to the emphasis on disasters, coups, revolutions, and other negative news from Latin America, Africa, and Asia.

Another topic of early INC study was propaganda, beginning with Harold Lasswell's (1927/1971) analysis of propaganda in World War I. No government, according to Lasswell, could control the minds of people without using propaganda; the mass media could thus move societies for good or ill (Bleyer, 1926). U.S. President Woodrow Wilson and scholars of the day such as Walter Lippmann (1922/1965) advocated using the mass media for the betterment of all people (Hellman, Nordenstreng, & Varis, 1980). The idealism of INC scholars in this early era about the media's role in improving the world continues to some extent today.

International Communication: Appearance of the Paradigm

World War II encouraged the further study of international propaganda (Lasswell, 1927/1971) and of persuasion (Hovland, Janis, & Kelley, 1953). Shortly after World War II, two important documents helped set the tone for future INC research and policy. In the United States, the Hutchins Commission on Freedom of the Press (1946) published *Peoples Speaking to Peoples: A Report on International Mass Communication*, which advocated a laissez-faire, free flow of information across borders to lead to a better world:

> What is needed in the field of international communication is . . . the linking of all the habitable parts of the globe with abundant, cheap, significant, true information about the world from day to day, so that all men [and women] increasingly may have the opportunity to learn, know, and understand each other. (p. 14)

This ideology reflected the high value on the First Amendment (freedom of the press) held by American journalists and by U.S. mass communication scholars of that day, extended to an international context.

A similar idealism led to the League of Nations after World War I and the formation of the United Nations near the end of World War II (Hellman et al., 1980). The United Nations Educational, Scientific and Cultural Organization (UNESCO) encouraged the free flow of information among nations. The 1946 UNESCO constitution, in its preamble, stated,

> Believing in . . . the free exchange of ideas and knowledge, are agreed and determined to develop and to increase the means of communication between their peoples and to employ these means for the purposes of mutual understanding and a truer and more perfect knowledge of each other's lives.

This policy also reflects the U.S. First Amendment.

UNESCO encouraged free-flow policies through international conferences and other activities. The Ford Foundation awarded the MIT Center for International Studies funding for its Research Program in International Communication. The center's research, guided by Lasswell's effects-oriented model (who says what to whom with what effect?) and the free-flow doctrine (Mowlana, 1996), involved communication scholars such as Ithiel de Sola Pool, Karl Deutsch, Daniel Lerner, Wilbur Schramm, and Lucian Pye. Influential publications of this era include Wilbur Schramm and John Riley's (1951) *The Reds Take a City*; Siebert, Peterson, and Schramm's (1956) *Four Theories of the Press*; and Schramm's (1959) *One Day in the World's Press*. The titles of these publications suggest the authors' general enthusiasm for the free-flow policy and their preference for American-style democracy.

The field of INC was conceptualized in the decade after World War II when the United States was involved in the Cold War with the Soviet Union. Behind the INC paradigm was a pro-Western, anticommunist ideology and a favored research methodology. Central to the INC paradigm were (1) the free flow of information across national borders, (2) an idealistic view of bettering the world through mass media communication, and (3) the empirical, effects-oriented research methodologies pioneered by Lasswell, Lazarsfeld, and Hovland.

International Communication: Normal Science

By 1960, the academic study of communication was becoming well established in many U.S. universities. In the decade after World War II, communication pioneer Wilbur Schramm founded communication research institutes and doctoral programs in communication at the University of Iowa, the University of Illinois, and Stanford University (Rogers, 1994). INC researchers came from doctoral training programs in communication primarily at Midwestern universities such as Iowa, Wisconsin, Minnesota, Northwestern, and Michigan State. Doctoral students from Latin America, Africa, and Asia traveled to these and other American universities to study, often conducting research on INC topics. Over half of the INC studies during the 120-year time period from 1850 to 1970 were completed during the 1960s, with the rate of production slowing somewhat after the late 1970s (Mowlana, 1973).

In 1974, the SCA published the first *International and Intercultural Communication Annual*. Important INC books were a reader, *International Communication*, by Heinz-Dietrich Fisher and John C. Merrill (1970), and Colin Cherry's (1971) *World Communication: Threat or Promise?* This invisible college of INC scholars also established specialized organizations such as the ICA's Intercultural Communication Division (later the

Intercultural and Development Communication Division). In the 1960s, the Association for Education in Journalism and Mass Communication (AEJMC) established an International Communication Division, which sponsored the Wingspread Symposium on Education and Research in International Communication (Mowlana, 1996). The International Association for Mass Communication Research (IAMCR), which received funding from UNESCO, was initially dominated by European scholars and emphasized a critical communication approach. The IAMCR helped internationalize the study of INC since the early 1970s.

INC courses were offered at many universities in the 1960s, and specialized degree programs in INC were established at Michigan State University, Stanford University, University of Minnesota, American University (in Washington, D.C.), and many other institutions.

International Communication: Anomaly/Exhaustion

In the 1970s, anomalies in the dominant paradigm for INC gradually appeared on two fronts. Herbert Schiller's books *Mass Communications and American Empire* (1969) and *Communication and Cultural Domination* (1976) strongly opposed the free-flow doctrine. Schiller, who was a critical communication scholar at the University of California, San Diego, argued that a laissez-faire policy on communication flows actually led to an asymmetrical flow. News and entertainment programming from Western nations dominated the media in Latin America, Africa, and Asia. Schiller (1969) introduced the concept of cultural (and media) imperialism, leading to investigations of how the media of one nation dominate other nations. A particularly influ-

ential study, funded by UNESCO, supporting the cultural imperialism argument was Nordenstreng and Varis's (1974) *TV Traffic: A One-Way Street?* Armand Mattelart, a Belgian critical communication scholar who became well-known while teaching in Chile from 1962 to 1973, conducted the most widely cited study of media imperialism, called, in English, *How to Read Donald Duck* (Dorfman & Mattelart, 1973). A survey of 100 Latin American scholars and a content analysis of eight Latin American communication journals from 1960 to 1984 showed Mattelart to be far and away the most influential scholar (Chaffee, Gomez-Palacio, & Rogers, 1990).

In the early 1970s, a growing number of the national leaders of developing countries recognized the imbalance, and cultural imperialism, in INC flows. Developing nations called for a New World Information and Communication Order (NWICO). UNESCO modified its policy stance from the free flow of information, established in 1946, to a free *and balanced* flow of information in the 1970s. UNESCO appointed an eminent panel of communication scholars and media professionals to investigate the imbalance in world news flows. This panel published the MacBride report, *Many Voices, One World* (International Commission for the Study of Communication Problems, 1980), which called for a more balanced flow of information among nations. Several Western countries, however, objected, and the United States and Great Britain withdrew from UNESCO, in 1985 and 1986, respectively, in part because of the NWICO debate. The NWICO debate eventually abated as a policy issue after the 1980s.

This debate, however, sparked considerable study by INC researchers in the late 1980s: Preston, Herman, and Schiller's (1989) *Hope and Folly*; Galtung and Vincent's (1992) *Global Glasnost*; Gerbner, Mowlana, and Nordenstreng's (1993) *The Global Media*

Debate; and Hamelink's (1995) *World Communication*. Influenced by Marxism and the Frankfurt school, critical communication scholars led the charge for a new paradigm of INC by critiquing the dominant INC paradigm, beginning about 1970. They pointed to the documented imbalance in worldwide information flows and assisted in creating a Third World news agency through the Yugoslavian news agency TANJUG. They pointed to paternalism and ethnocentrism in the West's idealistic approach to assisting developing nations with Western information and communication technologies (Mowlana, 1996, p. 14). They faulted the INC effects-oriented research methodology for overlooking the ideological, economic, cultural, and historical contexts of INC (McPhail, 1987). Mowlana (1993) suggested a revision of the Lasswellian communication model by advocating that the central question for INC research should be, "Who owns and controls the distribution of communication, and for what purpose and intent?" (p. 72). Today, critical perspectives are acknowledged by INC scholars and are often incorporated in contemporary INC research. The previous strong Western value on media libertarianism has given way to a focus on the media's role in social harmony and order (Merrill, 2000).

So the ideological foundation of the INC paradigm, originally proposed in the post-World War II era and emphasizing the free flow of information through the mass media, gave way in the 1970s to a focus on more balanced flows of media messages and to the study of media imperialism. The challenge by critical communication scholars to the Cold War paradigm for INC trailed off in the 1990s, after the end of the Cold War in 1989. Scholarly interests in the INC field shifted in an era of globalization, privatization, and informatization. Recent INC studies focus particularly on the role of communication satellites, telecommunication, and the diffusion of the Internet, its consequences, and on the digital divide between developed and developing nations.

DEVELOPMENT COMMUNICATION

Development communication (DC) is the study of social change brought about by the application of communication research, theory, and technologies to bring about development. *Development* is defined as a widely participatory process of social change in a society, intended to bring about both social and material advancement, including greater equality, freedom, and other valued qualities, for the majority of people through their gaining greater control over their environment (Rogers, 1976). For example, DC promotes social changes leading to improved nutrition, family planning, better health, higher literacy, and improved agricultural production in developing countries by means of more effective communication. The experts seeking to bring about this type of social change are typically different culturally from the people receiving the development assistance, so heterophily is involved. Histories of DC are Mowlana and Wilson's (1990) *The Passing of Modernity,* Rogers's (1976, 1989) reviews, and Schramm's (1964) *Mass Media and National Development.* The scholarly study of development began in the 1950s, about the same time as ICC, as nations in Asia, the Middle East, and Africa ended political colonization by European countries and sought to improve their socioeconomic conditions. The highest priority for these new nations was development, raising incomes and levels of living for rural and urban poor people.

Development Communication: Preparadigmatic Work

DC shares historical roots with INC. The development of societies is intrinsically tied to Darwin's evolutionary theory, Spencer's social Darwinism, and Marx's theories of societal development. Although writings on societal development have a long history, most scholarly work on development began after 1949 when the United States established the Point IV Program to extend the Marshall Plan to the nations of Latin America, Africa, and Asia in furthering socioeconomic development. Although investigations of development problems and of DC had been completed prior to World War II, these studies were scattered and did not advance conceptualizations in a coherent manner.

Development Communication: Appearance of the Paradigm

Two influential early books on DC were (1) Daniel Lerner's (1958) investigation of the role of literacy and mass media exposure in the individual modernization process in six Middle Eastern nations[5] and (2) Wilbur Schramm's (1964) synthesis and model of the media's role in development. The later book, especially, provided the paradigmatic statement for DC. Core elements in the DC paradigm are (1) the notion that the mass media technologies of radio, television, satellites, and the Internet can deliver informative and motivational messages to large audiences, especially of villagers and urban poor in developing countries, and (2) the research-based evidence that media exposure can change individuals' knowledge, attitudes, and overt behavior for economic growth and social advancement. Thus, the original paradigm for DC represented a certain degree of communication technological determinism and a communication effects orientation.

Development Communication: Normal Science

The field of DC attracted increasing attention by communication scholars in the 1970s and thereafter. By the mid-1960s, an invisible college of scholars began forming around the Lerner-Schramm paradigm, with these two scholars organizing their first DC seminar in Hawaii in 1964. Here the meaning of DC was defined and the nature of DC research was "framed" (Rogers, 1989, p. 68). Lerner and Schramm's (1967) *Communication and Change in the Developing Countries* and Schramm and Lerner's (1976) *Communication and Change* were important edited books. Schramm launched one of the first DC courses at Stanford University in 1966, about the same time that similar courses were being taught at Michigan State University and at the University of Wisconsin (Rogers, 1989). M.A. programs in DC were established at Stanford University, the University of Iowa, Cornell University, and Ohio University. Ph.D. programs and funded research in DC grew to strength at Stanford, Michigan State, Wisconsin, Texas, Florida State, and Pennsylvania. In 1982, the Intercultural Communication Division of the ICA became the Intercultural and Development Communication Division.

Early DC research projects dealt with how the expanding audiences for radio and television broadcasting could be harnessed in a developing country to reach its development goals. The introduction of new communication technologies played an important role in DC. The effects of instructional television projects for in-school teaching and for village development in Colombia, El Salvador, the Ivory Coast, and American Samoa (Schramm, Nelson, & Bethan, 1981) and in the 1975-1976 SITE (Satellite Instructional Television Experiment) Project in India were evaluated by communication scholars in the 1960s and 1970s. The impacts of new communication technologies, such as television, telecommunication satellites (Melkote, Shields, & Agarwal, 1998), and more recently, the Internet, have been investigated. In the 1980s and 1990s, the emphasis in development programs focused on sustainable development, as these programs sought to fulfill human needs without endangering future opportunities. Here the ability of a DC project to continue after initial funding and technical expertise ended became a key consideration, as did avoiding environmental pollution.

Development Communication: Anomaly/Exhaustion

Through a process of empirical investigation and self-critique, DC scholars gradually questioned their theoretical assumptions and modified their paradigm in important ways. Increasing attention was given to participatory development (Jacobson & Servaes, 1999) and to the realization that the mass media may not be directive in the development process (Hedebro, 1982; Hornik, 1988; Servaes, 1999; Wilkins, 2000), at least not to the extent originally thought. A recent meta-research of 209 DC studies from 1958 to 1996 showed that "the research conducted most recently has tried to account for the complexity of national development by downplaying the media's direct role in either individual modernization or social change" (Fair & Shah, 1997).

As in the case of INC, but even more so, DC study gradually became more internationalized (e.g., Hedebro, 1982). In Latin America, communication scholars turned away from models and methodologies imported from the United States, toward alternative models, such as the critical scholarship of Mattelart and Latin American cultural studies (Chaffee et al., 1990; Rodriguez & Murphy, 1997). Gradually, the study of DC became less America-centric and less ethnocentric.

By the 1970s, the Lerner-Schramm paradigm began to come into question, as some scholars faulted the older paradigm, especially the ethnocentric perspective of "modernizing" traditional peoples. The original DC paradigm was modified in important ways to account for these anomalies (Mowlana & Wilson, 1990; Rogers, 1989). To use Kuhnian terminology, the DC paradigm had experienced a pseudo-exhaustion.

The early focus on the development potential of broadcast media in the 1990s was redirected to newer communication technologies such as the Internet. Globalization, "informatization," entertainment-education, and organizing for social change gained the attention of DC scholars, particularly in the past decade. The global village is a world that is increasingly connected by communication technologies and that tends toward a global culture. Large cities across the world resemble each other, at least in certain superficial ways, such as in consumer product sold, movies, fast food, air conditioning, and traffic problems (Rogers & Steinfatt, 1999, p. 283). *Globalization* is the degree to which the same set of economic rules applies everywhere in an increasingly interdependent world. Often the economic rules center on capitalism. Writing in 1776, Adam Smith, in *The Wealth of Nations,* described competitive markets as the "invisible hand," the force that allowed the economy to operate in the most efficient way for the most people. Capitalism, the economic and political philosophy that reflected Smith's open competitive forces, spread from Europe and North America through much of the world during the past century, a trend punctuated by the fall of the Berlin Wall in 1989, which symbolized the end of the Cold War, and a move away from state socialism in many nations.

The concept of the global village was coined by Marshall McLuhan (1962, p. 31), the Canadian media guru at the University of Toronto. McLuhan's concept expressed his general position as a *technological determinist,* that is, in believing that technology (in this case communication technology) is the main cause of social changes. *Technology* consists of knowledge about how to accomplish some task. Many aspects of globalization are facilitated by the new communication technologies of the Internet. However, government policies, regulations, revolutions and other political actions, and public opinion may also be important factors in such social changes as globalization.

Informatization is the process of communication and social change made possible by communication technology that moves a nation more and more toward becoming an information society (Singhal & Rogers, 2001). For example, much wealth has been created since the early 1990s in such technopolises (technology cities) as Bangalore and Hyderabad in India. This rapid economic development was driven by the computer software industry, and it builds on India's competitive advantage in English-language ability and a well-developed university system in engineering. The Internet connects individuals and communities over great distances, speeding the globalization process. In developing nations, many individuals use the Internet through public access computers in "cyber-cafés" or telecenters, by paying a small fee per hour of use (rather than accessing the Internet via individually owned computers).

In recent decades, globalization was accompanied by privatization and commercialization of key institutions. An example is the privatization of television in India in the 1990s and the increasing introduction of American television programs (such as MTV and *Baywatch*) and Western products (such as McDonald's, Nike, and Coca-Cola), which are advertised on India's increasingly commercialized television system (McDowell, 1997; Singhal & Rogers, 2001). Important changes in Indian society have occurred; for example, a media image of the ideal Indian woman as slim and assertive has been conveyed to the rapidly expanding television audience (Malhotra & Rogers, 2000). With the increasing privatization of television in India, the entertainment function of television replaced its previous educational and development focus, as the private television networks in India compete for audience ratings and profits.

One means of combining the educational and entertainment functions of the media is *entertainment-education,* defined as the intentional embedding of educational messages in entertainment media in order to change individuals' knowledge, attitudes, and overt behavior (Singhal & Rogers, 1999). In recent decades, more than 100 entertainment-education projects have been carried out in Latin America, Africa, and Asia. The educational issues have included family planning, HIV/AIDS prevention, female equality, environmental protection, and other types of DC.

Early DC research dealt mainly with audiences of villagers and urban poor, who often constituted three fourths or more of a developing nation's population. These individuals had the lowest incomes, gravest health and nutrition problems, and lowest levels of formal education. By the 1990s, however, this audience focus shifted to the rapidly expanding middle class, particularly in the fast-rising nations of Asia and Latin America (Skinner & Kandath, 1998).

Scholars of DC recognized that development often entails system-level change as well as individual-level change and that organizational and social structures can facilitate or impede development. One outcropping of this focus on system change and of participatory development has been investigations of organizing for social change. Papa, Auwal, and Singhal (1995, 1997), for example, studied the empowering role of local groups of micro lenders in the Grameen Bank system of Bangladesh. Similarly, Papa and others (2000) investigated the process of how individuals in one Indian village, in response to their exposure to an entertainment-education radio program, organized themselves to combat the practice of dowry. Here the research shifts to analyzing discourse and to a focus on paradox and contradiction. Studies of organizing for social change bring together the theories and methodologies of organizational communication with the concerns of DC. Instead of studying Indian villagers as a relatively passive audience for DC messages (Freire, 1970), organizing-for-social-change scholars focus on the process through which individuals gain *collective efficacy,* defined as the degree to which individuals in a system believe that they can organize and execute courses of action required to achieve collective goals (Bandura, 1997). Combating dowry in an Indian village cannot be accomplished solely through individual activities. Nor is the process one of linear and direct movement toward a social change.

The DC field currently shows few signs of anomaly or exhaustion, although the main focus of scholarly attention now includes globalization, informatization, entertainment-education, and organizing for social change. In fact, the worldwide forces for globalization, privatization, and informatization led to increased scholarly attention to DC in the past decade. The general goals and conceptualizations of DC have been changed over the years in a flexible yet resilient fashion (Rogers, 1976), but the modified paradigm for DC continues.

CONCLUSIONS

"World War II had a tremendous impact on the field of communication" (Rogers, 1994, p. 10). As shown in the present chapter, the Second World War and the beginnings of the Cold War were turning points in the development of the fields of international and development communication and in the rise of the academic discipline of communication study. The key founders (Lasswell, Lazarsfeld, Hovland, and Lewin) were in Washington, D.C., in the early 1940s and/or were involved in war-related research, as was the founder of communication study, Wilbur Schramm. After World War II, as the United States emerged as a world power and as an increased global awareness became pervasive, the two specialized fields of communication study that are the focus of the present chapter were established. They are a product of their time, an era of the Cold War, internationalization, and Westernization, fraught with tensions and conflicts.

Both fields deal with the concepts of communication and culture and with interaction between culturally unalike (heterophilous) people. Both fields are related to important social problems of the world and, though theory oriented and based on empirical research conducted in a scientific manner, deal with implications for social action and social change. Certain key events of history, such as the launching of the Point IV Program and the Cold War, affected INC and DC.

The intellectual roots of the two fields can be traced to the great 19th- and early-20th-century theorists Darwin, Marx, and Freud.

Political science and international relations contributed to INC, and DC attracted the attention of scholars of education, particularly specialists in instructional technology. Both fields of study reviewed here are thus somewhat interdisciplinary in nature, although they are mainly centered in communication study.

NOTES

1. Frederick (1993) distinguished between *international communication* and *global communication*, with the latter including communication between non-state actors such as nongovernmental organizations (NGOs) and transnational corporations (Mowlana, 1996; Stevenson, 1994). We use the term international communication in the present essay to include all types of communication that occur across national boundaries, as is the usual convention.

2. Darwin's and Marx's theories, along with the theoretical contributions of Georg Simmel, were transported across the Atlantic and adapted to North American conditions through empirical research by the Chicago school (John Dewey, George Herbert Mead, and Robert E. Park) in the period from 1905 to 1935 (Rogers, 1994).

3. Contemporary nations that label themselves communist are actually socialist, according to Marx's use of these terms.

4. Frederick (1993) traced the history of international communication to ancient postal systems.

5. The Lerner (1958) book reported a reanalysis of survey data originally gathered to evaluate the audience effects of Voice of America broadcasts in the six Middle Eastern nations. Lerner reformulated the data to explore his theory of individual *modernization,* the process through which individuals gain literacy and education, have mass media exposure, become empathic with unlike others, and change their attitudes and actions. A number of modernization investigations were conducted in the 1960s and 1970s, but a meta-research of development communication publications showed that by 1987-1996, "Lerner's mod-

ernization model completely disappears" (Fair & Shah, 1997, p. 7).

REFERENCES

Bandura, A. (1997). *Self-efficacy: The exercise of control.* New York: Freeman.

Bleyer, W. G. (1926). The press and public opinion in international relations. *Journalism Bulletin, 3*(2), 7-20.

Chaffee, S. H., Gomez-Palacio, C., & Rogers, E. M. (1990). Mass communication research in Latin America: Views from here and there. *Journalism Quarterly, 67*(4), 1015-1024.

Cherry, C. (1971). *World communication: Threat or promise? A socio-technical approach.* New York: Wiley-Interscience.

Dorfman, A., & Mattelart, A. (1973). *Para leer al Pato Donald.* Valparaiso, Chile: Ediciones Universitarias de Valparaiso; translated in English in 1975 as *How to Read Donald Duck.* New York: International General.

Fair, J. E., & Shah, H. (1997). Continuities and discontinuities in communication and development research since 1958. *Journal of International Communication, 4,* 3-25.

Fischer, H.-D., & Merrill, J. C. (1970). *International communication: Media, channels, functions.* New York: Hastings House.

Fortner, R. S. (1993). *International communication: History, conflict, and control of the global metropolis.* Belmont, CA: Wadsworth.

Frederick, H. (1993). *Global communication and international relations.* Fort Worth, TX: Harcourt Brace.

Freire, P. (1970). *The pedagogy of the oppressed.* New York: Seabury.

Galtung, J., & Vincent, R. C. (1992). *Global glasnost: Toward a new world information and communication order.* Cresskill, NJ: Hampton.

Gerbner, G., Mowlana, H., & Nordenstreng, K. (1993). *The global media debate: Its rise, fall, and renewal.* Norwood, NJ: Ablex.

Hamelink, C. J. (1995). *World communication: Disempowerment and self-empowerment.* London: Zed.

Hedebro, G. (1982). *Communication and social change in developing countries: A critical view.* Ames: Iowa State University Press.

Hellman, H., Nordenstreng, K., & Varis, T. (1980, September). *Idealism, aggression, apology, and criticism: The four traditions of research on international communication.* Paper presented at the meeting of the International Association for Mass Communication Research (IAMCR), Caracas, Venezuela.

Hornik, R. C. (1988). *Development communication: Information, agriculture, and nutrition in the Third World.* New York: Longman.

Hovland, C. I., Janis, I., & Kelley, H. (Eds.). (1953). *Communication and persuasion: Psychological studies of opinion change.* New Haven, CT: Yale University Press.

Hutchins Commission on Freedom of the Press. (1946). *Peoples speaking to peoples: A report on international mass communication.* Chicago: University of Chicago Press.

International Commission for the Study of Communication Problems. (1980). *Many voices, one world: Towards a new, more just and more efficient world information and communication order.* Paris: UNESCO.

Jacobson, T. L., & Servaes, J. (Eds.). (1999). *Theoretical approaches to participatory communication.* Cresskill, NJ: Hampton.

Kuhn, T. S. (1970). *The structure of scientific revolution.* Chicago: University of Chicago Press.

Lasswell, H. D. (1971). *Propaganda technique in the World War.* Boston: Knopf. (Original work published 1927 by K. Paul, Trench, Trubner, New York)

Lerner, D. (1958). *The passing of traditional society: Modernizing the Middle East.* Glencoe, IL: Free Press.

Lerner, D., & Schramm, W. (Eds.). (1967). *Communication and change in the developing countries.* Honolulu, HI: East-West Center.

Lippmann, W. (1965). *Public opinion.* New York: Free Press. (Original work published 1922)

Malhotra, S., & Rogers, E. M. (2000). Satellite television and the new Indian woman. *Gazette, 62*(5), 407-429.

Markham, J. W. (Ed.). (1970). *International communication as a field of study.* Iowa City, IA: International Communications Division, Association for Education in Journalism.

Mattelart, A. (1994). *Mapping world communication: War, progress, and culture* (S. Emanuel & J. A. Cohen, Trans.), Minneapolis: University of Minnesota Press.

McDowell, S. (1997). *Globalization, liberalization and policy change: A political economy of India's communication sector.* New York: St. Martin's.

McLuhan, M. (1962). *The Gutenberg galaxy: The making of typographical man.* Toronto, Ontario: University of Toronto Press.

McPhail, T. L. (1987). *Electronic colonialism: The future of international broadcasting and communication* (2nd ed.). Newbury Park, CA: Sage.

Melkote, S. R., Shields, P., & Agarwal, B. C. (Eds.). (1998). *International satellite broadcasting in South Asia: Political, economic, and cultural implications.* New York: University Press of America.

Merrill, J. C. (2000). Social stability and harmony: A new mission for the press. *Asian Journal of Communication, 10*(2), 33-52.

Mowlana, H. (1973). Trends in research on international communication in the United States. *Gazette, 2,* 79-90.

Mowlana, H. (1993). Toward a NWICO for the twenty-first century? *Journal of International Affairs, 47*(1), 59-72.

Mowlana, H. (1996). *Global communication in transition: The end of diversity?* Thousand Oaks, CA: Sage.

Mowlana, H., & Wilson, L. J. (1990). *The passing of modernity: Communication and the transformation of society.* New York: Longman.

Nafziger, R. O. (1940). *International news and press communications, organization of newsgathering, international affairs and the foreign press: An annotated bibliography.* New York: Wilson.

Nordenstreng, K., & Varis, T. (1974). *TV traffic: A one-way street? A survey and analysis of the international flow of television programme material.* Paris: UNESCO.

Papa, M. J., Auwal, M. A., & Singhal, A. (1995). Dialectic of control and emancipation in organizing for social change: A multitheoretic study of the Grameen Bank in Bangladesh. *Communication Theory, 5,* 189-223.

Papa, M. J., Auwal, M. A., & Singhal, A. (1997). Organizing for social change within concertive control systems: Member identification, empowerment, and the masking of discipline. *Communication Monographs, 64,* 219-250.

Papa, M. J., Singhal, A., Law, S., Pant, S., Sood, S., Rogers, E. M., & Shefner-Rogers, C. L. (2000). Entertainment-education and social change: An analysis of parasocial interaction, social learning, collective efficacy, and paradoxical communication. *Journal of Communication, 50*(4), 31-55.

Preston, W. E., Herman, E. S., & Schiller, H. (1989). *Hope and folly: The United States and UNESCO: 1945-1985.* Minneapolis: University of Minnesota Press.

Rodriguez, C., & Murphy, P. O. (1997). The study of communication and culture in Latin America: From laggards and the oppressed to resistance and hybrid cultures. *Journal of International Communication, 4*(2), 24-44.

Rogers, E. M. (1976). Communication and development: The passing of the dominant paradigm. In E. M. Rogers (Ed.), *Communication and development: Critical perspectives* (pp. 121-149). Beverly Hills, CA: Sage.

Rogers, E. M. (1989). Inquiry in development communication. In M. K. Asante & W. B. Gudykunst (Eds.), *Handbook of international and intercultural communication* (pp. 67-86). Newbury Park, CA: Sage.

Rogers, E. M. (1994). *A history of communication study: A biographical approach.* New York: Free Press.

Rogers, E. M. (1995). *Diffusion of innovations* (4th ed.). New York: Free Press.

Schiller, H. I. (1969). *Mass communications and American empire.* New York: A. M. Kelley.

Schiller, H. I. (1976). *Communication and cultural domination.* White Plains, NY: International Arts and Sciences Press.

Schramm, W. (1959). *One day in the world's press: Fourteen great newspapers on a day of crisis, November 2, 1956.* Stanford, CA: Stanford University Press.

Schramm, W. L. (1964). *Mass media and national development: The role of information in the developing countries.* Stanford, CA: Stanford University Press.

Schramm, W., & Lerner, D. (Eds.). (1976). *Communication and change, the last ten years—And the next.* Honolulu: University Press of Hawaii.

Schramm, W., Nelson, L. M., & Bethan, M. T. (1981). *Bold experiment: The story of educational television in American Samoa.* Stanford, CA: Stanford University Press.

Schramm, W., & Riley, J. (1951). *The Reds take a city: The communist occupation of Seoul.* Westport, CT: Greenwood.

Servaes, J. (1999). *Communication for development: One world, multiple communities.* Cresskill, NJ: Hampton.

Siebert, F. S., Peterson, T., & Schramm, W. (1956). *Four theories of the press: The authoritarian, libertarian, social responsibility and Soviet communist concepts of what the press should be and do.* Urbana: University of Illinois Press.

Singhal, A., & Rogers, E. M. (1999). *Entertainment-education: A communication strategy for social change.* Mahwah, NJ: Lawrence Erlbaum.

Singhal, A., & Rogers, E. M. (2001). *India's communication revolution: From bullock carts to cyber marts.* New Delhi: Sage.

Skinner, E. C., & Kandath, K. P. (1998). International satellite broadcasting in India and other areas: A critical summary. In S. R. Melkote, P. Shields, & B. C. Agarwal (Eds.), *International satellite broadcasting in South Asia: Political, economic, and cultural implications* (pp. 295-315). New York: University Press of America.

So, C. Y. K. (1995). *Mapping the intellectual landscape of communication studies: An evaluation of its disciplinary status.* Doctoral dissertation, University of Pennsylvania, Philadelphia.

Stevenson, R. L. (1994). *Global communication in the twenty-first century.* New York: Longman.

Sumner, W. G. (1940). *Folkways.* Boston: Ginn. (Original work published 1906)

Taylor, P. M. (1997). *Global communications, international affairs, and the media since 1945.* New York: Routledge.

Wilkins, K. G. (Ed.). (2000). *Redeveloping communication for social change: Theory, practice, and power.* Lanham, MD: Rowman & Littlefield.

Author Index

Subject Index

About the Editor

Bella Mody is Professor in the Department of Telecommunications at Michigan State University. She was Chair of the Intercultural and Development Communication Division of the International Communication Association from 1999 to 2001. Her research interests include international media, communication technology application in developing countries, formative research for media campaign design, and gender, ethnicity, and class. She is coeditor of *Telecommunication Politics* and author of *Designing Messages for Development Communication* and several journal articles. She has edited special issues of the *Journal of International Communication, Gazette,* and *Communication Theory.* She is a consultant to international and nongovernmental organizations and has been an advertising copywriter and a civil servant in the government of India. An updated vitae may be found at www.msu.edu/~mody/

About the Contributors

Oliver Boyd-Barrett is Professor in the Department of Communication at California State Polytechnic University, Pomona. His research interests have focused mainly on international communication, with special reference to global news media and news agencies. He has authored or edited 14 books and approximately 100 articles. Books include *The Media Communication Book* (with Chris Newbold et al., in press), *The Globalization of News* (with Terhi Rantanen), and *Media in a Global Context* (with A. Sreberny-Mohammadi, et al.), among others.

Sandra Braman is Associate Professor in the Department of Journalism and Communication at the University of Wiconsin, Milwaukee. She has published widely on the macro-level effects of the use of new information technologies and their policy implications in journals such as the *Journal of Communication, Telecommunication Policy, Gazette,* and *Media, Culture & Society.* She coedited *Globalization, Communication, and Transnational Civil Society* and served as book review editor of the *Journal of Communication.* Currently, she is Chair of the Communication Law and Policy Division of the International Communication Association.

Edward Comor is a faculty member of the School for International Service, American University, in Washington, D.C. Among other publications, he is author of *Communication, Commerce, and Power* (1998) and an editor of and contributor to *The Global Political Economy of Communication* (1994). His research focuses on the political economy of communication and culture. He is a cofounder and former Chair of the International Communication Section of the International Studies Association.

William B. Hart is Assistant Professor in the Department of Communication and Theatre Arts at Old Dominion University. His dissertation at the University of New Mexico, *The Historical Contributions of Boasian Anthropology to the Interdiscipline of Intercultural Relations,* deals with the early history of intercultural relations (an interdiscipline including intercultural communication, cultural anthropology, cross-cultural psychology, etc.). He was the founding editor of the electronic journal *The Edge: The E-Journal of Intercultural Relations* (www.interculturual relations.com).

Robert Huesca is Associate Professor of Communication at Trinity University in San Antonio, Texas. His research interests include alternative media and participatory communication for social change. His research on international and development communication issues has been published in *Communication Studies, Gazette, Journal of Communication, Media Development,* and *Media, Culture & Society,* among others.

Thomas L. Jacobson is Associate Professor and Director of the Informatics Research Center at the University at Buffalo, State University of New York. He has been secretary of the Intercultural and Development Division of the International Communication Association and President of the Participatory Communication Research Section of the International Association of Media and Communication Research. His research interests focus on national development, participation, and new technologies. His most recent book, *Theoretical Approaches to Participatory Communication* (1999), was co-authored with Jan Servaes.

Won Yong Jang is an ABD in the Department of Communication, State University of New York at Buffalo. His principal areas of research address political communication, global communication, public journalism, and new information and communication technologies. Recent publications include (with T.L. Jacobson) "Rights, Culture, and Global Democracy," in *Communication Theory* (2001).

Anselm Lee is a doctoral student in the Mass Media Program at Michigan State University. He completed his master's degree at Emerson College in integrated marketing communication and his bachelor's degree in advertising and public relations at Boston University. He is interested in the impact of media on individual identity and self concept, and in international media and program flows.

Stephen D. McDowell teaches in the Department of Communication at Florida State University in Tallahassee. His research interests include new communication technology and society, telecommunications policies, and communication policies in North America and India. He has held fellowships with the Strategic Policy Planning Division of the Canadian Federal Department of Communications in Ottawa and the Shastri Indo-Canadian Institute in New Delhi, and held a Congressional Fellowship in Washington, D.C. His book *Globalization, Liberalization, and Policy Change: A Political Economy of India's Communications Sector* appeared in 1997.

Srinivas R. Melkote is Professor in the Department of Telecommunications at Bowling Green State University. He has published on topics such as satellite broadcasting in South Asia, communication for development and empowerment, mass media effects, and HIV/AIDS. His latest books include *Critical Issues in Communication* (coeditor) and *Communication for Development in the Third World* (2nd ed., coauthor).

Everett M. Rogers is Regents' Professor, Department of Communication and Journalism at the University of New Mexico. The chapter for this volume was written while he was on sabbatical leave as Visiting Professor in the Center for Communication Programs, Johns Hopkins University. He is author of *Diffusion of Innovations* (4th ed., 1995), *A History of Communication Study* (1994), and *Intercultural Communication* (with Thomas Steinfatt, 1999). While Chair of the Department of Communication and Journalism at the University of New Mexico, he helped establish a

Ph.D. program in intercultural communication.

J. P. Singh is Associate Professor in the Communication, Culture, and Technology Program at Georgetown University. He is author of *Leapfrogging Development? The Political Economy of Telecommunications Restructuring* (1999) and coeditor (with James Rosenau) of *Information Technologies and Global Politics: The Changing Scope of Power and Governance* (in press). He currently is working on another book titled *Communication and Diplomacy: Negotiating the Global Information Economy.*

Leslie B. Snyder is Associate Professor of Communication Sciences at the University of Connecticut. She has published articles in *Communication Research, Journal of Communication, Mass Communication and Journalism Quarterly, AIDS Education and Prevention,* and *Health Communication,* among other journals. She is principal investigator on a grant from the National Institute on Alcohol Abuse and Alcoholism to study the effects of alcohol advertising on youth.

H. Leslie Steeves is Professor at the School of Journalism and Communication, University of Oregon. Her research focuses on two areas and their intersection: women's roles and representations in the mass media, and communication in developing countries, especially sub-Saharan Africa. She has published a number of articles in these areas, as well as a book, *Gender Violence and the Press: The St. Kizito Story* (1997). She also is coauthor (with S. Melkote) of *Communication for Development in the Third World: Theory and Practice for Empowerment* (2nd ed., 2001).

She has had Fulbright grants for teaching and research in Kenya and Ghana.

K. Viswanath is Acting Associate Director of the Behavioral Research Program, Division of Cancer Control and Populations Sciences, National Cancer Institute. His research interest is in using a macro-social approach to the study of communication, with his most recent work focusing on mass communication and social change and health communication in both national and international contexts with particular focus on communication inequities and disparities. He has been involved with guided social change projects in India and the United States. He has published in such journals as *Gazette, Media Culture and Society, Health Communication, Journalism Quarterly, Communication Research, American Behavioral Scientist,* and *Health Education Research.* He has also co-edited *Mass Media, Social Control and Social Change* (with D. Demers).

Silvio Waisbord is Associate Professor of Journalism and Media Studies at Rutgers University. His research interests include culture and media globalization, media and development, and political communication. His most recent books are *Watchdog Journalism in South America* (2000) and *Latin Politics, Global Media* (co-edited with Elizabeth Fox, 2002). His work has been published in the *Journal of Communication, Critical Studies in Mass Communication, Political Communication, Communication Research, Canadian Journal of Communication, Gazette,* and other publications.

Karin Gwinn Wilkins is Associate Professor and Graduate Advisor in the Department of Radio-TV-Film at the University of Texas,

Austin. Some of her research on development and international communication can be found in *ReDeveloping Communication for Social Change* (2000), *Media, Culture & Society, Critical Studies in Media Communication, Journal of Communication, International Journal of Public Opinion Quarterly, Media Development, Media Asia, Journal of International Communication,* and the *Asian Journal of Communication.* She is Chair of the Intercultural and Development Division of the International Communication Association.

Liren Benjamin Zeng is a faculty member at the Centre for Communication Studies, Mount Royal College in Alberta, Canada. Prior to this he served as a copy editor for the *Pacific Daily News.*